"In the U[illegible] the developing
world. In t[illegible] Commission and
that there [illegible] ound the world.
But povert[illegible] roups of people
unreached [illegible]

"This book is a HUGE wake up call to the church in the UK. We desperately need to listen to the facts, figures, cultural knowledge and ministry wisdom that Mez has gathered here. Millions of souls, the health of the church, and the glory of Christ are at stake."

Matt Oliver, Pastor of Hardwick Baptist Church, Stockton-on-Tees

"Warning: this book may cause you to do something costly for God's kingdom. Written with the blood, sweat and tears of raw personal and ministry experience. A densely researched analysis of our nation's class, culture and economic systems that contribute to very real poverty. Providing a biblical framework, cultural insight and spotlight experiences from the trenches. A voice crying in the spiritual wasteland advocates for the poorest communities in our land. How long will the church look away from the poor? Leaving them to die in the devil's gutter whilst we look on from the safety of the church."

Fontaine Selway, Women's Worker for Gracemount Community Church, Edinburgh

"I suspect that most British evangelicals have little idea what life is like on a council estate; we rarely enter these communities and their people don't venture into our churches. This book is the insider's perspective the church needs, revealing what life is like in this hidden world. Mez gives in-depth explanations for the current disparity, and offers realistic solutions. I cannot recommend it highly enough and

pray that it will help the church reach communities that desperately need the Gospel."

Nathan Young, Pastor of New Life Church, Middlesborough

"Coming from a very middle-class background, being a part of 20schemes has turned upside-down almost everything I thought about mercy ministry. Many have wondered why we would move our young family into a scheme to plant a local church and this book goes a long way to answer why.

"In this challenging and sometimes hard to swallow read, Mez holds nothing back. He presents a well-researched overview of poverty in the UK, and intertwined with his own personal experiences and that of others, he uses the Bible to show why and how the church should step up and respond in taking the gospel to all people.

"Let this book provoke you for the sake of those neglected, and change you as you heed the call of Christ."

Lindsey Stewart, Pastor's wife, Hope Community Church Barlanark, Glasgow

"It is a great sadness that the UK evangelical church has not been able to effectively reach the UK poor with the good news of Christ crucified — even with generations of well-intentioned believers. We need to sit down and consider why and explore the issue of poverty more deeply. In his usual clear and concise way, Mez and his guest collaborators have gone some way to put an excellent resource in our hands.

"If you want a book that you believe is 100% right on everything, then buy a Bible. Inevitably you will be provoked and challenged as you read this book. But it is a vital voice in an area where we seriously, and collectively, need help. In it we have insight not just

from somebody who comes from a people group we are desperately trying to reach, but from somebody who has spent the past 20+ years as a believer seeking to do the same and seeing fruit. That gives us double the reason to listen. And that's before we get down to the serious research, testimonies and experiences of other gospel workers in deprived areas that make this book a valuable asset in reaching our deprived communities."

Steve Walker, Pastor of Hope Community Church
Middleton, Leeds

"Warning: this book my change you; it's a powerful, thorough, much needed challenge to evangelical church in the UK. Everyone needs to read this. It's easy to read but hard to swallow. With moving testimony and stark research, it helps highlight the disparity and challenges faced in reaching the least, the last and the lost in our society. The schemes, valleys and council estates of our nation need Jesus; they need healthy churches; and they need you to support those churches."

Will Savory, Pastor of Soul Church, Neath

"It is easy to say that we share the ambition of Paul to preach the gospel where Christ is not known. It is far harder to action that ambition when we discover that many of the places where Christ is not known are the poorest communities in the UK. The contributors to this insightful book share the conviction that our Lord Jesus reaches people in communities of all kinds (including those in the poorest areas) through healthy gospel churches. Prepare to be informed and educated; prepare to be reminded of the saving power and wisdom of Christ; prepare to be made to think differently; prepare to be challenged and rebuked; prepare to be driven to prayer and action. This is not a comfortable book to read, but it is a book that needs to be read. It reflects the heart of our Lord Jesus for those often neglected

by others. Spurgeon once said, 'The joy of Jesus is the joy of saving sinners.' This book calls us to believe that His joy is saving people who live in every kind of community, including the poorest."

Jonathan Prime, Associate National Director of FIEC (Local Ministries)

"I loved this book. Having lived my entire life in needy northern towns so much of it resonated with my experience, both within the church and outside. As someone planting a church in one of these towns, it highlighted almost every issue we've encountered as we've sought to build a team, find partners, raise support, and reach our community with the gospel. Mez's call for the UK church to recognise and repent of our historic neglect of forgotten places and people, to reassess where our helping might be hurting, and to renew an active and sacrificial support for those seeking to reach the least, the last, and the lost is exactly what we need right now. I pray the Lord might use it to build his kingdom and bring glory to his name."

Graham Thompson, Pastor of Spen Valley Church, Cleckheaton

"Working in a scheme, one experience people express repeatedly is the feeling of not being heard by the police, social workers, doctors and teachers. For too many generations in Scotland, the impoverished voice hasn't been heard in our seminaries, churches and culture. The Least, the Last and the Lost *is a significant book, as it steps in the right direction to equip people to listen for that voice. May this book launch many more like it. Mez has assembled a group of contributors, as well as giving you years of his experience and research. This has produced a resource for planters, preachers, and people in Kingdom work to read, process, and practice in the UK church."*

Chris Davidson, Pastor of Merkinch Free Church, Inverness

"As someone who comes from a poor coal mining family in the forgotten South Wales valleys, I've worked in dire poverty and also in middle class contexts. I feel like Mez: a class-chameleon! This book resonates with me in a big way. It's an overdue and honest clarion call to the UK church to wake up to the beautiful harvest on its doorstep that's so often neglected.

"Mez is doing a great service to the church here: speaking up for the poor and needy, gathering hard data to intelligently argue the cause of the gospel for those who have no voice. We all need to hear these challenges and not close our minds to gracious rebuke. It might sting, but rather than defending our positions, we must do some soul searching and ask 'What can we do to answer the call of God to the poor and oppressed?' Take this is opportunity to grow your love for God in loving the unlovely. Don't miss the blessing!"

Dr Joel Morris, Executive Director of Union School of Theology, Wales

"This is a great book. Insightful, challenging, practical and heartfelt. Mez uses facts, research, personal experience and the Bible to blow apart our common and damaging misconceptions about ministry to the poor. He has done us all a huge favour by refusing to talk about ministry to the poor on the terms set by middle class churches. This book packs a punch because it allows those on our schemes and estates to set the agenda for ministry in their communities. It is packed with good theology and practical wisdom but more than anything it is a cry to the rest of us to wake up to what's going on in our schemes and estates. Stunning insights, terrible tales, lived experience, and a radical rethinking of ministry to the poor are to be found in these pages. Read this book or shut your mouth."

Neil MacMillan, Pastor of Cornerstone Free Church; Moderator of Free Church of Scotland; Director of Church Planting Generation

"In this book, Mez has brought together current data, lived experiences and a pastor's love and longing for people in a way that will be a loving challenge and encouragement to many. A timely and important work that I know will be used as people plant and revitalise churches and bring the good news of Jesus to the millions living in the lost and forgotten communities of the world. This is a book that all church leaders should read."

Steve Robinson, Senior Pastor of Cornerstone Church Liverpool; Director of Cornerstone Collective, Acts29GB

"In The Least, The Last, and The Lost, *McConnell shares his razor-sharp analysis of the struggles of those living in poverty and how it has impacted the development of the church in modern Britain. More than just theological, this book charts the history of the church in the UK today. More than just sociological, this book points to a hope that is transcendent. More than just recounting grievances, this book sets out a vision for the spiritual renewal for those living in hard places. I truly believe that were church leaders to take time considering the conclusions of this book, then the result will be many more healthy churches in our poorest communities."*

Dr. Matthew Spandler-Davison, Director of Acts 29; Director of Church in Hard Places; Executive Director of 20schemes

THE LEAST THE LAST & THE LOST

Also by Mez McConnell:

Church in Hard Places
First Steps Series
Is There Anybody Out There?
The Creaking on the Stairs
Preparing for Baptism

MEZ MCCONNELL

THE LEAST THE LAST & THE LOST

Understanding Poverty in the UK &
the Responsibility of the Local Church

EP

Scripture quotations are taken from The New International Version NIV Holy Bible, New International Version Anglicised, NIV Copyright © 1979, 1984, 2011 by Biblica, Inc. Used by permission. All rights reserved worldwide.

Scripture quotations marked "CSB" are taken from the Christian Standard Bible
Scripture quotations marked "ESV" are taken from the English Standard Version
Scripture quotations marked "GNB" are taken from the Good News Bible
Scripture quotations marked "KJV" are taken from the King James Version
Scripture quotations marked "NKJV" are taken from the New King James Version

First published in Great Britain in 2021

British Library Cataloguing in Publication Data
A record for this book is available from the British Library

ISBN: 978-1-78397-328-6

Typeset by Pete Barnsley (CreativeHoot.com)

Evangelical Press (EP Books), an imprint of 10Publishing
Unit C, Tomlinson Road, Leyland, PR25 2DY, England

www.epbooks.org
epbooks@10ofthose.com

1 3 5 7 10 8 6 4 2

CONTENTS

FOREWORD

Please don't say that this book is thought provoking. It is – as much as anything I've read – but that is not its purpose.

Please don't say that it's informative. It is – I have learnt huge amounts – but that is not its purpose.

Please don't say that it's emotional. It is – I am not ashamed to say I have cried while reading it – but that is not its purpose.

This book introduces you to a joy that is spoken of throughout the Bible, a joy that has been known in the church for most of its history. But, somewhere along the line, certainly before I was born, Christians have forgotten it.

What is this joy?

It is a joy Paul describes as a fragrant offering in Philippians 4:18. It was an offering that was pleasing to God, but also a mark of the sincerity of the church's love towards him. Paul, speaking to the church at Corinth, said this to them: "God is able to make all grace abound to you, so that having all sufficiency in all things at all times, you may abound in every good work" (2 Cor. 9:8, ESV). He goes on in verse 9 to say: "As it is written, 'He has distributed freely, *he has given to the poor*; his righteousness endures forever.'"[1]

The ministry of this service was not only concerned with supplying the needs of the saints, but with overflowing in many thanksgivings to God. It reminded both the givers and the recipients of the gospel. Paul's aim for every church is that we would know this joy and blessing in our own giving to the poor.

As a church, we at Mount Pleasant felt that Scripture was clear on this issue. We wanted to partner with a church that was reaching the poor. We weren't sure what it would look like, but we did it initially because the Bible says we should. And so we formed a partnership with Niddrie Community Church in Edinburgh, Scotland.

We gave money because the Bible says we should. We prayed because the Bible says we should. We offered help because the Bible says we should.

Yet, what happened next was extraordinary. We started to *feel invested* in what was happening in Edinburgh. If they were blessed, we were blessed. If a soul was saved, it felt like we were involved. If an addict was doing a Bible study, we felt their excitement. If a new project started, it encouraged us. If they had a struggle, we wrestled in prayer.

In lockdown, we had a joint online prayer meeting. A lot of children from our church came to that prayer meeting and one little girl from a middle-class family sticks in my mind. She saw a young single mum speaking about how Jesus was changing her life and it moved her so much that she prayed for her. This little girl didn't see a charity case but a sister in Jesus – and it blessed both of them.

We have been blessed in so many ways by our partnership. It's not just about money. We have learnt and been challenged. We get more than we give. The partnership is real. One time we even received a financial gift from them, which moved our church. We have learnt about how to deal with people who are struggling. Our church plant in Neath, for example, which is reaching similar people to Niddrie, has felt strengthened by those in a similar spiritual battle.

When Mez came and preached, a large number of people in our church who are from council estates were just so thrilled one of "their own" was preaching. At first, I was frustrated by this. After all, I had been a church planter in one of the estates. But then a teenager who was in care sat at the back of the church listening. She'd been coming along for a while and every week I had tried to talk to her. Sometimes she would respond and often she wouldn't. It was a real struggle. But, after listening to Mez speak that day, she was friendly and chatty. I think it changed the way she saw our church. I remember feeling so happy at her laughing away with others after the service that I thought my heart was going to explode out of my chest.

I am so glad we are partners with Niddrie Community Church. I believe that our relationship blesses both churches in a way that is thoroughly biblical.

As you travel through Wales, you will see chapels of every theological stripe in many of our poorest communities. These buildings remind us of what Christians in the past felt about the poor. Their highest priority was to make sure these people had access to the gospel. Read your church history. William Tyndale, John Wesley, George Whitefield, Charles Spurgeon. All had a love for the poor. Wesley says,

> *We came to Newcastle about six; and, after a short refreshment, walked into the town. I was surprised: so much drunkenness, cursing and swearing, (even from the mouths of little children,) do I never remember to have seen or heard before, in so small a compass of time. Surely this place is ripe for Him who "came not to call the righteous, but sinners to repentance."*[2]

Our Christian forebears put their money where their mouth was. Where is the modern church in the UK putting its money? I believe a terrible sin has occurred in the UK church and nobody has noticed. When I worked in a church plant in a poor community, we had no money, and nobody asked us for any. Yet, when I went to a more affluent city-centre church, I was shocked by endless para-church groups expecting money from us. I regularly received begging letters from a host of spurious organisations. Why are local churches footing the bill for Christian agencies who claim to be helping the poorest members of our society? In my experience, some of these organisations are totally deceitful. Some of them get offended when I refuse their request to come and speak at our church. Some have even been known to turn up at our services to hand out leaflets or "prayer letters" encouraging members to set up direct debits. Even people who beg are never this rude. This is stealing from the church, from God and from the poor. It is as Campbell Morgan once observed: "One cannot help the conviction that many of our organizations are fungus growths, sapping the Church's life and contributing nothing to her fruitfulness."[3]

As you read this book, I would ask you to look at your direct debits and ask yourself if this is why God has given you money. Are we stealing from the poor to finance Christian para-church organisations? Pastors should look at their church budgets and honestly assess if their giving actually helps the least, the last and the lost.

How much of our giving is, in reality, stealing from the poor?

God has provided His people with enough money to help the poor and those serving in poor communities. Millions are going to hell in our poorest communities and, in some case, we are giving our money to nonsense.

The great commission is for *churches*. For 2,000 years, baptism has been done in *local churches,* regardless of denomination. Our giving should likewise be done through *local churches*. And our poorest communities are ripe for Him who "came not to call the righteous, but sinners to repentance".[4]

If we love God and if we love the least, the last and the lost, then we must demonstrate it with the money that God has given to us.

This book is written in a very easy style. It slowly but surely untangles the lies people believe about the poor. It is moving but not patronising. It is rigorous but still interesting. It creates sympathy, but at the same time it is brutally honest. It speaks from Scripture about the issue. Don't respond to it by being a hearer only. Be a doer.

We read in almost every page of the New Testament about God's concern for the poor. When the New Testament talks about giving, it talks of the rich church helping the poor church.

If you want to know the joy of God in your life, maybe it's time to think about the way you give, and to whom you give.

I pray that this book will encourage you to do that.

Steve Levy
Pastor, Mount Pleasant Church, Swansea, Wales

PREFACE

Before you scan the contents page of this book and then put it back on the shelf, can I just have your attention for a few moments?

It would be easy to look at a book like this and think to yourself: *This is just for pastors or missionaries or Christians in full-time vocational service.*

But you would be wrong to think that.

This book is the product of over 20 years of thought and thousands of hours of research. This book is for any and every Christian who has an interest in the poor and the oppressed.

I am hoping that includes you.

At heart, this is a book about how to love God better by loving the least, the last and the lost.

So, don't put it back. Take it to the counter. Pay for it. Take it home. Read it.

Ask the Lord to change your heart.

Who knows, maybe this book will inspire you to change the direction of your life to the glory of God.

Mez McConnell

ACKNOWLEDGEMENTS

I would like to thank all those who contributed to this book (not least, those who have written the Spotlight sections) and the Fellowship of Independent Evangelical Churches (FIEC) for financing the research behind the book. Every person who buys the book will have access to all of our data regarding poverty in the UK. They will also have access to details on the FIEC and where they are in relation to the least, the last and the lost. Particular thanks must go to Timothy Hein for his hundreds of hours of dedicated research. Without him, I wouldn't have a book. The real fruit of his labours can be found in that online resource.

Just a small disclaimer: some of the contributors to this book may not necessarily agree with me on every issue, just as I might disagree with them on some things. I was looking less for agreement in this book, and more for opening up a dialogue. To be clear, the FIEC funded the research, but they don't necessarily endorse every opinion expressed within these pages.

I would like to thank my wife, Miriam, and my girls, Lydia and Keziah.

Thanks also to my church and to those behind the scenes who have helped to make this book become a reality.

I thank Jesus most of all for my salvation because, without Him in my life, this work would not be now in your hands.

INTRODUCTION:

WHY HAVE I WRITTEN THIS BOOK?

When I pick up a book, several questions run through my mind. *Why has the author written it? What's the point of it? What does the author expect from me at the end of it?* They are reasonable questions, and I wouldn't expect any different as you now hold this book in your hands.

To fully appreciate my motives and objectives in writing this book, I want to take the time to share some of my life story with you. I'm hopeful that this will help answer the *why* question. As to the *what* questions, I pray that the answer to those will become more evident as the book unfolds.

A CLASS CHAMELEON

As I type these words on an expensive laptop, I am sitting in a nice house. What's even better is that it's my own house. I have been married for over 20 years to Miriam, I have two teenage daughters, three foster children and two dogs. My wife and children love *Downton Abbey* and correcting my grammar. My wife screws her face up in disgust when I say "bog" instead of "bathroom". My girls get annoyed when I ask what's for tea instead of what's for dinner. Both of my girls aspire to university degrees, with one hoping to be a teacher and the other a scientist.

So far, so typically middle class. At least, that is how it would appear from a material perspective. But my family and I live in a scheme (or council estate) on the east side of Edinburgh. We live and work within a community – Niddrie – which is designated "deprived" by the UK government (more on this later). Therefore, from a geographical perspective, we are anything but middle class.

I live and move, somewhat uneasily, between these two worlds. I feel most comfortable socially within the scheme culture, but I have learned to navigate, and even appropriate, some of the cultural sensitivities of the middle class. So, I like a chippie, a beer and watching the boxing with my pals on the one hand, but I also like reading all kinds of literature and have high educational hopes for my girls, on the other. This has left me as somewhat of a "class chameleon". I have no impulse towards upward social mobility (which sounds odd to the middle class), yet I have no problem if my girls want to leave the scheme and pursue their ambitions (which is seen as defecting to the enemy by the benefits/working class).

RAGE AGAINST THE MACHINE

It was all so much easier when I was younger. A quarter of a century ago, I was shivering in the cold outside Victoria train station in London. I was high. I was hungry. I was scared. I was so very angry at the world. I was full of rage but, had you asked me, I would have had no clue against whom, specifically, this fury burned.

I was paranoid and tired from trying to ward off the advances of a procession of male predators who wanted to have sex with me. Within weeks I would be doing 15 months in a Category A prison where I would grow angrier still, forced into terrible acts of violence out of fear and self-preservation. Always on edge. Jittery. Untrusting. Guarded. Instead of rehabilitating me, prison hardened me, and with unfettered access to every kind of drug, my habits spiralled out of control. I left prison far angrier than I'd entered it.

I was furious at the world, the system (whatever that was), and anybody who I thought had it better than me. I had been forced from my home in Ireland into a children's home in England, passed from foster carer to foster carer, separated from my only sister, beaten, ignored and, finally, spat out into the world at 16 years old – violent, vengeful and left to my own devices. My social workers and counsellors did me no favours either. I entered adulthood in a complete mess. I was a victim. Nothing was my fault. It was "my circumstances". It was the Conservative Party. They stole our milk in the 1970s and 1980s and we never got over it. Imagine the man I could have been if I'd just had milk! They killed the miners. They killed the manufacturing industry. They wreaked havoc across the northern working-class heartlands. All of it churning about in my head, driving my impulses and emotions.

Homelessness followed soon after. Park benches, disused houses, on friends' floors –wherever I could get my head down. All of it blotted out by more and more drugs. Dealing, stealing, burglary, violence, lying; whatever it took to get me what I wanted. Meaningless, monotonous jobs: putting lids on yoghurt tops, making nails, making cardboard boxes, making hairspray, labouring, cleaning toilets, and my personal favourite – putting Ghostbuster badges on birthday cards. Hating my life. Hating my existence. Making bad choice after bad choice. None of it my fault. All of it everybody else's. This is what society had made me. That's what I told myself. No one cared about me, so why would I care about them?

BROKEN BY THE GOSPEL

Then, one day I met with Christ in a violent and uncompromising way. I found a Matthew Henry commentary in the house I was staying in and came across the book of Romans. The book of Romans brutalised me far more effectively than my vicious stepmother ever did! The Apostle Paul forced me to confront my sin. My selfish choices. My self-righteous, self-absorbed, vicious cycle of sinful rebellion. I hated the book of Romans with all of my heart. If I could have, I would have beaten the Apostle Paul to death with a bat.

I wanted my social workers back. I wanted the kind-hearted old lady at the soup kitchen who was sympathetic to my problems and told me I was a good boy who just hadn't had the right breaks. I wanted to be told that I wasn't a bad person. That I was just damaged by a bad start in life. Yet, the Bible destroyed every barrier and excuse I had ever constructed over the years to justify my way of life. The Bible tore a hole through every argument I had for all the pain and misery I had caused to others. The Bible wouldn't let me off the hook. The Bible didn't want to hear that it wasn't my fault. God Himself, through the pages of Scripture, grabbed my head with both hands and forced me to look into a spiritual mirror to see what I really was and what I'd truly become.

I was a sinner. A rebel against God, His Word and His people.

Looking at my true self in that spiritual mirror was the worst experience of my life. Worse than a maximum-security prison cell. Worse than prolonged punches to the kidneys by playground bullies. I was crushed by the realisation of my sin. I fought with all my might to look away from my reflection. But God, in His mercy, forced me to keep looking, long and hard. Then, just as I was about to sink into total despair, He granted me salvation. That's when I first discovered what love really was. I had been told by a few people in my childhood that Jesus loved me, but I never understood it. *Why would Jesus love me? My own mother didn't even love me. Those placed in authority over me didn't love me. I didn't even love me.* It was only when I saw the true depth of my sinful heart, and the great mercy of a forgiving God, that I began to understand love.

Looking into that mirror, with no excuses left, I sank to my knees and begged for God's forgiveness. I begged to escape His just wrath. I threw myself on the mercy of Jesus. I confessed my sinful, proud rebellion against my Holy Creator. I threw my whole weight behind the Lord Jesus to save me, not only from myself, but from the sin that had separated me from God.

Against my wishes, I had become a Christian.

COUNTING THE COST

Usually, at this part of a testimony we get to the good stuff that God does next. I talk about how my life changed for the better, *blah de blah de blah*. Of course, my life has changed for the better in many ways, and I praise God for that. But I had to go through a bloody culture war first, something that very few people back then understood, and nobody had warned me about. It turns out that there really is a great cost to following Jesus.

By the time we get to Luke 14, large crowds are following Jesus. He has become something of a Middle Eastern superstar. Everybody wanted a piece of Him. Doubtless, His closest disciples were loving the buzz of being around Him. So, Luke records these words of Jesus to them at that time.

> *Large crowds were travelling with Jesus and turning to them he said: "If anyone comes to me and does not hate father and mother, wife and children, brothers and sisters – yes, even their own life – such a person cannot be my disciple. And whoever does not carry their cross and follow me cannot be my disciple."*[5]

Jesus is clear that He requires absolute devotion from all who claim the name "Christian". That's exactly what He goes on to tell them: Those of you who do not give up everything you have cannot be my disciples.[6] In other words, don't put your name to His if you are not all in.

This is a pretty straightforward set of verses in the Bible. They're not complicated in any way. But I soon discovered that different social classes interpret them in very different ways. I took Jesus's words to heart and immediately began to review everything in my life, including lifelong friends and family members, in order to discover who and what would hold me back from getting serious with Jesus. My new middle-class friends applauded me for my commitment. They encouraged me to leave behind all of my friends and family members who were criminals or drug dealers and/or users (not that they all were, you understand).

Don't get me wrong, there was no malicious intent. But what they were doing, inadvertently I'm sure, was asking me to leave my entire life and culture behind in order to assimilate to theirs. The issue was black and white in their minds. My culture was bad and theirs was good. My culture needed to be discarded and their culture was the one to which I should aspire. Of course, I lapped it up. *Why wouldn't I?* I wanted to get as far away from my old life as I possibly could. I was desperate to fit into this new Christian world, and so I walked away from it all – my family, my friends and my whole way of life.

As soon as I made this decision, a spiritual war broke out on two fronts simultaneously.

WARRING WITH THE CHURCH

Firstly, I discovered that a person can't just follow Jesus on their own. They have to be part of a thing called "the church". Or, more particularly, a local church. I thought churches were just places people went for religious ceremonies: baptisms, weddings, funerals and the like. I had no idea that Christians met together twice on Sundays and again during the midweek.

Then, on top of that, there was all the socialising and drinking copious amounts of Schloer.[7] I wasn't prepared for the cultural idiosyncrasies of the Christian world. It was intense. The problem was that I had no category for Christians. They were as foreign to me as an Amazonian tribe. I had never in my life met a working-class Christian. I had no idea what went on inside a church any more than I knew what went on inside a mosque or a synagogue. Despite the kindness of many church members, the cold reality is that, in the early days of my faith, I felt far safer, and more comfortable, inside a maximum-security prison yard than I ever did attending a Sunday morning service.

Let me reiterate, nobody was mean to me. In fact, far from it. I was saved into a congregation that was full, in the main, of some of the kindest people I had ever met. They were patient, godly saints, many of whom have prayed for me faithfully over the years (and still do). They weren't unlikeable or judgemental. Actually, the opposite was true.

Some people went out of their way to embrace me, and a godly couple even took me into their home for a time. They invited me to eat with them and welcomed me into their family. But it was pretty clear that in this Authorised Version-only, organ-only, predominantly suit-and-tie-wearing-congregation (as it was at that time), I was the odd one out. Even my attempts to fit in by wearing a shirt and tie in the early months of my conversion only heightened the difference and made me feel even more uncomfortable. It was clear by how I talked, how I walked and how I thought that I was very different to them.

The nicer these Christians were to me and the more I began to enjoy church life, the more anxious I became. I wanted to love these people. I wanted to be a part of the family of God. I wanted to sit around dinner tables with church members and laugh about my day. But I just couldn't face it. I felt dirty. I felt unworthy. I felt fake. I just wanted to be alone. I was fearful and anxious that these people would find out what I was really like, and then reject me as so many had before. I wanted to be accepted so much that I hated myself for being so weak.

Almost overnight, I became something of a local celebrity among Christians in the town. Everybody knew who I was. I was a novelty item. "A brand plucked from the fire" is how someone once described me. Soon, I became a man in demand. Everybody wanted to hear my story. They said, "Tell us how Jesus saved you" – but what they really meant was, "Tell us all the gory, heart-rending details of your past. Recount your time in prison. Tell us about your childhood abuse and your homelessness. Oh, and tell us about Jesus too."

They didn't ever put it quite that starkly, but I knew what was expected. They were an easy crowd to please, these Christians, and I was desperate for their acceptance. I wanted to belong. I wanted to be special. I wanted the attention. I was a willing participant. Their applause gave me meaning and made me feel significant. Their awe at my testimony gave me a special kind of pride. It made me feel like I was somebody important. It made me feel admired in a culture that, at worst, despised my friends and, at best, feared them. I enjoyed the acclaim. But, while I was fighting for acceptance within this new world, I was also fighting a war on another front.

WARRING WITH MY OLD LIFE

As soon as I professed my faith in Jesus, the dynamic of the relationship between my old friends and family members changed dramatically. Becoming a Christian on a council estate is akin to becoming a Conservative voter (back when northern towns exclusively voted Labour!) It was to deny your roots. It was to deny your own kind. It was to defect to the other side. I had committed the cardinal sin of appearing like I was trying to better myself. *How dare I deny my working-class roots? How dare I even think of getting out of my chaotic, abusive, self-destructive life?*

Many things could be forgiven within my culture. Finding myself in trouble with the police? Easily explained away – *youthful exuberance and, anyway, we all know the police are corrupt.* Experimenting with drugs? Easily explained away – *everybody does it, right? It's almost a rite of passage and, anyway, who doesn't like a little fun at the weekends?* Being sentenced to spend time in prison? Easily explained away – *maybe a disappointment to some, but to the majority it was a badge of honour. Certainly nothing to be ashamed about.* Becoming a Christian? Silence. *What? Hang on a minute. That's not right. What's that about? Why would anyone do that, let alone somebody from our walk of life? That's not just disappointing, it's bloody embarrassing.*

Indeed, you would have been hard pressed to find a single family member or close friend of mine who was not confused, bemused or downright angry at this step I had taken in my life. Discussions about Mez "turning Christian" were almost funereal in some circles. Finding God was pretty much equated with a mental illness, or something lifers and sex offenders did to ease their guilty consciences. I remember reading about the experiences of teenage girls getting pregnant in the 1950s and people whispering about them behind their backs. It was a cultural taboo. Back in the 1960s and 1970s, the majority of the British population were disdainful of relationships between people of mixed races. Becoming a born-again Christian was on a par with those things, certainly in the 1990s. I'm convinced that if I had come out as gay, I wouldn't have elicited such widespread hostility and profound disapproval. It was a very, very painful time in my life.

The upshot of these pressures was that I found myself walking the tightrope of trying to fit in with Christians, while trying to maintain relationships from my old life. I felt like John the Baptist, with one foot in the old world and one foot in the new. The pressure was further compounded because I had nobody with whom I could share my experiences, troubles, fears and anxieties. Most of the people in the church had come from a long-established Christian heritage that went back decades, often even longer. That meant that, while some Christian confidants could sympathise with me, I faced these spiritual battles on my own. I was always defensive and on edge. Because of my stunted emotions, and my unspoken fears and doubts – like Israel in the wilderness – I began to pine for my old life on the streets. I romanticised it. I conveniently forgot about all the reasons I had been desperate to leave it behind. I even began to seriously worry whether I was on the verge of losing my mind.

I remember the exact moment when all my emotions came to a head. I was on my own at the bottom of the garden in a house where I was lodging. This house sat on the top of a hill, overlooking the town below. As I sat on that garden wall smoking my roll-up, my mind was a mess. I knew it was either flight or fight. It was crunch time. Stay and take the risk on the Christian life that I could see spreading out before me, or run back to the cold, vomit-strewn doorways – a life that I at least understood. I had the devil whispering in my ear, coaxing me to run back to the life I knew. At the same time the Holy Spirit was urging me to stay and hold fast to my new life with Jesus. The constant mental to-ing and fro-ing was wearing me down. Thankfully, the Holy Spirit won out that day. The love of Christian strangers won out over the perverse allure of street culture, the devil and my own sinful desires.

The exact moment I made that decision to stay and fight for this new life was the day that everything began to change for me. I began to devour the Bible. I began to grow in my knowledge of and love for Jesus. I slowly grew more accustomed to the strange culture of the church. Most importantly of all, I began to question everything and everyone around me about all things biblical.

That's when my problems really began.

BITING THE HAND THAT DIDN'T ACTUALLY FEED ME!

I don't recall the exact day that the celebrity shine started to wear off for me. It was a gradual thing. Firstly, I began to grow in my knowledge of the Bible. Then, I began to grow in the knowledge of myself. As time wore on, instead of pride in my past, I began to feel shame. I wanted to run from my past. I wanted to leave it far behind. I didn't want to talk about it anymore. I felt like every testimony I gave kept me in bondage to the sin from which I was trying so hard to escape.

But, in church circles, everybody wanted me to keep regurgitating it. I began to feel that perhaps I should be doing more than just continuously telling my horror story for the entertainment of the (mainly) middle-class masses. So, I began to try to distance myself from my testimony. I said "no" to speaking engagements. I offered to teach the Bible instead. Invariably, this suggestion was met with bewilderment and, in some cases, open amusement. I was the church's testimony guy, not the preacher guy.

That's when I began to feel a distancing from the church. Subtly, you understand. Not mean spirited, but there, nonetheless. The invitations to speak dried up. It seemed as if the more I wanted to distance myself from my old life, the more the church kept me at arm's-length for anything else. These feelings were exacerbated further as I began to study some of the deep doctrines of the faith. To the surprise of many, I read book after book on a variety of biblical subjects. I remember when I first stumbled upon the wonderful doctrines of grace; it was like pouring petrol on the smouldering embers of my soul. My spirit burst into flame with the realisation of the absolute sovereignty of God over all things. So, of course, I wanted to talk about these things. But it wouldn't be long before somebody in the church would throw cold water over those fires. As one leader told me when I enquired about seminary: "Bible college isn't for guys like you, Mez. Just stick to loving Jesus and you will be okay."

The unspoken assumption seemed to be that guys "like me" didn't need to know the Bible that deeply. After all, it's not like we would become pastors, right? I told myself I was just being paranoid, yet everything I saw in the evangelical world confirmed my suspicions. For example, I never met a pastor from a council estate. In fact, I met very few pastors working in council estates. Also, I never heard a voice like mine, or met a person from my background in church, except if there was a testimony night somewhere. The Christian conferences I attended were the same. When I finally did go to seminary, I discovered the same thing there. When I brought the issue up, I was shushed. *What are you talking about? It's not true. It's just your imagination.* I noted the irritation whenever I spoke about it. It was made clear to me that if I wanted to progress into Christian ministry then I had better not upset the apple cart. "After all," one friend told me, "where's the wisdom in biting the hand that feeds you?" To my shame, I stopped talking about it. Not out of wisdom, but out of fear. The fear that I would be excluded from the middle-class club. I couldn't go back to my old life, that much was clear. *So,* I reasoned, *if I wanted acceptance in this new life, then I had better toe the line.*

STREET GANGS AND STRIPPERS

Despite my private frustrations and a recognition of my powerlessness within the evangelical world, I left seminary and went into full-time Christian ministry in 1999. My family and I would be working with street gangs in Brazil by 2003, and so I felt fulfilled in the work that the Lord had given me to do. *After all, what did I have to complain about?* I had a wonderful family and a successful ministry. I had come a long way from the pitiful figure sleeping in bus shelters and smoking discarded cigarette butts that I found on street corners or picked out of rubbish bins.

But, two phone calls, an off-the-cuff comment, a surprise party and a stripper changed the direction of my life – yet again – and reawakened all of the misgivings I had suppressed for so long. The first phone call was with my father, who I rang at least once a month while living in Brazil. There was nothing unusual about the call and I guarantee that he probably has no recollection of it whatsoever. Once the customary football chat was out of the way, I remember him asking me how things were going. I explained what Miriam and I were doing and, in a rare moment of emotional depth, he announced that he was proud of me. "It's all Jesus", I assured him. He grunted, the way he always does when I say things like that. I asked him, "Why don't you get yourself along to a church this Sunday, dad?" He simply replied, "I don't think so, son. I haven't got the bottle to do that." That was it. That's all that was said. Completely off the cuff. Nothing profound. The moment passed, and I hung up with the promise to call him the following month.

However, try as I might, I couldn't get his words out of my mind. My dad has been a builder for 50 years and has seen the rough end of life. He socialises in Miners' Clubs and is well used to being in bars and going to parties which, more often than not, end in violence and multiple arrests. To be clear, he is not a criminal, nor a violent man. My point is that he doesn't even blink in those situations, and yet here he was admitting to me that he was scared to go into a church! But, when I thought back to my own experiences of church in the early days, I began to appreciate what he meant.

Several months later, our little family returned from Brazil on furlough. We were tired, but extremely encouraged by the work we had established there. The ministry was blossoming, and all was well. That's when I received the second phone call. This time it was from a family member inviting me to a surprise birthday party for my dad. "Is there anything I can do to help?" I asked. "Oh yes," came the reply. "You can pay for the stripper." I laughed, but they were deadly serious. "I'm not paying for a stripper!" I said, "I will pay for the DJ." "Okay," was the reply as they hung up.

Of course, this now left me with a new dilemma. Do I go to my dad's party or not? I hadn't seen him for a couple of years at this point, and so I was leaning towards going. But now that I knew there was going be a stripper, where did that leave me as a Christian? Every Christian friend I asked counselled me not to go, citing a bad witness as the reason. Fellow pastors offered the same advice. But, after praying about it, and talking to my wife who would ultimately accompany me to the party, I decided that I would go and just leave the room when the stripper made her appearance.

The day of the party came and, as expected, the pub was packed to the rafters with family and friends I had not seen for years. It was loud, it was raucous, and it was (mostly) fun. It didn't take me long to spot the drugs being handed out in one corner, or the shady deals being made in another. The karaoke machine was being well used and, bang on time, the stripper made her entrance. As Miriam and I got up to leave the whole place started howling abuse and making fun of us. But we moved into the other bar and waited for the show to be over. When we returned, we received more than our fair share of scowls and snarky comments from people who thought our actions somehow communicated that we were better than them. Miriam and I retreated to a quiet corner with our drinks, planning to stay a couple of hours more so as not to appear rude.

Then, over the course of the evening, a strange thing happened. One by one, people who had been mocking my faith earlier in the evening came to sit at our table. Every person asked me about my faith and every single one regaled me with stories of their own broken lives and how empty they felt. By the end of the evening, there was a crowd around our table as people sat, some nursing their drinks, some smoking their joints, listening as I explained the gospel to them. A few made snarky, sarcastic comments, playing to the crowds, but the majority were taking in what I was saying. Instead of leaving early, we ended up being the last to leave. Of course, I was exhilarated by what had happened. I spent the next couple of days on a spiritual high. But that wouldn't last long.

QUESTIONS, QUESTIONS, QUESTIONS

Miriam and I were touring the country at this time as we visited churches to raise the profile of our work back in Brazil. Life was so busy that I had little time to think. But, in my few quiet moments, usually on the long car journeys, my mind drifted back to my family and friends at that party. *Did any of them come to faith?* Not to my knowledge. That wasn't what was troubling me. *What if one or more of them had come to faith? Where would they go to church? How would the church cope with them, and they with the church?* The churches I had been in struggled with one or two people from my background, so what would they do if multiple people came to faith? Then I thought about the party as a whole. *How many of those who were in attendance would ever come into contact with a Christian in their daily lives?* These were dustbin men, hairdressers, builders, scrap merchants, painters and decorators, electricians, plumbers and labourers. Never mind the criminal element, who were a whole other ball game. *When would any of them have an opportunity to hear the gospel proclaimed?* I knew the answers to these questions, and it depressed me. There was very little gospel light in my home town in Yorkshire (there still isn't) and, even if it did exist, it was not easily accessible by people from my cultural background.

It was then that I began to question whether I should return to Brazil. In the town where I worked, there were at least 10 solid gospel churches along a three-mile stretch of road near my home. One of these churches had 15,000 members! On the other hand, I reasoned (with myself), none of them were reaching the street gangs and local favelas. Yet, what they had in Brazil was far more than those living in the council estates and schemes of the UK. So, I asked myself, *why travel thousands of miles to bring Christ there, when my own people were toppling headfirst into a lost eternity right on my doorstep?* After much prayer and soul searching, Miriam and I made the difficult decision to leave our burgeoning ministry in Brazil and return to the UK to plant a church on a housing estate. At that point we had no idea where, we just knew that this was what we should do. Not long after that, a providential turn of events took us to Niddrie Community Church, on a housing scheme in Edinburgh where, in 2007, I became the pastor of a small congregation in need of revitalisation.

SPIRITUAL WASTELANDS?

Shortly before leaving for Scotland, one old saint took me aside and said, "It won't be like Brazil, son. Scotland is a spiritual wasteland and the people are hard to the gospel up there." I don't think he was trying to discourage me, rather to prepare me for the hard work ahead. Yet, when I got there, I found that the people were not hard to the gospel (although many were and are), they had just never heard it before, and certainly not from someone from their own background.

It wasn't long before we started to see conversions, and our church slowly grew. Instead of being a building full of outsiders, who were subject to the taunts and assaults of local youths, we became an intrinsic part of the community again. God was at work in Niddrie, and He still is. Not long after this, 20schemes was born.[8] Our idea was simply to revitalise or plant 20 gospel-preaching churches in 20 schemes across Scotland over 10 years. Despite lots of cynicism, opposition, ambivalence and a lack of support from the UK Christian church, our ministry flourished and continues to do so thanks to God's mercy and kindness. In one sense, the old saint was right when he said that Scotland is a spiritual wasteland. I would be even more specific by stating that Scotland's *schemes* are a spiritual wasteland. Not because of a lack of gospel opportunities, rather a lack of healthy, gospel-preaching local churches.

STAND UP AND SPEAK OUT

Once again, I had found my voice to speak up for the millions in our country who live, work and die in council estates and housing schemes. As I began to write and speak about these concerns, I was quickly denounced as causing trouble or, more popularly, of having a chip on my shoulder. I have prayed, cried, shouted, fought, studied, sacrificed my health and spent all my energy over two decades so that believers from council estates and housing schemes can have a voice in the reformed evangelical wing of the UK church. I've had to scrap my way through the system, as well as jump through all the hoops and barriers put in my way, in order to be accepted as credible in the UK church.

There is quite clearly a fault line in the UK evangelical world. All men and women are not equal when it comes to having access to the gospel and discipleship-oriented resources. I've seen it in everything from the heavy emphasis on student ministry, the speakers at conferences, internships offered at local churches, theological publications, books (specifically evangelistic material), and theological education. Let me be clear, the failing does not lie with para-church organisations or theological institutions and book publishers. They are only catering to, and for, the markets they have access to. The failing lies at the local church level. It lies with pastors and church leaders who, quite obviously, do not see gospel ministry to council estates and schemes as a priority in their towns, villages and cities.

Thankfully, it is not all doom and gloom. The FIEC, for example, have prioritised our communities in recent years, and have released a lot of money towards work in deprived communities across the country.[9] They continue to hold discussions with us, even if they often feel our approaches are somewhat "bull in a China shop"! Likewise, 10ofThose have proved a valuable ally to us and, along with Christian Focus Publications, they have enabled us to get our resources out to a wider audience.[10] Union School of Theology have sought to work in genuine partnership with us whereas, historically, other institutions have sought to control us.[11] In other words, there are slivers of light on the horizon, but every square inch we move forward is hard fought.

Some feel that there is altogether far too much talk concerning deprived communities in the UK right now – yet it's been 38 years since Roy Joslin wrote *Urban Harvest*.[12] His worry for the UK church back then was that it was leaving behind the working classes. Bearing in mind this was almost four decades ago, he writes: "Christianity in this country has become a middle-class movement."[13] In the intervening years, since those words were written, the church has become *more* middle class, not less, and the gap between the evangelical church and those living and dying in housing schemes and council estates is as vast as it has ever been. One theologically-minded book in nearly four decades hardly constitutes a massive swing in our direction!

Quite simply, if the church in the UK is not willing to listen to our pleas, then we will plant new churches and revitalise dying ones ourselves. It will take longer, and be more difficult, but we will do it. It is what we have had to do with 20schemes, and it is what is happening through Church in Hard Places in over 30 countries around the world.[14]

Why are those involved in planting, pastoring and revitalising churches in deprived communities finding it so hard for our voices to be both heard and taken seriously? Darren McGarvey, in his brilliantly provocative book, *Poverty Safari* gets to the nub of the issue:

> *In Scotland, poverty is dominated by a left-leaning, liberal, middle class. Because this specialist class is so genuinely well-intentioned when it comes to the interests of people in deprived communities, they get a bit confused, upset and offended when those very people start expressing their anger towards them. It never occurs to them, because they see themselves as the good guys, that the people they purport to serve may, in fact, perceive them as chancers, careerists or charlatans.*

> *They regard themselves as champions of the underclass and therefore, should any poor folk begin to get their own ideas, or, god forbid, rebel against the poverty experts, the blame is laid at the door of the complainants for misunderstanding what is going on.*[15]

Swap the well-meaning liberal left with the well-meaning middle-class Christian and we get to the heart of the problem. I could stand up in almost any church and conference in the UK, state that there is a problem with how the church is doing outreach and discipleship to people from deprived communities, and I will be ignored or castigated for being reactionary and divisive. God forbid that I say anything negative about the golden calf of UK Christianity – food banks! This, after all, seems to be the tool by which most middle-class churches gauge their love of the poor and the needy. Despite the fact that they are mainly disastrous (more on this later) and may, in fact, contribute towards poverty rather than alleviate it, most churches and leaders bury their heads in the sand when it comes to any kind of critique of their so-called "mercy ministries".

"IF YOU ALWAYS DO WHAT YOU'VE ALWAYS DONE, YOU ALWAYS GET WHAT YOU'VE ALWAYS GOTTEN"[16]

I will state, once again, what Roy Joslin pointed out in 1982 and what I have been claiming for the last decade or more. There is a problem in the UK church in how it does outreach into council estates and housing schemes. Do movement leaders, para-church leaders and theological institutions have the courage to call a moratorium on soup kitchens, food banks and any other poverty-related initiatives in order to produce a biblically thought through, and practical way forward, that will help us to reach and disciple those living in deprived communities more effectively? Can we just admit that being busy isn't the same as being effective? Your soup kitchen ministry may well be feeding 100 people per week, but that is clearly a sign of need, not necessarily proof that the ministry itself is effective for the kingdom in evangelising and growing disciples.

Pastors, how much of our energy and resources are we expending on reaching trainee electricians, hairdressers or builders in relation to the amount spent on evangelising students in our churches? How much money have we been earmarking specifically for church planting and revitalisation in the most deprived communities on our doorsteps? They're not hard to find. They are all around us.

Don't farm out evangelism among the poor in your community to para-church organisations. They may well do good work, but four decades of this has not seen the establishment of very many gospel-preaching churches in these communities. We need to pray for the courage to take the harder, longer, more expensive and self-sacrificial route of church planting and revitalisation. Local children need a healthy local church in their communities far more than they need our yearly holiday Bible clubs or weekly drop-ins.[17] If the evangelical church, and her institutions and systems, don't change, then what will close the spiritual and cultural gap between middle-class Christianity and the rest of the country? If we continue to do what we've always done, then we will continue to get what we have always gotten.

Nothing of substance.

Christian, as you read this book, please do so with an open mind and heart. If you're involved in mercy ministry and in the lives of the neediest souls in our towns, cities and villages then, trust me, I have no desire to crush you or to belittle your work. In fact, my intention is the exact opposite. I know all about the hard, often thankless, work that you do. I know how many of you have been battling away for years, bringing Christ to the fringes of society, and trying, often unsuccessfully, to incorporate them into the life of your churches. As one who was on the streets for six years, I thank you deeply for your kindness and self-sacrifice. My aim in writing this book is to encourage you to help your churches think more broadly, and more biblically, about your vital work.

If you are a church leader, or someone thinking about planting or revitalising a church, then I would urge you to use the statistics and stories within this book and on our website to help you to think more strategically for the kingdom. Think about that housing estate near you, or that community that seems cut off in your town or village. Review your church's ministry to the poor. *How effective is it in evangelising lost souls? How effective are you in keeping the saved, discipling them and then integrating them fully into the life of your church? How many men and women from council estates or schemes has your church trained for future ministry, whether vocational or not? How are you celebrating and encouraging those in your congregation who are battling on the front lines in deprived communities?* It's not an exhaustive list of questions, but it's a start.

Change is required. But we cannot change a system with which we are happy and comfortable. Therefore, we are going to have to think seriously, from the ground up, if we want to make a difference in the lives of millions of people in our country who will be born, live, love, work and die without any access to the gospel. Their only crime? They're not middle class and university educated. They live in our council estates and housing schemes. They live in the high-rise flats most of us pass on our way to work every day. They live in our picture-perfect country towns and villages. They empty our dustbins. They deliver our mail. They clean our office blocks. They mop the toilets of our favourite supermarkets. They cut our hair. They deliver our shopping and our takeaways. They cut our grass and paint our fences. They wash our windows and clean our gutters. They sweep our roads and labour on our building sites. They're everywhere we look, and yet they are hardly anywhere to be seen in our churches.

These are the reasons behind *why* I have written this book.

As to my *what* questions, the answers to those are much simpler and more straightforward.

What you have in your hand is the product of over 1,000 hours of dedicated research and over 21 years of ministry to the poor and/or marginalised in various contexts around the world. I was going to include a statistical breakdown of the whole of the UK, plus London (which is pretty much a country of its own in terms of population). However, I decided that this would make an already lengthy book even longer. So, in Appendix 1, there is a code which will lead you to a website. There you will be able to click on any country in the UK and have all the statistical research at your fingertips. We have also included a section detailing any and all FIEC churches that operate within, or close to, areas of deprivation.

When it comes to the statistical data, I have sought to be as independent as possible, so as to avoid any appearance of confirmation bias. I did that by hiring an American PhD student, who had no prior understanding of scheme or council estate life. In fact, he didn't even know what those terms meant! I gave him a simple objective: in each country, research the communities regarded by their respective governments as "most deprived". Understanding that even that term is loaded, I played no part in any of his research and did not interfere with his findings. He would send me regular reports of his progress, but I never made any comment or gave him any feedback. I wanted the information to arrive on my desk completely unvarnished. As a result, some of his findings were of great surprise to me, although much of it confirmed what I already knew.

Once that was done, he also attempted to map out where FIEC churches were to be found in relation to these communities. This research proved to be the most difficult to carry out. We sent out questionnaires to various churches. We surveyed church leaders at the FIEC Leaders' Conference in 2019. We talked to pastors working in deprived communities and to a host of others operating on the fringes. The results were complicated by a number of factors.

- Some pastors were unwilling to share any data with us regarding the cultural mix of their congregations.
- Some churches never responded to our requests for information and/or interviews.
- Some deprived communities, on paper, look like they are well served by a local FIEC church, when the reality is that the congregation is either dying, ageing and/or almost exclusively attended by people from outside the community in which their building is situated.

As you can imagine, the data gathered in each country was highly complex, multi-layered, and produced different results depending upon multiple factors, including the size of a particular community, the ethnic make-up of different areas and a host of other things. The reality is that I could have written a book on each country, plus London, with the information that was gathered. Such is the depth of our research that we have could have easily produced an academic textbook. But my aim has always been to produce a work that is both statistically rigorous, but also popularly accessible.

While recognising that the resulting discussions will be complex and nuanced, my aims are simple. Broadly, this book aims:

- To produce an informed and rigorous survey detailing the most deprived council estates and housing schemes across the UK.
- To seek to understand where evangelical churches (specifically FIEC) are to be found in relation to these communities.[18]
- To try to understand some of the issues facing people in these communities.
- To help the church understand the cultural and social make-up of these communities.
- To help the church to understand how people from these communities view the world and their place in it.
- To help the church to think through what effective evangelism and discipleship look like in these communities.
- To look at some of the failings of the UK church and the many para-church organisations who work with the most deprived people in our nation.
- To seek to galvanise a new generation of church leaders and women's workers who can take the gospel out to the least and the lost in the UK.
- To encourage the revitalisation and planting of gospel-centred churches in these communities by offering reliable research as to the geographical locations of some of the UK's least reached people.

- To help the wider Christian community understand the needs of gospel workers and / or churches already working in these areas or attempting to establish works.
- To provoke debate and to think about possible solutions to the current crisis of effective gospel outreach, meaningful discipleship and leadership training available and accessible to those from deprived communities.
- Finally, and most importantly, even if it does nothing else, I pray that it brings glory to our Triune God.

This book is the culmination of 25 years of thinking about, failing at and experimenting in what we, as Great Commission Christians, could do better to effectively reach and disciple the least, the last and the lost in our country (and beyond).

PART I:

POVERTY, CLASS AND CULTURE IN THE UK

CHAPTER 1:

WHERE DID OUR COUNCIL ESTATES AND SCHEMES COME FROM?

We all have particular places in our towns and cities and villages that we regard as "rough". Some are more populous than others and some are harder to spot. Very often, we drive past these places on our way to work and we teach our children to avoid these places – and certainly to be nowhere near them after dark. In most of the UK, they are known as *council estates* simply because most of the people who live there rent their home from their local council. In Scotland, they are called *schemes* and they have a reputation for housing society's undesirables. They are not *slums* as we would see in India, for instance (and in pre-industrialised Britain). Nor are they favelas as we would see in South America (both terms may seem similar to the Western eye, but I can assure you that a favela-dweller would take unkindly to you calling where they live a slum!).

But what is the history behind council estates? Whose idea was it to mass produce low-cost housing for the poor in the first place? To understand a people, we need to understand their history.

"HOMES FIT FOR HEROES"

This phrase – "homes fit for heroes" – was first coined by David Lloyd George, shortly after the end of World War I. He said,

> *What is our task? To make Britain a fit country for heroes to live in. There are millions of men who will come back. Let us make this a land fit for such men to live in. There is no time to lose.*[19]

Of course, these were not the only factors at play in the rise of housing development in the years immediately after WWI. Safe, affordable housing was certainly needed for our returning war heroes, but this was coupled with a fear of the rise of Bolshevism among the poor and working class. Far too many in the UK were living in substandard, slum conditions, evidenced by the fact that over 10% of conscripts in the war were rejected on health grounds as a direct result of squalid living conditions.[20]

Historians tell us that, prior to WWI, it was private builders who supplied virtually all the new housing in towns and cities.[21] All of this building activity came to a virtual standstill while the country was at war. By the time of the 1918 General Election, it was apparent that the country faced an acute housing shortage and that there were many slum areas that were not fit for habitation.

The problem, post-WWI, was that demand far outweighed the private sector's ability to produce good quality, affordable housing on a mass scale. The Addison Act, passed in 1919, sought to remedy this by charging local authorities to ensure adequate housing for the "working class". Lloyd George had a dream to build half a million homes in three years, but it was both unrealistic and unattainable. However, the number of people securing council homes began to increase year on year. In fact, before WWI, 1% of the population lived in council houses, but by 1938, that figure had risen to 10%.[22] By the late 1970s, it would rise to 50%.

The Addison Act soon gave way to Neville Chamberlain's Housing Act of 1923. A year later, it was replaced by The Wheatley Act. Half a million homes were built, but it took 16 years, not three, to achieve this figure. Great achievement though this was, there still remained two perennial problems:

1. Demand was constantly high and so builders couldn't construct quickly enough to cope with the demand.
2. The problems of inner-city slums were still very evident, even into the 1930s. Tenements (run down, overcrowded apartment-style houses occupied by multiple families sharing basic facilities), particularly in Scotland, were a blight on society and greedy landlords continued getting rich off the very poor by providing horrific living conditions at unreasonable rents.

The Greenwood Housing Act of 1930 was designed to address these specific problems. However, a worldwide economic slump meant that slums were not knocked down and replaced with quality homes quickly enough. Although an estimated quarter of a million slum houses and tenements had been cleared by 1939, there were still at least half a million slum houses in urgent need of demolition. Indeed, I personally remember still having to use an outside toilet as a child in the mid to late 1970s. Our houses were poorly built, mouldy, draughty and had asbestos roofs. Asbestos was still used in the building trade as recently as 1999.[23]

Despite the upside to these "homes fit for heroes" being built, it unsurprisingly caused a great deal of social upheaval. The ruling class and the rich were, obviously, largely unaffected – but not so the working class and the poor. They were uprooted from their homes – however slum-like – and shipped out (in their millions) to new council estates/schemes, which were usually on the outskirts of the city/town centres. Social surveys carried out during the inter-war period suggested that although tenants wanted new homes, many were reluctant to leave their communities where they felt secure amid the established family and neighbourhood networks, and where they could easily walk to work. Moving people to new estates involved the destruction of existing communities, created a sense of dislocation and isolation, as well as placing greater pressure on the family budget because of increased travel costs. Basically, as the cost of living went up, wages remained the same.

Many people were forced to move against their will. Although, it has to be stated that they were, in the main, relocated to far larger and more superior homes in cleaner, safer areas (though this point is arguable). Another positive was that many people had now escaped the clutches of tyrannical private landlords and were treated with more fairness, had greater legal rights, and had recourse to grievances being heard and acted upon by their local authority or council. Eventually, the political furore died down, people settled, and the future looked bright – bright, that is, until the intervention of war in 1939.

1945 AND ONWARDS: SOCIAL HOUSING

Despite all the policy changes and some great progress in the inter-war years, slum housing still remained a problem throughout the UK at the outbreak of WWII. The end of WWII brought with it a chronic housing problem due to widescale bombing and damage of many cities (over 25% of

British homes were destroyed). The government's so-called *temporary solution* at the time was to build factory-made, prefabricated houses to try to cope with the ever-increasing demand. However, many of these (often substandard) houses remained in use right up until the 1980s.

The New Towns Act was passed in 1946 and was meant to deal with the problem of slum housing and city centre overcrowding. In the UK, 14 new towns were planned in the 1940s and another 14 built in the 1960s. The new towns contained a variety of house types, shops, schools and leisure facilities – all within easy reach. New towns were built in Scotland at Cumbernauld, Glenrothes, Livingston, East Kilbride and Irvine.

The 1950s and 1960s saw wholesale changes to the British housing landscape as council after council demolished their stock of old, terraced houses and replaced them with high-rise flats (or tenements/apartments/"stairs"). In fact, they went on to become a central feature in most of the UK's council estates and schemes. Once again, community living took a back seat to social policy and many hundreds of thousands of people were left lonely and isolated in these buildings, even if they did live in far better conditions. Then, in the late 1970s and 1980s, the UK government introduced a "right to buy" initiative for many of the schemes, as well as seeking to redevelop these places through private housing associations and building contractors.

However, for most of the twentieth century, the responsibility for most social housing projects lay with central government and local authorities. From the inter-war period until the 1980s, social housing effectively meant local authority built, owned and managed housing. Of course, originally, these places were bastions of respectability for the working-class man and his family. They were marked by perfectly trimmed lawns and net curtains hanging from the windows.

URBAN BLIGHT[24]

Problems soon became apparent as houses were left to crumble because of a lack of local authority funding, unscrupulous landlords and feckless tenants. Urban blight set in and many of these communities and homes were left to decay and rot over a period of decades. Abandoned buildings became a feature, and I remember that at one point in my street, there were only two homes not boarded up and condemned. Council estates and schemes began to be marked by rising crime, violence, the explosion of the drug scene, gang culture and a lack of economic stimulation. This led to many empty properties becoming "squats" and places in which to buy, sell or take drugs.[25] The state's answer to these concerns was found in "gentrification".

GENTRIFICATION[26]

Gentrification is a phenomenon that is occurring in council estates and schemes all over the UK. It is a word that was brought to the fore in the early 1960s by a sociologist, Ruth Glass, who observed how middle-class people moving into traditional working-class areas often displaced the very poor. She writes:

> *One by one, many of the working-class quarters of London have been invaded by the middle classes – upper and lower. Once this process of "gentrification" starts in a district it goes on rapidly until all or most of the original working-class occupiers are displaced and the whole social character of the district is changed.*[27]

That quote sounds as if it has come out of a modern book when, in fact, it was written in 1964! Here we are, over five decades later, still seeing its effects being felt nationwide. The word actually has its origins in the old English word, "gentry" –

the land-owning social class of the UK. They were people who usually rented their land to farmers and thus enjoyed a generous income without having to do manual work themselves. They were regarded as high born and noble, but they were not aristocratic. They were respectable, but not within the upper echelons of polite society.

Gentrification is deeply divisive, but regardless of opinion, it almost always signifies profound changes in the social make-up of the communities in which it occurs. Usually, the first thing to be demolished is low-income housing, and the first people forced to move are the poor. Those who were living in homes earmarked for refurbishment would be temporarily moved out of the area and, if they were lucky, they would be allowed to move back into their newly refurbished property quickly (which meant within one or two years). The majority were not so lucky. Most people who were forced from their homes never came back. Whichever the outcome, gentrification always signals one of two things in council estates / schemes.

1. A rise in rents because of modernisation
2. A rise in private landlords

Whereas the gentrification of Glass's day was almost always the refurbishment of existing properties, modern gentrification is concerned with the destruction of buildings *en masse* and the redevelopment of previously booming industrial estates into flats.

Both higher rents and an increase in the number of private landlords are bad for the poorest people because they are forced to give way to wealthier residents who begin to move into the neighbourhood. The "problem people" – in other words, the tenants who fail to pay their bills and fail to maintain their properties – are then relocated, usually to another estate/ scheme somewhere else in the city.[28] On the positive side, there is often widespread building work and community regeneration of shops, businesses and parks. All of the above is happening and has happened to communities the length and breadth of the UK over the last few decades. However, it would seem that the south of England is being regenerated and gentrified at a far quicker rate than the North.

There is little doubt that the vast majority of middle-class people, small business owners, and the local authorities view the process as a good and healthy thing. It is often associated with "weeding out" the inherent social problems and "lifting up" the area in which it occurs. For all the good it brings to an area (rising home valuations for owners, new consumers for local shops, removal of drug houses, etc.), it also causes its fair share of problems.

Rising rents cause trouble for those struggling to pay existing ones. The rise of the local housing market also pushes out those not able to afford a mortgage. The real losers are the poorest, who find themselves compulsorily rehoused and moved to a new estate somewhere else and are often separated from decades-old roots and proximity to family members. Ultimately, gentrification ends up being good news for the "haves" and bad news for the "have-nots".

Some questions arise: *Has selling off council stock helped the poorest in society? Has it helped the neighbourhood being gentrified? Is it uniting communities or destroying them?* Depending on your point of view, the results are mixed at best.

THE PRIVATISATION OF SOCIAL HOUSING

Further complicating our efforts to locate the most deprived communities is the continued privatisation of council housing stock across England. Instead of each local authority being the landlords to their own particular stock, many have now, largely, sold them to private landlords, who could be any one of the following three groups:

- Private individuals
- Corporations
- Housing associations

This process has proved detrimental to many tenants, who have been pressured to leave and forced to transfer their tenancies to other areas. Regardless, far from saving local authorities money, these changes have ended up being prohibitively expensive. Reflecting on the National Audit Office's (NAO) examination of the financial costs and benefits of retaining a council housing property, versus transferring to housing associations, Norman Ginsburg writes:

> *[The National Audit Office] calculated that transfer was considerably more expensive for the taxpayer than retention and renovation by councils, possibly as much as 30 per cent more expensive. The NAO calculated that a renovation programme for one million council homes would cost £1.3 billion more if it were done through stock transfer rather than allowing the councils to do it. However, the NAO considered that the benefits outweigh the extra costs citing such benefits as "the transfer of risk, the accelerated achievement of improvements, the greater tenant participation" (NAO, 2003:32) associated with transfer. There is no question that improvements have been accelerated by transfer, but that is only because local authorities were prevented from doing them. There is undoubtedly increased tenant participation in the form of involvement in management boards, but whether*

tenants exert any more collective influence than they did within local electoral politics is highly debatable. The notion of "risk transfer" as a benefit involves taking a very narrow point of view on behalf of the taxpayer. It appears to be celebrating the loss of a public responsibility for meeting basic needs, and the transfer of risk to RSLs [Registered Social Landlords] and, implicitly, tenants.[29]

While the National Audit Office report focused on the prohibitive cost of privatising social housing and the failure to take public responsibility for meeting basic social needs, the British Housing Report findings highlighted some unexpected consequences of privatisation:

Outperformance of original transfer expectations seems to have been most marked in relation to regeneration. One measure of this is the extent to which – in many instances – demolition and replacement of substandard housing has turned out to be significantly more extensive than initially anticipated.[30]

THE GROWTH OF HOUSING ASSOCIATIONS (HAs)

Large-scale ownership transfers are transforming social housing throughout Britain, with over 180 new housing associations being created since 1989.[31] The upshot is that the move away from council-owned social housing has spawned, what the Joseph Rowntree Foundation (JRF)[32] calls "a new class of social landlord".[33] Furthermore, such is the success of these HAs, it is thought that "associations now manage over a third of all social sector dwellings – a threefold increase on the percentage in 1991".[34] According to the JRF report:

Since the transfer process began in earnest in the late 1980s,

> *more than 870,000 (tenanted) homes have been passed from state ownership (local authorities, new town development corporations or Scottish Homes) to housing associations (and, in a few cases, non-registered housing companies). By early 2003, 111 local authorities in England had transferred all their stock to housing associations. In addition, over forty authorities (twenty-three in England and nineteen in Scotland) have carried out "partial stock transfers", where a council disposes of a package of tenanted housing whilst also retaining stock in its ownership.*[35]

Typically, in England, the governing boards on the new HAs tend to be a mixture of tenants, local councillors and the prerequisite "independents". There is little doubt that lots of old council stock has, at worst, received extensive modernisation or, at best, been completely rebuilt. This is good for the tenants, but it almost invariably comes with an increase in rental costs. Perhaps more concerning is that transfers to HAs are often the prelude to gentrification. Tragically, those who are materially deprived in the neighbourhood are often the ones pushed out by a system that was meant for their benefit in the first place!

CONCLUSION

Opinions on housing schemes and council estates differ depending on your life history and your experience of them. I was dragged up through the gutter, so my view is somewhat coloured compared to a person who grew up in a "respectable" household (i.e. had a job and both parents) on the same estate.

Of course, there are great differences between a scheme in Edinburgh and a Catholic housing estate in Belfast. There are great differences between the old council estates that dominate the valleys of Wales and those in London. To some, our estates and schemes are places of horror; to some, places of terror;

to some, places of hopelessness – but, to many millions more, they are "home".

In fact, they are home to some of the poorest people in the UK. This begs the question: *Does poverty in the UK really exist, and if it does, what does it look like?*

CHAPTER 2:

HOW IS POVERTY DEFINED IN THE UK?

"Blessed are the poor; for they alone have not the poor always with them. The honest poor can sometimes forget poverty. The honest rich can never forget it."

G.K. Chesterton, *All Things Considered*

DEFINING POVERTY

This is a fundamental question for which, frustratingly, there is no simple answer. It is practically impossible to come up with a standardised definition that all interested charities and institutions agree on. That's before we even get to the biblical definition! Yet, we have to try to get beneath the surface if we are going to have a serious and sensible conversation about the issue.

The Labour Party made a pledge to the electorate in the 2019 General Election: "The next Labour government will wage war on poverty in all its forms, eliminating in-work poverty, ending austerity and raising living standards across the country."[36] The only problem with this grandiose promise was that they forgot to specifically define the poverty they promised to end. We shouldn't be too harsh on them, however, because formulating a clear and concise definition of poverty still eludes us today.

Poverty is so supremely complex and nuanced, that it has rejected all attempts to snare or tame it. The *Cambridge Dictionary* calls it, "A noun. The condition of being extremely poor."[37] The *Oxford Learner's Dictionary* calls it, "A noun. The state of being poor."[38] The *Collins Dictionary* informs us that synonyms of poverty are, "Scarcity, lack, absence, want."[39] But scarcity, lack, absence and want of what exactly? Money? Possessions? Home? Job? We do not know because the dictionaries go no further, other than to place the word in a few nebulous sentences.

Yet, the word is thrown around with such regularity that it has to mean something, right? Maybe, it's related in some way to the word "deprived" because they often turn up together at the same family gatherings. The *Oxford Learner's Dictionary* seems to think so. It defines "deprived" as, "An adjective. Without enough food, education, and all the things that are necessary for people to live a happy and comfortable life."[40] It even lists the word's solitary synonym as, "Poor".[41]

I know, from looking at the bookshelves in my office, that many before me have, with varying degrees of success, tried to tackle the themes of poverty and deprivation. I have books on worldwide urban crises, helping the poor, capitalism, socialism, social justice, cultural anthropology, abortion, charity, mercy ministries, theological frameworks for understanding poverty (more on this later), social class and poverty, giving, chavs, poverty and dependence, geography and poverty (fascinating subject), working-class worldview, race, and poverty and reconciliation.

How we define poverty (or "material deprivation") is vital to how we measure poverty. Again, it is notoriously difficult to get a cohesive and agreed definition of poverty and deprivation, simply because the institutions at the forefront of monitoring these issues in the UK tend to have their own definitions. The Central Government, for example, has a poverty threshold, that includes anyone who *falls below the UK's 60% median income.*[42] The Social Metrics Commission's (SMC) threshold is based upon what *a family financially needs to live reasonably.*[43] The Index of Multiple Deprivation (IMD) poverty threshold seeks to identify those persons, or areas, in the *lower 30% (Decile 3)* as "deprived".[44] This is in contrast to the European Union, which broadly defines poverty based on the possession of basic necessities required for living, like two sets of clothes and access to running water, etc.[45]

In effect, groups and institutions tend to define poverty in ways which suit their own ends. Not that this is necessarily bad or dishonest. End Child Poverty (ECP), for example, is obviously going to define poverty as it relates to children.[46] The IMD defines it in much broader terms.[47] Both groups have access to the same material sources, they will just highlight data specific to their goals and, sometimes, arrive at different – although not necessarily conflicting – conclusions about how to deal with the information.

DEFINING DEPRIVATION

"Deprivation", as with poverty, is not an easy term to explain and measure. "Poverty" has a wide-ranging impact on society, "creating problems of social isolation: low educational attainment: unemployment: impacting on mental and physical health and social interaction".[48] "Deprivation", on the other hand, "can be defined as the consequence of a lack of income and other resources, which cumulatively can be seen as living in poverty".[49]

Several factors are at work when attempting to define material deprivation. First, we must factor in *a nation's wealth:*

their overall global and local economic status, GDP, income, living expenses, and opportunities for growth, etc. Yet, we must be careful with this data, because the prosperity of a nation does not necessarily mean that every citizen within it experiences or possesses that same level of wealth. Being jobless or sleeping rough is bad anywhere, no less so in the UK than in any other country. Indeed, a rough sleeper in Edinburgh, Scotland, who is out on a freezing November night is far worse off (in one sense) than a homeless person on the streets of Rio, during their summer months.

Secondly, and crucially, we must factor in *the national structures and infrastructures* that allow or prohibit a prosperous life. Factors such as the stability of government and economy, reliable and accessible healthcare, affordable and safe housing, effective transportation, crime controls, etc.

Thirdly, the way a nation *measures poverty* is significant. A nation may measure poverty in their country by measuring it in terms of the median income of the whole – but that doesn't necessarily mean that people who earn more than that number are not poor. So, for example, let us take a family in the UK whose household income is £50,000. That is a lot of money if you live in Middlesbrough, in the north-east of England. That's more than enough to pay the average rent on a three-bedroomed home, pay the bills, clothe and feed the children, and still save up for a family holiday. Take that same £50,000 income and give it to a family in Central London, and they will be struggling to pay the bills and survive day-to-day.

The point is that in the world of material statistics, all that is seen is the amount of income and therefore, wrongly, some people will be defined as living above the poverty line, even though their personal experience is to live well below it. In other words, solely measuring income as an indicator of material deprivation is flawed. That is why, fourthly, it is actually *the cost of living* that is the greatest help in comparing and evaluating who lives in material poverty and who does not.

Fifthly, *opportunity for change* tends to be a greater factor than often considered, though it is more difficult to define. Let's consider Bob in Southend, England, and Josef in Mumbai, India. Both live within the 10% most deprived demographic in their respective countries, with regard to education, healthcare, employment, housing and crime/ safety, etc. Josef lives in a small hut on the edge of a massive slum. The area has no real infrastructure and he has limited access to the few resources that are available to him. There is very little opportunity for Josef to escape his situation in order to build a better life for himself.

England, on the other hand, has a very well developed infrastructure. However, Bob still finds himself in a similar situation to Josef. He struggles to pay the rent on his one-bedroom flat. In comparison to Josef's accommodation, it is luxurious, but this hardly matters because the electricity has been off for weeks because of non-payment. Bob's benefits have been delayed for unexplained administrative reasons, and he has gone a month now without any financial assistance to which he has full rights. He is unemployed and disabled, and his deep fear is that he will be evicted long before the benefits agency corrects this administrative mess.

In effect, though living in a so-called first-world country (England), Bob's experience of poverty is not all that different from Josef's experiences in Mumbai. *How* they experience deprivation may differ, but the net result is the same: powerlessness, frustration, hunger, fear and financial difficulties. The point is simple: a person can be materially deprived in any nation on earth. Regardless of which country it is, material deprivation is neither desirable, nor commendable – much less humane or even bearable – for a long period of time.

Lastly, it must be said that defining, quantifying and locating material deprivation is a massively complex issue. A common reaction is to see poverty as a "simple problem" or to minimise the impact it has on people's lives or to minimise the number of people. No report can produce data on the living conditions of every single member of the UK. Countless thousands – tens of thousands – may not have a place to sleep tonight or have had a proper meal today. Many thousands cannot get a job because of a criminal record. Many others care for a family member with a disability. Many thousands of children will be moving for the third time this school year or have parent(s) who do not care if they attend school and care even less about whether they do their homework.

And yet, none of them will be found on any report at all.

HISTORY, CULTURE AND TECHNOLOGY

As with many other words and concepts within the English language, the meaning of "poverty" and "deprivation" has changed over the past century. Even the basic tools for measuring poverty have shifted, first with the industrial revolution and, latterly, with the technological revolution. Both are defined and measured very differently in twenty-first-century Britain from how they were defined at the front end of the twentieth century. For example, as Danny Dorling notes:

> *In 1899 a young adult was seen as poor if he could not afford to buy a postage stamp to send a letter to a loved one. In 2009 a young adult was seen as poor if she could not afford a top-up to send a text to a loved one. It was The Young Foundation, in their major study of contemporary needs, which discovered that some of our poorest teenagers now often go without food in order to keep their phones working.*[50]

But are we really suggesting that poverty in the UK is when a young person cannot top up their phones unless they skip a meal? I am assuming they at least have the luxury of making that choice. How does that square up to a child in India forced to scrabble around in raw sewage and rubbish in order to find food? I remember speaking at a conference on poverty at a church in Northern Brazil, and the whole room burst into laughter when I showed them the pictures of brick houses in Niddrie (a scheme in Edinburgh where I live and pastor) and told them that this was a community designated "deprived" by the British government.

> *Assisting the poor is an important requirement of Christian belief and action. To do so, the poor need to be identified, a task that is probably easier in developing nations than in developed ones. Malnutrition, starvation, and proneness to disease are obvious signs of poverty in the developing world, but these qualities are less prevalent and are manifested less in the developed world. Disagreement has recently arisen among Christians about who the poor are in developed nations. Some Christians argue that material poverty and inequality are no longer problems because of the high degree of affluence in the West.*[51]

It does seem more than faintly ridiculous, at first glance, to suggest that poverty really exists in the UK in a world where:

- Three billion people live on less than $2.50 a day.[52]
- One billion children live in poverty, and 22,000 children die each day from hunger.[53]
- 750 million people do not have access to clean water.[54]
- Hunger kills more people worldwide every year than HIV/AIDS, malaria and tuberculosis combined.[55]

Little wonder that a room full of Brazilian favela dwellers laughed at my photographs of what we, in the UK, consider deprivation. However, the issue is not as straightforward as we might think. Darren McGarvey puts it succinctly: "Yes, it's certainly true that a Western child has less chance of dying of hunger, dysentery or malaria than a child in Rwanda, but that is little consolation when you are being verbally abused, beaten or sexually assaulted in an alcoholic home."[56] In other words, try telling a child from a Northern Irish council estate whose drunken, drug-addled stepfather beats his mother unconscious every night that he has it better than a child living in a shack in Brazil with two loving parents trying their best to provide for him. Try telling the child on a Welsh housing estate that he's not really poor when he's not had a hot meal for a week and been living off mouldy Rice Krispies and gone-off milk.

The issue of poverty is far more complicated than most of us can possibly imagine. The poor and deprived in the UK might well live within brick houses and modern council flats, but that does not negate the desperate struggles many are battling with behind their double-glazed windows.

HOW ARE STATISTICIANS DEFINING POVERTY AND DEPRIVATION?

For the Index of Multiple Deprivation, a person, household and/or community is suffering from poverty and/or deprivation if they fall below the standard minimum government parameters in each of the following seven areas:

- Income (22.5%)
- Employment (22.5%)
- Education, skills and training (13.5%)

- Health deprivation and disability (13.5%)
- Crime (9.3%)
- Barriers to housing and services (9.3%)
- Living environment (9.3%)[57]

Each factor is given a particular "weight" – hence the percentage figures – towards building a multi-layered deprivation consensus. According to the UK government: "The weights were derived from consideration of the academic literature on poverty and deprivation, as well as the levels of robustness of the indicators."[58] In effect, the domains reflect key areas of impact, and the weights help quantify the impact of those domains. Therefore, when we speak of poverty and deprivation, at least within the research part of this book, we will be using these same seven weights as our baseline.[59] We are not claiming that this is all there is to say about poverty, nor are we asserting that this is an exhaustive list of measurements. However, each of these weights is the product of multi-agency, up-to-date research and are, in our opinion, as reliable as is possible. It is because of this reliability that the IMD's findings are the main statistical source for almost every other agency in the UK when it comes to measuring poverty.

By using these seven domains, researchers can account for one factor's impact on the poor in relation to the others in various combinations: if a family lives in a community with a positive living environment but low employment opportunities or low education, are they more or less likely to experience poverty? This may well be a commuter neighbourhood, where people travel one hour to work and all have college degrees, or it could be a neighbourhood where living conditions are declining. These domains help sort such factors.

By weighting these domains, the research data keeps these domains in perspective, in reasonable relationship to each other. Notice that, "Income" and "Employment" are significant factors that can help someone keep out of poverty, but poor health or disability can easily find one unemployed or otherwise and therefore unable to make ends meet. If someone bought a "fixer-upper", or if the community is in a gentrification process, their "Living Environment" score is inevitably going to be low. But a high score in that alone does not signify that there is a problem, nor is it an indication that the neighbourhood is "poor".

Conversely, it is worth repeating that the IMD weighting system reveals a significant bias towards income and employment. Obviously, income and employment are two of the most significant factors contributing to poverty: no job or no money usually leads to financial poverty. However, education and health are essential for being able to work. So, too, is a home to come back to. This is why some are sceptical of what they see as an imbalance in the weighting system. This being said, we feel, given the use we make of other reports from a number of different agencies, that our research has righted any imbalance people feel may exist with the IMD's.

That being said, the IMDs of each country in the UK do not look into the reasons behind poverty, or its effects on different nations, communities and individuals. Indeed, even *how* poverty is experienced will differ according to the specific contexts and situations people find themselves in. In much the same way we view mental health issues on a sliding scale, poverty can be measured and experienced along its own scale, depending on the type of poverty being experienced.

HOMELESSNESS AND SQUATTING

Interestingly, while the IMD reports do single out housing as a factor, *homelessness* and *squatters* are categories of material poverty unto themselves. We must remember that when it comes to measuring these two groups, the statistics are estimates at best, because it is difficult to find and count how many people are homeless, how many are "squatters" and how many "couch surf".[60] Oftentimes young people, particularly, do not have a home and so "spend the night" – although it is often much longer than this – on couches with family, friends or otherwise. A lot of these people purposely stay off the grid and are only registered in the case of a medical emergency, a police report or if they register at a homeless shelter.

Further complicating matters is the declining use of the term "council estate(s)" and the declining use of council housing itself – with the government opting for a housing association model of government supported housing, as previously discussed.[61] This has meant that the government is only registering people who make use of their approved HAs – and that leaves countless thousands outside of the reach of our research and statistical analysis.

The central point is that locating the UK's most deprived is fraught with complications because of these issues. Relying on the available research, we press on to locate the UK's poorest by using the most reliable data that can be found by the IMD. Where helpful, that data is then corroborated with other reports.

CONCLUSION

Poverty cannot not simply be boiled down to statistics on a piece of paper. Nor can it be accurately measured solely by the results of surveys concerning income and expenditure. There are real people behind these numbers living in, and often with, distressing personal circumstances. To quote the World Bank:

> *Poverty is hunger. Poverty is lack of shelter. Poverty is being sick and not being able to see a doctor. Poverty is not having access*

> *to school and not knowing how to read. Poverty is not having a job, is fear for the future, living one day at a time. Poverty is losing a child to illness brought about by unclean water. Poverty is powerlessness, lack of representation and freedom.*[62]

To be sure, poverty is about a lot more than these things, at least from a spiritual perspective. But neither is it less than those things, as we shall go on to see.

CHAPTER 3

HOW ARE PEOPLE EXPERIENCING POVERTY IN THE UK?[63]

We've all seen the pictures of starving children in Africa and the horrors of mass immigration camps in Syria and other war-torn regions. I have personally visited and continue to mentor men in some of the poorest nations on the planet – people without any running water, electricity or access to a regular meal. Poverty is easy *to see* in these places. We don't have to quibble about the meaning behind, and the definitions of, words when standing in the middle of an immigration camp in Africa.

The UK, on the other hand, is a member of both the G7 and G20 and is rated seventh in world output by the International Monetary Fund (IMF).[64] Yet, according to Daniel Dorling and Bethan Thomas, in their book, *Bankrupt Britain: An Atlas of Social Change,* "It is well known that of all the countries of Western Europe, the UK has among the highest rates of child poverty and by far the highest rate given the wealth of the country."[65] It seems scarcely believable, but they remain convinced that, "Income inequalities in Britain are among the widest in the affluent world. The largest group of poor households living in Western Europe live in Britain."[66] They go even further in their damning indictment of poverty in the UK, by saying:

> *In no other large European country is housing as badly distributed as in Britain. In no other similarly affluent country do people live in such cramped and crowded conditions, with so little floor space for most people and so many children sharing a room with a sibling of the opposite sex in their teenage years. Housing in Britain is shamefully poorly used, badly repaired, seen as yet another way to get rich rather than as the means of satisfying everyone's need for a home.*[67]

According to Eric Jensen's study, *Teaching with Poverty in Mind*, there are six main types of poverty in the UK.[68] They are outlined below:

SITUATIONAL POVERTY

This kind of poverty occurs with the onset of a sudden crisis, outside an individual's control. The Global Financial Crisis of 2008 would be such an example, in that it led to the bankruptcy of many businesses and jobs worldwide.[69] Other events could be chronic health issues, environmental disasters and familial breakdowns. On the plus side, this type of poverty is often only temporary and those with savings and assets – typically financially secure, middle-class families – are able to ride out the storm and come out the other side. The less fortunate – those already suffering from a permanently low income – are described as having, "a precarious well-being".[70] The majority of people suffering from situational poverty do so in the knowledge that their situation is temporary at worst. In other words, they can see light at the end of the tunnel. Their situation is not completely hopeless and may well be reversible.

GENERATIONAL POVERTY

Generational poverty is a different beast altogether. It occurs in families where at least two generations have been born into poverty.[71] This poverty is not just financial. According to one report, "Families dealing with generational poverty are also challenged with three other forms of poverty: educational poverty, parental poverty and spiritual poverty."[72] Whereas those suffering with situational poverty at least have hope, those suffering with generational poverty are left only with a sense of hopelessness. "Without hope and the belief that life can be better, the motivation and energy needed to break the cycle are very low."[73] Families living in this type of poverty are just not equipped with the tools to move out of their situations.

Dr. Debra Kidd writes:

> *There are working-class children whose parents have aspirations for them, and there are working-class children whose parents are not even aware of what possibilities exist, and if they are, have no idea how to help their child to achieve them. The difference between situational poverty, where you've experienced something and aim to get back there, and generational poverty, where there has been nothing but poverty, create very different mindsets and circumstances.*[74]

I come from a third, even more perverse, brand of parenting that despised education and belittled any attempts that were made to study or better yourself. It was termed, "trying to get above your station" or "making out you're better than everybody else". So, even when I wanted to study, adult pressures and the prevailing culture of despair forced me to act up and perform poorly at school, despite the fact that I found the work both interesting and easy. Doing badly was celebrated as "sticking it to the man", whereas doing well was frowned upon as "sucking up to the establishment".

RELATIVE POVERTY

This refers to, "the economic status of a family whose income is insufficient to meet its society's average standard of living".[75] Habitat for Humanity define relative poverty in the following way:

> *Relative poverty is sometimes described as "relative deprivation" because the people falling under this category are not living in total poverty, but they are not enjoying the same standard of life as everyone else in the country. It can be TV, internet, clean clothes, a safe home (a healthy environment, free from abuse or neglect), or even education.*[76]

The UK government's measure of relative poverty "compares the households with the lowest incomes against the rest of the population *in that year*".[77] The term, "relative poverty" is often misunderstood or tossed about carelessly, particularly within the world of research. There is a widespread belief in the Western world that it is better to be *materially poor* in the so-called "developed" world, than in, let's say, the two-thirds world. The logic being that it is surely far better to be poor in the UK than in the slums of India. Yet, as we saw with Bob and Josef, people can still suffer from the effects of material deprivation in both countries, even though their experience of it is markedly different.

ABSOLUTE POVERTY

The Declaration of Copenhagen defines absolute poverty as: "A condition characterized by severe deprivation of basic human needs, including food, safe drinking water, sanitation facilities, health, shelter, education and information. It depends not only on income but on access to social services."[78] In the UK people are designated as being in absolute poverty, sometimes called "persistent poverty", if their income is 60% less than the national median income over a *sustained period of time*.[79]

URBAN POVERTY

Urban poverty occurs in areas with populations of at least 50,000 people.[80] According to Jensen, "The urban poor deal with a complex aggregate of chronic and acute stressors (including crowding, violence, and noise) and are dependent on often-inadequate large-city services."[81]

RURAL POVERTY

Rural poverty occurs in areas with populations below 50,000. The poor in these areas face multiple problems. For instance, "the job market in small towns is limited, which prevents people with an already low-income from improving their finances and gaining access to certain services".[82] The rural poverty rate is growing and has exceeded the urban rate every year since data collection began in the 1960s. The difference between the two poverty rates has averaged about 5% for the last 30 years, with urban rates near 10%–15%, and rural rates near 15%–20%.[83]

Therefore, in the light of this discovery, we must ask the question:

> *How are people experiencing these different kinds of poverty in one of the richest nations in the world?*

I ask the question because of research carried out by the World Bank.[84] They, like most Western institutions, measure poverty by *income*. They set the daily poverty line at $1.90 per day which means that just under 10% of the world live in abject poverty below this line. That amounts to just under 700 million people. One of the interesting things about their research is when they asked people who lived below this line the following question: "What is poverty?" The responses were startling insomuch as a high majority of the respondents talked about their poverty in terms of their *experience* of it. How it made them *feel*. If we were to ask the question in the financially rich Western world, the answers are instead almost exclusively centred around *lacking money, education* or *physical services* (schools, hospitals, etc.).

In light of these findings, we need to understand that for many people experiencing poverty in the UK, the issue is about *how they feel* and not always about a lack of physical and financial resources. It's important that we consider this before writing off people in the UK who we think of as not being poor merely because their income dwarfs that of somebody living in a shack in a Brazilian favela. The issue is more complex than that.

STATISTICAL EVIDENCE OF UK POVERTY

The most recent statistics back up the claim that poverty, in all of its types, is a serious problem in the UK. Research tells us that *14.2 million people experience material deprivation across the UK* – a number that has increased since the Social Metrics Commission report of 2018.[85] Consider the following:

COMPOSITION OF UK POVERTY IN 2016/17 (14.2 MILLION PEOPLE) BY FAMILY TYPE

Source: Family Resources Survey and HBAI dataset (2016/17), SMC Analysis.[86] *Figures refer to total people in poverty in different family types and depict SMC's analysis for 2016/17. The number of people living in poverty in the UK has risen since then.*[87]

Poverty, unfortunately, is alive and well and evident within the UK at different levels of society. The truly sad thing is that we don't even have to try too hard to uncover the facts. Indeed, research has proven that, within the UK:

- Women bear a disproportionate burden of poverty.[88]
- Children growing up in poverty are often permanently disadvantaged.[89]
- Families with children face high risks of poverty.[90]
- 48% of children in one-parent families suffer from poverty.[91]
- Twice as many women as men are in low paid jobs.[92]
- 30% of all children in the UK live in some form of poverty.[93]

- 37% of children in families where someone is disabled are in poverty, compared with 27% of children who come from able-bodied homes.[94]

When looking at people at risk of poverty, the UK ranks 13th among EU nations, with *17% of the UK population at risk of poverty*, which is virtually identical to the EU's overall rate of 16.9%.[95] It is important to note, though, that direct comparisons between the EU and UK are not entirely reliable as the EU and UK measure poverty differently.[96] The fact still remains: poverty is a reality in the UK for a great many people.

NOT ALL MEN, WOMEN AND CHILDREN ARE CREATED EQUAL

There is a widely held belief in the UK that poverty and homelessness could happen to any one of us at any time. The cliché is that any one working person in the UK is no more than three month's salary away from financial ruin and a slide into poverty. Research-backed reality, on the other hand, reveals this claim to be absurd nonsense and a gross oversimplification of what it means to live in poverty and deprivation in the UK.

Let's take child poverty and homelessness as two examples. In the 2018 UK Housing Review Autumn Briefing Paper conducted by Mark Stephens et al., their research discovered that childhood poverty has more explanatory power for early adulthood poverty than either poor health, support needs or drug use.[97] In other words, child poverty and homelessness very often happen to people through no fault of their own. Instead, the research revealed that homelessness is "systematically found in a set of identifiable individual, social and structural factors, almost all of which, it should be emphasised, are *outside the control* of those directly affected".[98]

Furthermore, the report estimates that a mixed ethnicity female who experienced poverty as a child, was brought up by a lone parent, left education at sixteen and has had spells of unemployment has a 71.2% probability of being homeless by the age of 30. On the other hand, a white male from a relatively affluent childhood in rural England, who graduates from university at 21, lives with his parents until he is 26 and has no partner or children has a 0.6% probability of meeting the same fate.[99] In other words, it matters *where you were born* and *to whom*. Of course, this information begs the question: *Where are all these poor people to be found?* The answers are at once surprising, yet also profoundly sad.

COMPOSITION OF UK POVERTY BY FAMILY TYPE SHOWING YEARLY CHANGE

	SMC 2018 report	SMC 2019 report	Change (%)
Single people with no children	3,100,000 21%	3,000,000 20%	-1%
People in lone-parent families	2,600,000 18%	2,600,000 18%	0%
People in couple families with no children	1,400,000 9.8%	1,400,000 9.7%	-0.1%
People in couple families with children	5,600,000 39%	5,900,000 41%	+2%
People in pension-age single families	700,000 5%	-	
People in pension-age couples with families	800,000 5.6%	-	

Source: Family Resources Surveys and HBAI datasets (2016/17 and 2017/18), analysis by the Social Metric Commission.[100] *Figures refer to total people in poverty in different family types.*

In SMC's 2019 report, it was found that 41% of people in poverty are couples with children and 18% in lone-parent families. Put another way, a total of 59% of people in poverty (8,500,000) are families with children – an increase of 300,000 people from the SMC's 2018 report.[101]

Looking for a more tangible, measurable definition of poverty is difficult. The SMC sets the "poverty threshold" at £251.95 per week (which is equivalent to £1,007.80 per month or £12,093.60 per year).[102] And, according to the SMC, the weekly expenses that a child needs in order to survive is £52/week. Taking those figures, poverty thresholds for various family types can be calculated.

ESTIMATED POVERTY LINE FOR HOUSEHOLDS – NET DISPOSABLE INCOME REQUIRED AFTER HOUSING COSTS (2017/18)

Household type	(£ per week)
Single, no children	£152
Lone parent, one child (under 14 years old)	£204
Lone parent, two children (under 14 years old)	£256
Couple, no children	£262
Couple, two children (under 14 years old)	£366
Couple, three children (two under 14 years, one 14 years or older)	£476
Couple, four children (two under 14 years, two 14 years or older)	£586

Source: Figures are adapted from the Social Metrics Commission's 2019 report.[103] Net disposable income figures are equivalised.[104] A child is defined as being under 14 years old.

The different impact a single adult experiences compared with a couple who have children is significant. Obviously, the larger the family, the larger the income needed to support a family. The "Households Below Average Income (HBAI) 2018" report clarifies such distinctions. To lie in the top half of the income distribution in 2016/17, a single individual needed a net income over £17,200, compared with a couple with two young children who required a combined net income over £36,000.[105]

As helpful as this analysis is, flaws inevitably exist. Some believe the SMC has significantly underestimated the actual costs to families.[106] Yet, I suspect there are many who can only *dream* of having so much weekly income! For example, a couple where both are employed and are paying a total of £125 per month for car costs will find it much easier to manage than a single mother will. The age and medical needs of a child vary widely: a family of three with two teens and an infant is vastly different from a family of two primary school pupils, yet the above reporting treats them largely the same. A family may be living in an inherited flat or home in London, but the cost of living in the area where that home is may evaporate the savings on housing costs if utilities, transportation, groceries, etc. are inflated compared with living outside the city and commuting.

CHILD POVERTY

Children experience poverty differently to adults. Namely, they often are on the receiving end of their parent's poverty with no recourse. End Child Poverty provides helpful analysis which shows that child poverty is on the rise.[107] Indeed, child poverty is also a helpful metric for identifying areas of greater deprivation, because where we have a child in poverty there is likely to be one or more adults experiencing poverty with that child.

The level of child poverty in the UK is nothing short of criminal. The statistics are as scandalous as they are frightening. When we are talking about children in poverty, we are typically referring to those who are dependent upon one or more adults, who themselves are poor, and who are unable and / or unwilling to support them adequately.

The 2018 SMC analysis reported that *4.6 million children in the UK live in poverty* – that is 32.6% of all UK children.[108] The highest concentrations of children in poverty are to be found in London, Manchester, Birmingham and other major urban areas. In fact, only one local authority – Wokingham – has child poverty as low as 10%, which was the rate suggested by the (now largely defunct) Child Poverty Act of 2016 as the target for every local authority in the UK.[109]

Child poverty is a major, and growing, concern in the UK. All the reports and indicators are that the number of children experiencing some form of poverty is expected to increase sharply by 2022.[110] Some local authorities have a huge crisis on their hands. Let's take Devon as an example. This popular British tourist destination is home to a number of local authorities where, incredibly, *nearly half of all children experience material deprivation.*[111]

The JRF provides us with a helpful summary:

> *Among families with children there are very different patterns of poverty depending on the number and age of children. Over the last 20 years, child poverty has been highest in families with three or more children. This rate decreased from 1994/95 to 2010/11 but has begun to rise again in the last few years to 42% in 2016/17 (even before the two-child limit on benefits and tax credits was introduced in April 2017). The child poverty rate for families with one child and two children in 2016/17 was 25% and 26% respectively.*[112]

Professor Donald Hirsch's report, "The Cost of a Child", for the Child Poverty Action Group in 2019 highlights the relative increase in the cost of bringing up children in recent years:

> *Families on low incomes have been particularly disadvantaged by cuts in benefits, tax credits and universal credit, affecting disposable incomes both in and out of work. The various elements of child tax credit and child benefit have grown by between zero and 3 per cent since 2012, whereas consumer prices have risen by 12 per cent. Many families have faced additional losses through the benefit cap, cuts in housing benefit and the introduction of the "bedroom tax". Working families have benefited from a modest rise in real wages … However, much of these gains are clawed back through the tax credit system … and losses through the freezing of tax credits … universal credit rates and the work allowance are not rising with inflation.*[113]

Alison is 10 years old and lives at home with her mum, her three younger brothers and her mum's on-off boyfriend. Her mum is often out with friends and leaves her to watch over the three boys.

Alison has been attending a before-school breakfast club for the past few weeks. She has been referred by social services. She sometimes turns up after school to the church youth group with her younger brothers. Often, they look dirty and hungry. We soon discover that Alison and the rest of her siblings are regularly left overnight to fend for themselves as her mother and her boyfriend disappear for days at a time. They leave no money for food, and there is sometimes no heating in their cramped two-bedroom flat. Alison does her best to look after the boys, but that often means missing out on school because the boys' school is miles away and she doesn't know how to get there on her own. Sometimes she hears banging on the door and people shouting her mum's name through the letterbox. They say they are social workers, but her mum has taught her to hide in the bedroom and keep quiet until they go away. She's scared that if she lets them in then they will take them all away and she will never see her brothers or her mum again.

THE WORKING POOR

Historically, poverty in the UK has been closely aligned with issues such as unemployment and homelessness. However, we are now seeing an emerging, and fast-growing demographic, labelled as, "the working poor". This term refers to families who are gainfully employed, often with two or three jobs, but their income is often insufficient to meet their daily needs. Such a family may even appear to be financially stable on paper but, in reality, their job(s) and finances are quite volatile. One unexpected bill, or an extended illness, could put them on benefits – although the likelihood is that many of them are already receiving some kind of benefit(s).

The problem isn't just that these people are poorly paid, but that they can't keep up with the rising costs of food, fuel and housing. Indeed, research by Pascal Bourquin discovered that the number of people in the UK categorised as "working poor" rose from 13% to 18% – an increase of 40% – between 1994 and 2017.[114] The point being that even those who are in employment in the UK have very little chance of escaping their poverty, and that through *no fault of their own*. In fact, the real tragedy in Bourquin's report is the irrefutable evidence that the gap between the working poor and the more affluent middle classes is growing wider with every passing decade.

The problems are further compounded as we discover that the UK government's decision in 2011 to reduce benefit entitlements for those in employment have actually led to an increase in "in-work poverty".[115] That means that, for many families, finding a job makes no economic sense, because all it does is just impoverish them further.

> Sarah and Steven work zero-hour contract jobs. What they earn has to be supplemented by social security benefits. Both of them have to pay monthly child maintenance to children from previous relationships.
>
> *Just before the national lockdown in 2020, Sarah and Steven were hit with a couple of large bills. But both of them were forced to stop working because of the pandemic and were no longer getting paid. Their benefits slightly increased, but not by enough to keep their heads above water. The lack of money coming in pushed them further into debt to the point that they now rely on food parcels from the local church. They have a large amount outstanding on their credit cards and, even when life returns to "normal", they think it is going to take some time to pay off the balance on their cards. Steven wonders about the point of working hard and still getting nowhere each week. Both are suffering from depression.*

THE UNEMPLOYED

Any talk of poverty and deprivation, at least historically, often focuses almost exclusively on one group of people in the UK: the unemployed. They are like the witches of medieval England, who weren't just burned to death and/or drowned for heresy by the church but were also blamed for every ill and evil in wider society.[116] The unemployed have certainly been one of the media's favourite scapegoats for the social ills of the UK. Back in the 1990s, as the country came out of a deep recession, poverty and unemployment were inextricably linked. According to a report by Larry Elliot in *The Guardian*, this was, "because the majority of poor people live in workless households".[117] The front pages of the mainstream press were often full of stories about benefit scroungers, single mums, drug addicts and immigrants.

On the other hand, recently released research shows that Britain's unemployment is below 4%, the lowest it has been since the mid-1970s. Our employment stands at just over 76%. The end result of this is that, in the UK, in 2020, you are more likely to live in poverty if you come from a working family than at any time in the past three decades.[118] It seems that the unemployed do suffer from poverty and deprivation in this country, but they are clearly not the cause of it.

Rob is in his early 40s and has spent most of his adult life receiving social security benefits.

"My first experience of work that I can remember is the YTS scheme.[119] It paid £29.50 a week, rising to £35 the second year. I started that when I left school at 16. Nearly everyone from our school was on the scheme and went on a YTS programme. To be honest, it was

just madness! Most guys were already starting to use drugs and drink, and we got up to all sorts of trouble. I did painting and decorating, brickwork, and ended up in a print shop during my time. I got bored easily and kept getting into trouble and so I was constantly being moved on. I lasted for about 18 months before I left. I was only interested in drugs and girls, and work just got in the way.

At 18, I discovered that people could get free money from the brew [social security], and the bonus was that it paid more than the YTS! So, I made the logical decision – to go on benefits.

After all, why work and be told what to do, when I could get free money off the brew and earn cash in hand on the side? The other benefit of being on the brew was that if you were an addict and prescribed methadone, your payments went up! An absolute bonus! Free money and prescription meds that I could swap for hard drugs. Life was looking up for me.

My mum and dad were always hard workers. My dad worked everywhere: tattie fields [picking potatoes], removals, slabbing, painting and decorating, the list goes on. My mum had three cleaning jobs, so I don't know why their work ethic bypassed me. I did pick up some jobs from time to time, but I couldn't be bothered to get out of bed and take orders from people. I decided my future lay in selling drugs.

I lived and worked in a subculture where claiming unemployment benefits, messing around with a job now and then, and selling drugs was deemed the smartest way to live. After all, why work hard when I could make easy money and receive free money? There were times when I got sick of my lifestyle, and I picked up a few labouring jobs. But the end result was always the same – I'd lose my job for either being under the influence of drink and drugs or being late due to my chaotic lifestyle.

There was an added problem with working as well. If I got a legitimate job, then I would have to declare it to the brew, and they would stop my money. Then I discovered that the government stole my money by taking tax off me! Then, if I lost my job, I would have to go back to the brew and sometimes wait months to get a payment. Luckily, I had a good doctor who would prescribe me methadone and drugs for anxiety, and this would speed the process up. Getting a sick note from the doctor was the holy grail, because it kept the brew off your back because you were deemed unfit to work.

Working was never a priority for me, or for most of my friends. If we needed money, we could do a couple of days' labour, cash in hand. Or, more easily, we could sell drugs or commit crimes. It's only since I came to faith in Jesus that I have started working full-time for the first time in my life, and now I take financial responsibility for my family in a legal way."

THE ELDERLY

It is estimated that two million pensioners live in poverty in the UK and, according to Age UK, that number is increasing yearly.[120] One third of black British and Asian British pensioners suffer from poverty, compared with 15% of their white counterparts.[121] Spiralling care needs, the rising cost of care homes, disability and poor housing are all cited as contributing factors.

Margaret is an elderly single lady with learning difficulties, who lives alone in a high-rise flat in Niddrie.

"I'm terrified to go into my stair [my flat] because I never know who's going to be there. I know the guy up the stairs is dealing. I'm not daft and he's not exactly subtle, but there is nothing I can do about it. If I grass, they will break my door down and set all my stuff on fire. Sometimes they start kicking off and fighting and the violence spills out into the stair. Nobody calls the police. Not in this stair anyway.

The other day there was a huge puddle of urine outside my front door. I cleaned it up, but they do it almost every night. It's the same in the lift. It stinks. Sometimes they poo in it too! And then there's the rubbish. They just open their window and throw it out onto the green below. Now we have rats everywhere. I don't know what to do. My support worker says I should report them, but she doesn't have to live here. My friend said I should make myself homeless, but I'm too scared to do that. What if they put me in some place worse? I don't know how long I can live like this."

IMMIGRANTS, REFUGEES AND ASYLUM SEEKERS[122]

Not everyone who is poor in the UK – regardless of family type – necessarily traces their family history to the UK. The racial compositions of these groups are a matter of great complexity (and beyond the scope of this book). However, helpful reporting is growing.[123] Immigrants, refugees and asylum seekers, second and third generation (or later) immigrant-citizens, and ex-patriots (though perhaps the least likely) may also be included. Often immigrants who are well-educated professionals in their home countries cannot find work in their field, typically due to asynchronous qualifications standards by the government or guilds, leaving qualified surgeons cleaning toilets and lawyers washing dishes.

The Joseph Rowntree Foundation (JRF), drawing on data from The Family Resources Survey,[124] have discovered that foreign born people living in the UK are at a higher risk of poverty than UK born people.[125] The JRF report shows that, on average, over the three-year period to 2013/14:

- Foreign-born people living in the UK made up 12% of the population.[126]
- One in three of these people were in some kind of poverty.[127]
- 45% of children with foreign-born parents were living in poverty.[128]
- 70% of these children were born in the UK.[129]

Mary arrived in London with her seven children in 2010. Her husband Mark came looking for work, along with many other men from their village in Eastern Europe.[130]

Mark had been out of work for a very long time back in his country of birth. There were so few opportunities for far too many men. But since 2004, when their country

In his second year, the government take away his financial allowance and replace it with a voucher scheme which he is allowed to spend in a shop for food. Eventually, after two years, Jacob hears from the Home Office that his asylum claim has been rejected. His solicitor immediately appeals the decision, which means that Jacob can continue in his accommodation until his appeal is processed.

However, Jacob has now been in the UK for three years and he has still been unable to work. Many of his compatriots, who are likewise seeking asylum, find themselves in a similar position. Because of the enormous financial and emotional strain and because they are struggling to provide properly for their family and relatives, many of these people are forced to find work that pays in cash off the books. The hours are long, and pay is criminally low, but it eases their financial burdens slightly.

Unfortunately, Jacob loses his appeal, and he is now liable for eviction, detention and deportation. Within three months he is evicted from his flat and he is made homeless. A friend offers him a sofa at his place temporarily. Jacob has no right to further appeal, no right to work, nowhere to live and no legal right to remain in the UK.

After consultations with various people who know about Jacob and his situation, a fresh asylum request is submitted to the Home Office. The claim is received and one year after the rejection of his appeal Jacob is back on the asylum scheme. He is once again provided with accommodation, but he is still not entitled to any form of paid employment. He can, however, access some training and so he signs up for English classes at a local college four mornings a week. Learning English is good but getting out of the flat four days a week is even better for Jacob's mental health.

Twelve months later Jacob learns that, yet again, the Home Office have rejected his claim for asylum. Once again, he appeals the decision. It takes a further two years to set a date for a hearing at the independent tribunal. However, this time the tribunal upholds Jacob's appeal. The Home Office appeals that decision and Jacob is informed that he has a period of a further three years' leave to remain in the UK until the matter is sorted out.

On the plus side, he is now legally entitled to work, to benefits and to full-time education. Negatively, he will lose his flat and the weekly allowance for rent and fuel. In effect, Jacob has been in the UK for over seven years and has not worked during this period. He has two options: find paid work or apply for unemployment benefits. He has no recognised UK qualifications and a hole in his CV for the past seven years. His only alternative is to find work in a takeaway.

So, he lives and works in the city with the threat of deportation hanging over him, earning a pittance and hoping that sooner or later he will be granted permanent leave to begin a new life in the city.

CONCLUSION

At one level, the most deprived in the UK are fairly straightforward to identify. They are those who have no money, no job (or a poorly paid one), probably on benefits, are highly medicated, are taking street drugs, have criminal records, and live in a scheme or a council estate. In all likelihood, they come from a long line of council estate residents.

However, the reporting that leads to identification of "most deprived" is riddled with complexities. Identifying a place where there is a high number of people *experiencing* poverty, does not necessarily mean that everyone there is *in* poverty. An area may be designated deprived, but there could be those within the community that own their own home, have a well-paid job and feel no compunction to leave (largely because of the nearness of family members).

The statistics can also be further complicated by other factors: *How many months/years has a person or family been financially struggling? What depth of financial poverty are they experiencing (are they still receiving benefits or not?)? Are they in full-time or part-time employment? Are they homeless? Are they in B&B or temporary housing? How many children do they have?* The answer to these questions varies from community to community and from home to home.

As with all research, the results very much depend upon the honesty of those being questioned. It is well known, within the world of poverty research, that many respondents, especially those on state benefits, are not always totally truthful out of fear that they will lose their income. Residents of schemes and estates are notoriously suspicious of outsiders, and particularly those looking to "get in their business".

Also, oftentimes, according to Brewer et al., people, "may feel that their responses to the survey may lead them to have higher tax bills or reduced entitlement benefits".[131] For most in scheme or estate communities, a deep-seated distrust of government (born of multiple generations of failed promises) certainly do not encourage reliable reporting – not to mention there will be a lively black market, with cash in hand business deals going on, as well as illicit or illegal activities.

When my family and I lived in Northern Brazil in the early 2000s, we would sometimes take boat trips up the Amazon River to visit missionary friends working in the interior. Chugging along on our dilapidated river barge, we would pass row after row of wooden shacks, each with distinctive bamboo roofs. Barely dressed children would line the riverbanks, smiling and waving as we went by. It was a magical time and it felt as if we were travelling through lands untouched by the modern world. Except for one thing. Every single shack, without exception, had a large satellite dish protruding out of its roof. These are people who didn't have much money; they didn't have much of anything. They had no furniture to speak of – maybe a couple of hammocks swinging from nearby trees. Yet, every single one of them had access to a satellite TV. The incongruity was startling.

There is a similar emotion felt by many in the UK when they hear the word "poverty", or when an area is designated "deprived". Drive through pretty much any council estate or scheme and you won't find anybody living in a grass hut. There will be cars parked on drives and youths walking around with designer trainers. People are walking to well-stocked corner shops, talking into their expensive smartphones. Nor is it hard to miss the glare of oversized flat screen TVs present in almost every home.

The following questions immediately come to mind: *How is this poverty? And if it is, then surely these people are squandering what they have on luxuries instead of necessities?*

SPOTLIGHT:

HOW ARE WOMEN EXPERIENCING POVERTY IN THE UK?

SHARON DICKENS,
DIRECTOR OF 20SCHEMES WOMEN'S MINISTRY

> *Gender inequality is one of the oldest and most pervasive forms of inequality in the world. It denies women their voices, devalues their work and makes women's positions unequal to men's, from the household to the national and global levels. Despite some important progress to change this in recent years, in no country have women achieved economic equality with men,* and women are still more likely than men to live in poverty.[132]

The research undertaken by 20schemes has proven that UK women are more likely to be living in deprived areas and struggling with poverty than men. However, we must be mindful that statistics only tell part of the story. People are much more than the statistics paint them to be. But at least they help us to highlight the need for more and more women to be theologically trained to reach the least, the last and the lost among the female population living in our council estates and housing schemes.

LONE PARENTS

In Scotland, one quarter of all families are lone-parent families.[133] Nine out of ten (91%) of those lone parents are women.[134] Shockingly, their average age is 38 years and not the imagined teenager many may perhaps have in their minds.[135]

The harsh reality is that almost four out of every ten of those families will be living in relative poverty, and about a third suffering in absolute poverty. Consider the following statistics:

- Poverty rates for children in lone-parent households are much higher than those for children in couple families (41% compared with 24%).[136]
- 39% of children in lone-parent families were in relative poverty, while 34% of children in lone-parent families were living in absolute poverty.[137]
- "A total of 41% of children in single parent families in the UK live in relative poverty."[138]
- "31% of children in lone-parent households were persistently poor (that is, they were in poverty for at least three out of the previous four years)."[139]

Obviously, lone-parent families live across the whole of Scotland, but lone parents "are more likely to live in urban areas".[140] Indeed, 53% of all lone parents living in Scotland live in its most deprived communities.[141]

> Jane is a single mother in her early 30s.
>
> *"My husband had an affair and left me with the kids and all the debt. We didn't have a lot of debt, but when you don't have anything and have no hope of ever*

finding the money, £6,000 is a crushing amount. I was working, but suddenly there was only one wage and the same amount of bills. Most months we barely make it to the next pay day.

One time, I can't even remember why, there must have been an extra bill, I had nothing – no milk or bread. It was so bad that I even asked my ex for money. He left me so humiliated that the £50 he gave me wasn't worth the price of my self-respect. I never asked him for anything again.

Things began to get on top of me and I turned to the doctors for anti-depressants. I could barely drag myself out of bed in the mornings and it was a struggle to get the children ready for school. I lost my job and had to go on full-time benefits. It was just so embarrassing. I never planned this for my life, but now I'm trapped. I want to get a job and start earning again, but it's hard to get a good enough job that lets me pay all the bills and feed and clothe the children. Even then I'd have to get babysitters and they cost money too. I'd need to earn a small fortune to cover what the social pay us, and I don't really want to lose my housing benefit. I'm trapped and there's no way out. I don't want to live like this anymore. And I don't want my children growing up like this – struggling to get by from one week to the next. What else can I do?"

DRUG-RELATED DEATHS

Let's dig a bit deeper. In Scotland, drug-related deaths have increased. Although men still remain the largest group to die from something drug-related, we discover that the largest increase over the last decade has been in the number of women dying.[142] Nor is this trend confined to Scotland. According to the Office for National Statistics 2017 report, England and Wales have seen a similar rise as "the average annual number of drug misuse deaths among women increased by 64%, compared to 28% for men".[143]

The figures are stark.

The evidence indicates that women start using drugs at an older age than men, and that they are generally more likely to be influenced by their family's and partner's use. What we see on the ground is reflected in the current research that "women are more likely to engage in non-medical use of prescription drugs, though this is not conclusive and may relate to their greater exposure to prescription medications with potential for misuse".[144] We observe women battling this in their everyday life as prescription drugs are being heavily misused in a bid to escape the daily physical and emotional pain. Women are "more likely than men to cite the alleviation of physical or emotional pain, social reasons, or having a drug-using partner… Among women interviewed … several made reference to the role of trauma in precipitating or sustaining drug use, which was often seen as a form of escape."[145] Sadly, it is very common for women with previous experience of child abuse or sexual violence to misuse substances.

One anonymous woman says the following:

> *I think women do it to block out what's happened in their life, like, abusive relationships, losing their weans [children] …To shut much of life out … because they're hurting from something.*[146]

Drug use doesn't happen in isolation. We see the impact that drug use has on many women and their families. Often the primary care of the children is undertaken by a grandparent, although we are discovering that more and more grandparents are themselves addicts – and/ or dealers – who are facing their own battles. In their twilight years, many grandparents are faced with the reality of bringing up their grandchildren full-time.

Having to face the everyday struggles of life, the challenges of old age, failing health and reduced finances pale in comparison when forced to choose to care for their grandchildren full-time or hand them over to the social services as mothers enter rehab or prison. These are difficult, and heartrending, choices. The number of lone parents receiving custodial sentences is rising in Scotland, leaving families even further ravaged.

MENTAL HEALTH ISSUES

There is a well-documented correlation between deprivation and diminished mental health. According to one report:

> *This link between poverty and mental health has been recognised for many years and is well evidenced. The relationship operates in two directions: being poor can bring about mental health problems (most commonly anxiety and depression), but mental health problems can also lead people into poverty due to discrimination in employment and reduced ability to work.*[147]

Research has indicated that the "prevalence of two or more depressive symptoms was much higher in the most deprived areas than in the least deprived areas (20% compared to 5%)".[148] Deprivation has a clear impact on mental health. Women from the schemes are four times more likely to suffer mentally than those in more affluent areas.[149] The evidence proves that women from poorer backgrounds are far more like to suffer from anxiety and depression than men.[150]

PERIOD POVERTY

Many women in the schemes have to make the decision between buying food and buying tampons and pads. Rent is usually the main priority, with food second and hygiene products falling low on the list. Many women and young girls simply can't afford feminine hygiene products. Period poverty is a reality, even in twenty-first-century Britain. Thankfully, Scotland has recently written groundbreaking legislation making it a legal requirement for local authorities, educational institutions and other relevant public services to make feminine hygiene products available to women free of charge.[151]

At our church in Niddrie, we make sure these products are available in the ladies' toilet. The lack of this one basic necessity highlights the reality for women in poverty everywhere. Almost a third (32%) say they've either been directly affected by period poverty, or they know someone else who has. In fact, 10% of girls in Scotland report that they have been unable to afford to buy feminine hygiene products.

VIOLENCE AND WOMEN

Violence against women almost constantly fills the headlines in the UK. During the national lockdown in 2020–21, domestic violence killings have doubled and calls to the helplines have surged. According to one report, "the number of women killed by men over the first three weeks since lockdown is the highest it's been for at least 11 years and is double that of an average 21 days over the last 10 years".[152] Women now have a special hand sign or signal that can be used to alert their family and friends if they are in serious danger and can't speak freely.

Interpersonal violence isn't going away. According to some reports:[153]

- One in ten women in Scotland have been raped.
- One in five women have experienced attempted rape.
- Only 12% of reported rapes where prosecuted – 6% led to a conviction.
- In 87% of cases of serious sexual assault, the victim knew the offender.
- There were 30,718 charges reported that related to domestic abuse in 2019–20. This is a 5.7% increase from the year before.[154]
- Domestic abuse charges included 35% threatening and abusive behaviour and stalking offences, 28% common assault, and 15% crimes against public justice.[155]
- Police Scotland data requested by children's charity NSPCC shows that there were 5,311 recorded offences against children in 2019–20 – an average of 15 a day and up 30% in the five years since 2014–15. This includes incidents of rape, online grooming and sexual assault.[156]

Frighteningly, many incidents of interpersonal violence, abuse and sexual assault go unreported. The Scottish Crime and Justice Survey reported that, *only 16.8% of people who were victim-survivors of rape reported it to the police.*[157] There are not adequate words to express the ongoing traumatic violence that many women and children face on a daily basis. From just a little bit of searching, the statistics are terrifying enough – but the truth behind the numbers is far more horrific.

For many, this has become a normal part of their everyday existence.

CHAPTER 4:
HOW DO WE MEASURE A THING LIKE CLASS?

"It was the best of times, it was the worst of times, it was the age of wisdom, it was the age of foolishness, it was the epoch of belief, it was the epoch of incredulity, it was the season of Light, it was the season of Darkness, it was the spring of hope, it was the winter of despair, we had everything before us, we had nothing before us."

Charles Dickens, *A Tale of Two Cities*

This is probably the most famous opening paragraph of any book that Charles Dickens ever wrote. He wrote this novel largely as a social commentary on the state of society, through the eyes of two men who experienced the French Revolution. Of course, he would go on to write the world-renowned *Oliver Twist*, which was his commentary on the much-despised Poor Law of 1834.[158] Dickens created the character of Scrooge – many believe his character was based on those in power in Victorian England, who persistently demonised and oppressed the working-class man and the indigent poor population.

In Victorian England, a person's class was clearly definable into the following categories:

- Part of the aristocratic ruling class (upper class)
- Part of the landed gentry (upper middle class)
- Part of the (new) rich industrialist community (new middle class)
- Part of the general labour workforce (working class)
- Part of the unproductive members of society (indigent)

However, these class distinctions have become somewhat blurred in twenty-first-century Britain. Of course, there are those who turn their nose up at the whole idea of class and refuse to either discuss it or accept its reality in our modern world. "Class" is such a small word. It's only five letters long, and yet it remains one of the most difficult words to quantify in the English language.

What does the word actually mean? What do people mean when they identify with a certain class? For some, it all comes down to a person's job. *Do you come home with your hands and clothes dirty and sit down to have your tea in front of the TV*? You're working class. *Do you work in an office with a decent pension and opportunities for moving up the career ladder*? You're middle class. *Do you get your wage paid in cash in a brown envelope every week*? You're working class. *Do you get paid monthly directly into your bank account*? You're middle class. Unless, of course, you just happen to be a working-class person who gets paid monthly. Or a working-class kid who did well at school, went to university and got an office job. So, who's in what class now? This, my friends, is where the trouble starts.

How do we even begin to identify and measure a person's class? There are a number of ways that institutions and sociologists have sought to categorise class and we should briefly consider each of them. But, before we do, we ought to pause briefly and recognise that we cannot have this conversation without referring to what Dr. Watson calls "economic, social and cultural capital".[159]

I will outline a brief definition of each below, and we will return to these categories again later in the book.

ECONOMIC CAPITAL

This is the amount of wealth a person owns, either through gaining a salary, through investments and the acquisition of property and/or businesses. In a small minority, there is also inherited wealth, titles and lands.

SOCIAL CAPITAL

Social capital is regarded as "a durable network of more or less institutionalized relationships of mutual acquaintance and recognition".[160] At its basest level, social capital is the connections we have with other people in our lives. That includes family, friends, neighbours, work colleagues and other associates we come into contact with within the circle of influence in our lives.

These are the people we naturally network with, the ones who recommend us for a good job, or a promotion. The ones that have the economic capital to help us get a business off the ground or dig us out of a financial hole. The wider our circle of influence, the greater our social capital becomes. Without even knowing it, this means that those of us with broad social capital have a huge advantage over those who have little or no social capital outside their own class and culture.

CULTURAL CAPITAL

This is the sort of capital that *money buys*, usually for others, and sometimes for yourself. For example, I may come from a working-class background and not have the cultural capital needed for me to rise in society and thus gain more social capital. But, if I pay for my daughter to learn a foreign language, and maybe to ride horses, I am opening up a world to her that I myself am not easily able to gain entrance into.

The sort of people who ride horses and speak foreign languages operate within social classes largely closed to my own working-class background. My daughter, on the other hand, because of my economic capital, has acquired the cultural capital necessary to improve her social capital. The thinking is that the more money you have, the easier it is for your children to gain cultural capital. In simple terms, your parent's economic capital *buys* your cultural capital, which you can exchange for a higher social status in society.

SOCIAL, ECONOMIC AND CULTURAL MOBILITY

The theory posits that all three work *interchangeably* to one degree or another in our lives and relationships. We must understand that every culture operates on these principles somewhat. Back in the 1970s, for example, if John lived on a council estate and left school at 16 with no real qualifications, the blow was softened by one or more family members who either worked down the mines, in the steel works or at the car factory. John's *social capital* was his uncle Ben who had been at the car plant for 30 years – he could have a word with the foreman. Or, better yet, his cousin Rob had been down the mines since he left school and he could have a word with his gaffer too. Even though he didn't know it, John was using his social capital to his own advantage.

The problem for John, and millions of other men and women from council estates and schemes, is that the steelworks have gone, the manufacturing mills have closed down and the mines have been shut for decades. Whole communities have been decimated as the local industries –the ones that employed the historic working class – have gone and have not been replaced. One of the places most affected by this has been the historic fishing towns of the UK. Historically bustling northern ports have seen the fishing industry decline so dramatically that many young people from disadvantaged backgrounds have little hope of finding meaningful employment. This, obviously, has an effect on the mental well-being of the population in these distressed areas. Compare the future outlook and ambition of the average university student with that of a school-leaving student from a council estate in Brighton, for example, and you will clearly see the difference in outlook, worldview and their thoughts on what the future holds for them.

There is very little doubt, then, that one of the important factors that distinguishes the classes today is this whole issue of *upward* (or not) *mobility*.[161] People from more affluent backgrounds can decide where they want to live, what job they'd like to take, and what school their children can be educated in. In short, *they have choices*. People who live in council estates have fewer choices, and often none.

It's important that we at least understand these sociological terms which largely underpin the whole discussion of class in twenty-first-century United Kingdom.

OCCUPATION, EMPLOYMENT AND SOCIAL MOBILITY

The National Statistics Socio-Economic Classification (NS-SEC) has sought to define a person's class based on their occupation and employment status.[162] They surveyed people aged 16 to 74 and placed them in one of eight groups. Where somebody lies on their scale determines their class. Their data breaks down as follows:

1. Higher management, administrative and professional occupation (doctors, lawyers, CEOs, clergy)

2. Lower management and professional occupations (journalists, nurses, schoolteachers)
3. Intermediate occupations (travel agents, police officers)
4. Small employers and own account workers (farmers, taxi drivers, hotel managers)
5. Lower supervisory and technical operations (train drivers, electricians, bakers)
6. Semi-routine occupations (scaffolders, dental nurses, traffic wardens)
7. Routine occupations (bar staff, carers, cleaners, bus drivers)
8. Never worked and long-term unemployed[163]

Note that the higher you are placed on the grouping scale, then the greater chance you have of *upward social mobility*. This means that those people operating from group one through to group six tend to be able to have opportunities for improving their employment status and, thus, improve their social status. Those who fall within groups seven and eight, on the other hand, have the lowest chance of upward social mobility. They are far less likely to improve their working situation and therefore they have little chance of improving their social status. This means that people in groups seven and eight would be regarded, at least by this study's metrics, as being working class and/or poor, deprived or indigent.

According to the NS-NEC, this scale tends to be fixed. That means that people from group eight, for example, could never normally hope to rise to group one. There are of course, exceptions to the rule (me being one of them), but if it does occur, it is regarded as a statistical aberration.

Their point is that the higher up the grouping, the greater your salary, the more responsibility you have and the more freedom of choice you have within your job market. With time and hard work, you can move up to a higher position of management and responsibility over others, or even change career altogether. This would enable you to move from being socially working class to socially middle class. Consequently, the lower down the scale you appear, the less freedom you have in career options and, thus, the less chance you have for social upward mobility. In other words, groups six, seven and eight tend to be static, with group six being the ceiling for any job or social advancement.

One thing to note about group one occupations is that they are disproportionately found to be in London and the south-east of England.[164] That means that many people who are qualified to be in group one but live outside of London (particularly in the North) find themselves working at a lower classification job. This can often mean that it's not the qualifications that you receive that get you a good job, but *where* you receive them that remains one of the keys to upward social mobility.

Not only that but, according to Darling, "People in higher levels of NS-SEC are likely to be paid more, be better educated, have better health, and live longer than those in lower levels."[165] In other words, *where* you were born matters very much indeed. It will affect your education and your chances of finding employment with good opportunities for personal development and advancement.

The issue with all of this, of course, is that as a minister of religion I find myself categorised as a group one individual, making me part of the highest social class in the UK! I think that those who know me very well would find this as hilarious as they would ridiculous. Nobody meeting me for the first time would classify me as coming from the higher echelons of society. Again, it shows the limitations of trying to identify class solely through job and/or employment status.

MONEY

Others try to identify class through financial income. Again, if we take the eight social groups as put forward by the NS-SEC, then the assumption is that if we work backward from eight to one, we will see an exponential lowering of income. Therefore, the theory goes, those in groups seven and eight can expect to be among the lowest wage earners, or recipients of benefits, in the country.

As a general rule, this is true. There is no doubt about that. However, there are many people I know who would be socially categorised in group eight, yet they drive around the scheme with a £50K sports car paid for in cash. They have no qualifications and no legal means of income, and yet their earnings (if we can call them that) often exceed those of many people who would fall into the group one category. In fact, I know many people in group eight who earn more in a week than many people who fall into the group one category could hope to earn in a month!

Of course, money is a factor in defining class, but it is surely not the *determining* factor. In fact, more and more, I am beginning to realise that class is less about what a person *earns* and more about how they *handle* money. Poorly educated, group seven and eight people often have disposable income, but it's their lack of budgeting and forward planning that gets them into trouble.

For example, I know a self-employed, barely literate, odd job man who can easily earn a couple of thousand pounds on a good week. Instead of planning ahead and putting money aside to buy new equipment, or to save in case he has a tough week, he will spend all of the money immediately. He will think nothing of blowing £500 on a weekend and come Monday morning he will be borrowing money from local sharks or online loan companies. Of course, this kind of lifestyle is not unique to the working and non-working classes. Middle-class people across the UK are in huge amounts of debt too. But they're far more likely to own their own home, have some form of pension and have access to family and friends with higher economic means than those from groups seven and eight.

GEOGRAPHY AND THE POSTCODE LOTTERY

Years ago, a friend of mine was flying into Edinburgh from London. He was a converted ex-Premier League footballer visiting our church to give a talk. He happened to be a very nervous flyer, and as his little propeller plane took off, the man in the next seat recognised him and sensed his nervousness. "Where are you going pal?" he asked my friend. When my friend told him that he was going to Niddrie, the man, who obviously knew the area, said to him, "Trust me pal, you're safer on this plane than in that place."

On another occasion an American friend was staying in a hotel in the centre of Edinburgh. He spoke to reception and asked for a taxi to Niddrie. The lady behind the desk refused to order it for fear of his well-being. When he said he was going to a church there, she recommended he go to a church in a safer area. Even though I found the stories amusing at the time, they do reveal something about the inbuilt biases that people have about certain parts of our towns and cities. Every person reading this will immediately think of an estate or a scheme in their city or town that they would hesitate to walk in at night. The great majority of us will have an opinion on these places despite the fact that we've never been there physically. Reputation alone is enough for us to make up our minds.

In Detroit, a city in the USA, you will find something called, the 8 Mile Road. It was actually made famous by the film, *8 Mile*, about the life of the American rapper, Eminem. In effect, it is a motorway that runs along the northern part of the city and serves as a protective border dividing the city's predominately African American urban core from the more white, upper-class suburbs to the north.

Now, your community might not have an 8-mile stretch of motorway dividing the rich and the poor, but I guarantee you that there are still dividing lines. Even if there isn't a physical wall separating "us" from "them", there are still boundaries that exist. There are certain lines of demarcation which let us know that we are now entering a housing scheme or a council estate. Maybe it's a mural if you live in Northern Ireland, or the proliferation of boarded up houses and hooded gangs on street corners in northern England. Maybe it's the social deprivation of the valleys of Wales. Or the postcode wars in London and Birmingham. In my community there is a small railway tunnel that serves as the boundary between Niddrie and the scheme next to us. The tunnel itself is only 100 metres long, but it may as well be 100 miles for some in our city who would never dream of crossing it.

Other barriers are not so visible. Three miles down the road from us is an exclusive area of the city. Nobody from Niddrie goes there and certainly nobody from there passes through our community (unless they're the police or social services). There's no visible dividing line, but there is an unspoken social and cultural one. It's visible by the size of the gated houses, by the artisanal coffee shops, by the high-end boutique clothes stores and the expensively priced restaurants. The kind of people who live in these houses, drink in those coffee shops, buy those clothes and dine in those restaurants do not, generally, come from schemes and would never dream of passing through one.

Make no mistake: the absence of an 8 Mile Road in your own town or city does not mean that walls of hostility do not exist. It's more likely that people share an unspoken agreement about the places where they do or do not belong. It's implicitly understood by people on both sides of the boundary, whether by race, class or culture.

Sometimes, these two worlds are so close to each other they are within spitting distance.

Take, for example, the two schemes next to mine in Edinburgh. They are called Bingham and Magdalene and the only thing that separates them is a main road. On one side of the road is Bingham and on the other is Magdalene. But, along the main road, in the middle of these two schemes, is a row of private houses. I'm unsure of what came first, the schemes or the houses. Regardless, these houses are valued at three or four times the price of a house in the scheme, even though they share the same postcode! Such is their disdain for the community around them that they do not associate with people in the schemes, or shop in the same places as them, or engage with them in any social context.

Social segregation is alive and well in the United Kingdom, and it is everywhere we look – if we would only have the eyes to see it. Even a simple thing like a postcode can have a devastating and detrimental effect on the lives of millions of people in the United Kingdom. In case you think this is all just exaggeration for effect, then let me point you to the 2020 Scottish exam results scandal.[166]

In March 2020, the Scottish government announced the cancellation of Scottish National 5 and Higher Examinations. The Covid-19 pandemic was at its height and every school had been closed. So, the decision was made to mark students on the grades their teacher *estimated* for each pupil, rather than through the normal examination route. So far, so reasonable.

However, the Scottish Qualifications Authority (SQA) had different ideas.[167] They decided that they didn't trust that teachers would be unbiased in their grading, and so they decided to rely on their own in-house marking algorithm. This meant that over 125,000 pupils had their marks downgraded from the grades their teachers had awarded them. As if this wasn't controversial enough, it turned out that the SQA had used a computer-generated algorithm which effectively penalised pupils who lived in Scotland's poorest communities. Instead of relying on their teachers, this algorithm allocated marks based on factors like postcode and a school's previous examination performance averages. In real terms, pupils who got predicted A grades were downgraded to an F solely based on the fact that their school fell within the postcode of a poor or deprived community.

One headteacher, who asked not to be named, said this about the scandal:

> *The most damning and dispiriting aspect is the treatment of pupils and schools from the most deprived areas. We have been working for years to improve the prospects for our most disadvantaged learners, families and communities. To now see the SQA decide to reduce the teacher assessments more in those communities, "for reasons of credibility" is a slap in the face to everything we have been doing to try and close the so-called "equity gaps".*[168]

EDUCATION

On the subject of education, we are laughably told by those who deny that class and social disadvantage is a reality in this country that "education is the great leveller". What they fail to realise, or just flatly deny, is that *where you were born* and *how you were raised* often determines *how well you do at school*. In fact, I would argue that very often intelligence isn't really that much of an advantage in excelling educationally and socially in the UK. It's *family life* and *social capital* that are the keys to getting ahead in the UK.

I passed my 11+ and went to a grammar school, where I was largely tormented by the other pupils and humiliated by teachers because of the state of my uniform and because of where I lived. My friends at school were going to university. Some were going to intern at their dad's business or a law office of a family friend. They had what I lacked: *social capital*. And I quickly learned that it is those things, much more than intelligence, that make the world go round. I was in the top 5% in the school in terms of grades, and yet I couldn't get past the first step of any serious interview because of my postcode and also my lack of connections. It seemed that where I lived, and who I knew (or didn't know), would determine my whole future, and there wasn't a thing that I could do about it.

My home life was another factor. When I wasn't in care, I was beaten for getting good grades. I was made to stand naked in front of strangers if a book was found in my possession (so I used to hide them around the house or out in the garden). My stepmother said it was to teach me not "to get ideas above my station". Maybe she thought she was saving me from a life of disappointment. I don't know. I never asked her. All I saw was the screwed-up face of scorn and hatred as she would hit me with my own schoolbooks and tell me I'd never amount to anything in my whole life.

What chance do children from housing estates and schemes have when education is scorned and intelligence is seen as a moral defect? What chance do they have when they come home from school with books to read and are faced with barely literate and disinterested parents? What chance do they have when all they're fed is a diet of violence and video games consoles? Or when they're groomed, almost from the moment they can walk, to carry "packages" (read: drugs) to different people around the estate? Or when they're sent out to buy a £10 or £20 ice cream from the ice cream van?[169] What chance do they have when they're told that school is "for faggots" and when they can earn hundreds of pounds a week in their early teens as "delivery boys/girls"? What twelve-year-old wants to sit in a classroom with these pressures and temptations constantly surrounding them?

CONCLUSION

We asked a question at the outset of this chapter: *How do we measure a thing like class?* The answer is: with great difficulty. As we have seen, it's not just about what job you work, or about how much money you earn. It's about geography and a person's postcode. It's about education and home life. It's about economic, cultural and social capital.

> *One of the ironies of modern Western societies, with their emphasis on meritocratic values that promote the notion that people can achieve what they want if they have enough talent and are prepared to work hard, is that the divisions between social classes are becoming wider, not narrower. In the United Kingdom, for example, figures from the Equality Trust (2017) show that the top one-fifth of households have 40% of national income, whereas the bottom one-fifth have just 8%. These figures are based on 2012 data.*[170]

The working classes are discriminated against on a range of different fronts, including their accents, the food they eat, the clothes they wear, the social spaces they frequent, the postcode of their homes and even their surnames.[171] But, probably the biggest, most disregarded and possibly most surprising and overlooked measure of class is, as with poverty, related to *feelings*.

SPOTLIGHT:

STORIES FROM THE ESTATES[172]

I ASKED A GROUP OF PEOPLE: WHAT DOES IT **FEEL LIKE** TO HAVE GROWN UP ON A COUNCIL ESTATE/SCHEME?[173]

Ian is a pastor from Middlesbrough. Here's how he answered that question.

As a child

"Growing up in a working-class family was something to be proud of. The working-class environment brought love, loyalty, security and strength. The family was at the centre of everything. I loved Sundays. Everyone would go round Nanna and Grandad's. My mam, dad, aunties, uncles, cousins and even drunk friends of the family would turn up for Sunday dinner. The women and kids got served first and the men ate as soon as the social club had shut.

Sunday dinner was a feast. Everyone chipped in. Nanna would buy the meat and grandad would cook the lunch to perfection using the veggies that he had grown himself in the back garden. There would be emergency chairs round the table and men with trays on their knees sat in the front room as they watched the telly.

All my family lived within walking distance of one another and we did everything together – from day trips to Whitby and holidays at Great Yarmouth. Friday nights and Sunday afternoons were spent at the social club, and there were often trips to the beach at Scarborough for all the family and friends that socialised there. To be honest, most of what we did was focused in and around the local social club – the "Big Chute".

Humour was also central to our family life and culture. The humour was often dark and brutal and, although it was self-deprecating, it could sometimes descend into a full-scale brawl if it went too far (which it often did). That's one thing that I witnessed among the working class growing up – a lot of black eyes, shared equally among the men and the women.

As a child, I witnessed a lot of fights and had quite a few myself. It is a little ironic but having a family that fought others, and among themselves, brought me security. In a funny sort of way, I felt protected. My family all fought hard and played hard. Yes, they loved a party and a good drink, but they worked harder than they ever fought or partied. My grandparents grew up in poverty, their kids didn't have it much better, and every single one of them had aspirations to get off the council estate and see the world.

British Steel employed most of Middlesbrough and most of my family, and so when the steel industry went into decline, so did family life. My memories are of my dad and uncles travelling the country joining picket lines and hating Margaret Thatcher. They would also use their union money to travel to Calais to do the fag and booze run.

As a child, being working class represented toughness, loyalty, security and fun. I was proud to be working class.

As a teenager

What a difference a decade makes! From the age of 8 to 18, the council estates changed dramatically. Large, tight-knit families were replaced by single parent families (of which I was a part). Those who were hard working used the right to buy their council house as a stepping-stone off the council estate. Those made redundant either retrained and used their redundancy to get off the estate or pissed it up the wall [used the money to get drunk] and resigned themselves to living there for the rest of their lives.

School was a nightmare. Travelling there and back required skill, speed and a sixth sense to avoid the inevitable kicking we would get from the gangs in rival schools. Even when I managed to get to school unscathed, I then had to use the same skills to avoid a good kicking for the six hours that I was at school.

I soon realised that getting the questions right in class wasn't worth it. For starters, the other students didn't take kindly to boffins who thought they were clever and the teachers were uninterested as most were just seeing their time out until retirement. The young, motivated teachers soon left as they realised that the school was going to get worse, not better.

Motivation to learn was diluted by the motivation to survive, and the thought of leaving school with as few kickings as possible was my main scholarly ambition. Partying and fighting hard was still a part of being working class, but it was being replaced with selling and taking drugs, watching Sky TV and riding motorbikes and twocked [stolen] cars across the local fields. I didn't fit in with this new working-class environment which now represented isolation, paranoia, violence and fear. I had a desire to get off the estate, but I sadly lacked the means. I was no longer proud to be working class.

I felt ashamed.

As an adult

From leaving school in May to starting college in September, I shot up about six inches. As I started boxing, kickboxing and weight training, the puppy fat disappeared and was replaced by muscle. I managed to get into a sixth form college and I was only one of a handful off the local council estate to attend. Most of the other students were from the posh areas of Middlesbrough. They were all middle class, academic and completely unaware of the fact that I used to be the little fat kid who would be bullied on a daily basis.

The lads thought that because I was from a council estate it would automatically make me hard and someone not to be messed with. The lasses thought I was a bit of rough and exciting and those that enjoyed a party thought that I would make an ideal friend because I had my own housing association flat, had access to drugs and was a bit mental. So now, for me, being working class and living on a council estate represented kudos, a reputation and a lot of posh friends. I was still ashamed of being working class, but I had learned to use it to my advantage.

I was partying seven nights a week with different social groups. I had my college friends and my council estate friends. My college friends worked hard and dreamed of good jobs. They had a focus. I just focused on partying and dreaming about the future. I started and quit several college courses, worked on oil and gas platforms in Europe, dabbled in fashion and retail, and even did a year at university! I ended up moving off the estate and managing a pub in a middle-class housing estate. Living and working in a pub added more kudos to my identity as a working-class man. The customers behaved themselves because I was edgy and unpredictable. The women still thought I was a bit of rough and everyone wanted to be my friend so that they could stay back after hours for a lock-in.

The majority of the customers were middle class or the old-school working class who had middle-class aspirations and had moved off the estate years ago. I had those same aspirations, and, because of my job, I lived in a desirable location. The pub was owned by an international leisure company, and I had opportunities to develop my career. Life was good! Some of my peers went on to manage some top restaurants, to own a pub, or went into regional management – whereas I chatted up the barmaids and customers, gambled on the fruit machines, had shut-ins every night, got drunk, took drugs and fought with customers who didn't follow the rules. I got into debt and, eventually, did a runner with the takings.

Although I had moved off the estate, the culture and baggage of being working-class had followed me. Now, being working class represented addiction, mental health issues and wasted opportunities. I was recently asked: "What does it mean to be working class?" and I didn't feel I could give an answer. I knew what it meant in a different era and I knew how it felt in different stages of my life. I knew that at times it gave me pride and protection, but at others, it brought me shame and fear.

All I can say is this: Your class isn't about where you live. It's an attitude or a belief. It is more about where your head is than where your home is."

Lacey is a young woman who has grown up and lived in the same council estate all her life. Her family have lived there for at least five generations.

"Growing up on an estate is a unique way of life. Like marmite, you either love it or hate it. It's either good or bad, with not much room left in between. You grow up in a community that's plagued by what most parents try to keep their kids away from. We're surrounded by drug and alcohol addiction, messed up and broken families, high levels of crime, all sorts of abuse, extreme displays of violence in the street and teen pregnancy.

Growing up on my estate, you learn fast that to be able to survive, you have to be able to defend yourself, no matter what it takes to do that and no matter who's coming at you. You have to stand your ground. You must never back down. Never show your gentle side, unless you're in your own house away from everyone else. Even then, you have to be careful, because you can still get a slap for being "soft".

You learn from a young age how to play the system and how to pull the wool over the eyes of every official and authoritative figure you ever come into contact with. You're taught that you should never lie to your mum and dad, but everybody else is fair game. This is especially true when it comes to the police and the social. No grassing. Ever.

It all becomes second nature and, before you know it, you find yourself, knife in hand, trying to stab another kid in the street for trying to make you look like a mug. Your parents – if you're lucky enough to still have them (or unlucky if they're really bad) – pretend to be telling you off in front of the authorities. But, once the front door closes, it's all smiles and congratulations for sticking up for yourself.

You soon develop a hard exterior. For example, a new family moved into our flat and it was obvious that the woman's fella was giving her a real hiding. The next day, I was playing in the street with her daughter. We were both about nine years old. She started crying and telling me about her dad beating and sexually abusing her ma. "Toughen up mate, it happens all the time here." That's all I said to her, and we carried on playing. She never mentioned it again even though I could hear her and her mum getting a pasting almost every night.

People on the estate are sceptical about outsiders that come into the community. They'll figure them out before deciding if they're acceptable to live among them or not. But in the midst of all the chaos, hostility and mental health issues, there is a huge heart for community. Once accepted, people get stuck in and help out with no questions asked. You grow up knowing that you can tap any one of your neighbours' doors and they will welcome you in. Whether it's to play with their kids or to feed you your tea. You learn to keep your circle small with people that have your back as much as you have theirs.

You learn that family doesn't always mean blood, but we always look after our own. The unwritten code is, if the police come calling, or if the social workers knock on your neighbour's door, you say nothing. You keep your mouth shut. You know nothing. You've seen nothing. You don't know where they are, and you don't know when they will be back.

Estates are typically full of big families that have lived on them all their lives down through the generations. When it comes to the summer or Christmas time, everyone rallies round to make sure the kids have a good time. People will spend ridiculous amounts of money and get in huge debt in order to give their kids what they never had growing up. But, at the end of the day, who you are matters more than what you have."

Rachel is in her late 20s and works for a church on the council estate she grew up in.

"Growing up on an estate has its pros and cons. Growing up, we were always playing outside with what felt like hundreds of other kids our age. We never had the best bikes or the most expensive trainers. We made do with hand-me-downs and sometimes 10 kids would take it in turns to ride the one bike that the street shared.

We didn't go on family days or days out, maybe the odd occasion, but it was rare. Holidays weren't a thing and most people were in the same boat.

We knew not to take friends home at teatime because our mum couldn't afford to feed everyone. When money was tight, we would go to our pals' house for tea. Sometimes, our friends would turn up at teatime and we fed them no matter what was in the cupboards. Nobody said anything, but we knew that if they were at our house for tea, then their mum was struggling.

Basically, we shared everything with those around us.

We also grew up learning not to ask for things, because the answer was always "no". It took me a few years to realise that it wasn't because our parents didn't love us, they just couldn't afford it. We walked to school to save money. We never got ice creams from the van. Or if we did, it was one between a group of us. It was one lick and pass it on. There were the rare times when we got a bus to school or got an individual ice cream. But mostly we learned never to ask. That way we were never disappointed.

I remember growing up very aware of how life was a daily struggle, full of stress, and a vicious cycle of constantly chasing your tail and hiding from debt collectors. It made me feel the need to create a better life for me and my own children.

Higher education just got in the way of my life. When it came to the choice of staying in high school or getting a part-time job to help feed the family, then there was always only going to be one winner. I didn't bother with high school, not because I didn't like it or because I wasn't bright enough. I did and I was. I didn't bother because the family came first. It's hard to foster ambition for the future when you're just trying to survive hand to mouth each week.

There was a constant tug of war for me, growing up. I was desperate to do the things I really wanted to do, such as pursue a better education and maybe get off the estate. But then there was the irresistible pull of my family's needs, and so I just let my ambitions slowly die.

There are many bleak things about growing up on an estate. Never having stability. Never knowing if the electricity is going to run out. Being exposed at an early age to sex. Being hungry. Feeling scared of strangers on the street. Having to elbow your way past gangs of drugged up lads outside the local shop.

But there are also many great things.

Learning to make your own fun and to play without the latest gadgets. Sharing what little you have. Working hard to help your family. The sense of community. Everyone looking out for one another. We wandered in and out of each other's houses. We stuck together, especially against the police, the council and the social. We were loyal to one another. And we loved one another in our own peculiar ways.

Growing up in a scheme ages you before your years. But the reality is that it's home. It's life. It's familiar. Even in the scary, violent times, it felt strangely safe. It's comforting. There are so many moments I can look back on and smile."

Angie is a mother of four in her late 30s who has spent her entire life on council estates.

"Estate life. Feast or famine. Food on benefits day. Empty beer cans and stale cigarettes strewn on dirty carpets. Dad (if you were lucky) at the bookies. The constant gnawing of hunger. Holes in shoes. Posh kids laughing. Not enough money in the metre to heat the water for a bath. Young mums and dads creating something to love, but not able to look after it. Cramped houses full of people wanting to escape their own heads. Loud music. Weed. Barking pit bulls. Ball games in the park. Running free. Staying out all hours to avoid going home. Loyalty. Sharing what little there was between each other. Survival. Hustle. Dreaming of a better life. Jealous of kids who go to ballet and whose mums and dads turn up to sports day.

Education? What's the point? Be a brickie. Be a hairdresser. Be a single mum. Be anything but in school. Sign on. No boundaries. Feckless parents. Violence. Sexual abuse. Crushed dreams. Scared boys trying to be men. Knives. Guns. Samurai swords. Drug running for pocket change. Marking your territory. Suspicion of outsiders. Hate the police. Hate the council. Hate social workers. Hate the blacks. Hate the foreigners. Hate the middle class. Hate the nonces. Sadness. Confusion. Denial. Lack of ambition. Scared to sleep. Hard drugs. Suicides. Overdoses. Murder. Kids in care. Mental breakdown. Silent screaming. Does anybody care?

Constantly wondering if there's anything more to my miserable life than this."

Sam is in his late 20s and grew up in a Welsh council estate.

"I'll be straight with you. I would say I didn't have a bad home life growing up and, in many respects, I stand by that today. I lived with my mum and younger brother, and my mum loved me the best she could. She was a single mum with some mental health issues and my younger brother was very different to me, especially when we were growing up under the same roof.

This meant at times I'd feel like I was on my own, which I preferred to be honest. But it was becoming apparent to others around me that I wasn't right in the head myself. I would have zero remorse for things, and had no problem killing animals. I would also get filled with rage over nothing and scare my brother. I would often fight with, or injure, the different men that had relationships with my mum. I felt like I had to protect her even though she said she didn't need it. Me and my mum would fight a lot because of this, and so home could be a war zone at times. Often, she would just lock me out. Looking back, I probably would have done the same. My behaviour was out of control.

By the age of about nine or ten years old, I'd figured out how the streets worked and started getting up to no good. The only men I knew well were gangsters, and they saw me as someone perfectly suited for that life. All I cared about was making money and making a name for myself.

I sometimes think that my life would have been a different life if I'd had a strong male role model in it. I have had my eyes opened to this recently as I've observed the influence Christian dads, especially, have on their kids as they are growing up. The first ten years are so vital. I wish I'd had that stability growing up.

I wasn't at home much from the age of about twelve, and I was making decent money by this point. My brother had started taking drugs too and so neither of us were home that much. When I did show my face, my mum would cry, but nothing changed. I had things to do, and I only really cared about myself."

SPOTLIGHT:

A STORY FROM THE SCHEMES – GROWING UP POOR

MY STORY

WHY SO EMOTIONAL?

There is very little discussion on what it *feels like* to be working class in the UK. Or what it *feels like* to be deprived. Yet, our emotions play such a large part in our social make-up. I can remember speaking at a conference in London on class, and one middle-class observer commented on being taken aback by the sheer *emotion* in the room from some of the working-class speakers. It caught him by surprise. He'd only discovered what we'd known for generations. Class is as much about *feeling* as it is about economics and geography.

Working-class people and those from council estates process the world and air their emotions and grievances, at least publicly, in a far more direct and emotionally charged way than the average, buttoned-down middle-class person. It's not that middle-class people don't have deep feelings and emotions. It's about how they are expressed and the manner in which they are processed.

How could we ever adequately describe the *feeling* of being working class? The feeling that no matter how hard you work, nothing ever changes. It feels like the world outside of the estate is outside of your control. It starts with what family you're born into. Outside of your control. What school you go to. Outside of your control. It's your high school teachers informing you that the best you are going to do in life is work in one of the factories or mills in the town (when they existed). It was sticking badges on birthday cards 10 hours a day for £1 an hour, just to help out at home. Or stacking kitchen units on pallets. Making cardboard boxes. Making hairspray. Putting plastic lids on yoghurt pots. Selling shoes. Picking orders for a department store warehouse. One soul-destroying job after another. Never staying more than a few months at a time. Not because the work was hard, but because it was mind-numbing. Not for me the robotic life of the factory floor worker. Why not? Because I was better than them? No. Because, I didn't want my options pre-programmed for me. Who were other people to say that I had to stay in my lane and not get above myself? That a boy from a council estate couldn't become a journalist (my dream as a boy) or even write books.

I think the issue is that I am probably not working class and probably never have been – at least not in the way that it has historically been defined. My dad is. He's been a builder for over 50 years and still goes out to lay bricks, rain or shine, at almost 70 years of age (more out of financial necessity than anything else). Despite his work ethic, I was brought up in a world of the underclass. The illiterate. The drunk. The promiscuous. The gamblers. The dole dossers. The lazy. The feckless. Take your pick. There are plenty of titles for us. There was no nice lawn or evening meal around the dinner table. There were no, "How was your day?" conversations. There was no help with homework. There was no reading books together or trips to the football. There was just torment, suffering and pain – and the deep, deep longing to escape. Just the determination inside of me to not live like this when I grew up and to not treat any children I might have in the same way.

The real working class where I grew up went to church on Sundays. Their dad brought the money home and the bills were paid on time. They might not have had much to spare, but there was always a yearly holiday to the beach. Their kids had clean shirts when they went to school. They had polished shoes, a schoolbag full of books and a packed lunch.

They were kings in our mind. Although my stepmother had other, more colourful names for them.

OWNING NOTHING AND OWING EVERYONE

Back when I was growing up in the 1970s and 1980s, real working-class men took care of their families and even if they lost their job, they would find another one, or two, and take care of business. If it meant moving away somewhere, that's what they did (many builders travelled to Germany in the 1980s to find work). They taught their kids the value of education and bettering yourself. They weren't angels. This isn't rose-tinted glasses stuff. But they were a different breed to the families (if I can call them that) that I grew up around.

But I thought your dad was a working-class bricklayer? He was. And still is. The problem was that he was a world-class drinker and a terrible gambler. He farmed out his parental responsibilities to a barely literate, drunken, child-abusing long-term girlfriend (they were together over 10 years). Her family were largely feckless, unemployable idiots and all three of her brothers, ultimately, committed suicide.

That meant that even though our next-door neighbours were committed Catholics, whose father worked on the bins and who went to church every Sunday, they may as well have lived on the moon. Such was the difference of our experience of life. We lived on the same street, but we inhabited entirely different planets. We were looked down on by them and we despised their snobbery. They stuck with their own and socialised in Miners' clubs and working men's clubs. We stuck to cheap whisky and lager in our houses and made our own entertainment (which usually meant several arrests at the end of the night).

They bought their house when the right to buy your council house became law in 1980.[174] It was a revolution on the estate. A bought house was usually for people who lived in the posh part of town. But now the respectable working-class man could buy his own house and so the gulf between neighbours widened.

Our problem was that we rented pretty much everything we owned. Even our TV set was from Radio Rentals.[175] There was a box on the side, and you had to put 50p in it to make the TV last for a few hours. We'd put a few 50p pieces in at the beginning of the week, but as the week wore on, we'd jimmy the box open with a knife and just keep putting the same 50p back in time and again. When the man came every week to empty it, we told him we hadn't watched much TV that week. He never questioned it. Not in a smoke-filled room full of hard-drinking, hard-faced northern women. The same with the insurance man. And the catalogue man. We seemed to own nothing and owe everybody.

Then there was the rent man. I only ever got a quick glance at his face, as his nose pressed against the front room window as we all hid behind the sofa. He knew we were there. We knew he knew we were there. That was the game we played (as our stepmother called it). We even had "rent man drills" to see how quickly we could turn the TV off and get behind the sofa. It was little wonder I'd often come back from school and see our few miserable belongings in the front garden as we'd been made homeless once again. A short stay in a homeless shelter, followed by some more substandard housing followed.

Sometimes, we moved to a different council estate, and sometimes we moved just a few streets away. The pattern was all too predictable, broken only by stints in a children's home or with foster parents.

Of course, we were emotional. *Why wouldn't we be?*

TRIPE, KERBIE AND THE *DAILY MIRROR*[176]

We kept a bucket of tripe under the kitchen sink, next to a tub of used lard left over from the deep fat fryer. We'd often sneak in to dip a finger into the gloopy mess and hope we managed to get some burnt bits as well to give it that lovely crunchy texture. It was lovely on bread, but there was hardly any of that around in our house, at least not for the children anyway. Every Saturday morning, I would have to go to the shop for my dad's cigarettes and a copy of the *Daily Mirror*. "The working man's paper," he called it. Anybody who read anything else was a Tory and I was under no illusion that they were scum and led by a wicked witch called Margaret Thatcher. I had no idea what a Tory was, but I knew they were the enemy of the working man. "The working man is a Labour man," my dad always said. They looked out for us, and they looked after us. Back then class defined who you voted for. Working class was Labour, and middle class and upper class were Tory. Now some people on our estate broke the rules and voted Tory, but they were traitors to their class and were jumped-up wannabe middle-class types (like our Catholic next-door neighbours). You knew who they were because they would stand frowning behind their net curtains watching the local children kicking a ball outside on the street.

Coming from an estate meant the chippie on a Friday if dad won on the horses (which wasn't very often). It meant Happy Shopper Cola and a 10p Lucky Bag of sweets. It was a time when Snickers were Marathons and bath night was on a

Sunday after Bullseye. It meant listening to your sister and her friends squealing as they tried, unsuccessfully, to tape the Top 40 off the radio.

It was the pop van, the fruit and veg van, the coal man, and the rag and bone man. It was nits and everybody knowing you had them because you had to have your head shaved bald at least four times a year. It was the smell of bed bugs as they crawled all over your face at night. It was sleeping on the floor because you didn't have a bed, it was peeling walls and creaking floorboards. It was queuing for free school meals while the posh kids brought packed lunches. It was hand-me-down clothes from charity stores from the social services. It was being sent to school with girls' shoes because there were no boys' ones left in the clothes box.

It was being sent to the shops at six years of age to buy cigarettes and beer with government issue milk tokens (and being served). It meant listening to the sounds of wild parties and watching violence in the streets every weekend. It meant becoming an expert at dodging a punch from your drunken stepmother and nicking cigarettes and money from her drunk friend's pockets. It meant leaving the house at 7 a.m. during the school holidays and not getting back until after dark. It meant watching police cars and vans arrest people you knew every single day of the week. It meant watching out for the old paedos and shoving dog dirt through their letterboxes. It meant going around the estate every November and collecting bits of old furniture for bonfire night. It meant ripping down fences and dressing up the youngest of your pals as a guy and wandering around asking for money. It meant worshipping the older teenagers who powered through the estate and up the fields on a selection of stolen quads and scramblers. It meant watching the older lads tinkering on cars in their back gardens that were over-run with motorbikes and parts. It meant the introduction of the rave scene with LSD, ecstasy and speed. It meant weekend binges and watching your friends graduate onto heroin, cocaine and crack. It meant a rise of burglaries and stabbings as the drugs epidemic took hold. It meant choosing between a life of dealing and crime or working in dead-end jobs for little money and no prospects. It meant accepting arrest and prison as a necessary evil in your life.

It meant watching grown men cry as the mines went to the wall and the industrial factories went bust. It meant the scrimping and the scraping of the financial bust of the late 1980s and early 1990s as the building trade went into freefall. It meant watching your dad forced to work for 12 hours a day, 7 days a week, just to earn what he used to earn in a day. It meant watching the light go out in a whole generation of men who felt let down by their country. It meant giving up on life and giving up on dreaming that, one day, it would all get better. It meant settling into a life of petty criminality, sexual promiscuity and the disintegration of family life (such as it was).

CONCLUSION

As I said at the outset, one of the distinctive traits of those from council estates and housing schemes is *how they feel*. Of course, we are emotional. Why wouldn't we be? If a young person grows up in a home that is violent, where education is sneered at, where money is tight – or, if it isn't tight, it is wasted – then their opportunities for advancement are limited. They are going to feel very angry about that. They are going to disengage from the world, from their teachers and from their peers. They *feel* that the world is against them. They *feel* that education is pointless. And as a consequence of these factors, they remain culturally insular and isolated from the rest of society.

When we take a child from a middle-class situation who is born with both parents, where money is not really a problem and where education is encouraged and reinforced, then their view of the world, how they *feel* about it, and their options for advancement look and sound very different. They don't *feel* that the world is against them. They *feel* like they have options to explore. They're more likely to want to explore and learn from other cultures without *feeling* threatened. Unless, of course, that other culture is housing estate or scheme culture. Then they probably *feel* completely disdainful, if they *feel* anything at all about the residents there.

As a man in his late 40s, I think that one of the main reasons for the rage of my generation is that we were forced to watch the death of the traditional working-class man. And there was not a single thing we could do to stop it.

CHAPTER 5:

THE DEATH OF THE TRADITIONAL WORKING CLASS?

"We are all middle class now."

John Prescott, former Deputy Leader of the Labour Party[177]

In 2016, the University of Oxford produced a report claiming that 60% of all British people considered themselves to be working class, despite the fact that only 25% of the population work in manual and/or low paid service jobs.[178] According to the BBC's 2011 Great British Class Survey, the true figure is closer to 14%.[179]

There's little doubt that just as the Industrial Revolution changed the face of the UK workforce, so too did the technological revolution, which began in the 1980s. As mines shut down, mills closed and the building industry was brought to its knees by a financial global crisis, the traditional working class began to slowly, but surely, die out. They began to feel left behind by a world they no longer understood.

As the above survey demonstrates, the traditional working-class professions have shrunk drastically in the past three decades, while there has been significant growth in middle-class managerial and professional jobs. On our scheme, the last of the old miners are almost extinct. Most of their friends have died from lung cancer and all sorts of other illnesses, doubtless caused by decades working in a hole in the ground. They're regarded as dinosaurs by a world that has passed them by. They are bemused by the idea that a man who has never done a manual day's work in his life, owns his own home, drives a modern car and has seen his children all go to university, would have the gall to call himself working class. He probably feels more irked, incidentally, about the young drug-dealing thug who lives in the flat below also referring to himself in the same way.

THE NEW CLASS SYSTEM[180]

"Working class" is generally accepted as a term categorising people in the nineteenth and twentieth century who earned a living labouring, building, mining, doing factory work and in farming. The differences between the working class, the middle class and the elite were quite clear in where they lived and communed and so on. Working-class people would have been described as, "disadvantaged through low wages, poor working conditions, poor access to health and living in inadequate housing".[181]

According to the findings of the BBC survey, the UK is now split into seven differing social classes ranging from an "elite", with an average annual household income of £89,000, to a "precariat" (those with insecure employment and/or income) who have an average annual household income of £8,000.[182]

In brief, the seven classes are:

The elite: These are people with very high economic capital (especially savings), high social capital and highbrow cultural capital. It is their high economic capital that sets them apart from the rest of society. They move easily between the top tiers of society.

The established middle class: These are the people with high economic capital, a greater number of high level social contacts and high emerging cultural capital. They are regarded as a gregarious and culturally engaged class. They have friendships and acquaintances among the elite and the technical middle class.

The technical middle class: Again, these people are marked by high economic capital, very high social contacts but moderate cultural capital. This is a new and small class, less culturally engaged. They have contacts within the new affluent workers (from which they probably came) and work hard at developing cultural capital within the established middle class.

The new affluent workers: These people have moderately good economic capital, moderately poor social contacts and a moderate, but good, emerging cultural capital. They are a young and active group. They most likely emerged from the traditional working class, having been sent to university by traditional working-class parents or grandparents. They have contacts within the traditional working class, but they tend to associate with friends within the technical middle class.

The traditional working class: These people have moderately poor economic capital, although may own their own home. They have few, if any, social contacts outside their own class, and therefore low cultural capital. The average age of this class is older than the others and they are shrinking year on year. They tend to socialise only within their own class, although they will undoubtedly have family members within the new affluent workers and almost certainly within the emergent service workers known as "the precariat". This is the group least likely to want to "better themselves", as they see it. This is viewed as a curiously middle-class obsession. Richard Hoggart observed way back in 1958 that: "Not all working-class people are on a ladder trying to scrabble up to the next rung; in all likelihood, they are more likely to fear dropping down."[183]

The emergent service workers: These people have moderately poor economic capital, with reasonable, if often unstable, household income, moderate social contacts and low cultural capital. This class are young and often found in urban areas. They tend to come from within families dominated by the precariat and they aspire to the new affluent worker's class. They very seldom associate with those of a higher class.

The precariat: These people have poor economic capital, poor social capital and negligible cultural capital. This group tends to contain the long-term unemployed, drug addicts, people with wide-ranging mental health issues and a hard core of those fit for work but unwilling to do it. They tend to socialise only within their own tight knit group. They have very little interest in socialising with people from other classes and have no ambition to rise above their current station in life.

UNDERSTANDING THE HIDDEN RULES OF CLASS

We were all raised in a particular way, whether by two parents, one parent or the state. The way we were raised influences the way we think and interact with the world. We all learned how to behave, what to believe and how to talk as children. Money doesn't tend to change these norms, which is why class is not really about money.

Some of the biggest influences in our formative years are our relationships to the role models in our lives. Who have been our main influencers as children? It matters if you were raised in a loving family unit or if you were raised by a violent, drunken and dysfunctional family unit. It matters if your parents nurtured and empowered you to function in the world or if you grew up with self-destructive adults who had no interest in your development.

When I first came to faith in Jesus Christ and joined a local church, it was like emigrating to another country. I did not know the rules or the cultural norms of evangelical Christianity. Thankfully, my not-yet-wife acted as my travel agent, in that she prepared me for the culture, warned me of the hidden traps and helped me to learn to navigate the cultural norms. I learned to pick up on social cues that I had never been taught and that were not readily apparent to me. Christians ate food that was alien to me. They ate at a table and put their food groups in different bowls rather than just pile it all on the plate and then serve. They dressed differently. They talked differently. They said "bathroom" instead of "bog". They didn't like it if you asked to eat your food in front of the TV. You even had to turn the TV off if a visitor popped by!

Each social group takes certain thoughts, patterns and behaviours as the norm. These include the following:

THE SCHEME/ESTATE WORLD

1 I know which churches have food banks and which are the best places to get free clothes.

2 I see the police as a threat, not a help.

3 I know not to trust any authority figure.

4 I am prepared to defend myself with any weapon that comes to hand.

5 I know how to get a gun or if I don't, I know somebody who does.

6 I know how to hotwire a car or if I don't, I know somebody who does.

7 I don't have a bank account.

8 I don't know my national insurance number.

9 I know how to survive without electricity and gas.

10 I know what to do if I have no money to buy food or pay the bills.

11 I know how to move out of my house within three hours.

12 I know how the benefits system works inside out.

13 I know where to buy almost any product that has been stolen.

14 I rent my house, or the council pays the rent for me.

15 I instinctively distrust people.

16 I have at least a dozen close family members who live within streets of my house.

17 I know the names of the main drug dealers on my estate. Even if I don't personally know them, I know who they are.

18 I know not to call the police if I hear the couple next door fighting.

19 I can hold a normal conversation in a room with the TV on in the background, full blast.

THE MIDDLE-CLASS WORLD

1 I know how to get my children into a good school.

2 I know how to set a table for dinner.

3 I understand life insurance, savings and pensions.

4 I discuss university options with my children.

5 I encourage my children to read and to do their homework.

6 I know how to get the best interest rates for my mortgage.

7 I help my children with their studies and feel able to contact the school should I have any worries about their education.

8 I have savings in my bank account in case of emergencies.

9 If I see a crime being committed, then I will report it.

10 If someone comes to visit, I will turn off my TV.

11 I would have no idea where to score hard drugs.

Here's the thing. If you are reading through the middle-class questions thinking to yourself, "Children know most of this stuff", then just remember most estate people are reading through their list and thinking the same. Both groups are looking at the other's list with a mixture of fascination and disbelief!

There are so many little differences that we don't really think about. Council estate people see money as a tool to be used immediately, whereas middle-class people see it as something to be managed and invested. Middle-class people put a high premium on saving for retirement, whereas many people in our estates see that as a waste of time because they're highly unlikely to make it to retirement, and if they do then the state will take care of them anyway!

Decision making on an estate is based on the feelings in the moment, whereas the middle class tend to think about the long-term ramifications of their decisions. That's why, "Generally, in order to successfully move from one class to the next, it is important to have a spouse or a mentor from the class to which you wish to move to model and teach you the rules."[184]

It is true that the term "working class" is a bit of a loaded term. It is demonised in some quarters as perpetuating social division, and yet in other circles (predominantly in the north of England), it is worn as a badge of honour. According to Floyd Woodrow, the phrase stands for, "having a strong work ethic, standing up for your work colleague and not letting anyone down".[185] As we've discovered, people of a certain age proudly think of themselves as working class even now, decades after the last mine closed. The builders still exist. As do the plumbers and roofers and electricians and all the other trades. None of them would regard a shop assistant in JD Sports as working class. "If you're not getting your hands dirty, then it's not work," as my dad used to say.

CONCLUSION

Men like my dad, the historic working class, have been left trailing in the wake of society's massive changes over the past 30 years – northern men who worked hard, drank hard and bet hard. Working life for the lower classes is now fraught with the uncertainty of how many hours' work they will get in the week. *Will there be enough work? Will I have to look for another job next week?*

When the "red wall" of northern England turned politically blue in 2019, the whole of the UK, particularly the London-based political and social elite, were left shell-shocked. Trust me, they weren't as shell-shocked as the miners of the 1980s who had fought in vain against the Tory government led by Margaret Thatcher. They collectively blamed Thatcher and the Tories for the wholesale destruction of their livelihoods and their way of life and for decimating whole mining towns, villages and council estates. Yet, it was proud Labour-voting men like these who voted *for* the Tories against the party they had once been slavishly devoted to.

It is these new working-class men and women who keep our country running. The delivery drivers. The bin men. The public transport workers. The carers. The plumbers. The electricians. What middle-class people don't seem to understand is that most of these people don't want another job. They don't want to "better themselves" (as middle-class people define it). They are happy with their life. They're not looking for upward social and cultural mobility. They would never dream of moving out of their communities. Their whole family and everybody they know live there and have done for generations.

Nothing showed up our class distinctives more than the lockdown of 2020–21. People were furloughed, which meant that many of the middle class worked from home. That wasn't a luxury afforded to the millions that worked in the service and hospitality industries. Many lost their jobs and their only real source of income. Listening to Radio 2 callers carping on about the loneliness and difficulty of working from home was sometimes hard to stomach. It wasn't that the middle-class people weren't struggling, they obviously were. But it's that their struggles were a world away from the experience of millions of other people. We share the same island. We speak the same language. And yet we inhabit, socialise and work within entirely different worlds.

Millions of men, women and children live in our schemes and council estates. Millions. *Who are they? What do they do? What do they dream about? What are their ambitions? How do they view the world and their place in it?*

CHAPTER 6:

WHAT KIND OF PERSON LIVES IN A HOUSING SCHEME?[10C]

UNDERSTANDING THE SCHEME COMMUNITY

If we want to understand the kind of people living in council estates and schemes, then we need to categorise the different social groups that make up the population. Some people may feel uncomfortable with this, but it is helpful in trying to capture the reality of who lives and works and dies in our communities. There is often a stigma attached to coming from a housing estate or scheme. People are often labelled as scroungers, layabouts, junkies, feckless, a drain on human resources. I have spoken in churches and been asked the question more than once: *Can the government not sterilise these people?*

Others critique my presentation of scheme life and culture and say: *We are all the same underneath. Dividing people into categories is not helpful, or even biblical.* Maybe that's how you feel, and I can respect that. I will seek to address the question of whether we are all the same in the latter half of the book when we begin to think about what the Bible teaches. But, by putting people into categories – or "labelling them", as some critics would argue – I am seeking to increase our understanding of the different kinds of people who make up our communities.

Let me emphasise that these are generalisations. However, I think that they are helpful ones. Any person who has grown up in, or who has lived on, a council estate for any length of time will immediately recognise the categories. Some of us fall into multiple categories at various stages of our lives. But, if we want to understand how people think in our communities, then we have to understand the breadth of people and cultures who live within our communities. Of course, there are differences. There are fewer black faces in Niddrie, for example, than in a London housing estate. There are greater religious and political undertones in a Northern Irish council estate than in a valley estate in Wales. Therefore, I am going to rely on the common sense of my readers to contextualise accordingly.

Think of housing estates the same way you think of prison. Each prison is different. For example, an Edinburgh jail is going to be full of far more white people than a Birmingham jail, due to the different social demographics of each city. But an experienced convict instinctively knows that while each place will have a different social make-up and different ways in which the jails are run, there are *rules of the jungle* that are common to every jail, no matter where you find them in the UK. There is a social order and a hierarchy within the jail, and everybody knows their place. The same is true in pretty much every council estate in the UK. You will generally find the same kinds of people who live in them.

THE TRADITIONAL WORKING CLASS

These are the retired men who worked down the pits, or worked in the heavy industrial mills and factories of the 1970s and 1980s. It includes women too – although many of them didn't officially work, they did do the odd cleaning job or mended clothes from home to earn a few extra pounds here and there. Some of them earn a bit of pocket money now to supplement their state pension by working the trollies at local supermarkets, and other, less physically demanding work. They are often hard-working, hard-drinking, hard-gambling, honest and decent people.

THE SKILLED WORKING CLASS

These are younger men and women who work full-time in a variety of jobs: builders, plumbers, electricians, joiners, mechanics, forklift and other heavy machinery drivers, lorry drivers, painter and decorators, fencers and roofers. They've normally done some form of apprenticeship or learned the trade on the job, although they don't necessarily have any paper qualifications. Nurses and those in the caring profession, including fostering children and young people, would also be included within this group.

THE UNSKILLED WORKING CLASS

These are the people who often work long hours as shop assistants in supermarkets or sports shops or cafes. It also includes those who work in factories as order pickers, packing food, making cardboard boxes and putting lids on yoghurt tops. It includes warehouse operatives and assembly line workers. Taxi/Uber drivers fall into this category (although major city cabbies require a higher skill set than small town and highland villages ones). These people deliver our shopping, food and other online orders. They would include bin men, window cleaners, office cleaners and the labourers for the skilled working class.

THE SELF-EMPLOYED ENTREPRENEUR

This category includes the person who has turned their back garden into a makeshift garage and repairs cars, motorbikes and pretty much anything else electrical. Others buy and sell goods online. Still others collect and sell scrap for a living – or maybe used cars, knock-off tracksuits and trainers, tobacco and alcohol. We have mobile hairdressers, dog groomers and tattoo artists. Schemes and council estates very often have a booming micro-economy.

The local entrepreneur generally falls into three categories.

1. The legal entrepreneur: They set up a small business such as a mobile hairdressers or gardening business and they do it legally. They declare their income and pay taxes, etc. The successful ones will have more than one small business on the go at any one time.
2. The cash-in-hand, on-the-record entrepreneur: They may do things like odd jobs, painting and decorating, fencing, etc. They work exclusively cash-in-hand and are also in receipt of social security benefits such as having their rent paid for by the local authority. Some of these people will trade in black market and/or stolen goods.
3. The cash-in-hand, off-the-record entrepreneur: They operate a cash-in-hand small business or businesses, but these people do not take receipt of any social security benefits. They choose to remain completely off-the-record. However, often their partner will be in receipt of benefits. Indeed, one of the reasons few of this generation marry is because of the detrimental effect it could have on their benefits if they registered another adult at their address.

THE SHORT-TERM UNEMPLOYED

These are people who are never out of work for more than a few weeks or months at a time. They often move from unskilled job to unskilled job, never staying at each for more than a few weeks or months at a time. Sometimes, this is due to mental health or addiction issues. At other times, it is because they cannot accept taking orders. Sometimes, it is because of the health of family members. Frequently, it is because they live chaotic lives and simply cannot work to an ordered time structure.

THE LONG-TERM UNEMPLOYED

Quite a significant minority of people fall into this category. They are usually found within the 30 to 60 age bracket. These people are fit to work but refuse to do so and use a number of excuses, generally relating to their physical and/or mental health. They tend to claim benefits, and indeed many of them know the benefits system inside out. It is not uncommon for somebody on the estate, unfamiliar with the benefits system, to be schooled on what they are and are not entitled to by a seasoned professional. Some even charge a small fee for this service!

THE DRUG DEALER

This category needs no real explanation. There are levels to drug dealing. There are the simple cannabis dealers who do exactly that, and only that. Then there are those who will sell pretty much anything and everything: heroin, crack, coke, speed, LSD, ecstasy (if you like your drugs old school) and pretty much every prescription drug you can think of. These include Valium (a clear favourite), methadone, most anti-depressants and every opioid available. There are three main categories of drug dealer:

1 The dealer who uses his own supply: These are at the bottom of the drug dealing food chain for obvious reasons. They buy some drugs with the intention of selling, but they use their stash and end up in serious debt with their own supplier(s). These drug dealers are only ever used by other bottom feeders or if you have no other resort left open to you. They are the most likely to get you killed – or kill themselves, because they cut up their drugs with pretty much anything in order to make more money. They will use horse tranquilisers, disinfectants, cattle de-wormers, and even acid. It is no surprise that a large number of these types of dealers kill both themselves and their customers on a regular basis.

2 The dealer who doesn't use his own supply: This is the dealer with enough brain cells to know that you can't make money if you get high on your own product. This dealer will sell the same product cut different ways, depending on the person in front of him. If he's selling cocaine to outsiders (for example, students, etc.), then he will cut his product, but not too much. Competition is stiff and he wants to keep them returning. But, if he's selling to the bottom feeders and addicts, he will give them the highly cut stuff. They make up a large proportion of his business and profits, but they're always desperate and they always come back, no matter how badly cut the drugs are. They never deal one-to-one and always employ a group of young people to sell the drugs for them. The younger the better, because they are less likely to be stopped by the police. And if they ever are caught, they are too young to face prosecution. The reality

is that even if they are caught with a few grams on them, the police usually take it off them and let them go, once they realise that they won't talk.

3 Those who shift weight: These are the people who don't deal in grams and ounces. They deal in kilograms. They are known by name, but they are never seen in the community. These are the more serious players, but they are by no means anywhere near being the top dogs.

THE DRUG ADDICT AND THE ALCOHOLICS

Drug addiction is a problem across all of society, but those living in Scottish housing schemes are 18 times more likely to die of an overdose, than anywhere else.[187] The drug addict and the alcoholic are viewed as the most hopeless cases on the estate/scheme. Locals often have far more sympathy for the drunk than for the drug user (even though both are addicts). The alcoholic will often be seen stumbling around the community, muttering incoherently. Their drink of choice is cheap lager and cheap cider. Spirits are a rare treat, usually saved for giro day or a rare win at the bookies. They either live alone or with an alcoholic partner. More often than not, their flats have been taken over by drug dealers in a process known as "cuckooing". This is when local gangs and drug dealers use the homes of the vulnerable as bases for cutting drugs, storing stolen property and safeguarding weapons.

The drug addicts will be seen queuing outside the local pharmacy, waiting for their prescription drugs, namely methadone or, more recently, Subutex. Both of these prescribed medications act as substitutes for heroin and other opioids. The idea being that they act as an intermediate drug to help the withdrawal from street drugs, heroin in particular. However, the reality is that they are swapped on the local black market for Valium, heroin and other prescription drugs. Many pharmacies are now in the habit of providing a room in the back of the shop for the addict to swallow their prescribed medications under observation from the chemist. This is being done to combat users selling or swapping their prescription and to try to lower the high number of assaults on drug addicts from other addicts stealing their medication outside chemist shops.

As a rule, drug addicts are inveterate liars, thieves and manipulators. This is a fact almost without exception. It is probably why they are, without any doubt, the most despised group within council estate life. They really are the lepers in council estate culture. They are the lowest of the low. And it is little wonder when their entire existence, from morning until night, is taken up with stealing, borrowing money or fencing stolen goods in order to feed their habit.

I only have to walk a few hundred yards from my home to the local pharmacy every morning to see the queues of, quite literally, hundreds of pasty anaemic and toothless looking ghosts, all waiting to receive their morning prescriptions of methadone, Valium, anti-psychotics, and all sorts of other tranquillisers they use to anaesthetise themselves during their slow walk to the grave.

One thing is certain though. In the hierarchy of scheme/council estate life, these people are the bottom feeders. The scum. Looked down upon by almost everyone. It's not shameful to be a drug dealer in our communities, but it is to be a drug addict. Cocaine is okay, but heroin and Valium, they're the dirty drugs. Once they have their hooks into you, you've just entered the bottom of life's food chain. And once there, the only way out is a prison van or a coffin.

THE BENEFITS CLASS

This group is only slightly higher than drug addicts in the minds of the traditional and skilled working classes. The thinking goes that at least a non-benefit-claiming drug dealer is trying to make an honest living! On the other hand, there are those who think of the benefits class as the unsung and misunderstood Robin Hoods of our day. Stealing from the rich to give to – well, themselves! That argument sort of falls down if you look at it too closely. Demonised by the media and the focus of the UK's recent obsession with poverty porn, this group also falls into a couple of subdivisions.[188]

1. The genuine: Here are those who have genuine disabilities and those who cannot work to look after the (often multiple) health needs of close family members. Some even act as full-time carers for struggling neighbours.
2. The hustlers: These are the ones who know how to play the system and milk the system. These are the hardcore minority that are portrayed in the media and cause untold damage to the many millions in real and desperate need in our communities.

THE TRAVELLING COMMUNITY

It is reported that there are around 300,000 travellers in the UK and they are one of the most disadvantaged and demonised, ethnic groups in the country.[189] Some groups are extremely suspicious of outsiders and therefore it is often hard to discover their core beliefs and how they view the outside world.[190]

They tend to fall into the following categories:[191]

1 Those who regularly move around the country from site to site and enjoy constantly being "on the road".

2 Those living permanently in caravans or mobile homes, on sites provided by the council or on private sites. We have a static community on a site next to our scheme in Niddrie.

3 Those living in settled accommodation during the winter or school term-time, who then travel during the summer months.

4 Those living in "bricks and mortar" housing, settled together, but still retaining a strong commitment to gypsy / traveller culture and traditions.

We have a few travellers that attend our church in Niddrie and, from conversations with them, it is clear that there are different factions within the community. So, for example, some don't like to be referred to as gypsies and others don't like to be referred to as travellers. So, it can be a bit of a spiritual and cultural minefield for the uninitiated when seeking to understand them.

> Kelly is a married, self-identifying traveller from Edinburgh.
>
> *"I was brought up in the schemes of Edinburgh, the fifth child to Thomas Stewart McCallum and Rebecca Kennedy McMillan. The reason I say these names is to prove that I'm a full gypsy / traveller, which is a big deal among the gypsy community. If you're not a full gypsy, you are called a "buck" which means a half-traveller.*
>
> *I don't have a lot of memories of every scheme I lived in because there were a few different ones. I do remember*

them being very rough. There were seven of us in our family growing up, which is another sign of travelling culture. Travellers can be a very close community, but there are also issues of class among us as well. Those who lived in houses could be looked down upon as not being real travellers, *and there was a lot of competition in proving how pure your family line was.*

Our family always had a house, but we would go camping in the summer with the rest of my dad's family. My mum didn't work and my dad would often go hawking, which means going round the doors looking for work. He would deal in gold and scrap and he and my brothers were also gardeners for years. I would often help, sitting in the back of the pick-up while they were on jobs.

Life was fun and there was lots of freedom, but there was always a fear of trouble. We were often racially abused, called names like "gypsy scum" and "dirty thieves". We were sent letters asking us not to steal clothes from people's washing lines (stealing clothes from washing lines was very popular back in the 1980s and 1990s). We have been threatened with petrol bombs and we have had our house smashed up by football hooligans because of who we are. For these reasons, travellers tended to stick together. We had some good non-travelling friends, but mostly we stuck with our own people.

It was definitely a tough life. My dad had to fight a lot to protect us. My mum was also very tough, and they wouldn't tolerate anyone looking down on us. I was always frightened of the police because they also abused us. My dad got attacked by them a few times and that left us with the feeling we had no protection from the authorities. On the other hand, we weren't completely innocent. My mum and dad did what they could to earn a living, but they also stole like a lot of people in the schemes.

We moved in my teen years to a new scheme and a new school, and yet again we faced prejudice. The problems weren't just caused by the other children but by teachers who made it very clear of their dislike of the travelling community.

When I met my non-travelling husband, he was warned to stay away from me because of who I am. Thankfully, he chose not to listen and we have a great life and a happy marriage. He has never been racist to me, although myself and other travelling family and friends have been to him.

None of my siblings are married to travellers, but we have raised our children to be respectful of our cultural heritage. We do not accept racism and, thankfully, our children embrace their roots and are not embarrassed by them.

I feel gypsies are the last ethnic minority where people still feel like it's okay to say what they like about us. We are human beings, made in God's image.

Many of us use a secret language which we will use when in the presence of an outsider, or when we don't want non-travellers to understand what we are saying.

> *We call it the words of the Cant, a sort of mixture between our own language and Gaelic."*[192]

THE SEX WORKERS

We have a proliferation of sex workers (both men and women) on our schemes and estates. Some voluntary and some forced. As you can imagine, the people forced to go down this path in life are often very often serious drug addicts, or they are run by serious criminal enterprises. It is not unusual for men living in the high-rise flats to pimp out their girlfriends to their friends and neighbours.

IMMIGRANTS, ASYLUM SEEKERS AND REFUGEES

Each city and town in the UK will experience the rise of immigration differently. The problem for many immigrants entering the UK is how they are portrayed in the media. Depending on your politics, they are either taking our housing or taking our jobs, or both. In Niddrie, we have seen a sharp rise in the number of immigrants being housed in our scheme in the past five years. Where once we were almost exclusively white and British, we now have people from Poland, France, Russia, Nigeria, Sudan, Brazil, China, Romania and countless other places. This is slowly changing the make-up of the community and many of the older residents of our estates find the issue problematic. There is very little doubt that many in housing estates and schemes are racist and xenophobic. Sometimes, tensions run very high. But the voices of those who complain the loudest that these new immigrants are "taking our jobs and our houses" tend to belong overwhelmingly to those who don't work, won't work and are not interested in ever working. We find that those who are from the traditional, skilled and unskilled working class are far more accepting and tolerant.

Take a walk down the main street of our community now and you will find shops that were not there five years ago. There is a Polish shop, a barber's run by men from Iran, a Turkish cultural centre, two African churches – all alongside the usual corner shops run by Pakistani families.

THE MIDDLE CLASS

The standard joke is: *What do you call a middle class person on a scheme? Your social worker, your support worker, your drugs counsellor or the police.* These people are a far bigger problem in the eyes of many local people than immigrants ever will be. These are the people locals blame for gentrifying our communities at frightening speeds. In Niddrie, most of the old social housing has been knocked down and the land sold to private developers who have built modern flats and town houses.

We knew something was going on when a new hospital suddenly appeared, closely followed by a state-of-the-art modern library and brand new schools. All of the things that locals had campaigned for going back decades now suddenly became available. Even our old street names were changed to make them sound more desirable to the incoming middle class and the upward mobile. "Greendykes Lane" became "Greenacres" overnight. Starter houses were being sold at ridiculously high prices. Those who had once lived in the old council houses, and were promised new homes by the developers, suddenly discovered that there was no place for them in the estate where their entire family had lived for generations. They were shipped off to other schemes and made to start again.

The young, middle-class professionals, looking to get a foothold in the housing market, flocked to the new builds. But, once they realised the community that they have bought in is in a notorious housing scheme, they soon leave. The current average length of stay in a new build home in my scheme is reputed to be less than 12 months.[193]

In our scheme, the new middle-class inhabitants form their own neighbourhood watch groups instead of joining the pre-existing local ones. They shop outside the scheme. They socialise outside the scheme. They study and work outside the scheme. They contribute nothing to the fabric of our community. In many ways, they have been responsible for the slow death of community life – and all in the name of so-called "progress". Instead of integration, all we have is more hostility and even greater division.

CONCLUSION

Life on a council estate is never dull and it is certainly never quiet. From the barking dogs, the loud music, the screaming matches on the street, the revving of car engines and motorbikes, there's never a moment's peace. But it's not an oppressive noise. There's something comfortable and familiar about it.

People are generally affable. Kids are cheeky but amusing with it. Neighbours are, well, neighbours. There are good ones and there are bad ones wherever you live and whatever your class.

There are many decent, hard-working, family-conscious people who live here. There are also many who are not so decent, not so hard working and not so family conscious. There is little doubt that there is a hardcore of those we can only describe as an underclass (in which I was raised). These people follow no laws. They have no sense of civic responsibility. They change sexual partners with alarming frequency. They are also responsible for a large proportion of the crime on the scheme.

Yet still, there are those of us who love scheme life. On the other hand, there are those who cannot wait to get out. Even if the older, traditional working class refuse to leave, they openly encourage their children and grandchildren to leave and make a better life elsewhere. There are many who work several jobs, scrimp and save, and encourage their children in their schooling.

They dream of a better life. They dream of having choices and upward social mobility. Too few of them will make it. Their dreams and ambitions will, slowly but surely, be sucked out of them. An ill parent. An unwanted pregnancy. Their education giving way to the financial needs of the family. And so, they will enter the merry-go-round of long hours, poor pay and very little chance of escaping the grinding economic poverty of the unskilled working class.

Maybe a handful of the really resourceful and bright make it out. A few others may start a successful small business and find steady work. Others will slip into drug abuse and alcoholism and become the very people they despised when they were growing up. There'll be children along the way. There always are. And if they're lucky, some of the girls will find a man who will stick by her and not knock her around. The others, not so much.

But that's life on a scheme. At least there's family nearby when things get rough. They can't take that away from us. Until, that is, they do. Soon a nice couple, with a Honda Civic and two sweet children are living in a new house on the site of where your Aunt Babs lived for 50 years. And one day, you wake up and look around and realise that this place isn't the same as the one you grew up in. It's changed. It's full of strangers now. A better class of strangers. Some of them even have exotic accents and speak in strange languages. But strangers all the same.

SPOTLIGHT:

WHY I LIKE PASTORING IN A HOUSING SCHEME

ANDY CONSTABLE,
CO-PASTOR, NIDDRIE COMMUNITY CHURCH, EDINBURGH

I live and work in Niddrie. In recent years the area has been regenerated but, as one of the most deprived areas in Edinburgh, many of the historical social issues remain. The most frequent sight from my children's bedroom is of police cars and hardly a night passes without the sound of a police chopper overhead. Then there are the half-dozen drug dealers on my daily pilgrimage to church from my house. There's the pervasive smell of weed which hangs like a cloud above our homes. There is the sight of children, some as young as seven or eight, roaming the streets and causing needless vandalism.

But that's not all that our community is.

It would be easy for me to focus on the negatives – but Niddrie is so much more than its social problems suggest.

Niddrie is my home. My children go to school here. Our neighbours are our friends. Many of the people who live here are like family. I love pastoring in this community. Let me give you some specific reasons why:

First, I like pastoring in my scheme because of the *community spirit*. Many families in Niddrie have lived here for generations. People are born, they go to school, make friends, make a life for themselves and die here. In that way, it's a settled community. This is quite different to the transient nature of more suburban communities. The middle class tend to have a more individualistic outlook and often move around for job promotions, or to buy bigger houses, or settle in different cities, far from family and childhood friends.

However, in the schemes (and among other poor communities I've visited), there is a more communitarian outlook. People watch out for one another. They care for one another. There is a group identity. Each day, I walk from my home to the church and I will *always* bump into at least one person I know and have a conversation with them. Often, I am able to talk about my faith or at least find out what is going on in their lives. When I was living in suburbia, it would be difficult to get a smile and a nod, let alone a conversation.

And once you are "accepted" on the estate, people are fiercely *loyal*. Those who are born and bred in my scheme will have your back once you are their friend. They will seek to protect and provide for you. A few weeks ago, an intern from the church had his bike stolen by one of The Young Team (a teenage gang). As soon as one of our neighbours heard about it, she immediately started a group on Facebook to raise funds for a new one. Within 48 hours, the money was raised – and it was all by local people. None of them were Christians but they wanted to show their appreciation for the work of the church.

I like pastoring on a scheme because of the brutal *honesty*. People, in the main, let you know how they feel to your face; you know where you stand. This can take some getting used to if you are from a "more polite" culture. The culture I grew up in taught me to be polite to someone's face but gossip behind their back. It taught me to keep my feelings to myself and not to share too much. If you were not happy about something, then you didn't shout but instead gave people the cold shoulder. On the scheme, people tell you exactly what they think. This can be brutal in the moment – but at least you know where you stand with someone. Further, it means the problem is out in the open and you can sort it out. It's not swept under the carpet which means you can get on with resolving the problem.

On the scheme, there is a *spiritual openness* that I've not found anywhere else. There is constantly an open door for evangelism. In my student days, there was lots of debate around philosophical issues, and even then, it was very difficult to engage with people who were just so comfortable in life. Hardly a day goes by in our community without an evangelistic conversation with an unbeliever.

In the schemes, we can get straight to the gospel. There is a common belief in some sort of God. There is a belief in the supernatural. There is a fear of death. They are aware that they are sinners. Our communities are open to hear what we have to say about heaven, hell, Jesus and a whole load of subjects from the Bible. Yes, they have their own barriers. Yes, they are blinded by their sin. But there is a revolving door of broken people who at least give a hearing to the gospel, even if they deny God's command to repent.

I like pastoring in the scheme because I get a front row seat to see *lives transformed by the gospel.* Now I know that every single conversion is a miracle. Conversion is a supernatural work of the Holy Spirit. However, there is something precious about seeing a prodigal come home. To see someone whose life has been a complete train wreck being transformed by Jesus. To see a person that society has written off being used powerfully in God's kingdom.

And in our hard places, we get to see the change up close and personal both outwardly and inwardly. From someone abusing their bodies with drugs to being clean. From uncontrollable anger to peace. From fear to security. From hopelessness to hope. To see someone who looked like a zombie look human again and have life back in their spirit! To see depression lifted. To see someone who has been rejected their whole life coming to know the infinite love of Jesus Christ.

Listen to some of these testimonies, and praise Jesus…

> Charlene
>
> *"My life was in the gutter, and I was on a one-way track to hell, caught up in a world of addiction. I was alone and had nothing. But since coming to Christ, I am free from my bonds of addiction and have been given eternal life. Surrendering to Christ was the hardest, but greatest, experience of my life – BUT now I live to serve Him, and He has blessed me in ways I never thought possible!"*

> Lee
>
> *"My life before Christ was without meaning. I was paralysed by fear and I had become an expert at wearing a mask. I was dying inside. After I gave my life to the Lord, my life had meaning and I could finally make decisions for life and move forward. Praise to Jesus."*

> Sam
>
> *"My life before Christ was full of murderous rage, constant evil and emotional numbness. Life in Christ is so different. I am calmer, more peaceful, hopeful. I am happy. I feel alive!"*

This is what the Lord is doing in our community.

Finally, I enjoy working in the scheme because I get to see *people discipled and transformed into the image of Jesus Christ*. There is a huge discipleship problem in the UK evangelical church. The problem isn't a lack of quality materials but a lack of willingness for many Christians to open their lives up to others. People from our poorest communities often get saved and then are only wheeled out for a testimony evening now and then.

But, when we disciple people as we ought, we get to experience the joy for ourselves of seeing the seed of the gospel grow and produce fruit. What a privilege to be involved in helping young believers become more like Christ and then watching them blossom as they use their God-given gifts for the strengthening of the local church.

It's a joy to see someone who was once hopeless speak to their friends and family about the hope they have found in Christ. It's a joy to see someone written off by society preaching a sermon. It's a joy to see someone who used to live just for themselves now serving selflessly in the community. It's a joy to see people's minds transformed and their spirits renewed by the Word of God.

Ministry in our community sometimes takes a heavy toll. It can be painful. It can be tiring and soul-destroying. But what a blessing to be a part of it to the glory of God. Let's open our eyes to what the Lord is doing across the UK in our housing schemes and council estates. It may be an overused cliché – but the fields really are "white unto harvest" in these places.[194] We have tens of thousands of estates and schemes across the UK and very few willing to deny self, take up their cross and take the gospel into these places.

If you're not here, you really don't know what you're missing.

CHAPTER 7:
UNDERSTANDING SCHEME CULTURE – I

"They are moreover possessed of a racy and salty speech, touched with wit, but always with its hard grain of common sense."

Richard Hoggart, on working-class life[195]

UNDERSTANDING WHAT SCHEME CULTURE IS NOT

If we want to understand scheme and council estate culture, we must first understand what it is not. When I first came to minister in Niddrie in 2007, I came to join a small group of believers who were meeting in a new building and had seen little fruit from their labours over many decades. One of the first things that was handed to me by one of the (very) middle-class leaders at that time was the result of a survey that they had conducted in the community. It was titled: "Understanding the Niddrie NED".[196]

"What's a Niddrie NED?" I asked him. "A Non-Educated Delinquent", he responded. I looked down his survey and discovered that people in Niddrie:

- Never got out of bed until after 1 p.m.
- Only ever watched Jeremy Kyle and reality TV shows[197]
- Never read books
- Were drug addicts
- Liked modern music
- Were overwhelmingly unemployed and claiming benefits

At that point in time over 8,000 people lived in Niddrie. My question to this leader was, "You're telling me that is how every resident of Niddrie behaves?" "More or less. There are always exceptions to the rule, of course."

I was incredulous and deeply offended. "Have you shown this to anybody in the community?" I asked him. "No. This is just an in-house study so that we can identify with the locals and reach out to them with the gospel in a more informed manner." "Listen, mate." I said to him. "You'll be reaching out with a broken jaw if any of the locals see this!" I sent him home – which was miles away from the community – to delete the offending file from his computer while I binned his piece of so-called community research.

This man – and whoever else had conducted this piece of research with him (I never asked) – had bought into the narrative that council estates/schemes are all terrible paces to live, and inhabited by the drug addicted and the feckless. The truth is more like this:

- Most people are up and out of bed early doors. Very few people (who are mainly weed-smoking middle-class students) get out of bed after midday.

- Jeremy Kyle was popular. We will take that one. We like a reality show too.
- We read. This is the biggest lie perpetuated by middle-class outsiders and so-called cultural observers.
- Yes, there are plenty of drug addicts. But, if we were to add prescription abuse into the equation, then a massive percentage of middle- and upper-class people are drug addicts too.
- Who doesn't like music? Reggae. Rap. UB40. Madness. Garage. Hardcore. Even Justin Bieber! Take your pick.
- Yes, there is higher than normal unemployment in schemes and council estates. And yes, many people do claim benefits. But there are many more who work hard to provide for their families – and even to help the families of their struggling friends and neighbours.

Here's what *wasn't* in this man's report.

- Many people get up early to go and work hard at physically demanding jobs. My neighbour, for instance, often leaves the house at 5.30 a.m. to get to a building site in a neighbouring town or city.
- Many of the people in council estates and schemes work in the care industry as nurses, carers and home helps. They work long hours for a minimum wage, looking after the old, the sick and the vulnerable relatives of the same middle classes who disparage them and where they live.
- Some of us love to talk about art and philosophy. We love to read books, write poetry, make music and take

photographs. Behind the scenes of most estates and schemes is a thriving artistic community.

- If you run out of milk, sugar, gas or anything else, your neighbour will help you out if they can.
- There's always somebody nearby who can fix your car, plumbing or electrics.
- People acknowledge you in the street and take time to stop for a chat.[198]
- The older, traditional working-class residents always keep their gardens in immaculate condition.

Of course, there's a lot more I could say, but you get the point. Council estate and scheme culture is not all *Trainspotting* and NEDs.[199] Not everybody is a hoodie-wearing hooligan. Not everybody is a drug addict and a waster. There is so much more to life on a council estate than that.

A SMALLER WORLD WITH A WIDENING GAP

In many ways, the world of the twenty-first century is smaller than it's ever been. The internet has connected people from all over the world. We can talk with people from multiple places right from our computers or phones. Technology has certainly narrowed the cultural gap for many people. Cheap travel is another factor in the growing multiculturalism of modern societies. We can fly practically anywhere around the globe for less money and in less time than at any point in human history. Our supermarkets are stocked with exotic products and we can order a takeaway from our bedrooms for just about any food in the world.

And yet.

It feels like the class divide in the UK has never been bigger. The things which divide us appear to be outdistancing the things that unite us. This is certainly true for white, working-class men who feel particularly left behind by a country that seems embarrassed by them. In mainland Britain, the north of the country seems cut off from the south, particularly from the champagne socialism of London. If Brexit proved anything, it was that the chattering classes have not been listening to the concerns of those from the council estates of the north of England. Nor have they taken them seriously.

The Equality Trust calculates that 10% of UK households hold over 44% of all of the wealth.[200] The Office for National Statistics also claims that the gap between the richest 20% and the poorest 20% is widening year on year.[201]

"HOUSTON, WE HAVE A PROBLEM!"

The problem is not only found in the world of politics or economics. It is true within the church too. Forty-five years ago, Dr. Martyn Lloyd Jones spoke at the Westminster Conference and said these words:

> *The impression has gained currency that to be a Christian, and more especially an evangelical, means that we are traditionalists, and advocates of the status quo. I believe that this largely accounts for our failure in this country to make contact with the so-called working classes. Christianity in this country has become a middle-class movement; and I suggest it is so because of this very thing. Nonconformity is by no means clear on the question. In the last century, and in the present century, far too often, as Nonconformist men have got on in the world, and made money, and become Managers and Owners, they have become opponents of the working classes who were agitating for their rights.*[202]

How prescient those words now sound in 2021. Yet, if I was to stand up at any major Christian conference in the UK today and say the exact same thing, I would be called divisive and wrong. I am also constantly amazed at the middle-class Christians that I meet who insist that there is no such thing as class on the one hand, yet when I offer proof, quickly change tack to assure me that either:

- They were born on a council estate
- Their parents were working class, or
- They have working-class friends

It's like the people who want to prove they're not racist by telling you how many black friends they have. Or they're not homophobic because of all their gay friends. I remember speaking once to a group at a Christian conference in England and I asked how many people in the room considered themselves working class. Quite a number stood up. Then I asked how many of them lived on council estates. The whole room sat down apart from one man in a tweed jacket and some coloured corduroys. Anyway, he began to get very red in the face and said to me in very clipped tones that he didn't appreciate what I was doing and that he was very much working class. His poor, desperate wife was tugging at his sleeve and hissing at him to sit down. It was so painful that even I felt embarrassed for him. He huffed and puffed about all men being equal, when that quite obviously isn't true.

Why is it that the Christians who say that dividing people into class and tribes is wrong have no problem doing it when talking about overseas missions? We talk of reaching "people groups" and "tribes" and the speakers of particular languages. Denying the reality of the gap between the middle-class-dominated UK church and those living on council estates is not going to solve anything. As Joslin says, "Sin does not go away if we choose to ignore it. We have to face reality in order to deal with the problem."[203]

The UK is quite obviously divided into different social groups and factions: upper class, middle class, working class, benefits class, black, Asian, immigrant, Catholic and Protestant. People who think the topic somehow isn't biblical or godly need to re-read the Bible. God's Word deals with divisions and class hierarchies time and again throughout history. The early church was awash with such issues among the Jews, the Greeks, the rich, the poor, the slave and the slave owner. Just because your church has a black elder or a multi-cultural flavour doesn't mean it doesn't have a class issue!

SUMMARY

If we want to narrow that gap and if we seriously want to take the gospel of Jesus into the council estates and housing schemes of the UK, then we need to accept that the problem exists. And if we are going to reach the people in the schemes and estates, then we had better try to understand them.

CHAPTER 8:

UNDERSTANDING SCHEME CULTURE – II

"Along with disengagement from the society, there is a hostility to the basic institutions of what are regarded as the dominant classes. There is hatred of the police, mistrust of government and of those in high positions and a cynicism that extends to the church. The culture of poverty thus holds a certain potential for protest and for entrainment in political movements aimed against the existing order."

Oscar Lewis, *The Culture of Poverty*[204]

Although the social and cultural make-up of schemes and housing estates varies, there are aspects and beliefs that are common to all.

AUTHORITY FIGURES

All government institutions are intuitively distrusted by those living on schemes. The police are regarded with a hatred that often borders on the fanatical. While I was growing up, it was drilled into me that the police were the enemy of the working-class man. The nightly pictures on the evening news of miners being mercilessly beaten by the police only cemented that view.

Sir Robert Peel founded the first police force in London in 1829.[205] They were funded, in large part, to protect the interests of wealthy industrialists and the middle and upper classes. At the time, there was great fear of a popular revolution due to the appalling living conditions of many of the working class and the indigent poor in London's slum areas. That feeling of the police protecting the economic and cultural elite from the rest of us has always persisted, even to this day.

POLITICS

It would have been historically easy to measure the political voting patterns of the working-class populace 50 years ago. Working men voted Labour and that was it. No discussion and no argument. But the voting habits of low-income people are probably more volatile and changeable than they've ever been. For example, I never thought I would live to see the so-called "red wall" of the north of England turn blue, and yet it did.[206]

In Scotland, Labour was a dominant force for many decades. They managed to deliver a Scottish Parliament in 1999, but then began their demise.[207] The schemes of Scotland, slowly but surely, became died-in-the-wool SNP voters. In 2014, record numbers of scheme voters deserted Labour by voting in their millions for an independent Scotland.

When the surprise (to the elite) results of the 2016 European Referendum came in, the Joseph Rowntree Foundation published some key findings, including the two below:

- The poorest households, with incomes of less than £20,000 per year, were much more likely to support leaving the EU than the wealthiest households, as were the unemployed, people in low-skilled and manual occupations, people who felt that their financial situation had worsened, and those with no qualifications.

- Groups in Britain who had been "left behind" by rapid economic change and felt cut adrift from the mainstream consensus were the most likely to support Brexit. These voters faced a "double whammy". While their lack of qualifications put them at a significant disadvantage in the modern economy, they were also being further marginalised in society by the lack of opportunities in their low-skilled communities. This made it extremely difficult for the "left behind" to adapt and prosper.[208]

Of course, this fed into the narrative that Brexit voters were all dole-dossing, lazy racists who couldn't possibly have voted to leave on sound economic and political rationale. It used to be a generally accepted fact that the poorer the voter, the more left they leaned. Again, this is a generalisation. I know of a lot of working-class people who voted for Margaret Thatcher (albeit secretly) but that was not the norm. My own community, Niddrie, recently voted in a Conservative councillor for the first time in its history! The indigenous local people were in dismay. The consensus has been that the poorest didn't vote and that the incoming middle classes and immigrants – who do vote – voted this person over the line. It seems, in our world at least, that the poor vote is up for grabs. If somebody can convince them, their vote could easily change the political landscape of the UK once again.

I remember voting Labour when I turned 18 and my dad being so proud of me. Labour was what you voted around our way. They fought for the working class and the poor. Nobody voted Tory. Margaret Thatcher was a hate figure in the north of England and all across Scotland. We called her the 'milk snatcher' for bringing an end to free milk in schools (largely my only nutrition as a small boy). We despised her for closing down all the mines and decimating communities all across the north of England and Scotland. So, to vote Tory you were either a posh southerner or a cultural turncoat. Rich people voted Tory and nobody voted against their own people when I was growing up. I couldn't have told you one thing about the Labour Party when I first voted. That wasn't the point. "We" (council estate folk) voted Labour, and that was that.

RELIGION AND SPIRITUALITY

On leaving Brazil, where I served as a missionary for four years, I was told that Scotland was a spiritual graveyard and that the schemes were the worst of all. The truth, however, is far different. There is a genuine spiritual openness in our culture – although not always to the truths of the gospel. However, it is generally far easier to gain an evangelistic hearing in a scheme or a council estate than it is in a middle-class context.

However, there is an interesting phenomenon among those living in council estates and schemes when it comes to the topic of religion. Leaving Northern Ireland to one side for a minute (for obvious reasons), it is more common to find middle-class people in a nonconformist evangelical church and the upper middle classes in Anglicanism. You will find very few people from the traditional working class in any of them. People from the poorest end of society are less likely to go to church than the middle classes, although they are more likely to believe in God. Indeed, you will find very few atheists (outside the middle classes) on a council estate or housing scheme.

I think that, if anything, people are overly spiritual in our communities. In Niddrie alone, we have witch's covens, self-declared Satanists (although they don't seem to agree on what they mean), and a whole list of mediums and spiritualists. Throw in an African prosperity church, the local Catholic church, the Church of Scotland and us, and what you have is a heady brew of spirituality. Overwhelmingly, the white indigenous population of Scottish schemes identify as either Catholic or Protestant. And this will be further stamped on their consciousness by which team they support. Hearts and Rangers if you're Protestant and Celtic and Hibs if you are Catholic (even though the overwhelming majority of supporters wouldn't be seen dead inside a church of any denomination).

Women, in particular, are as likely to go to mass as to go and see a medium. Although our church is somewhat of an exception, Christianity is seen largely as a female and/or middle-class pastime. And the only time anybody has any real need to go to church or to contact a minister is in the event of a funeral, a baptism or a wedding.[209] There is obvious confusion among the populace of Niddrie about the differences between Roman Catholics and Protestants, and I am often approached to conduct child baptisms by those who would identify as Catholic. They are usually shocked when I explain the difference to them and why, as a Baptist, I don't baptise babies. Nor is it uncommon for me to be asked to conduct a prayer service at the graveside of the dead on a particular anniversary!

CLOTHING

Clothing is interesting to observe from a sociological perspective. The older, traditional working classes, immigrants and the genuine benefits recipients would never dream of spending £130 on a pair of trainers, certainly not for themselves. Almost every other group in the scheme, on the other hand, would think nothing of spending that kind of money, regardless of how little income they have coming in.

Richard Hoggart writes:

> *Cheap mass-produced clothing has reduced the immediately recognizable difference between the classes ... A closer glance*

> *from an expert of either sex, from a middle-class woman or a man particularly conscious of clothes, will usually be sufficient even nowadays for them to "place" most people around them.*[210]

There is huge pressure for young, single mums in particular, to make sure their children are seen to be dressed in the "right" clothes. That means expensive trainers and premium branded clothing. The only people who don't do this are the drug addict, the alcoholic and the long-term unemployed deadbeats, who don't even feed their children properly, let alone clothe them. And nobody wants to be put into that category!

MONEY

Several years ago, I was asked by a fellow pastor what my "retirement plan" was. I had no idea what he was talking about. He asked me, "Are you setting money by for investments or a good pension scheme?" I just shrugged and said "no". I think the church was paying into a salary scheme for me, but I didn't have any savings. We spent what we earned and that was it. Shortly thereafter followed a crash course in saving money for a rainy day.

My experience tends to typify the attitude towards money of the average person in a scheme, especially those of us who grew up in the poorest households. We would prefer to spend less money on clothing and more on food and we would always like to have a little stash of cash put by in case of emergencies.

Money is easy come and easy go. The elderly retired traditional working class tend to be the best savers – well, at least those who didn't blow their entire lifetime of wages down at the bookies! The travelling family have always got cash stashed away for a rainy day. It won't be in the bank. Nobody trusts the banks and very few of them can even get a bank account. Hoggart writes:

> *There are many husbands [or partners] who regard all the family's money affairs as a shared concern, who hand over their wage-packet on Friday night and leave its disposition to their wives. ... But ... There are many households where the wife [or partner] does not know how much money the husband earns.*[211]

Drug dealers are notoriously poor with money, unless they're the ones that deal in weight and don't use their own kit. The rest of them tend to be terrible with money and think nothing of blowing their entire weekly wage over the course of a weekend. Of course, most are in debt up to their eyeballs and have maxed out every credit card they can get their hands on, in addition to owing family members – and then there's the high interest loan sharks. Money doesn't tend to stay in their hands for very long!

Hoggart says:

> *There are many thrifty working-class people today, as there have always been. But, in general, the immediate and present nature of working-class life puts a premium on the taking of pleasures now, discourages planning for some future goal, or in the light of some ideal.*[212]

Contrast this with the middle-class savers who have pension plans and ISAs and all sorts of other saving plans that are foreign to, and seem way beyond the reaches of, working-class people. "Wage-packets come in weekly and go out weekly. There are no stocks, shares, bonds, securities, property, trade assets."[213]

Things such as beer and cigarettes, which would have a low priority in many middle-class homes, would be given a high priority. After all, why shouldn't a man who has worked 80 hours this week, in the wind and the rain, not have a few creature comforts at the weekend? Why not try your luck on the horses, the dogs, "the pools" (as was), the Lottery, or whatever other raffle you have spent a few quid on? Luck is a big part of working-class life and some people have an almost mythical status, for being renowned as particularly lucky. The ultimate prize on payday, if the horses came in, was "the Friday fish supper". That was the treat for all the family and is a staple of almost every working-class family in the land (before the emergence of takeaway food from around the globe).

COMMUNICATION

It is a common mistake to confuse people speaking the same language as you with seeing the world the same way you do. Many, but not all, inhabitants of council estates and schemes appreciate directness of speech. They value relationship by speaking honestly. On the other hand, middle-class people value relationship by tempering their speech. So, for instance, a working-class man and a middle-class man hear the same sermon. Neither of them likes it. The working-class man is likely to say "it was boring" if asked directly about it. The middle-class man is more likely to find something positive to say about it even though he agrees with the working-class man. As a result, one side looks rude and brutal and the other looks wishy-washy.

The middle-class man thinks, "Why does he have to be so rude?" The working-class man thinks, "Why is he lying?" This leaves Christians from council estate and scheme backgrounds (where they exist) confused by the church. They don't understand why middle-class people get upset at them for speaking the truth plainly, and yet these same people appear to have no problem with lying! Language and culture are very complicated things, even in the English-speaking world.

Working-class people are often seen as "straight talkers" and can, at first glance, appear rude and unfeeling.

> *Working-class manners are more abrupt, less provided with emollient phrases than those of other groups: their arguments are often conducted in so rude a way that a stranger might well think that after this, at the worst, a fight would follow, and at best a permanent ending of relations.*[214]

SEX AND RELATIONSHIPS AND BLENDED FAMILIES

According to the *Cambridge Dictionary*, single-parent families and blended families now outnumber traditional families.[215] This is in large part down to the revolution in the UK towards sex and family life over the past three decades. Back when I was growing up on a housing estate in the 1980s, homosexuality wasn't taboo, but it wasn't completely understood either. Promiscuity was widely accepted and encouraged, and it has become even more so today. Those under 30, in particular, very rarely settle into monogamous relationships. Obviously, there are exceptions, but even if they do settle down with one partner, they still sleep around. If anything, it is the traditional working class and the skilled working class who are more likely to be faithful to one partner and parent their children well.

The family dynamics on council estates and schemes works very differently than from those in middle- and upper-class circles. Of course, family breakup knows no social or economic bounds, but there are certain factors that make family breakups that much harder in our communities. One of the biggest issues is that if a father decides to leave the mother of his children, his precarious employment status (if he even works) means that his options to move away are so limited that he often only moves in a few streets down the road with a family member. Often, we will find a mother with four children whose three fathers live in the same scheme, and all know each other and are even friendly to one another! The middle-class divorcees can at least afford (in the main) to locate far enough from their estranged spouse so as not to bump into them on a daily basis! This, obviously, creates real issues when it comes to discipleship and helping young men and women to take responsibility for their actions. Past sins are often messy and complicated and there are no easy answers to this.

My dad aside, I never saw a woman get treated with much respect during my whole childhood. They were beaten, cheated on, spat on, sexually abused and even, in some cases, murdered. The neighbourhood I grew up in would ring with the screams and shouts of couples smashing the house and themselves to pieces on a Friday night after a few drinks. But if the police went round, it wouldn't matter if the woman's face was half hanging off, she stood by her man. Try to tell her that she was the victim of domestic abuse, and she would have laughed in your face (and probably punched you for good measure).

It's not unusual for cousins to have children by the same man. Vary rarely is marriage discussed or thought about in the under 30s. It's why men, in particular, can jump from one sexual relationship to another, fathering a number of children.

Family feuds are commonplace and alliances are made and broken on a weekly basis. This is important to bear in mind in our discipleship. For example, a mother may come to you complaining that her son is physically abusing her and stealing her pension money for drugs. If you counsel her to kick him out, you will be met by a barrage of abuse on the street and your windows are likely to be smashed. To top it off, the mother will turn on you for badmouthing her son, conveniently forgetting that she instigated the whole situation!

CHILD ABUSE

Nobody talks about it and yet so many adults in my church, and many more associated with it, have suffered physical and/or sexual abuse as children. According to research published in the *Journal of Interpersonal Violence*, "Poverty is strongly associated with an increased odds of a child reporting … being sexually abused, coping with parental separation, or their parents experiencing issues with mental health, drug or alcohol abuse."[216]

There are a number of research papers studying child abuse and poverty and their results are terrifying. The figures being tossed around are almost incomprehensible but are borne out by the experience of many of us who have not only suffered abuse, but who work in communities where it is rife.

The statistics for the rest of the UK are frightening. The NSPCC reported that in 2018–19, there were over one hundred thousand children in care, and the number has increased year-on-year since 2010.[217] In fact, in the five years to 2020, the number of children being placed in care increased by 10%. The majority of these children were removed because of abuse and/or issues of neglect. According to a report carried out by the McDonald Charitable Trust on how best to tackle child abuse in Scotland:

> *Children who are abused experience significant repercussions, including mental illness, poor physical health, academic underachievement, and an increased likelihood of committing crime later in life. Child abuse also has serious social costs, including the cost of healthcare, productivity losses, criminal justice costs, and government expenditure on childcare and protection.*[218]

What makes the figures more frightening (and speaking from personal experience) is that the majority of child abuse incidents are never reported. This means that most of the people we come into contact with in our daily lives have more than likely been abused in some form during their early childhood and formative years. There is a lot of guilt and shame around the issue, which makes discipleship a slow process that can take up an inordinate amount of time, and therefore requires a high commitment from those doing the discipling.

THE HELPERS, CARERS AND SUPPORT WORKERS

This is big business on council estates and housing schemes. Darren McGarvey explains it well.

> *There is now a much-enlarged constituency for liberal views: the legions of helpers and carers, social workers and therapists, whose incomes and careers depend crucially on the supposed incapacity of large numbers of people to fend for themselves and to behave reasonably.*[219]

These people are generally quite popular because they don't tend to challenge offending behaviour and nor do they have the power of social workers to remove their children. They are largely seen as do-gooders who are good for a nice trip away or a few quid to help them buy the weekly shop. In Niddrie, one person has been known to have up to five different people from different charitable and local council organisations speaking into their lives!

SOCIALISING

People do not tend to socialise at home, unless with close family and friends on special occasions such as significant birthdays, weddings, baptisms and funerals. There is no real concept of sitting around the table having a family meal outside of the traditional working classes. People do sit and eat meals together, but normally around the TV. Very often, though, people get their tea and retire to their own space in the house. Hoggart observes:

> *He [the working-class man] has his pub or club, his work, his football matches. The friends of [him or his wife] at all these places may well not know what the inside of their house is like, may never have "stepped across the threshold".*[220]

That would be largely true today. I have buried people's family members and children and the only time I would get inside their home would be for a funeral. Most socialising is conducted outside. On a rare occasion, there may be a house party but even then, that would be held in the garden and spill out into the street.

The local pub is *the* place to meet up and socialise. Also, the bookies. Then there is the plethora of working men's clubs (miners, etc.) which offer cut price drink and bingo evenings. These are seen as the family-friendly alternative to the men-only pubs and bookies.

> *A working-class man goes to his club to drink, and usually gets his beer a little more cheaply than in a pub. But this is not the only attraction; often he will pass the evening there and spend very little, especially in mid-week. He will talk and play a game of darts or billiards or cards or dominoes; he may take a ticket out in one of the draws; he may have a half or a pint. Naturally, on weekend nights he is more likely to drink more, and about these nights there is a pervading air of "having a good time", and the club will have arranged a concert (usually a musical act of varying ability). At weekends, and especially*

for Sundays, many wives attend, usually as guests, they find the club "very sociable".[221]

SUSPICION OF OUTSIDERS AND THE MEDIA

Housing estates and schemes can be very dangerous places for outsiders. Family name and patriotism is all (whether you are English, Scottish, Welsh or Northern Irish). There is an inbuilt suspicion of "outsiders", especially posh ones buying up all the new build houses and gentrifying the community. And in our world, it is always easy to spot an outsider by the way they dress, the way they talk and even by the way they walk. A middle-class person in a scheme stands out in much the same way as a lad from a council estate at a cheese and wine party. Each group knows who does and doesn't belong. All classes have their cultural markers, even if they are not fully aware of them.

Author J.D. Vance sums it up well:

We can't trust the evening news. We can't trust our politicians. Our universities, the gateway to a better life, are rigged against us. You can't believe these things and participate meaningfully in society ... If you believe that hard work pays off, then you work hard; if you think it's hard to get ahead even when you try, then why try at all?[222]

Of course, the enemy in no particular order are, the police, social workers and the dole office. We then have cultural outsiders, often dismissed as posh people or the middle class.

In our communities, fights between women are common. Fights between men are common. And fights between the sexes are common. That's not to say they are right or acceptable, but they are commonplace. Death is another accepted fact of life. Suicides and overdoses are so commonplace in our communities that they barely raise an eyebrow anymore. If they were to happen in the same numbers in more affluent areas, there would probably be widespread media reporting and public enquiries.

SPORT

Football is a huge part of life in Scottish schemes and other UK council estates. In Northern Ireland and Scotland especially, religion and football intertwine. Team loyalties run deep, and often reflect religious backgrounds – but that's not to say that the football fans have any interest in the religion of their forebears.

Hoggart again: "In areas where rugby league is played (generally northern towns), the home team is also an important element in the group life of the district."[223]

One recent article argues that, as an anti-establishment sport, rugby league is a symbol of the problems facing northern towns:

> *As a sport with a deeply anti-establishment heritage … [rugby league is] a game that began as a revolt, created in 1895 when clubs from industrial Lancashire and Yorkshire split from the public-school men who ran rugby union. Resentment of the English rugby union establishment – centred on London, closely connected to fee-paying schools – remains strong among the game's supporters, as does anger over its neglect by the London-centred national media … The "whole culture surrounding the game" reveals much about national politics … While many were surprised by the Brexit vote and nature of the Tory election win years later, "if you've been knocking round in rugby league circles – which is still, despite the game's best efforts, very much a working-class, northern concern in this country – you probably wouldn't have been quite so surprised".*[224]

BAPTISMS, FUNERALS AND WEDDINGS

People will spend many thousands of pounds to make sure their relatives are buried "properly". This is a big thing in scheme culture. People have a respect for the institution of the church – but to them it is a middle- and upper-class thing. Very rarely are working-class voices heard from any pulpits, and indeed when I came to Niddrie, people were incredulous that a lad from my background had been allowed in the church.

By far the biggest request I receive on the scheme is for funerals. I have done very few marriages outside of my church. Again, I think there are financial considerations behind this. Most people don't want to lose their benefits by getting married or disclosing a partner in the home who works.

HEALTH

The health of a person is dependent upon a lot of factors, but class is still one of the defining factors in the health and lifespan of a person. Bennett et al. agree, "Social position remains an important determinant of health: 'differential health status is probably the most enduring and incontrovertible indication of class.'"[225]

Analysis by the Health Foundation has shown that, even before the pandemic, people in the poorest tenth of the country were three times more likely to die prematurely than some in the richest tenth.[226] According to their research, Covid-19 is only going to exacerbate these problems. And, as Professor Jackie Cassell, a public health expert at the University of Brighton, says, "The government is talking about the civic duty of people to do their bit, but that is harder for some than others."[227]

She says there are many complex factors at play:

> *If you haven't got a car or you are in ill health, it may not be easy to get to a vaccination centre. We can't assume it is because people do not want to be vaccinated – it may be about access. And if you live in crowded housing, are on a zero-hours contract or have to provide care to an elderly relative, isolating when you have symptoms is not easy. If we don't find a way to address these challenges, it will be devastating for the most deprived. They will be left behind.*[228]

Some of the results of the Health Foundation's research are startling. This includes:

- People living in the most socioeconomically deprived areas of England face a higher risk of death than people living in the least deprived areas. Someone younger than age 75 in the poorest tenth of the country is around three times more likely to die in the next year than someone of the same age living in the richest tenth.
- In terms of mortality rates, if everyone in England were brought up to the average of the least deprived half of the population, the Health Foundation estimate that there would have been 77,000 fewer premature deaths in 2018 – or one life saved every 7 minutes. The effect of Covid-19 was expected to increase this figure for 2020.[229]

Basically, people in more socioeconomically deprived areas are at greater risk of death at a given age. Looking across all age groups in 2018, women in the poorest decile were 86% more likely to die in the next year than those in the richest decile; for men this figure is 93%.

This means that, in the least deprived areas, 20% of deaths for women were among those younger than 75 ("premature mortality"). But in the most deprived areas, this increased to 36%. For men, these figures are even more striking. In the least deprived areas, 28% of deaths were among men younger than 75. In the most deprived areas, the figure rose to 52%.[230]

WHO NEEDS SKOOL?

In the schemes, education is seen as getting in the way of life, whereas in the middle-class world, it is *the* means of bettering yourself.

Because many children from our estates come from chaotic backgrounds, this translates into how they perform at school:

- They will frequently lose their homework and not get permission slips signed.
- They have a list of excuses for why they haven't completed assignments.
- They rarely do their homework.
- They become aggressive if challenged in front of the class.
- They prefer to joke around rather than apply themselves to study.
- They can read but struggle to comprehend.
- They struggle to be academic self-starters and independent thinkers. But put them in a crisis situation in the home (mum unconscious on the bathroom floor again) and they excel.
- They find discipline amusing and ignore it.
- They will work hard for a person they like, but not for somebody they don't.

- They dislike all authority figures and will rebel against anybody they see as trying to dominate them.
- They like to verbally interact and do not understand the rhetoric which is often used as a teaching device by the middle class.

It is not hard to see how these behaviours are transferred into youth clubs and clubs for middle-class children which are generally run on a classroom model of learning.

Education is seen as a luxury by some, a waste of time by many, and the hope of escaping the estate by still others. One of the biggest sins in the scheme is to be book smart. It's almost on a par with being a junkie for some. Street smart – now that's good. That's something to aspire to. Getting one over on social workers or the police or whoever else likes to poke their nose into your business. That's the sort of smart that is lauded and celebrated.

But book smart. You're just asking for a hiding. And so, the smart kids tend to hide it. They often tend to be the aggressive ones. The ones that refuse to do homework and make a scene in class to overcompensate for their bookish intelligence. It's the law of the jungle. And it is depressing. Our prisons are full of intelligent young men and women from housing schemes and estates who could have had a better life if they hadn't succumbed to the pressures of their peers.

WORK

Back in the early 1990s, Rover was still a British Car Company and one of the slogans at the local factory was "a job for life". Nobody got laid off at Rover. And if your dad or uncle or cousin had a job there and were willing to vouch for you, then you were almost assured a job on the factory floor. A decade or so later and that slogan turned out to be a flight of fancy. Thousands were made unemployed, the Germans took over the company, forcing many people out. It meant that many thousands of young people who had a skill on the factory floor but didn't really finish high school were on the scrap heap in their early 20s and needed some way to retrain or go back and get a decent education. Many never bothered and settled for a life on the dole, doing cash in hand jobs or, as the 1990s progressed, turned to drug dealing to make easy money.

MENTAL HEALTH

The poorer you are in the UK, the more likely you are to suffer from some form of mental illness. This is borne out by the pastoral experience of those who live and work in these communities and by a growing body of research. According to the Mental Health Foundation:

- Children and adults living in households in the lowest 20% income bracket in Great Britain are two to three times more likely to develop mental health problems than those in the highest.
- Children from the poorest communities in the UK are three times more likely to suffer from severe mental issues than those from wealthier families.
- Those on housing benefit are more than twice as likely to have a common mental health problem than those not in receipt of it (35.1% compared with 14.9%).[231]

According to one report, people with mental health problems are at increased risk of economic hardship. They are likely: to be in debt; to live in poor neighbourhoods with high rates of crime, environmental neglect and poor transport; to live in social housing or poor-quality housing; to be unemployed; to have limited education or training; to have small social networks; to be in poor physical health; and to have less access to essential services. A study of people with first ever contact with mental health services for schizophrenia showed that they were between 2.7 and 3.5 times more likely to experience multiple features of disadvantage than the general population. These disadvantages are risk factors for the whole range of mental health problems, including intellectual disabilities, substance misuse and suicide.[232]

The really scary thing about these statistics is that once the fog of the Covid-19 epidemic has lifted, we are going to face a crisis of mental health which is unprecedented in our nation's recent history.

CONCLUSION

There seems to be an unwritten rule for many in the middle-class world that the key to happiness and self-fulfilment is to do better than your parents, to move up in society and to move out of the area in which you were born. There's little doubt that social and geographical mobility work. Many middle-class people today will often speak of their humble, working-class parents and the cramped house they grew up in. They themselves left these roots long ago and now live in a nice house, with a car, holidays, friends and a lifestyle beyond their forebears' wildest dreams.

I write this paragraph on a MacBook Pro which cost more than my first car! I have travelled the globe and have contacts worldwide. There is no doubt I have benefited from social and geographical mobility. But I can't help feeling that it has been to the detriment of my roots.

One of the reasons I moved back to a scheme in Scotland 13 years ago was to take my new-found skill set and abilities back into a deprived community – more than that, to take the gospel back. To grow and model a church in the middle of a poor community that could show people what a working-class Christian looked like. And to be there for those who, when coming to faith, would need hand holding through all the culture shock and learning they would need to do.

But the current church mirrors the social mobility of the world. Take the gospel into a community and then assimilate the new converts into the church, where they quickly learn that to get on, they need to move on and move up. What would really be more beneficial to the community and the indigenous converts is to stay and be a light on their own particular hill, difficult though it may be.

SPOTLIGHT:

CONFESSIONS OF A MIDDLE-CLASS PASTOR ON A WORKING-CLASS ESTATE

ANDY PRIME, PASTOR,
GRACEMOUNT COMMUNITY CHURCH, EDINBURGH

A while back, a video went viral. It featured a man in a field in the US who'd lined up a group of young people for a race. The winner would get a hundred-dollar bill. But before he said, "Go", he said,

> *I want you to take two steps forward for each of the following statements that apply to you. If they don't apply to you, stay right where you are.*
>
> *Take two steps forward if both of your parents are still married.*
>
> *Take two steps forward if you grew up with a father figure in the home.*
>
> *Take two steps forward if you had access to private education.*
>
> *Take two steps forward if you never had to worry about your cell phone being shut off.*

Take two steps forward if you never had to help mum or dad with the bills.

Take two steps forward if you never wondered where your next meal was going to come from.

He makes it clear that every statement he makes has nothing to do with anything the young people have done, or any decision they have made. It has everything to do with factors largely outside their control. By the time he'd finished his list of statements, it is clear that there are some who were much closer to the $100 bill than others. In fact, some of the young people hadn't even moved from the start line.

Personally, I would have ended up closer to the money than most of the young people in the experiment. That video taught me a simple, but powerful, life lesson about my privilege. I have grown up wonderfully blessed and had advantages over a large swathe of others in the UK. I have had a head start in life afforded to very few people.

Regardless of how we feel, in the UK there is an "us" and there is a "them" when it comes to life and social mobility. The fact that we have housing schemes and council estates is brick-and-mortar evidence of this.

But the differences aren't just in our postcodes, it's beneath our clothes. The differences are not just in our bank statements but hardwired into our reflexes. And you will struggle as a middle-class person on a housing scheme if you don't recognise that.

My initial struggles as a middle-class pastor planting a church in a housing scheme didn't come because I didn't understand the privileges I'd had. Importantly, I didn't appreciate the emotions that these privileges provoked. There are a number of things I have come to understand as I have lived and worked in a housing scheme.

DON'T UNDERESTIMATE THE EMOTIONS BEHIND THE LANGUAGE OF "US AND THEM"

What are the emotions of someone back on the start line towards someone like me? There's a rightful sense of injustice. There's understandable anger towards the privileged.

We're walking into a community that has assumptions, and has drawn conclusions, and has created a caricature of who they think you are based on these emotions. If you're middle class and you're going into my housing scheme, you're walking into a community that sees you as the cause of much of this injustice and so also the target for their anger.

You're walking into a community that has a pathological suspicion of outsiders like you.

You don't come in neutral.

You definitely don't come in as a hero.

You probably come in identified as an enemy.

On both sides – middle class and working class – we often operate on the basis of emotionally-fuelled, generationally-instilled, inaccurate assumptions and exaggerated caricatures of what "they" are like. When I was around 18, I was asked to go and play guitar at Niddrie Community Church to help them out for a Sunday morning. When I told my dad, his instant reaction was, "You're not taking my Audi and parking it outside that church." When I told a pal in my scheme that I used to work for a church in the city centre and that it had about 500 members, his instant reaction was, "Where in Edinburgh is there space to park 500 Range Rovers?"

Both generalisations. Both caricatures. But both instinctive. Both emotive.

THE HERO AND THE VILLAIN

In your world, you're the hero and they're the villain. In their world, they're the hero and you're the villain. All this is to say, don't underestimate the struggle it is when these two worlds collide. You may only be crossing a street, but you're also crossing cultures. You may still be in your own city, but you're probably on foreign soil. Don't be ignorant of that.

DON'T UNDERESTIMATE HOW LONG IT TAKES TO EARN PEOPLE'S TRUST

I asked a pal of mine in my scheme, "What is the biggest struggle for somebody like me coming into a housing scheme like this?" Within hesitation he answered, "Trust." On our estates, trust is by works, not by grace. Trust is earned slowly but can be lost quickly. If you're not a person of your word, even in relation to the little things, you'll struggle. And distrust is a learned defence mechanism, particularly linked to authority.

So, in a community that's instantly suspicious and instinctively rebellious, you'll need to think carefully about how you introduce, talk about and appoint church leaders. How are you going to show that eldership and their authority can be a good thing, a noble thing? Don't underestimate how long that will take.

DON'T JUST PREACH AND TEACH BUT EAT AND DRINK

If you're trying to attract middle-class Christian people to help in your church plant, you'll probably gain their trust by being a gifted, able Bible teacher. But for the people we're desperate to reach with the gospel on our housing estates, that's not going to cut it. Trust won't be earned by a slick presentation from a pulpit. It's earned over banter about a football match, or tears at a kitchen table, or sharing bereavement at a graveside, or watching *The X Factor* final with a curry, or simply being there when needed.

I've struggled with this.

One, because I'm an introvert and would prefer to be safe in my study with a bunch of books written by dead people rather than vulnerable with people who don't trust me. Two, because it doesn't feel like an efficient use of my time. I've been programmed for productivity and some of these things can feel like a waste of time. Three, because in the busyness of ministry I feel guilty simply hanging out with the lads because I barely get any time to hang out with my wife and boy.

But it's important that it was said of Jesus in Luke 7:34, "The Son of Man came eating and drinking", to the point that people label Him "a glutton and a drunkard, a friend of tax collectors and sinners". Has anyone in your community ever described you as a glutton and a drunkard? You'll probably need to get there before people are willing to call you their preacher and teacher.

Does anyone in your community call you their "friend"?

Nobody will listen to a word you say from a Bible if you've not listened to them over a butty.

You're unlikely to have the joy of inviting someone to the Lord's table for the first time if you've never had them round your kitchen table. Prepping for preaching will most likely take up a pretty minor part of your time. The message is you.

All of you.

YOU'LL STRUGGLE IF YOU SEE EVERYTHING IN BLACK AND WHITE AND ARE UNABLE TO HANDLE GREY

My wife Sarah had been doing youth work in our scheme for years before I got involved. When we got married, I started helping at some of her youth clubs, having done tons of youth work, albeit with very affluent Christian young people. I thought I was God's gift to my wife's ministry.

But everything, for me, was black and white.

A kid came to an after-school club who'd skived school that day. I wanted Sarah to make a rule that to come to the after-school club they had to have gone to school. Another kid came in and their behaviour was all over the place, and my instinct was to discipline them immediately. Another time two kids started fighting, and Sarah sent one home and let the other stay. I wanted to take her aside and implement some consistency in discipline.

Everything was black and white.

But Sarah, patiently but firmly, schooled me. The kids who've played truant from school shouldn't be banned from our club. They're most likely the kids who need our club the most.

The kid whose behaviour was off-the-wall didn't need disciplining, he needed a chocolate spread sandwich. Him and his brothers never get breakfast in their house. What are you like when you're hangry?

And the kid in the fight who didn't get sent home? His dad just died of an overdose. Today, he needs to stay in the club.

I was only seeing the behaviour. I wasn't seeing what lay behind the behaviour.

What's true in youth groups with little kids is true of any discipleship relationship, pastoral situation or church discipline scenario. Don't just see the black and white. Slow down, understand, appreciate, listen to the grey. Remember where people are starting from and that repentance is never easy and straightforward for any of us, but costly and complex.

DON'T BE NAIVE TO THE POWER OF A DOMINANT CULTURE

When I worked in a large, gathered, affluent city-centre church, I felt like a fish *in* water. I don't just mean that I felt comfortable. Like a fish in water, I didn't know anything different. The culture didn't exist to me because it was just my natural habitat.

When I moved to Niddrie, I suddenly felt like a fish out of water. I felt like I didn't belong, I didn't fit in. I didn't just feel like an outsider, I felt like a child. Although I couldn't see my own culture, I could see this one very clearly. And I could see this wasn't my home.

Those feelings showed me that the easiest way to do church is to stay among your own. Existing in homogenous units is easy. Let's all just stay among our own and achieve unity through uniformity. Those feelings showed me how hard it must be for someone from a council estate to walk into, let alone stay, in a church where the dominant culture is middle class. And by the way, if you don't think your church has a dominant culture, then your church's dominant culture is your culture. That culture may be invisible to you, but it is not insignificant and it may well be intimidating.

So, if you're a planter or a church from the outside wanting to plant in a council estate, don't just drop a group of your members into an estate and start a service. You need to take time to listen to, understand, discern the culture, where possible letting those indigenous to the culture take the lead. Your community's culture needs to become the dominant culture. If it's in their community and you're an outsider, you're the one who needs to adapt and they need to feel at home.

According to the gospel, we must not expect the weak to adapt to fit in with the strong, but the strong are to become weak for the sake of the weak.

DON'T OVERLOAD BECAUSE YOU'RE AIMING FOR PEAK EFFICIENCY

I know for a fact that if I want to get something done efficiently, I'm best to do it alone. No interruptions. No questions. No distractions. Just me, and the task.

But if that's my approach to ministry, then my ministry will be limited to me and it will die with me.

In any context, to see leaders emerge you've got to: (a) take people along with you to observe your leadership; but (b) under-lead, by leaving things undone, allowing other people to step in, step up and take responsibility. And this is a struggle for a leader in any context, because productivity drops and standards drop.

But I need to constantly remind myself: the goal of this gig is not peak efficiency. It's to make much of Christ as a disciple-making-disciple who pastors a church-planting-church. Over-leading may mean an efficient, faithful church in this generation but will lead to a dead church in the next generation.

Under-leading may result in an unproductive, messy church in this generation but may well lead to multiple faithful, living churches in the next generation. But the truth is, this under-leading is both harder and more important when you're crossing cultures.

It's *harder*. Give me your average graduate from a theological college like Oak Hill to train and it would be easy, because we are both fish from the same pond. Put me with an indigenous believer from a council estate and we both struggle, because we are fish who both struggle to survive in each other's ponds.

It's also more *important* to under-lead when you're crossing cultures. That's because our desire should ultimately be for ourselves as outsiders to increasingly become less, and the indigenous insiders to become more.

Cross-cultural missionaries are to be midwives of the indigenous: Do your job. Pass it over. Be forgotten. In all the emotions, the distrust and the greys, hear this:

> *Here there is not Greek and Jew, circumcised and uncircumcised, barbarian, Scythian, slave, free; but Christ is all, and in all. Put on then, as God's chosen ones, holy and beloved, compassionate hearts, kindness, humility, meekness, and patience, bearing with one another and, if one has a complaint against another, forgiving each other; as the Lord has forgiven you, so you also must forgive. And above all these put on love, which binds everything together in perfect harmony. (Col. 3:11–14, ESV)*

SPOTLIGHT:

CULTURE CLASH – WOMEN IN THE SCHEMES

SHARON DICKENS,
DIRECTOR OF 20SCHEMES WOMEN'S MINISTRY

I'm a storyteller. I get it from my dad. He used to tell us the most amazing stories when we were kids. He'd just make them up on the spot, which sadly meant that they could never be repeated. My mum always told him to write them down, but he never would and now they are lost for ever.

But I love making up stories and interweaving plots. Growing up, I'd always wanted to write a book, but it was a pipe dream for a girl with dyslexia and no understanding of English grammar! When I finally got the opportunity to write one, I had this idealistic image of the writing process. I thought that I would open my laptop and the words would come flying out of me effortlessly. I thought I could use the process to express all of my frustrations concerning UK Christian church culture.

The reality was very different.

Writing has been one of the most difficult things that I have ever done in my life. Just you alone in a room, trying to translate your deepest thoughts and emotions on to a page. Yet, there is nothing quite like the editorial process for beating any hint of pride out of your character.

It's often humbling.

It's sometimes humiliating.

It's often downright frustrating.

Thankfully, not all editors are the same and I've been grateful for the last two female editors that publishers have assigned to me. I had this naive expectation that, as the author, I'd get to write what I wanted, how I wanted. But the publisher knows from experience what sells and what's not helpful. Let's face it, we write books so people will buy them and read them.

I recently wrote a book entitled, *Relationships – How Do I Make Things Right?*[233] It was my second book and so I had a fair idea of what to expect when the first edits came back. I had called one of my chapter headings, "When It All Hits the Fan". This clearly did not sit well with the editor. I was politely asked to change it. I refused. They explained – very robustly but ever so politely – *why* it should be changed. I wrote back that I understood their point but, in my context, this language was absolutely acceptable, and noone would be remotely offended. A flurry of emails went backwards and forwards, neither party willing to give up ground. Eventually Mez, the series editor, intervened and asked me to change it in order to keep the peace. I grudgingly submitted to his request.

Now, before you think this is some weird passive aggressive attempt to get back at the publisher of that book, I have a deeper motive for sharing this experience with you. This situation reveals is a classic culture clash, one that we see all the time as we partner with people who are not from our context. I find it particularly bizarre that when we discuss the cultural differences between women living on council estates and middle-class women that the latter deny that any such differences exist. Yet, this minor issue between myself and my publisher only proves my point. In all walks of life, especially in the UK church, the majority culture rules.

Every time.

Maybe you're thinking to yourself: "Calm down, Sharon, it's just a chapter title. What does it matter?" It doesn't matter in the grand scheme of things. What I find absolutely fascinating is not what caused the offence, but what didn't. In the same book I use an illustration of a man physically abusing a woman and not a single objection was raised. How can the title of a chapter that doesn't contain a swear word elicit such a strong reaction, and yet a graphic illustration of a man abusing his mother elicits none? I'm not suggesting that domestic violence isn't offensive in suburbia. But, if you were to ask somebody on a scheme what was more offensive, the title of a chapter or the abusive illustration, I can you assure that the latter would cause the most offence in our culture.

One of my responsibilities within 20schemes is to teach a class called, "Expectations and Transitioning Well". We have a number of international missionaries coming to serve and we want them to be prepared for the reality of life in our communities. In the Christian missionary world, we don't think twice about preparing our missionaries for the culture they're about to enter. Yet, we don't have the same mindset when we cross the boundary from suburbia to scheme. Denying that there are clear cultural differences is unhelpful and is perhaps one of the reasons why the UK church is so ineffective in our communities.

Several years ago, I managed to get some tickets to the FIEC Women's Workers Conference called "Thrive". Three of us went and two of the women I took with me were new Christians from the scheme. They'd never been to a conference in their lives! When we arrived, the venue was stunning. The women in attendance were all very nice and welcoming. But it was clear from the off that our girls were like fish out of water.

Mealtimes bordered on the hilarious. One of the girls complained really loudly about why somebody would put cucumber on a pizza, until someone politely informed them that it was courgette. That information was met with a blank look of incomprehension! They then complained about the lack of chicken in their soup and were mystified to discover they were actually eating a vegetarian chickpea curry. All they cared about was getting *some real food*, and they couldn't quite believe that there wasn't a local chip shop that would deliver to the door.

"Where have you brought us, Shabba? No smoking allowed. Weird food. No chip shop. Posh old ladies with strange accents. What's going on?" Perhaps the funniest scene was watching them trying to play croquet on the lawn. Picture the scene: They are playing with this really adorable, well-spoken woman called Julia. She's trying to teach them the rules of the game, but they just want to swing their mallets like golf clubs and are smashing the ball all over the place. One of the girls shouts out to Julia who is about to take her shot: "C'mon Julia, give it some wellie!" She responds, "I'm trying my dear." Even now the memory of it still makes me smile. Two worlds literally colliding at the end of a mallet.

Different doesn't mean bad or necessarily sinful – it's just different. But, to ignore the differences and pretend they aren't there is both short-sighted and potentially damaging. Some women from middle-class or international contexts have really struggled with the cultural transition to our communities. In fact, some couples have actually moved on because the culture was too hard for them to navigate. Not everything in the schemes is hard. Some of the cultural differences are amazing. I love the fact that children still play on their bikes and play with their pals on the green next to my flat. I love it in the summer when someone opens the hydrants in the road and the children dance through the water fountain. It's noisy and riotous. People are out on their balconies, shouting across the street to each other. It's not neat, tidy or serene. It's not hidden behind private gardens. People don't organise play dates. Children just tap on the door to see if their pal is coming out to play.

UNDERSTANDING THE SOCIAL CUES

The thing about being indigenous to the culture is that I don't need someone to interpret a situation, phrase or explain why we do something a certain way. I just know – it's familiar, comfortable and easy. The unspoken, subtle nuances of the middle-class world are foreign to me. Stick me in a city-centre church as a woman's speaker where, after I have spoken, I am served tea in a bone china cup and saucer, and I'm out my depth. I need an interpreter in that social circle. Of course, I know what's expected of me because I'm churched. I've been saved for decades and so I have had to make some adjustments to the majority culture.

In my years of observing Christian middle-class and council estate cultures, I have observed notable differences in a couple of key areas:

HOSPITALITY

In our context, the way we spend time together is generally differently to the way the middle classes do it. We are constantly in and out of each other's homes several times a day. Life is often fluid and unstructured. This has caused no end of problems for middle-class women who have moved into our communities and brought with them their particular concepts of "me time" and "free time".

Some women outside our culture act like the dinner table is off limits for any but the immediate family unit. People who are precious about their free time and personal space tend to struggle the most. The middle class have made going on holiday and "getting away from the stresses of ministry" the eleventh commandment.

This is completely foreign to our culture. We always cook extra for the uninvited guests who will turn up at mealtimes or who are invited to stay on a whim, without a prior appointment (gasp!). Holidays can quickly become a time for people from multiple households to share the same space, thus saving money. None of these things have detrimentally affected my relationship with my children. In fact, I would go so far as to say it has been beneficial for us. We've often had deeper gospel conversations because of the other people who have been encompassed into our family.

Hospitality has even extended to people living with us. One lady I was discipling used to stay at the weekends (with her child) and she spent so much time with us she felt like family. My daughter, especially, loves her still. Even now, a decade later, when I'm away from home, I know if the children need help, they can contact her for a more "adult" opinion. On the other side of the coin, I've been ripped off, lied to, things have been broken (lots of things) and the house has been left in a mess (worse than having teenagers). But, in the main, it's been amazing to see people grow and a privilege to be able to speak biblical wisdom into their lives.

This fluidity and the lack of structure, the crossing of personal boundary lines and the invasion of personal space, is just too much for some to tolerate. It's not like suburbia, when the phrase "pop round anytime" is not meant to be taken literally. When we say it, we mean it. And people will take us up on it, anytime of the day or night. It's not uncommon for me to have people for dinner and someone turns up unexpectedly (with her children) and ends up eating with us. Cultural outsiders who prefer structure, routine and scheduled meetings struggle with this. They think of themselves as hospitable. But it is usually hospitality put in the diary well in advance and on their own controlled terms.

LANGUAGE

Our love language is mockery. The more we like you, the more we tease you. There are people who can take it and there are those who hate it. Some cultural outsiders think that our humour is sinful and can be a bad witness. I don't think it's sinful, in the main, but it can degenerate into sin if taken too far. On the other hand, some of the dour stiffness of the middle class can also be sinful. There is nothing worse than the proud, stiff-necked judgement of someone without a sense of humour.

There is much about the way we communicate on the schemes that many middle-class women have struggled to understand. We are direct in our speech. If we have something to say, we say it. This is in contrast to the middle-class culture of UK Christianity that circles the garden so many times it's hard to appreciate what is and isn't being communicated. It's very frustrating.

Scheme women may come across as harsh and uncaring, but they are trying to respect you by giving honest answers to questions. If you ask them how they feel, they will tell you how they feel. That's how they value the relationship. Again, contrast this with the passive aggressive way some middle-class women show their unhappiness. Saying, "I'm not angry," politely, while it oozes out of every well-enunciated pore, is simply dishonest. Sometimes it's absolutely exhausting working out what they really mean!

Granted, this style of communication doesn't sit well with everyone. I remember years ago, in a mostly middle-class small group, we were at the "sharing for prayer" section of the meeting. That usually meant little depth and praying for vague and innocuous things, nothing remotely personal. I had a couple of scheme girls with me and when it came to their turn to share, let's just say that they grasped it with both hands! Everything poured out of them, from their fights with boyfriends, to issues with their children and feuds with their neighbours! Several of the middle-class ladies drew in sharp breaths at certain points and others looked awkwardly at the floor, obviously embarrassed. The girls hadn't shared anything out of the ordinary from our cultural perspective, they just weren't *au fait* with what was deemed as acceptable sharing at these meetings.

The real encouragement was that, over time, our scheme girls learned wisdom in how much to share, and the middle-class girls learned to share beyond the vague and superficial. And because of this, deep spiritual bonds were formed. Even though the cultural differences are very real, the good news is that in Christ they can be overcome with effort on both sides.

PART II:

THE BIBLE, POVERTY AND HELPING THE POOR

CHAPTER 1:

WHAT DOES THE BIBLE HAVE TO SAY ABOUT POVERTY?

In the first part of the book, we have sought to understand poverty and deprivation from the perspective of:

- The history of the working class in the UK
- Various modern research agencies
- The emotions and worldviews of people living in our poorest communities

It is important that, as Christians, we engage with the research, listen to the thoughts and seek to understand the worldviews of those living in our council estates and schemes. However, the Word of God is the *ultimate authority* in the Christian's life when it comes to understanding issues like class and poverty. We want to establish what the Bible teaches, before we begin to suggest practical solutions concerning topics we don't fully understand and before we seek to help people with whom we are not used to regularly socialising.

It is of fundamental importance therefore that, as Christians, we get to grips with the biblical understanding of poverty. If we are serious about reaching the least, the last and the lost, then we better be serious about understanding God's Word and God's perspective on things. *Why?* Because if we are not careful, those of us who are well meaning and want to help the poor can, ultimately, ending up causing more damage to them.

Let's take the Western obsession with donating clothes to charity shops as an example. Superficially, it seems like a well-meaning gesture. People want to help clothe those who are less fortunate than themselves. Unfortunately, it is now well documented that instead of helping the poor around the globe, the charity clothing industry in the West has cost many tens of thousands of poor people their jobs across Africa.[234] The problem is that much of our responses to poverty and deprivation are often knee-jerk and we almost never think about the wider, often negative, consequences of what we are doing.

Therefore, we must have *a biblical framework for poverty* if we are going to help people *biblically*. If we are to have any real hope of making a lasting difference in the lives of the poor around us, then we have to be able to answer the question: *What does the Bible teach us about poverty*? How we answer this most basic of questions will determine every ministry and outreach that we engage in going forward. Our presuppositions about poverty matter because they are the things that will drive any ministry we engage in among the least, the last and the lost.

HOW DOES THE BIBLE USE THE WORD "POVERTY"?

The poor are referred to over 400 times within the pages of Scripture, and the word "poverty" used a further 200 times.[235] There are a number of different Hebrew words used in the Old Testament to convey poverty. One of the most frequently used is the word *dal* which is used to describe a gaunt and hungry looking person, such as in 2 Kings 25:12. The word *ebion* is used to describe a poor beggar in Exodus 23:6, 11.

Yet another word, *ani*, is used to describe a person whose health is failing and who lacks neither influence nor power.[236] Almost invariably, the word *ani* has a multifaceted meaning in the Hebrew language including:

- The most vulnerable and oppressed in society
- A lack of material possessions
- Poor health and education
- Poor quality of life
- A low view of a person's place in society
- A poverty of spirit and faith in Almighty God

New Testament Greek, on the other hand, recognises three kinds of poverty. Firstly, it uses the Greek word, *penes,* to describe the precarious financial state of a person or people. The word is used to describe the widow in Luke 21:2. The meaning is related to a person who lives day-to-day and has nothing spare to fall back on.

Secondly, the New Testament also uses the word *ptochos* to describe a state of absolute destitution. This word is used in the story of the rich man and Lazarus in Luke 16:20–21. These would be the people that Jesus says we will always have with us in Matthew 26:11. They are completely dependent upon the charity of other people for their continued survival. These people include blind Bartimaeus in Mark 10, and the crippled beggar at the Beautiful Gate in Acts 3.[237]

Thirdly, there is the Greek word, *tapeinos*, which is used to describe those who are *lowly in spirit and humble*. We find the word used in 2 Corinthians 7:6 to speak of God comforting the downcast, and again in 2 Corinthians 10:1 to speak of the humility and gentleness of Christ Himself.

Therefore, when we take the biblical data as a whole into consideration, we discover that poverty is a multifaceted phenomenon and can be experienced in many different ways:

- Material needs: A lack of basic foodstuffs needed to eat. Or a lack of access to clean water and a roof over your head. A lack of money and access to a well-paid job.
- Health: It can mean a lack of access to basic healthcare services such as a doctor or a hospital. A lack of access to basic medicines.
- Education: A lack of schooling and access to basic educational facilities.
- Power: A lack of representation in the political arena. Having nobody to speak up for you or your interests. It can be sexual oppression and slavery. It can be child prostitution. Anything that is a loss of a person's power and personal freedoms. Anything that is unjust and seeks to oppress the most vulnerable members of our society.
- Relationships: God created Eve because it was not good for Adam to be alone. There are so many people in modern society cut off from other human contact. This has been exacerbated by the restrictions of Covid-19 and has led to a huge upsurge in mental health problems. The housing schemes and council estates of the UK often contain large family units that have lived there for many generations. They have a strong relational bond. When somebody comes to Christ in this context, that bond is often severed by angry family members (more on this later).
- Spiritual life: It can be a lack of faith in God. The irony here (and we shall look at this later as well) is that

this can affect the materially rich people in society perhaps even more than it does the materially poor people in society.

THE CAUSES OF POVERTY

According to the Bible, people fall into material poverty for four main reasons. They are:

- Oppression.
- No-fault disaster.
- Laziness and/or self-inflicted poverty.
- Gospel poverty.

OPPRESSION AND EXPLOITATION

Oppression is often seen in how the rich abuse the poor, often exploiting them for financial gain. Whether it's overcharging them for the sacrificial animals in the Temple as in Matthew 21, or not paying them a fair day's wage for a fair day's work, hence the warning of Leviticus 19:13. We see an example of oppression and exploitation in Nehemiah 5 when rich Jews were charging their own people exorbitant interest rates on loans to buy food for their families. Indeed, the situation was so critical that some of them were forced to sell their own children into slavery.

NO-FAULT DISASTER

Another cause of poverty is no-fault disaster. This occurs when people become poor because of a calamity that is no fault of their own. We are told, for example, in James 1:27 that pure religion involves providing for orphans and widows in their distress. Quite obviously the parents or husbands have died and left family members in need. Back in Jesus's day, there were no social services to pick up the slack and step in with financial and practical help for those who'd been unexpectedly bereaved. If they didn't have family and friends to help them out, they were on their own, unless the church stepped in as James instructs here.

Persecution could also fall into this category of poverty from no-fault disaster. Paul speaks to the church in 2 Corinthians 6:3–12 and lists some of the hardships he suffered for the sake of the gospel. These include troubles, hardships and distresses, beatings, imprisonments and riots, hard work, sleepless nights and hunger, dishonour, bad report, being regarded as impostors and regarded as unknown, dying, sorrowful, and having nothing.

LAZINESS AND/OR SELF-INFLICTED POVERTY

The Bible is full of warnings for the lazy, and they are categorised in a number of ways.

- The idle: Proverbs 24:33–34 says, "A little sleep, a little slumber, a little folding of the hands to rest – and poverty will come on you like a thief and scarcity like an armed man." They are warned again in Proverbs 28:19, "Those who work their land will have abundant food, but those who chase fantasies will have their fill of poverty." These are people who may well work but do the least amount possible to get by.
- Those who refuse to listen to wise counsel: They are told in Proverbs 13:18, that this could lead to "poverty and shame".
- Those who refuse to work: Paul was very clear to the church in Thessalonica about how these people were to be treated. He gives them this one rule in 2

Thessalonians 3:10, "The one who is unwilling to work shall not eat."

- Gluttons and drunks: Proverbs 23:21 says, "drunkards and gluttons become poor, and drowsiness clothes them in rags."

Some people find themselves in poverty because of their own selfishness, greed and stupidity. People often turn up on my doorstep begging for money because they have lost everything gambling on the horses or down at the casino. In other words, they are responsible for their own current, desperate situation.

GOSPEL POVERTY

Some people are financially poor because that is the path they have chosen to follow for the sake of the gospel and mission. The early disciples walked away from everything to follow the Lord Jesus. Many follow their example even today. A highly qualified doctor, for example, gives up a lucrative career to help refugees in a war-torn region. There are countless others who spurn the riches of this world to become missionaries in far-off places around the globe. In reality, these people may be cash poor, but they are spiritually rich. Of course, Jesus is our supreme model in this regard, as He leaves the riches and glory of heaven for the poverty and humiliation of this world, as revealed in Philippians 2. We read this of Jesus in Matthew 8:20: "Foxes have dens and birds have nests, but the Son of Man has nowhere to lay his head."

SUMMARY

In biblical language, poverty can be financial, physical and social. It can refer to social and spiritual exclusion, as well as those suffering exploitation at the hands of the rich and powerful. The Bible recognises at least three kinds of poverty.

- Precarious poverty: People who live hand to mouth, perilously close to abject poverty.
- Abject poverty: People who are completely dependent upon the charity of others in order to survive.
- Spiritual poverty: This poverty afflicts people of all social classes, rich and poor alike. The spiritually poor are those who refuse to turn from their sinful rebellion against Almighty God.

Because there is not one reason for poverty, the Bible recognises that neither is there one solution either. Some people find themselves destitute through no fault of their own, while others are poor because of laziness or bad choices that they made.

Poverty, in whatever form, is not easily resolved. While we in the UK may not suffer from the same widescale material need that was apparent in Jesus's day, we still live in a country with huge social problems and tremendous spiritual poverty. Not only do people reject God in the UK, but many of our materially and socially poor have very little access to the gospel at all.

So, what does God think about poverty? What does He have to say to us on these matters?

CHAPTER 2:

HOW DOES GOD INSTRUCT HIS PEOPLE TO RESPOND TO POVERTY? – I

THE OLD TESTAMENT

One thing is clear from the Old Testament, and that is God's love and care for the poor. God was very clear to Israel in Deuteronomy 15:4 when He declared: "there need be no poor people among you, for in the land the LORD your God is giving you to possess as your inheritance, he will richly bless you".

Proverb after proverb lays out God's feelings on those who fail to take Him seriously on this issue. In Proverbs 14:21 we are told that, "It is a sin to despise one's neighbour but blessed is the one who is kind to the needy." In Proverbs 14:31 we read that, "Whoever oppresses the poor shows contempt for their Maker, but whoever is kind to the needy honours God." We are told that neglecting the needs of the poor affects our prayer life in Proverbs 21:13, "Whoever closes his ear to the cry of the poor will himself call out and not be answered." In Proverbs 31:8–9 we are told to, "Speak up for those who cannot speak for themselves, for the rights of all who are destitute. Speak up and judge fairly; defend the rights of the poor and needy."

According to Graves, in the Old Testament, there are nine Hebrew words (with multiple variations) used for poverty.[238] They are:

1. The poor as oppressed, downtrodden, humiliated.
2. The poor as powerless and diminished.
3. The poor as yearning and insistent.
4. The poor as defenceless and open to exploitation.
5. The poor as needy and in want.
6. The poor as subject and dependent.
7. The poor as diminished and impoverished.
8. The poor as destitute and bereft.
9. The poor as dispossessed and evicted.

Because our God is a God of righteousness and justice, He opposes anyone and everyone who oppresses or ignores the suffering of society's most vulnerable people. Psalm 140:12 reminds us that, "The LORD secures justice for the poor and upholds the cause of the needy." We see the Lord's concern for matters of righteousness and justice revealed in two main ways in the Old Testament – in the Mosaic Law and in the message of the Prophets.

THE MOSAIC LAW

The Lord communicated His concern for the poor in the various laws He set out for the nation of Israel with regard to their treatment of them. For example, we observe the following laws and principles.

THE PRINCIPLE OF GLEANING[239]

We see this enshrined by God in Leviticus 19:9–10, "When you reap the harvest of your land, do not reap to the very edges of your field or gather the gleanings of your harvest. Do not go over your vineyard a second time or pick up the grapes that have fallen. Leave them for the poor and the foreigner. I am the Lord your God."

Again, we read of the principle in Deuteronomy 24:19, "When you are harvesting in your field and you overlook a sheaf, do not go back to get it. Leave it for the foreigner, the fatherless and the widow, so that the Lord your God may bless you in all the work of your hands" We see this principle beautifully illustrated in the story of Ruth and Boaz.

THE PRINCIPLE OF THE SABBATICAL YEAR

This was to occur every seventh year. The Lord instructs His people in Exodus 23:11, "during the seventh year let the land lie unploughed and unused. Then the poor among your people may get food from it, and the wild animals may eat what is left. Do the same with your vineyard and your olive grove."

Again, we see the principle being applied in Leviticus 25:6, "Whatever the land yields during the sabbath year will be food for you – for yourself, your male and female servants, and the hired worker and temporary resident who live among you."

Deuteronomy 15:12–15 is even more specific about this:

> *If any of your people – Hebrew men or women – sell themselves to you and serve you six years, in the seventh year you must let them go free. And when you release them, do not send them away empty-handed. Supply them liberally from your flock, your threshing floor and your winepress. Give to them as the Lord your God has blessed you. Remember that you were*

slaves in Egypt and the LORD your God redeemed you. That is why I give you this command today.

THE PRINCIPLE OF THE YEAR OF JUBILEE

The principle is recorded in Leviticus 25:8–31. And God says this in Leviticus 25:39–42.

> *If any of your fellow Israelites become poor and sell themselves to you, do not make them work as slaves. They are to be treated as hired workers or temporary residents among you; they are to work for you until the Year of Jubilee. Then they and their children are to be released, and they will go back to their own clans and to the property of their ancestors. Because the Israelites are my servants, whom I brought out of Egypt, they must not be sold as slaves.*

THE PRINCIPLE OF NOT CHARGING INTEREST ON LOANS

In Exodus 22:25 we read, "If you lend money to one of my people among you who is needy, do not treat it like a business deal; charge no interest." In other words, no loan sharking!

THE PRINCIPLE OF BEING GENEROUS TO THE POOR AND NEEDY

In Deuteronomy 15:7–11 we read,

> *If anyone is poor among your fellow Israelites in any of the towns of the land the LORD your God is giving you, do not be hard-hearted or tight-fisted toward them. Rather, be openhanded and freely lend them whatever they need. Be careful not to harbour this wicked thought: "The seventh year, the year for cancelling debts, is near," so that you do not show ill will toward the needy among your fellow Israelites and give them nothing. They may then appeal to the LORD against you,*

> *and you will be found guilty of sin. Give generously to them and do so without a grudging heart; then because of this the* Lord *your God will bless you in all your work and in everything you put your hand to. There will always be poor people in the land. Therefore I command you to be open-handed toward your fellow Israelites who are poor and needy in your land.*

THE PRINCIPLE OF PAYING WORKER'S WAGES ON TIME

In Leviticus 19:13 we read, "Do not hold back the wages of a hired worker overnight." This was especially important for the working poor who lived and fed their family day-to-day. God is even more explicit in Deuteronomy 24:14–15.

> *Do not take advantage of a hired worker who is poor and needy, whether that worker is a fellow Israelite or a foreigner residing in one of your towns. Pay them their wages each day before sunset, because they are poor and are counting on it. Otherwise, they may cry to the* Lord *against you, and you will be guilty of sin.*

THE PRINCIPLE OF SUPPORTING THE HELPLESS POOR

In Leviticus 25:35–37 God says,

> *If any of your fellow Israelites becomes poor and are unable to support themselves among you, help him as you would a foreigner and stranger, so they can continue to live among you. Do not take interest or any profit from them, but fear your God, so that they may continue to live among you. You must not lend him money at interest or sell them food at a profit.*

THE PRINCIPLE OF TITHING FOR THE BENEFIT OF THE POOR

We read of this practice in Deuteronomy 14:28–29.

> *At the end of every three years, bring all the tithes of that year's produce and store it in your towns, so that the Levites (who have no allotment or inheritance of their own) and the foreigners, the fatherless and the widows who live in your towns may come and eat and be satisfied, and so that the LORD your God may bless you in all the work of your hands.*

Also in Deuteronomy 26:12–13, we read:

> *When you have finished setting aside a tenth of all your produce in the third year, the year of the tithe, you shall give it to the Levite, the foreigner, the fatherless and the widow, so that they may eat in your towns and be satisfied. Then say to the LORD your God: "I have removed from my house the sacred portion and have given it to the Levite, the foreigner, the fatherless and the widow, according to all you commanded. I have not turned aside from your commands, nor have I forgotten any of them."*

PROVIDING FOR THE ALIEN

The Lord didn't just make provision for poor Israelites. In His great grace and mercy, He also made provision for many of the non-Jewish poor living in the Promised Land. Exodus 22:21 says, "Do not ill-treat or oppress a foreigner, for you were foreigners in Egypt."

Again, in Exodus 23:9, God tells them, "Do not oppress a foreigner; you yourselves know how it feels to be foreigners, because you were foreigners in Egypt."

In Leviticus 19:33–34 God warns His people, "When a foreigner resides among you in your land, do not ill-treat them. The foreigner residing among you must be treated as your native-born. Love them as yourself, for you were foreigners in Egypt. I am the LORD your God."

In Deuteronomy 24:14 we read, "Do not take advantage of a hired worker who is poor and needy, whether that worker is a fellow Israelite or a foreigner residing in one of your towns."

And in case anybody thought that the Lord was not serious about these matters, Deuteronomy 27:19 reminds them, "Cursed is anyone who withholds justice from the foreigner, the fatherless or the widow."

Sadly, by the time we get to Ezekiel 22:29, it is apparent that God's people have ignored His warnings as we read: "The people of the land practise extortion and commit robbery; they oppress the poor and needy and ill-treat the foreigner, denying them justice."

This leads us to the second main way that God demonstrated His concern for the least, the last and the lost in the Old Testament.

THE MESSAGE OF THE PROPHETS

A cursory glance through the history of God's people in the Old Testament reveals that time and again they consistently disobeyed God in two main ways: they turned to idolatry and they oppressed the poor and needy in the land. In response to this disobedience, God sent prophet after prophet to call them back to repentance and faith in God.

Listen to Amos's indictment of God's people in Amos 5:11–12.

> *You levy a straw tax on the poor and impose a tax on their grain. Therefore, though you have built stone mansions, you will not live in them; though you have planted lush vineyards, you will not drink their wine. For I know how many are your offences and how great your sins.*

Nobody withstood the withering gaze of this prophet of God. Consider his words to the rich women of Samaria in Amos 4:1.

"Hear this word, you cows of Bashan on Mount Samaria, you women who oppress the poor and crush the needy and say to your husbands, 'Bring us some drinks!'" Imagine hearing that preached at a woman's conference in our modern world!

God is very clear about what He thinks of those who love all the pomp and ceremony of religious practice but have no concern for the neediest in society. We can almost hear Amos's booming voice speaking for God in Amos 5:21–24:

> *I hate, I despise your religious festivals; your assemblies are a stench to me. Even though you bring me burnt offerings and grain offerings, I will not accept them. Though you bring choice fellowship offerings, I will have no regard for them. Away with the noise of your songs! I will not listen to the music of your harps. But let justice roll on like a river, righteousness like a never-failing stream!*

Isaiah 1:10–17 echoes Amos sentiments almost exactly:

> *Hear the word of the LORD, you rulers of Sodom; listen to the instruction of our God, you people of Gomorrah! "The multitude of your sacrifices – what are they to me?" says the LORD. "I have more than enough of burnt offerings, of rams and the fat of fattened animals; I have no pleasure in the blood of bulls and lambs and goats. When you come to appear before me, who has asked this of you, this trampling of my courts? Stop bringing meaningless offerings! Your incense is detestable to me. New Moons, Sabbaths and convocations – I cannot bear your worthless assemblies. Your New Moon feasts and your appointed festivals I hate with all my being. They have become a burden to me; I am weary of bearing them. When you spread out your hands in prayer, I hide my eyes from you; even when you offer many prayers, I am not listening. Your hands*

are full of blood! Wash and make yourselves clean. Take your evil deeds out of my sight; stop doing wrong. Learn to do right; seek justice. Defend the oppressed. Take up the cause of the fatherless; plead the case of the widow.

SUMMARY

If we had to sum the Lord up in a single Old Testament verse then it would have to be Psalm 145:8. "The LORD is gracious and compassionate, slow to anger and rich in love." This God places a high priority on *how* He should be worshipped. We are to approach Him reverently, with honour and respect. He is jealous that, as His people, we worship *only* Him. But He is just as deeply concerned with how we treat others, *especially* those who find themselves at the fringes of society and reliant on the charity of others.

God goes to great lengths, through both the Mosaic Law and the ministry of His prophets, to ensure that compassion, mercy and love remain high on the agenda of those claiming to worship Him as Lord and Father. He will not stand for oppression or indifference when it comes to the least, the last and the lost. In the words of Jeremiah 22:16, God wants His people to copy the attitude of King Josiah who, "defended the cause of the poor and needy, and so all went well".

CHAPTER 3:

HOW DOES GOD INSTRUCT HIS PEOPLE TO RESPOND TO POVERTY? – II

THE NEW TESTAMENT: JESUS AND THE POOR

As we turn to the New Testament, we see that, at the outset of His ministry, Jesus visits His local synagogue in Luke 4:16–19 and we read these words.

> *He went to Nazareth, where he had been brought up, and on the Sabbath day he went into the synagogue, as was his custom. He stood up to read, and the scroll of the prophet Isaiah was handed to him. Unrolling it, he found the place where it is written: "The Spirit of the Lord is on me, because he has anointed me to proclaim good news to the poor. He has sent me to proclaim freedom for the prisoners and recovery of sight for the blind, to set the oppressed free, to proclaim the year of the Lord's favour."*

SPIRITUAL POVERTY

Who exactly were these poor to whom Jesus had been sent to proclaim the good news? The passage Jesus speaks from in Isaiah refers to the meek, or the poor and lowly in spirit.

It is clear from the context that he's *not* talking about material poverty. Jesus is talking here about what a person *is*, and not what they own.

If we look closely at Luke 21:1–4, we read:

> *As Jesus looked up, he saw the rich putting their gifts into the temple treasury. He also saw a poor widow put in two very small copper coins. "Truly I tell you", he said, "this poor widow has put in more than all the others. All these people gave their gifts out of their wealth; but she out of her poverty put in all she had to live on."*

We see the word *poor* used first in verse 2 and, secondly, in verse 3. When we read this text, we automatically assume that the word means the same thing in both verses. But, in fact, they are two different words in the original Greek. In verse 2 the word translates as: "having very little". The word in verse 3 translates as: "having absolutely nothing".

It is the word used in verse 3 that Jesus uses in Matthew 5:3 when He tells us that "the poor in spirit" are blessed. In effect, Jesus is saying, blessed are those who recognise the depth of their spiritual poverty, who realise that they are hopeless sinners. Blessed are those, says Jesus, who are, quite literally, *bent double* by the weight of their sin.

The truly poor in spirit sympathise with Isaiah when he has a vision of the Lord and cries out in desperation: "Woe is me! ... for I am a man of unclean lips" (Is. 6:5, ESV). They cry out as Peter does in Luke 5:8, when he realises that he is in a boat with God. "Go away from me, Lord; I am a sinful man." They recognise, as Paul does in Romans 3:10, that "There is no one righteous, not even one." In Psalm 34:18 we are told: "The

LORD is close to the broken-hearted and saves those who are crushed in spirit." In Isaiah 57:15 (CSB) we read: "For the High and Exalted One, who lives forever, whose name is holy, says this: "I live in a high and holy place, and with the *oppressed* and *lowly* of spirit, to revive the spirit of the lowly and revive the heart of the oppressed" (emphasis mine).

Notice what Jesus's priorities are as He speaks to the people in Luke 4. He has come to proclaim the good news of the kingdom of heaven to the spiritually poor. Whatever else Jesus would go on to do, this would be the *primary ministry* in His life. All of the gospel writers record Him preaching the gospel of the kingdom and calling people to repentance, wherever He went (Mt. 4:17, 23, 9:35, Mk. 1:14, 38, Lk. 4:43, 8:1, 16:16).

Jesus confirms this Himself in Luke 19:10 when He says, "For the Son of Man came to seek and to save the lost." That being said, His concern for people didn't just stop at their eternal souls. He was also deeply concerned with the physical and social well-being of the most vulnerable members of society. When the rich young ruler approaches Jesus in Luke 18, the young man asks Jesus what was required for him to receive eternal life: "Sell everything you have and give to the poor," was Jesus's reply.

PHYSICAL POVERTY

A running theme in Luke's gospel is Jesus's compassion for Gentiles, Samaritans, women, children, tax collectors, sinners and others often regarded as outcasts in Israel. Luke repeatedly shows in his gospel how the Great Physician ministered to those most aware of their need (cf. 5:31, 32; 15:4–7, 31–32; 19:10).

Indeed, almost everywhere He went His preaching was accompanied by miracles of one sort or another. For example, in Matthew 9:35–36 we read of Jesus's deep concern for the physically poor and downtrodden: "Jesus went through all the towns and villages, teaching in their synagogues, proclaiming the good news of the kingdom and healing every disease and sickness. When he saw the crowds, he had compassion on them, because they were harassed and helpless, like sheep without a shepherd." This compassion showed itself in a wide variety of situations among people from all walks of life and ethnicities.

- In Luke 7:1–10, it was the servant of a Roman centurion who was healed by Jesus.
- In Matthew 15:32, we read of Jesus's compassion for the hungry crowds who had come to hear Him teach.
- In Matthew 8, He breaks with all social and religious convention, by touching and healing a leper.
- Later on, in the same chapter, we read of Him healing the demon possessed and many who were sick (Mt. 8:16).
- In Matthew 20:34, He gives sight to the blind.

The point is that Jesus was not oblivious to poverty in all its multifaceted forms as He came upon it. He was *moved deeply* by suffering.

This leads us on to the early church and how they interpreted Jesus's commands to preach the gospel and show compassion to others.

THE NEW TESTAMENT CHURCH

Clearly, New Testament Christians are not literally bound to the Mosaic Law and the warnings of the Prophets in the Old Testament. There were particular laws and prophecies that were immediately applicable to, and specifically addressing, God's chosen people in Israel at various points in her history.

The church of Jesus, however, is not restricted to a particular land mass or country and nor is it subject to a ruling monarchy or a human High Priest.

That being said, in Matthew 5:17, Jesus says: "Do not think that I have come to abolish the Law or the Prophets; I have not come to abolish them but to fulfil them." The responsibility of the New Testament Christian is therefore to work hard at identifying the principles behind the Old Testament laws and prophecies regarding our social and spiritual obligations to the poor. We have a duty to proclaim the gospel and a responsibility to care for the working poor and the genuinely destitute.

When John the Baptist was preaching in the wilderness in Luke 3:8, he challenged the watching crowd to "produce fruit in keeping with repentance". Upon hearing this, the crowd asks him in verse 10: How do we do that? He tells them in verse 11: "Anyone who has two shirts should share with the one who has none, and anyone who has food should do the same." He then goes on to instruct the tax collectors to stop overcharging people, and the soldiers to stop extorting the people for money.

In James 2:14–17, Christians are encouraged in the following way:

> *What good is it, my brothers and sisters, if someone claims to have faith but has no deeds? Can such faith save them? Suppose a brother or a sister is without clothes and daily food. If one of you says to them, "Go in peace; keep warm and well fed," but does nothing about their physical needs, what good is it? In the same way, faith by itself, if it is not accompanied by action, is dead.*

Paul, speaking to the church in Romans 15:26, was sorry that he couldn't make it to the city, and told the church that he was on the way to Jerusalem with a financial gift for the poor believers in the city there from generous believers in Macedonia and Achaia. In Galatians 2:10 he encourages the church to "continue to remember the poor".

Perhaps the most famous example of the early church taking responsibility for those in need among their own number is found in Acts 2:42–45.

> *They devoted themselves to the apostles' teaching and to fellowship, to the breaking of bread and to prayer. Everyone was filled with awe at the many wonders and signs performed by the apostles. All the believers were together and had everything in common. They sold property and possessions to give to anyone who had need.*

Paul emphasises this when he reminds the church: "Share with *the Lord's people* who are in need" (Ro. 12:13, emphasis mine). He reminds Timothy, similarly, to teach them "to do good, to be rich in good deeds, and to be generous and willing to share" (1 Tim. 6:18). The Apostle John is even more pointed when he says: "If anyone has material possessions and sees *a brother or sister* in need but has no pity on them, how can the love of God be in that person?" (1 Jn. 3:17, emphasis mine). Paul teaches us this in Galatians 6:10, "Therefore, as we have opportunity, let us do good to all people, especially to those who belong to the *family of believers*" (emphasis mine).

Indeed, most of the New Testament was written to people who were either enslaved, impoverished or persecuted for the faith. Much of the need of the early believers was because of oppression and some of it was down to unfortunate circumstances outside of people's control. Sometimes the Apostles weren't very quick on the uptake when it came to dealing with issues around the weakest and most vulnerable within some of the early church congregations. For example, in Acts 6, the Apostles were faced with an issue about the social care and needs of Hellenistic Jews. There was an accusation that their widows were being overlooked by the Hebraic Jews when it came to getting aid. As a result, the first ever deacons are elected to deal with the more practical matters of the church.

Again, in 1 Timothy 5:9–10 we discover the rules for local widows being put on a list for social care. In fact, Paul is very clear as to the qualifications needed in order for a widow to be eligible for aid from the church: "No widow may be put on the list of widows unless she is over sixty, has been faithful to her husband, and is well known for her good deeds, such as bringing up children, showing hospitality, washing the feet of the Lord's people, helping those in trouble and devoting herself to all kinds of good deeds." The point is that there were clear parameters set for giving aid to those in need who had suffered through no fault of their own, and who were known well by the local church.

PUTTING THE PRINCIPLES INTO PRACTICE

We've clearly established that *God's* concern for the poor should be *our* concern for the poor. No right-minded Christian is going to suggest otherwise. The issue, then, comes down to *how* we put some of these biblical principles into place in the life of the church in the UK. For instance, what do we do with the Old Testament principle of gleaning in modern society? Does that only apply to Christian farmers? Or are we supposed to let people wade through our vegetable patch in the back garden in the hope of finding something edible?

Some of the biblical principles are easier to apply than others. I mean, we can get behind lending people the odd tenner and not charging interest. That seems reasonable. But, what about the *helpless* poor? Who are they? Do they even exist in the UK? We can understand this working in rural Africa or the slums of India, but even the poorest person in the UK has access to financial assistance from the government, surely?

We could attempt to work through every Old Testament principle and come up with reasons not to continue with them in the modern world. But it gets a bit trickier to do that in the New Testament. There are still those, however, who feel that the principles in Acts about everybody sharing sounds a little bit like communism! Also, the argument goes, isn't the principle of sharing that is put forward by Paul in 1 Timothy 6 irrelevant in the modern age of taxation? We pay our taxes so that the vulnerable members of society can receive financial aid and, therefore, we are fulfilling the law of what Paul says here.

So, how are we supposed to determine who to help and who not to help? Should we just help everybody indiscriminately and leave it up to the Lord concerning who is genuine and who is not? Kevin DeYoung wrote a helpful article for 9Marks on how we navigate the minefield of helping the poor in our Western culture.[240] He outlines what he calls his "concentric circles of responsibility" and I have summarised his advice below.

In responding to God's call to help the poor, Christians should work from the most important to the least important when engaging with those in need.

1 Your immediate family: We see this clearly in 1 Timothy 5:8. "Anyone who does not provide for their relatives, and especially for their own household, has denied the faith and is worse than an unbeliever." What is Paul saying here? That I have to feed my lazy cousin Bob who just lies on the sofa all day smoking weed? No, he is not saying that. Paul's point is that if we have any family members who are really

struggling, through no fault of their own, then we have a responsibility to step in and help them. If we do not, then we are worse than pagans!

2 Our immediate church family: In Galatians 6:10 Paul tells us: "Therefore, as we have opportunity, let us do good to all people, *especially to those who belong to the family of believers*" (emphasis mine). Again, he is not talking about helping those who refuse to help themselves or have been brought to a point of need due to their own laziness or life choices. But, if a fellow church member is in dire need and we don't help them, then, again, our behaviour is anything but Christian. In Hebrews 10:33, for example, believers cared for fellow Christians who had been imprisoned for their faith.

3 Christians from other churches: This would include any church, anywhere in the world. We are not commanded to financially support Christians in other places, but it is something we see happening in the New Testament – for example, as we see with Paul taking a financial gift from Macedonia and Achaia to the struggling church in Jerusalem.

4 Other people outside the faith: These would include the "all people" in Galatians 6:10. I would say that the principle here is to help people in *desperate and immediate* need, especially if they are in danger. However, if, for example, a man blows his money on the horses, but his partner and children are starving, does that mean we shouldn't feed them? No, it does not. We should feed them and deal with the immediate need. What we shouldn't do is continually feed them for that will only be empowering him to

gamble further and not provide for his family. (We shall look at bad examples of mercy ministry later.)

CONCLUSION

We can say, therefore, without any hesitation that God loves the poor. He loves the poor who struggle day-to-day to pay the bills. He loves the poor who are completely destitute and depend upon the charity and good will of others. He loves the feckless poor. But, most particularly, He loves those who are poor in spirit and who are aware of their poverty of spirit in relation to His perfect holiness. And He requires that His people love these people too. So far, so straightforward. Not many of us will oppose anything said thus far. This is not new, or even groundbreaking information.

- God loves poor people. Check.
- God expects His people to love poor people too. Check.
- Christians should speak up for the vulnerable in society. Check.
- Christians should be involved in ministries of mercy and poverty alleviation. Check.

There are not very many right-minded Christians who are going to disagree with anything thus far. *So, what's the problem? Why the need for this book?*

The problem is not that Christians in the UK *haven't* responded to God's call to be merciful to the poor, or that they *haven't* attempted to show needy people the love of Jesus. They quite clearly have. Millions of pounds a year are donated to various para-church organisations and institutions seeking to help the poorest in our nation. There are some amazing things going on in the name of Jesus.

But much of the so-called help in this sector of society isn't actually helping at all. In fact, as I shall go on to demonstrate, it is often hurting us and not helping us over the longer term. Our current strategies to help the poor are simply not working. Poverty is not being alleviated in our country, despite our best efforts. In fact, the situation grows worse year-on-year, not better. More children are going hungry. More women are being abused. Many of our council estates and housing schemes have not had the gospel preached in them for many decades.

My concern is *not* that the church isn't *trying to help* – but that the help it is giving is *not working*. How we are doing mercy ministry in the UK is often not very merciful at all. How we are showing the love of Jesus is, in many cases, not loving at all. In fact, I would argue that much of what we do for the poor is done to salve middle-class guilt complexes, rather than being something that is well thought out, biblically-based and has a clear long-term strategy for helping people to move forward in their lives.

My challenge to the UK church, then, is to fight your knee-jerk reaction to the preceding paragraph and to stick with me until the end of the book. If you are in a local church that has any kind of mercy ministry to the poor and vulnerable, then I am asking you to *stop* what you're doing and *re-evaluate everything* in the light of the following critique.

PART III:

EXPOSING THE FAULT LINES OF UK EVANGELICALISM

CHAPTER 1:

THE MALEVOLENT GENEROSITY OF CHRISTIAN MERCY MINISTRY

In the mid-1970s, radical thinker Ivan Illich coined the term "iatrogenesis" to describe what he saw as, "a relentless increase in disease induced by doctors".[241] His main point was that doctors, trying to alleviate the problem of illness in patients, very often caused more serious health issues *because of* their intervention. He would often cite the many patients who received surgery as part of their treatment but died because of complications not related to their original illness.

One of the dangers that well-off, educated Christians need to guard against, when they come to minister among the poor, is giving the impression that they have all the answers and know what's best for those they are seeking to help. There is a confident assumption that they know better than those they are helping when it comes to providing solutions for poverty alleviation. In fact, it is well documented that those who enter poor communities around the world have a hard time trusting vulnerable and struggling people with any kind of leadership at all. This is coupled with the fact that many Christians have spoken and unspoken prejudices about people who come from housing schemes and council estates. They think they have the answers and the solutions to all the perceived problems in these areas, and that local people just have to listen to them and uncritically receive their largesse. Any attempt by the locals to question this is met with condescension and disdain.

RIGHT QUESTION, WRONG ANSWER

It is one thing to understand what the Bible says about poverty, but it is quite another to practice mercy in a way that is helpful, not hurtful. I travel the world speaking on issues of poverty and the local church, and I always ask people the same initial question: *What is poverty*? Almost without exception, I am met with a barrage of answers including:

- A lack of resources
- A lack of money
- A lack of a good education
- A lack of political will to help society's most vulnerable

There is a noticeable difference in the answers I receive from those who live in the West and those who live in the two-thirds world. In their book, *When Helping Hurts*, Brian Fikkert and Steve Corbett observe the following phenomenon:

- People from *financially richer* nations often describe poverty in terms of *a lack of money or physical resources*.
- People from *financially poorer* nations describe poverty in terms of their *feelings and experiences*.[242]

It is supremely important that we understand the difference between these two observations, because our presuppositions always affect our practice in these matters. The international aid and development community generally divide mercy ministry into three standard areas:

- Relief
- Rehabilitation
- Development

RELIEF

In a situation requiring relief, the poor are truly unable to help themselves and need *temporary, immediate aid*. Relief is only appropriate after a natural or man-made crisis plunges people into a downward spiral, such as after an earthquake, a medical emergency or some kind of personal trauma. This kind of intervention is *very rarely participatory*.

REHABILITATION

In rehabilitation, *people participate* in returning their lives to pre-crisis conditions, contributing to improving their own situation.

DEVELOPMENT

In development, *people participate* in improving their lives beyond what they were prior to the circumstances that led to their situation of need.

Many Christians and churches often fail to recognise these distinctions, continuing to provide relief to people long after they should have been moved on to rehabilitation and development. Let's think about these three terms using biblical language.

- Relief as evangelism
- Rehabilitation as discipleship
- Development as service

EVANGELISM

Let's use the example of a church opening a food bank twice a week in their building. The initial thinking behind the venture has to do with showing the love of Jesus and evangelising those in need. The types of people attending these ministries are very rarely found to be in membership of our churches. Initially, there are a few users who attend, making it easier to spend some quality time with people in an effort to understand their history and establish some human connection with them which would otherwise never happen over the normal course of our life and social interaction.

But over the weeks and months, numbers begin to steadily increase. Word of mouth has done its job and, before long, there are now queues of people waiting to use the facility. More packages are going out and, on paper, more people are being helped. However, the reality on the ground is that there is less time than ever to connect meaningfully with people and to get too closely involved in their lives. The ministry begins to subtly shift into crisis management and relief because of the larger number of people in attendance. Sometimes there is space for small gospel conversations, but the busyness of the ministry means that there just isn't enough time to go into greater depth or to follow through with people.

DISCIPLESHIP

In the event that somebody does make a profession of faith through this mercy ministry, they are encouraged to attend your church service or maybe even a small group. This is where we should be naturally moving away from evangelism and into an active discipleship relationship. The individual concerned has moved on from hearing about their need of Jesus and is now taught the basic doctrines of the faith as well as being introduced into their new Christian family.

Herein lies a fundamental problem. For most churches, their idea of discipleship is woefully flawed and completely insufficient to meet the complex needs of people from poor communities. Once again, the reality on the ground looks very different than the idealism we talk about. The fact is that the average person saved through some kind of mercy ministry – be it a food bank, soup kitchen or debt advisory service – ends up on the fringes of our churches at best, and completely ignored and isolated at worst. Most middle-class congregations have very little idea of how to do biblical discipleship with those on the fringe – and particularly when it's with people who come into the church family with a raft of mental and physical health issues. As a result, far too many of them disappear through the cracks and end up jumping from church to church.

This is the phase in which we ought to be teaching people that they are not just recipients of our mercy, but they are also disciples who are required to work and participate in their own spiritual growth and development through the power of the Holy Spirit.

SERVICE

According to Paul, one of the objectives of all pastors, is "to prepare *all* God's people for work of Christian service" (Eph. 4:12, GNB, emphasis mine). Every single member of the body of Christ has been saved to serve God in one capacity or another. For some of us it is vocationally and for others it is as full-time missionaries and evangelists in our workplace, families and communities. This includes those of us who are unemployed or have never finished high school. Evangelism that leads to conversion should always lead to discipleship, with the ultimate aim of equipping people for service to the glory of God.

THE GLASS CEILING OF MERCY MINISTRIES

My experience of over 20 years observing and participating in para-church and church-based mercy ministries to the poor and vulnerable is that we rarely get past evangelism, if that even occurs at all. Para-church organisations are not churches and, therefore, provide no serious ongoing discipleship in order to equip their "clients" for Christian service. Most are either disconnected from local churches – despite their protestations to the contrary – or work in areas where there are no local churches for any converts to attend. And those churches who do operate their own in-house mercy ministry have no plan in place outside of providing immediate relief.

As a result, by giving handouts to low-income people over an extended period of time – especially to those who are capable of helping themselves – churches and para-church ministries are actually contributing to the materially poor's sense of shame, helping to fund various addictions and even undermining their capacity to work. If our outreach into poor communities has no long-term strategy or a clearly defined roadmap from evangelism to discipleship to service, then those we are seeking to help will stay trapped in their helpless and hopeless situations. Even more seriously, we will be guilty of making the situation worse, and prolonging their suffering and shame.

The tragedy is that those who are *really looking to change their lives* get lost in the chaos of overstretched volunteers trying to feed, clothe and counsel the endless queues of people knocking on our doors looking for handouts. We *must* have a system in place that enables us to encourage people to not only get out of their present crisis, but also to move towards improving their lives and making a better future for themselves and their loved ones, both physically and, more importantly, spiritually.

If the most many people can hope for from us is a food parcel, clean clothes, a hot shower, a sympathetic ear, a gospel tract and an invite to a Sunday service, then it is not really mercy ministry at all.

MALEVOLENT GENEROSITY?

My fear is that much of what is packaged as mercy ministry in the Christian world is little more than *malevolent generosity.* Much of it, instead of creating a culture of local autonomy and ownership, has left us with a crippling dependency and an impotent approach to developing local leadership. Thanks to Tim Keller, mercy ministry is back in vogue among evangelicals but – and this is not his fault – much of it is unhelpful and not thought through at the level of the local church.

Many mothers come to me, for example, to talk about their drug-addicted children. Very often they will admit to me that they will often buy wraps of heroin for them. "Why?" I ask, even though I know the answer. "I just love them. I cannot help it. I just want them to be safe." Just because an act is borne out of love, doesn't mean that it is helpful. In fact, in many instances, it is singularly unhelpful and even dangerous and destructive. I often find that the most poisonous presence in a heroin addict's life is not the substance, but his family members, who undoubtedly love him but have enabled his behaviour for far too long.

Far too much of modern evangelicalism's obsession with "loving the poor" looks more like a desperate mother scoring drugs for her son in the vain hope that she is helping him, rather than the sort of tough love often required. We need to ask ourselves the following questions about any help we are offering to those from poor communities and difficult backgrounds:

- Are we giving/providing people goods and/or a service that they either do not need or could acquire on their own or through other legal means (e.g. their local council)? If we are then we may well be guilty of *resource paternalism.*
- Are we slow to offer leadership to people from poor backgrounds because of the unspoken (or even unthinking) assumption that we have more to offer than they do? If so, then we could be guilty of *spiritual paternalism.*
- Do we automatically assume that we have all the answers and the best ideas on how our mercy ministry should operate? Do we see ourselves as the teachers and the people we are seeking to help as the students? If so, we could be guilty of *knowledge paternalism.*
- Do we do work for the materially poor that they could do for themselves? Cleaning or painting their home, for example. When I was a missionary in Brazil, as an example, I would receive visits from foreign (church-based) mission teams who would come and do "work" in our street child project (painting walls, fixing fences, etc.) More often than not I had to hire local workers after the teams had left to undo the damage they caused. It ended up costing me more time and money than if they'd never come, but at least they had some good photos for Facebook and Instagram. If this is true of your work, then you may well be guilty of *labour paternalism.*
- Do you often take leadership away from the poor by insisting that they do things "your way" because it is "better" or "more efficient"? If so, you could well be guilty of *managerial paternalism.*

SUMMARY

The problem in many Christian circles today is that we are responding to poverty and social issues in ways that are not actually helpful and are not meeting the perceived needs of people on the ground. If we misunderstand poverty then we are going to misunderstand how to tackle it in a way that is biblical, helpful and long-lasting. The problems of our communities are not going to be solved easily. They are certainly not going to be solved by a two-week mission team, or by hit-and-miss approaches to social issues.

A doctor can make two mistakes when treating the sick.

- They only treat the symptoms of the condition, rather than the underlying cause; or
- They misdiagnose us altogether.

In both cases, the patient doesn't get better. In fact, they might even get worse. The same can be true in our efforts to help the poor. If we only treat the symptoms of poverty, or if we misdiagnose its root causes, then we can end up hurting the poor, despite our well-intentioned efforts to help them.

Therefore, it is my contention that many of our current forms of Christian outreach and ministry to the least, the last and the lost in the UK *do not go far enough*. They are far too often packaged under the banner of "showing the love of Jesus" and used as a pretext for evangelising a people who are both foreign – and, very often, frightening – to the membership of many evangelical churches. Sadly, this approach has put the cause of Christ back many decades in many of our poorest communities around the UK.

Sadly, it gets even worse.

CHAPTER 2:
MERCY MINISTRY: A SLOW DEATH TO THE SOUL?

Darren McGarvey, in his bestselling book, *Poverty Safari: Understanding the Anger of Britain's Underclass* wrote the following:

> *In Scotland, the poverty industry is dominated by a left-leaning, liberal middle class. Because this specialist class is so genuinely well-intentioned when it comes to the interests of people in deprived communities, they get a bit confused, upset and offended when those very people begin expressing anger towards them. It never occurs to them, because they see themselves as the good guys, that the people they purport to serve may, in fact, perceive them as chancers, careerists, or charlatans. They regard themselves as champions of the underclass and therefore, should any poor folk begin to get his own ideas or, God forbid, rebel against the poverty experts, the blame is laid at the door of the complainants for misunderstanding what is going on.*[243]

Likewise, in the UK the mercy ministry industry – and it is an industry – is dominated by well-meaning Christians and churches who are, quite literally, spending millions of pounds per year trying to tackle the problems of poverty.[244] Hundreds of churches and thousands of Christians are easing their consciences by giving money, or farming out mercy ministry, to para-church organisations of every stripe and theological conviction. And any critique of this practice is met with anger, confusion and offence. How dare anybody question their motives? How dare someone from a council estate lecture them on helping the poor?

McGarvey made this observation when he began to speak out about poverty from his own personal experience.

> *What I learned was that no matter your background, you were cast out the second you offended the people who are in charge of your empowerment ... the minute you start telling your story in service of your own agenda and not theirs, you're discarded. Your criticism is dismissed as not being constructive. Look out for the people. The people who pay wonderful lip service to giving the working class a voice, but who start to look very nervous whenever we open our mouths to speak.*[245]

Middle-class Christianity is happy as long as you are saying what they want you to say, or if you are critiquing them, that you are doing it in the way that they liked to be critiqued. Woe betide you if you speak out against the status quo, or if you turn up to their conferences and don't follow the party line. You become the problem child or the "one with the chip on his shoulder". The conversation around mercy ministry is completely dominated by middle-class Christians and rich, powerful churches and institutions, and they tend to only allow speakers from poor backgrounds into the conversation as long as they don't go off-script. Any attempt to challenge them or the system and you are cut off.

McGarvey, again, nails the issue.

> *The conversation about poverty is usually dominated by people with very little experience of being poor. It's this deficit between those who tend to lead the conversation and those who experience the issue that not only impedes progress but also leads to people in poverty feeling misrepresented or excluded by "culture".*[246]

It is frustrating for those of us who have grown up in poverty on council estates to be secondary to the conversation on reaching our own communities. Instead, middle-class leaders lead the conversation, and write the books and articles, with next to no knowledge whatsoever of our cultural heritage or worldview.

I have been saying the same thing now for almost two decades. Every church, and every Christian in the UK, needs to *stop* whatever ministries of mercy they currently support or are involved in. I speak as one who grew up on a sink housing estate in Yorkshire and has spent most of my life living and working in areas of deprivation. What the UK church is doing, when it is doing anything at all, IS NOT WORKING.

STOP WHAT YOU ARE DOING.

Immediately.

YOUR MERCY MINISTRIES ARE NOT HELPING US.

Doubtless, they are offering us short-term relief. But decade after decade of doing the same thing over and over again has left our communities with very few healthy gospel churches and next to no indigenous leaders to carry the baton of the gospel forward into the next generation.

A SLOW DEATH TO THE SOUL?

Your love is killing us. Your mercy is disempowering us. Don't just take my word for it. Even unbelievers are beginning to come around to the idea that maybe, just maybe, everything that we in the West have ever believed and practised concerning charity is just plain wrong and dangerous.

Several years ago, I read a book written by Canadian activists Nick Saul and Andrea Curtis, called, *The Stop: How the Fight for Good Food Transformed a Community and Inspired a Movement.*[247] When the book first came out, it made quite a splash in the UK, because Saul made the contentious claim that the food bank model of help is often nothing more than, "privileged people helping the underprivileged, perpetuating an us-and-them atmosphere".[248]

The Guardian newspaper wrote the following concerning the central message of the book.

> *For Saul, 47, a community organiser in his home town of Toronto, the problem – he believes – is that traditional food banks don't really help the needy. Their food "handouts" are often of dismal quality, and the "transaction" – the silent, humiliating transfer of the food parcel – does nothing to help clients' dignity or self-esteem, get them a job, help them out of poverty or improve their health and well-being. For a moment, food bank clients are not hungry – but not for long.*[249]

Well-meaning volunteers aren't the only people in his sights either. Saul also targets big business, particularly supermarkets, who (he claims) like to jump on the bandwagon so that they can give the appearance of being a good "corporate citizen". Indeed, Saul claims that the whole concept of food banks is largely a conscience-easing exercise across the board.

In Saul's opinion: "The only person who is not benefiting is the person who this was set up to help. Most people who have to visit food banks say it is a slow, painful death of the soul."[250]

WORKING THE SYSTEM

As a Christian, I was particularly struck by that last line. It's haunting. I used to visit all sorts of homeless projects when I lived on the streets in my late teens and early 20s. Across most cities, I could easily find places that would give me breakfast, clean clothes, a shower and some food. Like pubs, I had my favourite haunts and so did my homeless friends.

Those of us who lived and breathed within this largely invisible subculture knew all the "good places". We knew what time the doors opened, what time the "good stuff" came out, and we knew what we had to say and how we had to act according to who was giving out the goodies. Churches were particularly good because the people were generally nice, kind and sympathetic, while also being less savvy than government-run agencies. We quickly learned that all we had to do was sit through some God-talk, maybe take a booklet, and then we could be away for the day with bags full of food and clothing.

Although I didn't realise it at the time, these places were indirectly funding my drug habit and making it far easier for me to stay on the streets. Without motivation to find work to pay for my survival, I lost the will and inclination to be bothered to get myself out of the hole I was in. These places had, inadvertently I'm sure, become enablers for my largely selfish, sinful and completely destructive lifestyle.

Over time, government cuts (not just a new invention) closed a lot of our established council-funded haunts and we became more and more reliant on the "God squad". In the beginning, the constant stream of questions about our souls was annoying but, if handled like a job-centre interview, these people were easily placated. They would get to say their bit about Jesus, and I would get what I wanted or whatever goodies they had in store that day. Everybody was happy. They'd shared "the love of Jesus" with a poor person and I got to spend the money I earned from selling their second-hand clothes on drugs. The added bonus (in my mind) was that the money I saved from not having to buy food, fuelled my descent into my almost constant, drug-induced oblivion.

Put simply: I knew how to work the system and the people in it.

LITTLE CHANGE

Twenty-five years later, having worked in areas of urban derivation as a minister around the world for the best part of 20 years, I would *like* to say that much has changed. But it hasn't. The poor are still with us. The need for food banks and soup kitchens and a multiplicity of other ministries of mercy is perhaps greater in our country than it has been for generations. In the evangelical Christian world, there has been an explosion of interest in "mercy ministry" and "helping the poor" and, in truth, much of it makes me sad. I sit in conferences and listen to well-meaning young pastors and planters talking about "generous justice". Time and again, I am running into church leaders and/or Christians who are saying that they opened a food bank or a soup kitchen, and it "transformed" their church.

Or, even more offensively, young Christians, who boast of being "missional", join an existing work helping the poor so that they can serve the unfortunate in their city and/or witness to (highbrow) unbelievers about their "good deeds" at the same time.

Unbelievably, some Christian church planters have turned helping the poor into nothing more than an evangelistic strategy to reach the hip, modern unbeliever who like to have their "social justice" box ticked. Much of the chatter when this topic is discussed in these circles consists of phrases like: "It has brought people together." "It has transformed our community." "It has brought us into contact with the unchurched."

The reality, I fear, is somewhat different once the hype dies down. The people it usually brings together are either fringe Christians who have found something that fulfils them, or older/retired believers with more time on their hands to volunteer. Sadly, the cold, hard reality is that our poorest communities are not transformed by these endeavours. Sadly, far too many churches and Christians are more of a hindrance than a help to the poor.

They are often guilty of paternalistic outreach often packaged in the guise of a successful mercy ministry (when success is measured by 40 people turning up weekly for a food parcel). They measure their success in the numbers of food boxes delivered, rather than the number of converts being discipled within local churches. These so-called ministries of mercy go on, almost in perpetuity, serving largely the same constituents, with many of them never really moving on from their life situations. They are trapped, and many Christians, churches and para-church organisations are often guilty of keeping them trapped.

NO LONG-TERM PLAN

My phone often rings with pastors and other leaders asking me for help. The conversation invariably goes along these lines: "Mez, we have this man/woman here who has recently come to faith through our work with the homeless/addicts/poor. The problem is, we're not sure what to do with them now. Our church is not really geared up for this kind of person. Can you help us?"

Herein lies the fundamental issue for many churches and Christians working among poor communities. They simply do not have a plan outside of meeting what we deem *crisis intervention.* They have started a ministry without any real long-term planning and objectives. Serving needy people food is one thing but having to deal with them and their complex needs on a daily basis is quite another.

The bottom line is that most churches just haven't thought through the long-term ramifications of their ministry to the poor. It is staggering but true that many churches haven't thought about what they are going to do with somebody who comes to faith through their mercy ministry. *What is the discipleship strategy? Who will care for them in the local church? Who will hold them accountable? How will we move them forward in their walk with Jesus? How will we move them from a position of dependency to independence? How will we prepare them for whatever works of service God has called them to?*

The reality is that the queue every Thursday for parcels, or whatever we dole out, is so long in many places that we can do nothing more than hand stuff out and move on to the next person. Maybe we have people around who can stop and chat over a coffee but conversations are brief, superficial and don't move anywhere fast. Those who really do need our charity are often too embarrassed to stick around for long, and those who know how the game is played usually stay and take up as much time as possible. Soon, a routine comes into effect and, over time, as we tire of the same old stories, we just focus on the charity. Soon we enter into the most depressing phase of any mercy ministry, our familiarity with the regulars. Is there anything sadder in the world than seeing *a regular* at a soup kitchen? It is a travesty.

Very often, people we are supposed to be helping are not being moved on. They are not being helped. They are not, *horror of horrors*, being challenged to *help themselves*, largely out of a middle-class guilt complex (which often underpins much volunteering in this sector).

Church leaders, we need a plan. We need a plan bigger than just crisis management every week. We need a plan to share the gospel, see people come to faith, be discipled and then trained. *How many of us have that strategy built into our mercy ministries? How many people do you know that have gone from soup kitchen to pastor? Or to any meaningful employment?* I suspect that the answer to that is: not too many of us. Those of you with a handful of happy tales are few and far between. Certainly, the lack of meaningful results does not justify the millions being spent on these enterprises by churches up and down the country.

We have to be honest. There is a glitch in the system. Many (not all) of our current strategies for reaching the least, the last and the lost in our country are not fit for purpose. Nor do we do ourselves any favours by burying our heads in the sand. We really need to call a moratorium on mercy ministry among evangelical church leaders in the UK.

I am not calling for an end to mercy ministries. I am calling for them to be made better. I am calling for them to be more reciprocal, less one-sided and thought of more as a stepping-stone on the road to serious Christian discipleship *within a local church*. My contention is that generous justice and mercy ministry is *not enough* on its own. *Having a heart for the poor* is not enough. We need to ask ourselves some hard questions. We need to ask whether what we are doing is really helping people move forward, or merely servicing ourselves and our programmes. We all want ministries that bring spiritual life to souls walking the cruel pathway to eternal death. Maybe a helping hand is our first point of engagement. But for too many churches, it also seems to be our last.

SUMMARY

The sad fact is that after decades of mercy ministry, mission and giving, Christians have very little to see for it in our poorest communities. Yes, people may well have been helped in their immediate need. But where are the churches in our communities? Where are the indigenous leaders? What do we have to show for three decades of this way of doing mercy?

Our research shows that *wherever we find the most economically deprived people in the UK, we will also discover a dearth of gospel-preaching churches.* As evangelical Christianity has shrunk over the past three decades, it has done so within a largely middle-class culture. This means that very few Christians and evangelical churches live and operate within council estates and housing schemes. They may have a building nearby, or on the outskirts of several poor communities, but they have no real connection to the people that reside there. Any contacts they do have are invariably because of some form of mercy ministry that takes place there.

- A food bank or clothes bank that operates once or twice a week
- A children's pre-school breakfast club or after-school club for disadvantaged children
- An annual Holiday Club for children and/or young people
- Debt counselling services

Many of these initiatives do good work. I have little doubt that many Christian volunteers for this kind of work are genuinely seeking to help people. My concern is that far too many self-styled mercy ministries are anything but, and instead of helping the poor and the marginalised in our society, they are (often inadvertently) hurting them.

People on the fringes of society are seen as recipients and clients (by para-church agencies) and our relationship with them is almost always from a position of power and control, rather than as a real and lasting friendship. Many of us help poor people, but not many of us know them intimately. Sharing a cup of tea and a sandwich with them is not the same as sharing life with them. Many Christians have heard about a rough part of our town, but not many know what it's really like. We don't live there. We don't share life with others there.

What if we are doing mercy ministry all wrong? What if our good deeds aren't showing people the love of Jesus? What if the ministry to the poor that we are involved with, or that our church operates, isn't really helping people at all? What if the only real benefit behind what we are doing is allaying our guilt and feeling good about helping? What if what we do is only enabling laziness and addiction? What if we are contributing to society's social ills, rather than helping to end them?

Are you willing to listen? Are you willing to accept some insight from the other side of the serving hatch? Are you willing to turn from the blind acceptance of how your church does ministry to the poor, and open yourself up to new possibilities of doing it better?

If we're already doing a mercy ministry or if we want to start one (and you should if it's contextually appropriate), I want us as church leaders to think about the purpose behind it. Go deeper than the usual, "We want to show God's love to people." I am not belittling that but I am saying we need to have a broader vision than that.

I have been in churches with amazing mercy ministries and yet have not seen one "client" (their term not mine) in any of their services. I know churches that run separate services for the homeless and/or needy. My aim is not to judge but to get us to question ourselves as believers.

Is this really helping? If so, how? Who is being discipled and moved on? What is our plan when someone comes to faith? How will we begin to engage with them and offer them a pathway into our community but also into serving our community and, ultimately, being a sent one for the glory of God?

SPOTLIGHT:

HOW SHORT-TERM MISSION TRIPS HARM POOR COMMUNITIES

THE STORY OF AN ANONYMOUS PASTOR

Let me tell you a story about a pastor called John who lives in a small town in Scotland.[251] You've never heard of him and you've never heard of his community. Where he lives, unemployment is high, drug abuse is off the charts and life is hard and short for many of its inhabitants.

John was saved about 10 years ago on a holiday abroad. There was no evangelical church in his home town and so he struggled to grow in the faith. Not long after, his wife and children were saved along with a couple of his friends and neighbours. With no other options, they started meeting every Sunday at John's house. He had no theological training. He hadn't even finished high school. But John did the best he could with the tools he had.

Soon they outgrew the house, so they rented a little hall in the middle of the neighbourhood. Times were hard. Money was scarce. People would profess faith but would fall away after only a few months. Back to the drink. Back on drugs. Enticed away by a member of the opposite sex. Sometimes the group would swell to about 30 people and then sometimes it would sink back down to half a dozen. John was often lonely and didn't really know how to handle some of the difficult pastoral problems that came his way.

He tried to get support and counsel, but it was difficult to come by. Pastors in nearby towns were suspicious of him, especially because he lacked theological training, so they kept him at arm's length. He spoke at a few churches in other cities about his need for financial help, personal mentoring and about his need for mature Christians to move into his community to help him. People listened politely, even sympathetically. Some gave him money now and then. A few young families even came to his town to have a look at his work. But a tired, run-down man with a young family, half a dozen semi-literate converts and no musicians meeting in a draughty old hall put them off.

The months and years went by with John slogging his heart out – giving it his all – trying to reach his community and his town for Jesus. Then one day, out of the blue, John heard that a large church in the next city was thinking of planting a church in his town. John was elated, so he rang the pastor to ask if it was true.

"Yes," he said. "We feel a burden for the town."

"Me, too!" said John excitedly. He'd been working on his own for almost a decade at this point. "Would you be interested in doing the plant in partnership with us?"

Awkward silence.

"We have other plans. We want to plant in the city centre, next to the university campus. We have a team of about 30 and a young pastor ready to go. We want this plant to become a pioneering centre for a ministry movement across the city. Maybe we could do something together."

John hung up, devastated. He knew what that meant. He'd heard it before. He spent the rest of the day in a deep depression. He was glad that a gospel witness was coming to town, but it wouldn't be coming anywhere near his community, that much was certain.

What more could he do? He couldn't compete with this new church plant with their huge budget and massive online presence. Their little church didn't even have a website. He struggled to get enough money to pay for his children's clothing, never mind build an online presence. He didn't attract young people because he didn't have any young people. He struggled to pay the monthly electricity bill, never mind finance an internship programme. He felt defeated. He felt dejected. He felt ignored. He felt angry. No one was coming to help him. His little church wasn't growing. Maybe he should just pack it all in.

GLORIFIED GAP YEARS

John's experience is typical of pastors, church planters and church revitalisers, not only in Scotland but in poor communities around the UK. There are countless men and women who, like John, work in some of the hardest places in our country with little money, no support and a lack of solid theological training.

They're fed up of going cap in hand to middle-class churches and institutions looking for support, prayer and people but instead finding themselves ignored and isolated. And so, desperate to attract support, they put on "poverty safaris" so that middle-class teenagers can wander around their communities, taking selfies and updating their profiles on Snapchat.

They wince as they realise that a church will drop thousands of pounds on mission trips for their young people and then prevaricate over supporting them for a few hundred pounds a month. If any young people do show an interest in the poor, they are quickly lured away by well-financed multi-million-pound para-church agencies only too happy to offer them a year out before they continue with their university education.

The system that is used to recruit gospel workers, women's workers, pastors and church planters is broken. There is a fault in the matrix but nobody seems too keen to fix it because, after all, many are realising their dreams of working to help alleviate poverty and bring good news to the least, the last and the lost. Forget men like John, who've grafted for over a decade. His church is not sexy enough. Why go and help out at a struggling congregation that doesn't have a band and a great youth group, when you can go on mission with people your own age and have a great time together painting fences, handing out food parcels and running kids camps for underprivileged children. That's where the real action is!

The UK church has a duty to educate the next generation. Forget the glorified gap year with a group of likeminded young people. The best thing they can do for the least, the last and the lost in the UK's poorest communities is to go out and find men like John in their towns, cities and villages. You'll find them in the areas of your town that you would usually avoid, struggling away, invisible among all the bells and whistles of the modern evangelical mercy ministry money machine. If you really want to serve the least of these, then go and do a free internship in a place like that. Serve God and that community in anonymity. Turn off your iPhone. Delete your Twitter account. Keep off Instagram.

Millions of people in council estates and housing schemes are slipping into hell in the UK. Some of them live lives of desperate pain and poverty. There are areas in the UK that have less access to the gospel than even some of the least reached people groups in the world. There are some communities that haven't had a gospel-preaching church in them since the 1960s.

People need more than their garden digging or their local park painted. They need the gospel. They need to hear about Jesus Christ, the sinless one who came to earth to live a perfect life and die a humiliating death on the cross so that sinners like us could live in eternal bliss with our Heavenly Father. After three days He rose again and now sits at the right hand of the Father and someday soon He is coming again to collect His people up into His loving arms.

SUMMARY

Stop telling your children that the best life for them is the one that starts once they have their university degree. The best life for them starts when they take the command to go into all the world with the gospel, seriously. We should be encouraging them to lay down their lives for the sake of Christ. We should be teaching them that there is nothing greater they could do with their life than move into a housing scheme or a council estate and give their entire lives to the people that live there.

We need to teach them that the true heroes of the Christian faith aren't the big name preachers at the global conferences. The real heroes are soldiering on in difficult, heart-wrenching conditions, unseen by all except their God, silently working, doing the hard work of mission among the poor. Even if all they have to show for a lifetime of labour is a small congregation. Even if the singing isn't done very well. Even if they struggle to keep their head above water. It matters. They matter. The church of Jesus matters. The next generation needs to be inspired to do that. They need pioneers and examples to follow. They need somebody to be first over the trenches.

The current short-term mission trend is failing the UK poor. It's failing the young people who want to help, it's failing the people on the ground who are actually helping and it is failing the very people that they think they are helping.

And it gets worse.

CHAPTER 3:

THE FAILURE OF THEOLOGICAL EDUCATION IN THE UK

Imagine the CEO of a company, which you have shares in, announcing to the board that he has spotted someone with star potential working within the company. He's convinced that this individual has a golden future and, if given the right investment and training, could prove invaluable to the company in the coming years. But, instead of promoting the person and training him in-house, he has decided to send him away for three years to get further training.

What would your response be? What if the CEO said, "This young man is so good that I have even recommended him to another company who can take him on and train him in their business." What would be your reaction to this news? Surely, the best business sense would be to recognise the young man's abilities and then to offer him in-house training which would enable him to grow and develop and ensure that his skillset and potential are not lost to the company, thus enriching all parties.

Now, I have always been bemused in evangelical circles by:

- The practice of sending our "best" people away to Bible college for further training

- Importing pastors and assistant pastors into congregations they have no prior affinity or relationship with

In effect, what happens is that those with great potential in local churches are sent away for three or more years to pursue theological study and then end up at some other church entirely. We have been convinced that sending our best men and women away to be trained largely in a classroom setting is somehow beneficial for the local church. Only in the Christian world do we seem to take this bizarre approach to developing our future leaders.

In Niddrie, we are taking a multi-level approach to training and developing future, potential leaders. So, for instance, if a person approaches me and says they would like to "go to Bible college", I immediately want to know their reasons why. Then I want to challenge them to consider taking time out to serve our local church in some capacity in order to gain some "hands on" experience of ministry realities in a pressurised context. You soon get to see who is called to the work in the cut and thrust of real-life, gospel ministry. That's when the real heart of a person comes to the fore. That's when we get to see character exposed in all its inglorious sinfulness.

In my opinion, too many Bible colleges are no longer servants of the local church. They are, instead, often servants of whichever local authority ratifies their degree courses. This has left many of them basically operating without any real accountability at the local church level at all. A service that was originally supposed to meet the needs of the local church, in reality, often does no such thing.

So, at Niddrie we train our people in-house through our Ragged School of Theology. A huge issue for those of us working in housing schemes is that the current theological system in the UK is weighted in favour of the literate, erudite, reading classes. What about my illiterate evangelist guy? What about my local convert who would never cope with writing a "degree level" paper but has such a keen insight into the local culture that just needs to be refined and nurtured with the right discipleship? Sending them to a traditional Bible college would be counterproductive at many levels. That's why, for us at least, a comprehensive, in-house training programme is the answer.

So, would I never send one of my people to Bible college? No, not unless they tested their "calling" with us first. Of course, there are exceptions to this – for example, if somebody had the gifts needed for a specialist ministry, such as a Bible translator or a pilot. But I would still test their calling through in-house experience in the local body. I am not decrying intensive theological training. In fact, I am advocating it. But, certainly not in the context in which it is currently, almost exclusively, offered.

The fact that a godly, gifted young man with poor literacy skills wouldn't even get shortlisted for a job in 90%+ of evangelical churches in our country. This I question. The fact that a BA at the end of somebody's name now carries more weight in the evangelical world than actual character and giftedness. This I question.

My core ministry team consists of post-graduates. But importantly, it also consists of those who don't have any formal qualifications and even those who never finished school. Because at Niddrie we are seeking to be a training church, I strongly believe that both groups can learn from one another. Both groups recording their experiences. Both groups preparing to train the next generation of indigenous leaders coming through. We need the educated middle class at Niddrie. We need their money, their structure and their discipline. But they need the less educated just as much. For too long, men and women with backgrounds like mine are paraded at "testimony evenings" in some random middle-class church and yet we have been denied a place in church leadership.

One of the reasons, I believe, why the church is nowhere on housing schemes and council estates is because we have a system that encourages converts to:

- Stay stuck in testimony mode; and
- Get out of their schemes at the first opportunity. Too many have, sadly and ironically, gone to Bible college and have never gone back.

In middle-class circles, they look for the cream of the crop as it rises to the top, but in housing schemes, we have to dig that extra bit harder because the nuggets often sink to the bottom. Gold is often hidden in the dirt, the muck and the crap. It takes time and effort to sieve through it and pull out a gem. Jesus knew that. We forget how rough and ready the early disciples were.

That's why one of the things we are offering at Niddrie Community Church is an internship scheme for local people. So, they get to do jobs around the church, work in the cafe or do some admin, etc. If they work for a year without hassle, then they can join our full-time Ragged School of Theology (RST). For others, it provides a confidence booster, and for yet others, maybe even a way back into other employment. It is very early days, but we are trying to look at how we develop the next generation of "indigenous" leaders through our modelling approach. So, everybody on my core team has a local person to mentor and train. It encourages a two-way learning system and not merely a passing of knowledge in a passive manner.

Is it foolproof? No. Is it perfect? No. But we are trying to record our lessons every step of the way so we can pass our wisdom on. It's very experimental but it is better than the nothing that is currently going on in leadership training in too many of the housing schemes and council estates of our nation.

NEW PATHWAYS FOR MINISTRY TRAINING

In 1972, John Frame wrote an article entitled, "Proposal for a New Seminary".[252] Three things struck me about the article:

- Its radical nature despite the fact it was written four decades ago.
- The fact that the author was a Professor of Systematic Theology and Philosophy at a highly regarded American Bible college.
- How much it resonated with what I am trying to communicate in this book.

Concerning the inability of a Bible college to provide balanced, spiritual development as well as rigorous academic training, Dr. Frame traces the problem back to Princeton in the mid-1800s. There, the Rev. Gardiner Spring, who had been a board member at Princeton for 34 years, saw a marked difference between a seminary-trained minister and one trained in a local church setting. As a result of this, we learn that:

> *He [Rev. Gardiner Spring] advocated (1) that the seminary faculty maintain close supervision, not only over a student's academic progress, but also over his social and spiritual development; (2) that the seminary faculty itself consist of men with extensive pastoral experience; (3) that no student*

be ordained to the ministry until he has spent a time of apprenticeship with an experienced pastor.[253]

Now, I know that a lot has changed in the past 40 years, with many Bible colleges in the UK now offering "placements" to their students, along with "mission trips" and other "hands on" initiatives, as a means to helping get ongoing training and experience. This was certainly the practice of my Bible college 20 years ago. However, that which sounded good on paper, was often very different in reality. In my case, the workload was so heavy (a BA Hons degree) that it sometimes affected my ability to do anything meaningful in my placement church. I may have led the odd service and helped out in the youth work but that was about it.

The local pastor I was seconded to was much too busy for me and I received next to no hands-on counsel and spiritual help from him. This is not a criticism of the man but just a weakness of the system. Many of my friends had similar experiences. We were assigned personal tutors as well who were meant to be a sort of spiritual mentor to us. The gentleman I initially received was too busy to see me as regularly as I needed (he was both an administrator in the college and had at least 20 other "students" to care for) and also lacked pastoral gifting.

I see now that the one man who did play a major role in my life was just about the only experienced "pastor" on the staff. The rest were a mix of women, youth workers, children's workers, missionaries and evangelists. Good people, in the main, but of no help in terms of preparing me spiritually for the world of pastoral ministry.

This is how Dr. Frame describes it:

Worst of all, it seems to me that most seminary graduates are not spiritually ready for the challenges of the ministry.

> *Seminaries not only frequently "refuse to do the work of the church," they also tend to undo it. Students who arrive expecting to find a "spiritual hothouse" often find seminary to be a singular test of faith. The crushing academic workload, the uninspiring and unhelpful courses, the financial agonies, the too-busy professors, the equally hard-pressed fellow students all contribute to the spiritual debilitation. I have known a number of students who have stopped going to church while in seminary and others who wander from church to church in a fruitless search for genuine Christian fellowship, yet unwilling (some of them would say "unable") to give enough of themselves to others to make such fellowship possible.*[254]

He was talking decades ago, and I have to say that not much has changed in modern Bible colleges. If anything, the intellectual rigours have increased in many places with the rise of degrees being ratified by secular universities. Even from my own experience of having had several Bible college students doing their placements with me, I can tell you that the academic pressure on them was so enormous that they were practically useless in the church, particularly as exam deadline day approached! Again, this is not a criticism of some great young people (and some not so great), but a fault of the current system which now places so much emphasis on a paper qualification as the key to the door of pastoral ministry.

I believe that there needs to be some form of moratorium between evangelical churches and Bible colleges in our country. We need to ask some tough questions. *Who exactly is serving whom? Who are many of our Bible colleges actually accountable to? What figures do we have that show us, in real terms, just how successful these places are at ensuring people graduate to go into full-time pastoral ministry at some level? How can a Bible college realistically assess a person in terms of their spiritual character, devotion to the Lord, prayer life, love for the saints, perseverance through trial, etc.?*

As Dr. Frame points out:

> *The academic machinery is simply incapable of measuring the things that really matter – a man's obedience to God's Word, his perseverance in prayer, his self-control, his ability to rule without pride, the spiritual power of his preaching in the conversion of men and the edification of the church.*[255]

It has been my experience over the past two decades that those with Bible college degrees have been less useful to me in terms of evangelism, discipleship and pastoral care than those I have trained without any formal qualifications. Whatever Bible colleges think they are training men and women for, I can assure you it is not for ministry in the housing schemes and council estates of the UK. It is laughable to think that because somebody has a handle on Greek or church history that, somehow, they are better prepared and more qualified to face the temptations and trials of spiritual battle in the coalface of a housing scheme. More often than not I have to help people "unlearn" the Bible college mentality of academia and help them to work on the practical realities of godly living and ministering to people at the coalface.

Dr. Frame, 40 years ago now, makes an interesting proposal.

> *Let us then consider a positive alternative. A church or denomination establishes a kind of "Christian community" where teachers, ministerial candidates, and their families live together, eat together, work together; where they all really know each other; where their lives (their habits, their tempers, their talents, their loves, their hates, their struggles, their sanctity and lack of it) are known to all. The teachers*

> *and older students would thus be "examples" to the newer and the newer would be under the scrutiny of the older. The community is not a monastic escape from the world; rather it is mobilized for the purpose of establishing and nurturing churches throughout its locality. Each teacher, student, wife and child is to be deeply involved in the work of developing churches, through visitation, neighbourhood Bible studies, public meetings, street preaching, and then (as churches are established) through Sunday School teaching, preaching, church youth work, church administration, etc.*[256]

This, to my mind, encapsulates what we are trying to achieve through our Ragged School of Theology. With this system we get:

1. To train our people theologically at a very high level
2. The bonus of observing them, coaching them and discipling them in the particular field in which they want to serve ultimately. So, they get to learn and grow from serving alongside actual practitioners rather than from textbooks and through writing theoretical papers.

In Frame's alternative to Bible college, he envisions the following:

> *There will be no set "number of hours" after which a man is entitled to graduation. Teachers and older students involved in teaching will meet from time to time for intensive evaluation of each student's progress in life, skills and knowledge. These meetings will determine whether a man will be dropped from the program (either because of doubt concerning his call to the ministry or because of doubt concerning the ability of the*

> *program to deal with the student's problems), or whether he will be promoted to new levels of responsibility, or whether he will be "graduated" and recommended to the churches for the ministry. No man will "graduate" unless the teachers are convinced that he has the character, skills and knowledge that the Scriptures require of church officers.*[257]

At Niddrie, we are constantly developing our programme to ensure that people are:

1. Constantly getting good feedback. That means both positive and negative constructive criticism.
2. Subject to a high level of spiritual accountability with intensive one-to-ones and a designated accountability partner and/or mentor.
3. Given opportunities to serve in a variety of practical areas, including teaching, and are given wide-ranging feedback which will help them to nurture and develop gifting.
4. "Sifted" through the intensity of the process as underlying character defects and sins are brought to light and are dealt with.

Bible colleges tend to assess the suitability of men for ministry largely through the prism of academic ability. I remember a very intelligent intern we were training at Niddrie some years ago. He was super smart and, because it was in the days before our RST, we sent him to a local seminary for a part-time degree. He wrote some amazing papers and was a very good communicator. The college faculty loved him. The problem was that as we observed him in the daily setting of church life, it became clear that he had a serious character defect that we knew would prohibit him from pastoral ministry. The college disagreed with our assessment as we removed him from their programme. Their reasoning was based on his ability to communicate well and his excellent written papers. That is the nub of the problem – and it is a problem that seminaries are not capable of resolving, no matter how much they protest to the contrary.

Problems also usually appear when a person is designated unfit for ministry by the leaders of the local body, so they move on to a new church and turn up with the intention of going to "Bible college". I have lost count of the many people over the years who have randomly turned up at church for a few weeks, asked to meet me and then informed me of their desire to go to Bible college. When I ask them what the pastor of their "home" church thinks, I usually get a reply along the lines of, "Oh, he doesn't understand me… that church is awful" – or words to that effect. I personally tell them that I won't be signing off on a reference until they have been with me for a few years, and I have seen some sort of evidence of spiritual life, growth and leadership gifting. They are usually off down the road to the next church on their hit list, doubtless writing me off as one of those "terrible pastors" as well!

If, as evangelicals, we are serious about trying to encourage and grow a new generation of leaders to work in our housing schemes and council estates, then we must face the facts that Bible college is not the future for our people. Colleges have a vested interest in their own self-propagation. They're not going to lower academic standards even if a man has excellent spiritual credentials. They are going to fail him because they have to. Well, there are part-time courses, you may say! There are. But why would they be any more superior to initiatives like ours which, in my opinion, puts theological training back where it belongs. In the hands of local churches and local church leadership.

Please be clear that I am not advocating the end of Christian scholarship, but what use are scholars in training pastors and housing scheme/council estate church planters? Not much, I can assure you. Their benefit lies more broadly than that. I think that today, more than ever, if we are to grow future leaders who will be effective in housing schemes and council estates, then we must develop theological "hot houses" in our local congregations, work at sharing resources like the Ragged School, sharing experiences and lessons learned between local church practitioners, and offer valuable hands-on experience where possible. If I am going to send my best people anywhere, it will be to plant another congregation or grow them into teaching and leadership positions in order to train others also.

SUMMARY

What do the Scriptures say a man must be? I can't find Bible college or seminary graduate in 1 Timothy 3 or Titus 1 (or 2 Timothy 4:1–5 or 1 Peter 5, for that matter). It just isn't there.

A man must know the Word and be able to use it to silence those who are contrary (Tit. 1:9). He has to be able to teach (1 Tim. 3:2), and not just teach but teach well enough to train other teachers (2 Tim. 2:2). He has to be skilled in learning the Word (2 Tim. 2:15).

Can a person learn what they need to match those qualifications without going to a Bible college? Most of the textbooks we use are from men who died long ago. Often, they're more useful than the live lecturer when it comes to helping us contextualise what we are learning for our context!

Who says Bible colleges are the only place a person can gain a solid and working knowledge of God's Word? It's true that they can add some value to those who want to pursue a more scholarly ministry. *Why, therefore, do they have a stranglehold on the Christian church when it comes to training men and women for ministry? Why has the local church devolved her power and authority to others, allowing them to declare who is and who is not fit for ministry?*

One thing is for certain, the current training paths for ministry available in the UK are not helpful for people either from our context or for those wanting to work in our communities.

CHAPTER 4:

THE LIE OF THE TRICKLE-DOWN EFFECT

In his book, *The New Urban Crisis: How our cities are increasing inequality, deepening segregation, and failing the middle class – and what we can do about it*, Richard Florida states:

> *London is growing away from the rest of the United Kingdom and the rest of the world. It is almost a country unto itself; Londoners have more in common with the wealthy, plugged-in global citizens of New York, L.A., San Francisco, Paris, Tokyo, Singapore, and Hong Kong than they do with people elsewhere in the UK.*[258]

Florida clearly sees that the surprise Brexit vote of 2016 was a sign of the growing economic distance and social divide between the classes in the UK. He calls the UK, "a country so imbalanced it has effectively fallen over".[259]According to Florida, far too many people in our cities are locked into poverty. Surprisingly, one of the groups which is hardest hit, in his opinion, is the middle class. As he has monitored global cities, he has observed a pattern emerging where the advantaged and the disadvantaged in inner cities are becoming much more separated geographically. Accordingly, he claims, we have now entered into an era he calls the "new urban crisis". It is defined by five dimensions:

1. THE GROWING ECONOMIC GAP BETWEEN A FEW "SUPERSTAR CITIES" AND THE REST OF THE WORLD

According to Florida, these cities – London, New York, L.A., etc. – have a disproportionate amount of the world's high value companies and talent. He pinpoints the UK specifically as having the worst income inequality in Europe, with the centre of London having almost unbelievable amounts of wealth. If we compare this to the rest of the country, particularly in the North, with many communities marked by disturbing levels of deprivation, we begin to see the problem Florida is highlighting.

All of this means that there is now a huge, and growing, cultural and economic chasm between London and the rest of the UK. So, for example, when it came to the recent European Union referendum, he noted that over 60% of London voted "Remain" compared with 70% of the East Midlands voting "Leave" (the figures being almost as high across large parts of the North).

2. EXORBITANT HOUSING COSTS IN SUPERSTAR CITIES COMPOUNDS THE INEQUALITY

Most of the centres of these superstar cities have unoccupied properties that have been bought merely as investments by multi-millionaire / billionaire tycoons who have no intention of living there – over 750 properties which are valued at £5 million plus in London currently lie uninhabited.[260] As this practice has pushed housing costs up, the blue-collar and service workers have been forced to move out of the city due to unaffordable housing and rents.

3. INEQUALITIES LEADING TO SHRINKING MIDDLE-CLASS NEIGHBOURHOODS

According to Florida, two-thirds of the population of the UK identified as middle class in the 1980s. It is less than half that today. In the same period, poverty has jumped 10%, to 27% of the population. He writes:

> *In place of the old class divide of poor cities versus rich suburbs, a new pattern has emerged – a Patchwork Metropolis in which small areas of privilege and large swathes of poverty and distress criss-cross city and suburb alike.*[261]

4. HIGH CRIME AND POVERTY RATES, AND RACIAL AND CLASS SEGREGATION IN THE SUBURBS

So, for example, nearly all the poverty in London was once in the urban centre. But now, according to Florida, "60% of poverty in Greater London is in suburban Outer London".[262] In the old world order, the poor were largely found in cities and city centres, which were a hotbed of crime and other social problems, and the emerging middle class and the rich moved to the suburbs to escape the social problems. Statistics show us that this is now being reversed, particularly in the superstar cities of the world.

5. A CRISIS OF URBANISATION IN THE DEVELOPING WORLD

Developing countries think that if they build more cities, they will become rich like the Western superstar cities. But the problem is that this was never true for most Westernised cities. In fact, most of the West's global output comes out of only a handful of its superstar cities. "Superstar cities, in effect, form a league of their own, often having much more in common with each other than they do with other cities in their own nations."[263]

THE PROBLEM OF GENTRIFICATION

According to Florida, this new urban crisis is also fuelling much of the gentrification going on in and around many of the world's cities. "Generally speaking, gentrification describes a process in which a neighbourhood gains wealth and sees its population become more affluent, whiter and younger."[264] Gentrification is occurring in schemes and council estates across the UK. We are observing young, affluent, middle-class people of all ethnicities moving into our communities, often at the expense of the indigenous population. The effect has been mixed and includes:

a) Local identity stripped away: Historic street names are being changed to market the area to new, affluent buyers. For instance, as I've mentioned, the scheme next to mine in Edinburgh – known as "Greendykes" and famous for containing the blocks of flats where the two *Trainspotting* movies were filmed – was recently demolished and re-developed. It was been renamed "Greenacres" in an attempt to woo more affluent families and first-time buyers. A similar sort of thing happened in London with local authority planners renaming "council estates" as "neighbourhoods".[265]

b) People forced out: The fact that the cost of living in Edinburgh's city centre is so high, coupled with a chronic housing shortage, means that the local authority is gentrifying our scheme in an effort to tempt the educated middle classes to buy here. They've built a state-of-the-art library (a sure sign of gentrification, according to Florida), a shopping centre, supermarkets and new schools. Note that none of these things were available to the indigenous populace until the affluent needed somewhere more affordable to live.

Council houses were bought and sold off to developers with the promise that a certain percentage of uprooted residents could move back. That is rarely, if ever, happening. Instead, many of the houses are going to immigrants, which is causing racial tension. Alongside this, house prices have gone through the roof, so it is practically impossible to get on the housing market if you work in a service industry or other low-paid employment.

In the next decade, Niddrie will no longer be a scheme and most of the indigenous population will have been "re-homed" on to other schemes or have been forced to relocate further north to places like Fife, where house prices and rentals are much cheaper. The new, incoming middle class will know nothing of the deep history of the area and nothing of the old house and street names. Nor will they care. They will just swarm the community and the dominant class will ultimately hold sway.

All the while, we are meant to be grateful because these policies have "made things better". The reality is, they've made things better for those that can afford it. Those who can't will be brushed aside and, for many (if not all), their lives will not really have improved at all.

c) Problems not solved, just relocated: Thirdly, gentrification assumes a top-down approach to housing and social policy (at least in the UK – but this is generally true worldwide). By improving a geographical area in terms of housing and services, the idea is that the poor indigenous populace will benefit by default. It is called the "trickle-down effect".[266] The reality is that while there are improvements to many of these communities, the poorest remain poor and are forced out of their homes and communities. The problems are not solved, they are just moved on.

WHAT DOES ANY OF THIS HAVE TO DO WITH THE CHURCH IN THE UK?

The problem, as I have observed it over the last 20 years, is that much of the church-planting and revitalisation movement (around the world) has followed global sociological and economic trends rather than the Bible. In fact, much of it mimics gentrification. Let me explain what I mean.

Many evangelical church leaders in the UK, indeed, across the world, continue to maintain that our evangelism and missionary efforts should be concentrated on the leaders, politicians, artists and culture-shapers in our societies. Tim Keller is not the originator of this idea, but he is certainly one of the main voices responsible for its popularity among middle-class and hipster church planters. In effect, they believe that if Christians pump their finances and strategies into the upper and creative classes, this will ultimately have a trickle-down effect when it comes to reaching the poor. Poor and vulnerable people should not be used as some sort of evangelistic tool to impress rich and powerful people who are looking to tick the social justice box.

Some call it "planting upstream".[267] In other words, let's plant churches in financially rich communities and then, in the future, we can fund work in poorer areas. With money and influence, the thinking goes, we can have more effect planting one of these financial powerhouse churches than five poorer churches that drain resources. It sounds logical enough. It even sounds feasible. Except it doesn't work. And if the leaders advocating this approach don't know it, then they ought to. The reality in church circles is the same as the reality in gentrification. The people who end up suffering the most are the very people everybody claims to be helping – the poorest and most vulnerable members of society.

Somebody recently challenged me on this issue and said that there were more evangelical churches in rich communities doing mercy ministry than ever before, so how could I even make these claims? My answer is that much of the mercy ministry being carried out by richer, middle-class churches is nothing more than relief. While good in the immediate and short-term, it damages people in the long-term if there is no comprehensive and long-term strategy to welcome converts into the church, properly disciple them and equip them for godly service. It's no good proving to the non-Christian movers, shakers and culture-shapers what a great church you are because you feed the homeless once a week, while no real and lasting change is taking effect.

Indeed, in my experience of trickle-down Christianity, the further it trickles down, the more diluted the truth becomes. In effect, all that's left for us are the Christian oddballs and theological heretics.

Regardless, the plain fact is that so-called "upstream churches" are not financing church planting and revitalisation ministry in the UK in council estates and schemes in anything like the numbers required to make a dent. There may be those who have helped the odd work or maybe even planted one or two churches (rare, even if it is happening). We need to see funding on a huge scale, over decades, before we even begin to make up the ground that we have lost over the past 50 years.

Upstream churches with upstream budgets fund upstream building projects before they will fund downstream Christians to plant in schemes and council estates. That's the reality.

20schemes is almost entirely supported by Christian individuals and small churches (50–100 members) outside of the UK and not by rich, upstream churches. We have a few examples of large churches that regularly financially support us, but only a handful in the UK.

In short, I do not know one church planter working in the council estates and schemes who has been helped by this trickle-down model at the local church level. Brothers in schemes and estates are all struggling for money and for volunteers willing to move in and help them form teams. Larger churches may throw them a few pounds now and again, but nothing like what is needed to fund a church planter and his family properly and for the long-term.

Through my work with Acts 29 and our Church in Hard Places initiative, we have begun to gather a small group of men from around the UK working in difficult and deprived communities.[268] All, to a man, are struggling to get by with little financial support and are certainly not being helped sufficiently by larger, wealthier churches around them. On a recent call, I told them all:

> *No real help is coming for us from some of these major planting networks and upstream churches. We are going to have to band together to help one another. We are going to have to help each other train our own interns and future leaders. We are going to have to club together to fund one another. We may get the odd bone thrown to us now and again, but we are largely on our own.*

As practitioners in poor communities, we have to begin the slow work of rebuilding churches and growing leaders in our local areas. There is no significant "trickle-down" help coming our way anytime soon, and I very much doubt we will see it at all – unless a seismic shift takes place in the thinking of UK churches, denominations and financial institutions.

THE "SALMON" APPROACH

Unless I've missed something, I don't see how this "top-down" approach is biblical anyway. Surely, if the Lord wanted to use that strategy to reach the poor with the good news, he would have come down as a Roman governor or even the Emperor. That would have had a trickle-down effect! Instead, He came as a northern Jew who was dirt poor and insignificant in the eyes of the world. Shepherds and women (not at all the "culture shapers" of society) heralded His coming. His ministry was among the poor and the outcast.

Therefore, it seems to me that a much more biblical approach would be the "downstream church". Maybe we ought to be thinking about a "trickle-up" approach to church planting? Maybe we could call it the "Salmon approach", upstream and against the tide. Let me be clear. I am not arguing against planting "upstream" (although I despise this terminology and what it represents). What I am advocating is church planting and revitalisation across cultures – especially across the class divide. I am saying "planting upstream" as a strategy to reach the poor does not work and has little biblical merit or basis.

In 1857, Charles Spurgeon, preaching a sermon called, "Preaching for the Poor", said the following:

> *It is one delightful mark of Christ's dispensation, that he aims first at the poor ... It was wise in him to do so. If we would fire a building, it is best to light it at the basement; so our Saviour, when he would save a world, and convert men of all classes, and all ranks, begins at the lowest rank, that the fire may burn upwards, knowing right well that what was received by the poor, will ultimately by his grace be received by the rich also.*[269]

TALK IS CHEAP

In the past few decades, evangelicals in the United Kingdom and the United States seem to be working on different church-planting and evangelism criteria than that of the Apostle Paul, who told the Corinthians: "Not many of you were wise by human standards; not many were influential, not many were of noble birth" (1 Cor. 1:26). Too often, the church reflects the values and methodology of the materialistic culture around us. We talk about the poor. A lot. But what do we do? Very little.

I have developed a principle – let's call it the "trickle-down theorem": The richer the church, the more likely they are to talk about the poor and marginalised. But in reality, we prefer the millionaire's tithe to the widow's mite and we console ourselves, saying, "At least we hand out soup." But the poor need the gospel even more than they need a full belly. Biblical love – love that respects and sees all human beings as equally made in the image of God – is needed. Not the twenty-first-century version of charity.

I know the objections already. I know the charges of socialism, hypocrisy, liberalism, etc. I know that there are in the Bible examples of the Lord calling the wealthy, the elites, the powerful and the privileged. But these are the exceptions. The "not many". The biblical strategy is *not* to reach the wealthy that we might reach the poor; it is to reach the poor that we might reach the wealthy (who in reality are the hardest to reach).

But we don't believe that. It's why I can get any number of church groups from the United States to come and church plant in central London, Oxford, Edinburgh and St Andrews. But ask them to come to, or finance work in, Doncaster, Dartford or Dundee, and they are not interested. Apparently, these are not places of "influence" (like Nazareth!). We have reversed the biblical criteria and then claim that we are doing so in order to be faithful to the Bible!

This is how Florida sees it:

> *Our class geography no longer follows the old pattern of rich suburb and poor city. Highly paid knowledge workers, the affluent, and young people have been returning in droves to*

> *urban centres over the past decade or two, while growing numbers of the poor and disadvantaged are being edged out into the suburbs. ... Our class geography is now being reshaped into a more complex and variegated pattern that I call the Patchwork Metropolis ... that is being split into areas of tightly clustered zones of concentrated advantage and even larger swathes of concentrated disadvantage that crisscross cities and suburbs alike.*[270]

SUMMARY

There is a clear problem with the top-down approach to evangelism, church planting and church revitalisation in the UK. We have followed the worldly pattern of the trickle-down theorem. And by doing so we have thrown the least, the last and the lost of the UK onto the spiritual scrapheap and left them cut adrift in the wilderness.

SPOTLIGHT:

THE FREE CHURCH AND THE POOR

DAVID ROBERTSON, FREE CHURCH MINISTER[271]

THE FREE CHURCH'S HEART FOR THE POOR

The Free Church was born with a heart for the poor. In the early 1980s, I was studying history and politics at the University of Edinburgh. I had been attending Morningside Baptist Church – and indeed had been baptised there – but, through reading the Bible, I became what is called "Reformed", even though I did not know what that was! I began to look for a church that taught this biblical theology but also practised it too. Then I came across the Disruption in my historical studies.[272] The Disruption of 1842 was when leading evangelical Rev. Thomas Chalmers and over 400 colleagues indicated their willingness "to walk away from their jobs, their incomes and their homes in pursuit and a Kirk that was free of patronage and state interference". I was fascinated by a church which was theologically sound and passionately cared for the poor. I heard one lecture in which it was argued that the west of Scotland, and especially the Highlands, did not have an Irish style starvation with the potato famine because the church bought a ship of grain from Russia. Most of all, I was so impressed by Thomas Chalmers' views of church planting for the poor. Here was a church that was both biblical and passionate about the poor.

I was thrilled.

I discovered the ministry of Robert Murray McCheyne who, every year, in November, on the anniversary of his ordination to St Peter's, preached on Isaiah 61:1–3, "The Spirit of the Sovereign Lord is on me, because the Lord has anointed me to proclaim good news to the poor. He has sent me to bind up the broken hearted, to proclaim freedom for the captives and release from darkness for the prisoners ..."

The Free Church has always been a church of the poor, whether it was Thomas Chalmers in St John's in Glasgow, or Thomas Guthrie in Edinburgh with his Ragged Schools, or Hugh Miller advocating for the poor in the Highlands, or Alexander Duff fighting for the poor in India. This was not something that we did as a hobby. It was not virtue signalling. It was our very heart because it is the heart of the Lord: "Blessed are the poor, for theirs is the kingdom of heaven" (Matt. 5:3).

LET US COME FORWARD TO THE PRESENT DAY

Poverty is relative, but it is real. In many of our housing schemes and rural communities, there is real poverty of spirit – broken and dysfunctional families – as the poor pay the price for middle-class, bourgeois morality being imposed by the elites on the whole of society.

Drugs and alcohol abuse. Unemployment. The working class becoming the benefits class. Perhaps above all, mental health issues. These are also very violent places. And largely we stay out of them, apart from the occasional foray, or the gathering of Gaelic-speaking islanders in some of the Glasgow estates. There are notable exceptions – I was once told that the three worst areas in the Highlands for poverty were the Ferry in Inverness, Milnafua in Alness, and Brora. I was proud that the Free Church has significant work in all three. Recently, we have seen churches started in Govan, Charleston in Dundee, and the Ferry in Inverness.

But here is the problem. We have sent them out into the most difficult of situations. They don't drive in and leave. They don't do hit and run. They are long-term. They cannot grow by gathering people from other churches or becoming the "hip and happening" place in their area. They can only grow by conversion and then, when people are converted, there is a long process of discipleship. This is hard work. This is messy work. This is, in many ways, thankless work. This is long-term work. This is not perceived to be influential – influencing the gatekeepers.

And we have sent our men into these situations poorly funded and leave them to fundraise and largely support themselves. They need to be properly funded for the long haul. Given the job description, I think to add to it that you have to fundraise almost your whole support is an added pressure that is not helpful and conducive to church planting.

I once had a conversation with Mez McConnell in which he stated that he was not sure that Free Church plants would need 20Schemes because we were Presbyterians. Well, in my view, our Presbyterianism has failed. He should have been right. Most of all, I am utterly ashamed that I and my own church have not been able to offer the kind of support in different ways that Charleston, our daughter church in Dundee, needs.

It should be a matter of shame to Scottish Presbyterians that Americans give more to church planting among the poor than we do. Now I appreciate and am very grateful for the support of the Americans, and I have worked in bringing American missionaries to Scotland, but there is a downside. Firstly, our church planters have to spend significant time fundraising. They need around $50,000 per year from US churches. That's a drop in the ocean for many of these churches.

And raising American support comes with another cost as well. Although there are Americans who are culturally sensitive and biblically sacrificial and have been a fine example to me, I find that the general culture often operates on the principle of, "he who pays the piper calls the tune". "We'll give you $5,000 – can we send over a mission team?" Also, it's not wise to be dependent on American workers – we have had some excellent ones – but they usually go home and our work is long-term. Plus, the connections that we have with the United States are far more likely to see some of our best ministers going there rather than them coming to us.

SPIRITUAL TRICKLE-DOWN THEORY

Furthermore, the American churches in the Presbyterian Church of America have been greatly influenced by what some people call "spiritual trickle-down" theory. They believe that if we reach the wealthy and influential then there will be a trickle-down effect to the poor. When I was the team leader for Mission to the World (MTW) Scotland, it was MTW's policy that, because they were largely middle class, they should reach the middle class.[273] As a result of this attitude, it's relatively easy to get money and people for church planting in Edinburgh and St Andrews – the cultural and media centres. But what about Cowdenbeath, Charleston, Ferguslie Park, Merkinch and Govan? Everyone seems to think that if you evangelise the wealthy and powerful, you will then be able to reach the poor.

But what if it's the other way round?

THOMAS CHALMERS' PROPHECY

Thomas Chalmers foresaw that this would happen and I'm certain he would be appalled at our current practice. In his six lectures to the House of Lords in 1838, he warned that if everything was left to individual voluntary giving, the middle-class suburbs in our towns and cities would have an abundance of churches and the poor would be left out.[274] In Dundee, we have 70,000 people living in our schemes – these schemes need radical gospel churches, not charity. With the collapse of the Church of Scotland and its drift into, and toleration of, a "gospel" which is no gospel at all, we cannot rely on the Church of Scotland to reach housing schemes.

CHARITY OR LOVE?

We have also gone to a charity mentality – we think that people in housing schemes need food banks and soup kitchens more than the biblical gospel. It's easier for us to offer the charity of this world, rather than the charity and love of Christ as described in 1 Corinthians 13.

SO, WHAT PRACTICALLY CAN BE DONE?

Here's an idea from our history. McCheyne had a sermon once a year where the collection went towards provision for Gaelic schools among the poor in the Highlands. Why don't we have an annual Schemes Day in all our churches – where the collection goes to support existing Presbyterian works in some of our poorest communities? Who knows, maybe this will encourage others to take up the cause of church revitalisation and planting among the poor?

I started with McCheyne, let me finish with him.

> *Ah! Why am I such a stranger to the poor of my native town? I have passed their doors thousands of times. I have admired the huge black piles of building, with their lofty chimneys breaking the sun's rays – why have I never ventured within? How dwelleth the love of God in me? How cordial is the welcome even of the poorest and most loathsome to the voice of Christian sympathy! What imbedded masses of human beings*

are huddled together, unvisited by friend or minister! "No man careth for our souls," is written over every forehead. Awake, my soul! Why should I give hours and days any longer to the vain world, when there is such a world of misery at my very door? Lord, put thine own strength in me; confirm every good resolution; forgive my past long life of uselessness and folly.[275]

CHAPTER 5:

THE LEGACY OF NO EVANGELISM AND POOR EVANGELISM

Years ago, I received an invitation to speak at an evangelistic event for a big church in England. The day before the event the pastor rang me to go over some of the details. "We are hoping there will be lots of unbelievers there," he said. "Brilliant," I said. He went on, "I just wanted to let you know that we are looking for something a little low-key in the talk." "What do you mean?" I asked. "Well," he said, "We have a lot of unbelievers coming and they're all at different stages of their spiritual journey and so we were just hoping for a low-key gospel message." "What does that mean?" I asked. He began to sound a little tense. "You know, we want to be sure we win people not offend them. We'd rather just avoid mentioning offensive words and upsetting people we have been trying to reach for many years. We just don't want them to be put off the church." "What are the offensive words?" I asked, genuinely perplexed. "You know," he said, "hell, wrath, sin, stuff like that."

I took a deep breath.

"Let me get this right. You want me to give an evangelistic talk, but you don't want me to mention sin or hell. What can I mention then?" He sighed. "Talk about God's love and the forgiveness of Jesus. Things to build up and encourage. We want to be moving towards people in love. And we want to avoid the language of condemnation." At this point I am boiling with rage, so I change tack. "Do you believe that people are sinners?" "Yes," he said. "Do you believe that sinners go to hell unless they confess their sins and put their faith and trust in Jesus?" A slight pause. "Yes," he said. "Yet you are telling me it would be unloving to mention either of those things? You want me to ignore the very real danger sinners are in and just talk to them about love? How is that loving?"

Silence.

"Look, I think you know exactly what I am saying. There's no need to be difficult." "I'm not being difficult," I said. "You just want me to focus on God's love and the forgiveness of Jesus, right?" "Yes," he replied. "But the forgiveness of Jesus for what exactly?" I asked him. "What do you mean?" he said. "What has Jesus forgiven people for exactly?"

Long silence.

"Listen," I said to him. "If you want me to come, then I am going to talk about sin and hell and wrath and repentance and all the other offensive words. I am going to point people to the Bible, and I am also going to hold out the love of God and the life-saving good news of Jesus. I have never heard of a low-key gospel in my life, and, in fact, it smells like a sell-out to me. Low-key gospel presentations might win you friends, but it won't make Christians. If you can't accept that then I'm not coming. Simple as that."

He rang off saying he would pray about it, which is middle-class speak for, "There's no way you are speaking at our event, but I don't have the bottle to tell you to your face." An hour later one of his assistants rang me and said that they had found another speaker.

TWO BIG PROBLEMS

There are two big problems in the middle-class, evangelical world when it comes to evangelising the least, the last and the lost. The first is that they've made *being offensive the ultimate cultural taboo* when dealing with the non-Christian world. They want people to feel warm and welcomed in their churches and the price for doing that has been soft-sell evangelism. Being nice to and being liked by unbelievers is far more important to many Christians than being straight with them about the fact that they are living their lives under the wrath of God. They tell themselves that it is the gospel that should offend, not the messenger, yet in the Bible the message and the messenger are inextricably linked. This soft-sell evangelism has trickled down to the poorest communities in the UK. Middle-class people (already feeling guilty because of the advantages they have enjoyed in life) feel less than motivated to tell a woman with four children, whose partner is a heroin addict and sells her to his pals for a hit, that she is under the wrath of God and condemned to hell unless she repents of her sin and puts her faith and trust in Jesus.

It has left us with loads of do-gooders and social justice warriors wandering around our communities handing out bread and sympathy and telling us that God loves us and boosting our self-esteem. Many of these people have no idea of the gospel and much of what they say is meaningless psychobabble on the one hand and destructive heresy on the other. This is what happens when churches leave evangelism to para-church organisations who employ practically anybody with a pulse to come and serve God among the UK's poorest. They lack basic biblical doctrine. A lot of my time – and that of others in similar estates across the UK – is taken up with teaching these people the very gospel they think that they have come to proclaim!

The second problem for most middle-class evangelicals is that they have *overcomplicated evangelism* – so much so, that many churches find it necessary to run courses on *how* to evangelise the lost. They are obsessed with finding the right materials to study and discovering the silver bullet for effective evangelism. And the result of these two problems is that there are very few people from the schemes being converted in middle-class, evangelical churches today. Lots of people are being saved, no doubt. Usually those with a connection to the church or who perhaps come from Christian families. But certainly not from communities like ours. There are exceptions to this, but they are very few and far between.

The problem with Bible-believing, middle-class, evangelical churches is that they have forgotten what the Bible says. I've got three straightforward biblical truths that most middle-class, evangelical churches have lost sight of:

1. THERE REALLY ARE ONLY TWO WAYS TO LIVE

Middle-class churches are well schooled in the fact that there are only two responses to the message of the gospel – but most of them don't actually believe it!

Read through the book of Acts and you find acceptance or opposition. You find repentance or disobedience. You find faith or disbelief. That's the way it has always been and it is how the early church was born. People were amazed and astonished. They were pierced to the heart. They repented and believed in their thousands. They were in awe when the Apostles performed miracles and taught them. The priests, the captain of the Temple guard and the Sadducees were greatly disturbed. The jealous High Priests throw the Apostles in jail, yet other priests believe the gospel message. Some people were "cut to the quick and began gnashing their teeth" at Stephen's preaching while others respond to the gospel message by persecuting the messengers. We have Saul, whose dramatic and supernatural conversation with the risen Jesus, turns his priorities upside down – and he goes from murdering Christians to facing death threats himself. We have countless examples of people who believe – including the government official from Ethiopia, multiple Gentiles, multiple Jews and a few witches too. We see how the gospel message causes division, disagreement, persecution, agitation, rejection, opposition, terror. We see how the gospel cannot be quashed by the rich and powerful, by the influential and impressive. We see the preaching of the gospel that is the power of God to save.

What you *don't* find in Acts is anyone whatsoever who, after hearing the gospel proclaimed, just shrugs their shoulders and goes off ambivalent. It's acceptance or rejection. Sometimes converts outnumber opponents – but most often, opponents outnumber converts. Yet the book of Acts ends with Paul continuing to preach the kingdom of God and teaching people about the Lord Jesus.

But the way that many evangelical churches do evangelism shows that they don't really believe that there are only two responses to the gospel of Christ. Many of us have come to think that a wishy-washy non-response to the gospel is normal and acceptable. It is not. That a "low-key" gospel talk is evangelism. It is not. That unbelievers responding with a polite "I really enjoyed that" after a wine and cheese pre-evangelistic event is encouraging. It is not.

2. WE SHOULD EXPECT OPPOSITION AND HOSTILITY TO THE GOSPEL

We know that we should expect opposition and hostility in response to the preaching of the gospel. But that knowledge fails to prepare and strengthen some of us and, instead, opposition makes us ashamed of the gospel. But Paul tells us that we must *not* be ashamed of this message (Rom. 1). We must not shrink back from it. We must not try to water it down. We must not try to make it "relevant". In fact, we must not mess with it in any way.

Why? Why is it so important that we don't mess with the truth of the gospel? Paul makes it really clear in Romans 1:16 (ESV), "for it is the power of God for salvation to everyone who believes". This is why Paul is not ashamed of the gospel – because it is the power of salvation to all who believe. It is also the reason we must not water it down or soft soap it. If we do not preach the *full* gospel of Jesus to lost people, then they will never experience the salvation they need in order to be saved.

When someone responds to the gospel with opposition and hostility, it is most likely that it is the offence of the gospel that has riled them – the offensive and unacceptable message that they are a guilty sinner who needs to bend their knee to Almighty God. Too many of us have been infected by the political correctness of the world around us, by the requirement not to offend, by the need not to express our convictions too strongly for fear of disrespecting others, by the need to keep quiet if our beliefs do not mesh with what society has deemed acceptable. We have allowed opposition and hostility to make us ashamed of the glorious gospel of Jesus Christ.

3. WE HAVE LOST CONFIDENCE THAT THE HOLY SPIRIT WILL WORK THROUGH THE WORD OF GOD

How can we have lost confidence that the Holy Spirit will work through the Word of God? Haven't we been taught that "The Word does the work"?[276] That if we preach the Word, God will do the rest. That the Bible is "able to make you wise for salvation through faith in Christ Jesus" and means that we are "thoroughly equipped for every good work" (2 Tim. 3:15, 17).

What has happened to our confidence that the Holy Spirit will work through the Word of God? Paul is clear about this in 1 Corinthians 1:17–25.

> *For Christ did not send me to baptise, but to preach the gospel — not with wisdom and eloquence, lest the cross of Christ be emptied of its power. For the message of the cross is foolishness to those who are perishing, but to us who are being saved it is the power of God. For it is written: "I will destroy the wisdom of the wise; the intelligence of the intelligent I will frustrate." Where is the wise person? Where is the teacher of the law? Where is the philosopher of this age? Has not God made foolish the wisdom of the world? For since in the wisdom of God the world through its wisdom did not know him, God was pleased through the foolishness of what was preached to save those who believe. Jews demand signs and Greeks look for wisdom, but we preach Christ crucified: a stumbling block to Jews and foolishness to Gentiles, but to those whom God has called, both Jews and Greeks, Christ the power of God and the wisdom of God. For the foolishness of God is wiser than human wisdom, and the weakness of God is stronger than human strength.*

God saves people through the foolishness of what is preached – not through the cleverness of human wisdom (verse 22). In fact, we read that God is well pleased with His method of delivery (verse 21).

Culture and fashions are always changing and therefore we have to try harder and harder to keep relevant if that is our methodology. If we just open the old, old book and preach the old, old message, it remains the power of God for salvation throughout all generations.

Notice where the power lies in verse 18. The *gospel* is the power. The power doesn't lie in our ability to decide. The power doesn't lie in our ability to devise or use a beautifully crafted, exquisitely filmed, evangelistic resource. The power to be saved rests entirely in the gospel of Jesus. People cannot be saved unless the gospel is preached in all its fullness.

There is no such thing as low-key salvation or half saved. We are either children of God – or children of the devil. We are either fully saved – or we are not saved at all. The gospel is either music to our ears – or it makes our blood boil.

CHAPTER 6:

WHOM SHALL I SEND? AND WHO WILL GO FOR US?

So far my critique has focused on the problems surrounding "mercy ministries", some inadequacies of theological education, the myth of the "trickle-down" effect and the legacy of non-evangelism. Now we turn to issues surrounding funding and personnel. Let me start by suggesting a couple of reasons for why men and women working in churches in our most deprived communities run into funding and personnel issues time and time again.

THE CHURCH IS OVERLY FOCUSED ON STUDENT MINISTRIES

A report in *The Guardian* recorded that a record high of 30% of 18-year-olds applied to universities in 2019.[277] But that means 70% of 18-year-olds in the UK *do not* go on to higher education. Yet, I would suggest the figure is, at the very least, reversed in most evangelical churches. This is not to suggest our children shouldn't go to university. Of course, they should if they want to. Both my children have taken that route, albeit one in another country.

My issue is that, when we look at the pattern of church planting in the UK and also around the world, there is a disproportionate number of churches being planted in student areas. Couple that with the millions being poured into student ministry every year and we have a startling imbalance in who has access to the gospel and to Christian finances.

What is being done to reach the *70% of young people* who either go on to do vocational training, some form of apprenticeship or other work? What if church-planting strategists and financial institutions and grant-making bodies poured 70% of their people and their money into *these* young people? How much would that change the spiritual landscape of the UK in the next decade?

Al Gooderham, a pastor in Yorkshire, says this:

> *What if we invested as much in reaching the 18-year-old in work as we do the student at university? Even within cities like Leeds and Sheffield, the student populations make up less than 15% of the population. What are we doing, as evangelical churches and Christians, to reach the other 85%?*
>
> *45% of the population of the UK is working class.*[278] *Yet how many of our UK evangelical churches reflect that? How many of the leaders reflect that? What about our outreach and our church planting? How often are we doing it in working-class and/or deprived communities? Yet so much of Yorkshire, and the UK, is like that.*[279]

It is clear that there is a spiritual deficit in some of the neediest council estates and schemes of our land. I see it in the valleys in Wales, in the paramilitary (of all stripes) housing estates in Northern Ireland. The problem is huge in the council estates of the UK, where the north of England is practically a spiritual wasteland. In Scotland, we can drive past scheme after scheme with little or no established gospel churches.

Something needs to change. Denominations need to review their church planting and revitalisation strategies. The UK church needs to wake from its (largely) middle-class slumber. Its institutions are middle class. Huge amounts of funds and personnel are poured into middle-class planting ventures and para-church organisations. And those of us working in poor communities with little financial support and boots on the ground are being left in the dust.

CHURCHES, GRANT-MAKING BODIES AND CHRISTIANS PRIORITISE PROJECTS OVER PEOPLE

Recently, 20schemes began a new initiative called "Retrain".[280] Our intention is to provide meaningful employment opportunities (through small business start-ups and buying small cafes, for example) for Christian men and women from the schemes who may not have ever held down a job, have been long-term unemployed, and/or have faced (or still face) long-term addiction and mental health issues. But the main purpose behind the venture is to use the profits to fund our main mission of church planting in Scotland's poorest communities.

Here's what I have observed while raising money for some of our projects. In December 2020, we began a month-long funding initiative to raise start-up capital. We raised almost a quarter of a million pounds in less than four weeks. When we have needed to raise funds for building projects in some of the schemes, the money (running into the hundreds of thousands) has been relatively easy to find. Yet when I compare that to raising funds for a church planter and his family, or for an intern or woman's worker, the money dries up. The process takes much longer, and it is more difficult to raise finances for people than it is for projects.

Grant-making bodies and funding institutions want to see "measurables". They're used to funding para-church ministries that can provide tangible "results". For instance, they like to be able to tell a funder, "Your donation fed 1,000 families this year." It doesn't have quite the same ring to it when a church planter says, "Your donation enabled me to speak to 30 people this year about Jesus. None were saved. But they took away a book." Funders want to see, "A bang for their buck." One funder openly admitted to me that if I got creative and marketed the ministry more like a para-church organisation, then we would get more money. "Find out how much crime has gone down in your area and put that in a report", he said to me. "Keep track of the number of tracts you hand out. How many meal packages you hand out. All these things help."

What on earth are we doing in the Christian world when I am being asked to "get creative" with my reporting in order to gain funding?

Perhaps the most difficult part of trying to plant and revitalise churches in the schemes and council estates is the lack of middle-class Christians willing to come and join us in the work. This leads us to one of the most pernicious sins of the modern UK Christian.

Sharon Dickens is Director of 20schemes Women's Ministry.

"Every time our women go to a conference to speak about life on the schemes, someone always asks them, 'What about your children? Aren't you worried bringing them up on a scheme?' At some point, Miriam McConnell, our 20schemes Ministry Wives Co-ordinator, will respond by saying, "If God has called you to the schemes, then he's called your children as well.'

Middle-class Christians have an obsession with their children which borders on idolatry. One of the most offensive books I have ever read on our communities was written by a middle-class pastor. In the book he interviews a middle-class man working on a council estate and asks him about some of the ways in which he has counted the cost in his ministry. He responded by saying that he was resigned to his teenage daughter becoming pregnant in her teens! He considered that to be part of the hardship of taking the gospel to the estate he was on. To say that I was angry and offended was an understatement!

I doubt it was meant to come across as offensive as the way it had been (badly) written. But all too often the subtext of what middle-class people are communicating is, 'Why would we put our children in communities that risk teen pregnancy, drug addiction and poor educational options?'

I've lived my whole life on a scheme and raised my children here too. Both my children went to university (Edinburgh and St Andrews), both are over 25 and don't have any children as yet. Neither do drugs. Both drink alcohol, but only recreationally. The only shame they have caused me is by attending Comicon conferences! The reality is that my children have had more access to drugs, sex, porn and alcohol from their middle-class, affluent friends than they ever did spending time in the schemes.

Yes, there may be times when we have to navigate complicated situations, especially if your child's best pal is the local drug dealer's child, and they want to have a sleepover. Yes, your child may hear and see things at the park that might need some discussion afterwards. They may get picked on or hear words that are unacceptable. We can't pack our children in bubble wrap, separated and excluded from the world around them. We need to teach them to navigate the world with Christ at the centre. The Christian women who struggle to even contemplate moving their family to a scheme for ministry tend to be the ones who have made their children, and not Christ, the centre of their universe."

COUNTING THE COST

I (Mez) have spoken to many churches over the years about church planting in housing estates and schemes. I have talked to more elder boards than I can remember about some housing estate or another that their church straddled. Everybody agrees that the problem is serious. Residents from these communities are not present at Sunday worship. Any contact they do have is either through children or some kind of outreach, such as a food bank, homeless shelter, etc. They all agree that something needs to be done. Here's where the conversation ends.

Every. Single. Time.

"What do you think we should do about it?" That's the question I get in one form or another. So, I follow up by asking the same question. Every time. "Do you think these people are going to hell outside of Jesus?" "Of course, we do!" they say, "But we can't find anybody in the church willing to do the job." "You do it, then", I say. "Sell all you have and get every leader in this church move into the community. That will make a statement to your people. That will show them where your true priorities lie." Every single one of them, without exception, will look at me as if I have gone quite mad. Then, I will get almost the same response, regardless of where I am in the UK. "Oh no, we couldn't do that. My wife would kill me." Cue polite chuckling and the conversation comes to an end.

I have lost count of the number of times I have spoken to men with a real heart for ministry in a council estate or housing scheme and yet, when they have gone home, their wives have talked them out of it. They don't want to count the cost. They're quite happy for somebody else to do it, as long as it isn't them. They'll move overseas, if it only means that they don't have to move into some run-down community on the edge of town. They'll tell themselves that they're only being good parents. That their fears about schooling and crime and the state of the housing are sensible and not down to a complete lack of faith and trust in Almighty God.

There are a lot of middle-class Christian women in the UK who have a lot to answer for, and they bear a great deal of responsibility for the lack of personnel coming to join the frontline ministry on council estates and housing schemes. Millions are perishing without Jesus because they are more worried about their children's standard of education, or whether or not their house may get burgled, when millions are going to a lost eternity. When Jesus tells us "to count the cost", I'm pretty sure that he doesn't mean stay at home, live a nice life, have some children, see them into university, get them married, get a few grandchildren, retire and then die.

Consider Jesus's words in Luke 9:56–62 (ESV):

> *And they went on to another village. As they were going along the road, someone said to him, "I will follow you wherever you go." And Jesus said to him, "The foxes have holes and the birds*

of the air have nests, but the Son of Man has nowhere to lay his head." And he said to another, "Follow me." But he said, "Lord, let me first go and bury my father." And Jesus said to him, "Leave the dead to bury their own dead. But as for you, go and proclaim the kingdom of God." Yet another said, "I will follow you, Lord, but let me first say farewell to those at my home." Jesus said to him, "No one who puts his hand to the plough and looks back is fit for the kingdom of God."

SPOTLIGHT:

THE LACK OF FUNDING AND PERSONNEL

IAN WILLIAMSON, PASTOR,
NEW LIFE CHURCH, MIDDLESBROUGH

WHY IS FUNDRAISING SO HARD IN THE UK?

All of our church staff team had given up good jobs to be self-funded gospel workers, working full-time on less than the minimum wage. We were doing ministry in an area that was described by both Acts 29 and the FIEC as a *gospel priority area*. Despite this, neither Acts 29 nor the FIEC was able to offer me help when it came to fundraising and recruiting personnel. "It's very difficult to attract people to a town like Middlesbrough," they said. "If you want to plant a church there, then you will have to do it on your own."

Even though they supported in principle what I was trying to do, neither of these bodies (at the time) released funding for church planters. That left me trying to plant a church in the UK's poorest town, pastoring people with complex social and mental health problems and trying to network and raise finances for our fledgling work.[281] It was hard, backbreaking, soul-destroying work. I applied for grant after grant. I made short films promoting our work. I went to conference after conference on church planting to try to make the case for a gospel church in Middlesbrough's poorest communities. I sometimes got the odd handout. But it wasn't much and it was not nearly enough to sustain the ministry.

In five years, I got nowhere.

I was tired, discouraged, angry and just weeks from shutting the work down. I was frustrated that even though our ministry was praised by Christian networks, denominations and media, we still didn't have the financial support and backing that was needed to pay a pastor.

Fortunately, a small council estate church in Hardwick, Stockton bailed us out and gave us three months of funding, and then Niddrie Community Church in Edinburgh partnered with us and agreed to fully fund my salary for the foreseeable future.

Church planting is tough in any context. In my life, I am surrounded by need. Drug addicts. Suicidal people. Failing schools. Crime. Violence. Yet, my toughest battle is, and always has been, finding financial support and people willing to lay aside their middle-class aspirations and join us in our battle to bring Jesus to the people of Middlesbrough.

Pastoring troubled people is not my biggest distraction. Nor is it the case for brothers in similar contexts in other towns and cities across the UK. We are driven to distraction and exhausted trying to raise financial support and attract Christians to help us on the front lines.

Why is this?

COUNCIL ESTATE CHRISTIANS ARE ANONYMOUS TO FUNDERS

When starting out in ministry, I was self-funded and was encouraged to attend a training course called, "Funding the Family Business". It was run by Stewardship, a Christian financial support services charity.[282] This training is well regarded and many people who have attended it have found it hugely beneficial. So, when I signed up for the training, I was very excited and I really believed that it would be the answer to my fundraising issues.

My excitement soon faded when I realised that the training focused on encouraging the delegates to seek most of their personal support from Christian family, friends and churches with whom they were connected. We were taught that we should use our pastoral contacts in order to gain opportunities to share about our ministries in Sunday services or midweek prayer meetings. It was all about building partnerships with local churches.

This was all helpful stuff, but only for those who had grown up in a church environment and who had lots of pre-existing Christian friendships and contacts. I was a first-generation Christian from a council estate. I didn't come to faith in Jesus until my late 20s. I didn't have lifetime Christian friendships. Many of the delegates at the training were able to make lists of friends and contacts forged in their home churches, Christian camps, university and Christian conferences.

My piece of paper was largely blank.

I hadn't had any of those experiences in my life and I had never really come into contact with Christians or their subculture. That meant that the traditional way of raising money and attracting personnel was closed to people like me.

COUNCIL ESTATE CHRISTIANS HAVE NO CULTURAL CAPITAL

I was never invited to speak at churches about our church plant because I just didn't have the contacts or social capital. I was left to email churches, make telephone calls and badger network leaders to get a five-minute hearing. This approach took up a lot of time and, initially, I was regarded suspiciously by pastors who had never heard of me. Even if I was given a five-minute slot to share, I was told that the church already had mission partners.

Even though I began to get noticed by networks such as Acts 29 GB and the FIEC, there was still no clear pathway to funding and personnel. People protected their funders with paranoid zeal and would not share their contacts with me.

Even now, after over 10 years of fundraising for our work, I am still finding out about funding streams that I can apply to. In the Christian world, it's not what you know, but who you know that makes all the difference.

COUNCIL ESTATE CHRISTIANS ARE TOO HONEST

Funders are rarely encouraged by what we do. In fact, they are shocked at what we don't do. And, perhaps most surprising of all, they are shocked by our honesty.

Firstly, after applying for funding, we are very rarely asked about the work we do in the local pub, cafes, library and hairdressers. Instead, we are asked why we don't do things like a CAP Centre, a food bank, an Alpha or Christianity Explored course. But funders don't like it when we say, "Because these things are useless and don't work in our context." They listen to us speak about building community relationships and they tune out. They want numbers and measurable statistics. This is further exacerbated by the small number of converts we see in the short to medium term. Then, when we speak about the high number of backsliders, we are seen as too much of a financial risk and not a viable investment.

I know exactly what funders want me to say to gain their money, but I refuse to massage the figures and present the work in a way that keeps these people happy and interested. It's hard, brutal work and they need to know it upfront.

COUNCIL ESTATE CHRISTIANS ARE TORN BETWEEN PROMOTING MINISTRY AND DOING MINISTRY

In the early days, my main financial support came from other small, struggling council estate churches. But this wasn't enough to fund the work. I needed to look for ways to build partnerships with some bigger, wealthier churches and networks. I started writing blogs and doing videos to post online. I argued with people on social media. I made a noise about the work. Before long, I was travelling the country sharing about our work, which meant that I was spending more time writing and talking *about* the ministry and less time actually *doing* the work.

Preaching was taking second place to writing. Evangelism was getting in the way of me buttering up a pastor of a wealthy church. Before I knew it, my fundraising had become more important than my ministry. I was left with a dilemma. Concentrate on the church and risk it failing because of a lack of funding? Or concentrate on fundraising and risk the church failing for lack of gospel faithfulness?

I chose the latter.

The real crime is that I am forced to do so by an evangelical funding and recruitment system that is not fit for purpose – it totally fails to aid the poorest pastors in the poorest communities of the UK.

SPOTLIGHT:

WE HAVE A PROBLEM RESOURCING THE CHURCH IN DEPRIVED COMMUNITIES

STEPHEN KNEALE, PASTOR, BETHEL CHURCH, OLDHAM[283]

We have a problem with resourcing the church in deprived communities. Let me state, in the plainest possible terms, what it is that most under-resourced churches need.

PRAYER

I do not mean generic prayer like, "We pray for Deprived Church on the Crack Den Council Estate. We pray they would get whatever it is they probably need (you know what it is, Lord, we don't because we didn't ask them) and that you would provide it miraculously entirely apart from our having to do anything."

I mean real and informed prayer.

Get in touch and ask how you can pray for us more intelligently. It may shock you to know that some of us find it quite embarrassing asking others to pray for us apropos of nothing. A lot of middle-class people have never had to contend with the sheer awkwardness of going cap in hand to those who may graciously choose to offer some help. As such, it is so heartening when people ring or email you to ask how they can pray for you in a more informed manner. It means we are not foisting ourselves upon you, rather that you have actively sought us to see how you might be able to partner with us in prayer.

SUPPORT

Again, I do not mean cursory support. Despite what anybody says, and as helpful as it can be, a Christian fraternal does not qualify as credible support. These things, at best, offer an opportunity to meet those with whom you might *become* friends. Real friendship and support is likely to be found *outside* of the fraternal itself – the meeting being just that, a meeting.

Real support means real friendship. It means speaking with people outside of these meetings, going for a coffee and discussing how we might actually help one another. I have said it before and I'll say it again, fellowship cannot be reduced to little more than meetings. If the extent of our fellowship is sitting next to someone in a meeting at which someone else speaks, and then engaging in a bit of small talk afterwards, we are doing it wrong.

MONEY

We are all pretty familiar with the phrase, "Put your money where your mouth is." It is quite tiresome to hear lots of talk about support and help that, invariably, never extends to our bank accounts. We're very happy calling our members to "give generously" to our church – but then, as churches, tend to be less generous in giving it out.

As a small church running on a continual deficit (I was informed at our most recent meeting with the church treasurer that for the last quarter it was nearly £5,000), we still give regularly to mission partners and affiliate bodies. In deprived communities, it is hard to rely upon the wealth of those converting to give substantially to the church. Despite the fact that most do give from what they have, when it comes to supporting the work of the church, it is unreasonable to expect asylum seekers and those on benefits to fund the entirety of the ministry. We would need huge numbers of them to maintain a church on their ability to give alone.

We have had some people from outside the church give us financial support (for which we are extremely grateful), but it is simply not enough to support the work on its own. Churches in areas like ours need outside supporters to help us survive.

WORKERS

Ultimately, and perhaps even more importantly than financial support, we need workers to come and settle. Workers will bring their own finances. Either they will be funded by sending churches, or they will simply be people in secular work with a gospel heart coming into the area. An influx of workers would both help the financial situation of the church and increase the ministry of the church. Ultimately, we want people to come to know Christ and, to do this, we need workers who are able to commit to the town and share Him with those that live here.

The problem is that churches in deprived communities are getting almost none of these things. Churches and organisations do nothing to encourage workers to move to deprived areas. We may put up adverts for ministry trainees and church planters, but due to a lack of funds, we are asking people to do their own fundraising. It is hard enough getting people to move to deprived areas as it is, without having to ask them to pay for the privilege of living somewhere most people are trying to leave. It would be great if someone, or several someones, would set up a fund that would pay workers for one or two years to live, work and/or train in deprived towns like Oldham. We simply aren't able to fund it ourselves.

Without putting too fine a point on it, we have no outside supporters giving financially to the work of the church. We have not seen a single penny from any organisation to which we are affiliated, nor from any other church. There are even so-called "resourcing churches" who have shown precisely no interest in sending us either financial support, or workers to help in existing ministry, or those who might come and plant on local unreached estates.

Support has been lacking and the only thing we have received from anywhere is prayer. I do not want to denigrate how important prayer is to the work, we truly covet prayer, but doesn't John say, "let us not love in words or speech but with actions and in truth" (1 Jn. 3:18)? Didn't John also say, "If anyone has the material possessions and sees a brother or sister in need but has no pity on them, how can the love of God be in that person?" (1 Jn. 3:17). Is "We'll pray for you" alone a legitimate response to John's words?

We have members who don't know where their next meal is coming from and who cannot afford to turn on the lights at home unless we help them out. There are people in Oldham who will not hear the gospel, and who face a lost eternity, but for the fact that our church is here. How do John's words stack up when weighed against the building projects and extension plans of churches up and down the country for extra seats and a bit more storage space?

Let us not be satisfied with loving simply in words and speech. Let us love with actions and in truth.

CHAPTER 7

HOW MODERN CHURCH PLANTERS HEAR THE CALL OF THE WORLD MORE THAN THE CALL OF THE LORD

MEZ MCCONNELL

RACE AND PLACE

David P. Leong has written an incredibly helpful book entitled, *Race and Place: How urban geography shapes the journey to reconciliation.*[284] Despite the fact that it is written from the perspective of American racial injustice, I found that it spoke to our UK class problem in profound ways.

I briefly touched on this subject in an earlier chapter but I feel the need to return to the topic because it is so prescient in our current discussion on poverty, class and church planting. I remember a few years ago some black church-planting brothers from Atlanta came to visit Niddrie and they were shocked to discover that gentrification was happening in white neighbourhoods in the UK. In their experience, it was overwhelmingly a black problem, rather than a problem for deprived communities.

The problem with gentrification is that it is both good and bad. There is little doubt that our community in Niddrie has benefitted enormously from gentrification. We have new schools, a new hospital, a library and a shopping centre. Crime has gone down significantly. But it has also gutted the life out of our community. Many people have been rehoused against their will, and the local indigenous population have not been involved in any of the decision-making processes.

Yes, there are better facilities, but only for those who can afford them. Rents are sky high and no local could even think about affording a new-build home. What is worse is that there is a huge separation between the newcomers and the locals. Niddrie is well over a century old, and many families have been here for generations. Newcomers have no sense of the local pride and history of the place. They just see that a dump (in their eyes) has been cleaned up and made habitable for them and their aspirational middle-class families.

Leong describes the process in American terms:

> *Whole communities (almost always communities of colour), who for decades had been abandoned by white flight and public neglect, were suddenly in the cross hairs of many economic opportunists who saw dollar signs in the dirt.*[285]

What is particularly galling for those of us from the schemes is that the reason for making our communities better (at least in developers' eyes) is not for our benefit – it's not to make *our lives* better. Rather, it is for the benefit of the incoming middle classes and the young professionals looking to get a foothold on the housing ladder. As Leong notes, "Of course gentrification seems like a good thing to those who benefit from the changes and see them as normal and desirable."[286]

Those moving into our communities give no thought to the fact that their new town house sits on the site that was treasured by somebody's grandparents and great-grandparents. Nor are they interested in associating with the locals. The fact that they form their own neighbourhood watch committees, work in the city, socialise with their (largely university-educated) friends outside the scheme and, at the first opportunity, sell their new-build home for the promise of a bigger and better one across the city is a clear indication that they are not invested in bettering our community, but in bettering their own lives.

In fact, they are only interested in protecting their assets and ensuring their offspring go to a good school. Leong sees the same thing in the USA: "Perhaps the greatest cost of gentrification is the inevitable erasure of communities and histories that occurs through transition and displacement."[287]

THE GENTRIFYING CHURCH

What is truly offensive for me, as a planter/pastor, is listening to city-centre churches who now see our gentrified community (or at least the new builds) as fertile grounds for church planting. They never saw our communities that way before money and the middle class came to town! But all of a sudden, we look like a more desirable prospect.

It is inescapable that most church planting and revitalisation in the UK follows the money and the geographical places where monied people are located. Leong's challenge to the UK church is as follows:

> *If we follow the geography of grace in the cities, then one place I believe we'll find ourselves is not primarily with the "movers and shakers" above us, but "underneath the bridge with the moved and shaken".*[288]

Let's be honest about the church planting and church revitalisation strategies of most middle-class churches and denominations. I can tell you from cold, hard experience that the least, the last and the lost communities of our nation are very far down their list, even if they are on the radar at all.

Some churches protest and say that their Sunday gatherings are made up of people from all walks of life. But that Sunday attendance is not necessarily indicative of an integrated community life. Meeting together on a Sunday is not the same as being one in Christ. Leong says, "If the church is going to offer some real good news in broken communities, it has to be committed to a place."[289]

We will not be able to build friendships across social divides if we don't live near one another, socialise outside the Sunday gatherings and share life together regularly. Surely, we are only truly in community together when we worship together, pray together, study the Scriptures together, live together, shop together and love each other?

HEALING THE CLASS DIVIDE

According to Leong, if we want to heal the social divide in our churches, then we need to ask ourselves some serious questions:

- Where do we experience belonging, and why?
- With whom do we most identify, and what does that mean for those of a different class/race?

How have we located our lives – residentially, socially and vocationally – in ways that may simply reinforce our preconceived understandings of identity and community? It is going to take painful steps for those of us across the class divide to bring healing in our communities and churches.

Decades of neglect and misunderstanding will not be resolved overnight. That much is obvious. But we have a

Saviour who died to save us and to bring down these walls of hostility. We have a great responsibility to the gospel and to one another. *Can it be done?* I believe it can. But it will take a radical awakening, a lot of faith, some pain, a bucket load of tears and a confidence that the local church is God's only plan to manifest His manifold wisdom to the watching world.

If you are a church leader, then ask yourself these questions:

- Where are the poorest parts of my city and could we plant/revitalise a church there?
- Is there a pastor/planter struggling in a poor community that we could come alongside to help practically with finances and/or people?
- How many people from poor communities are being trained for leadership in our church?
- How many of our interns come from council estates/schemes?

If you are a denominational leader then think about these questions:

- Are our training days and/or conferences really open to people from poorer communities? Or are they priced out of them?
- Do the people we put on platforms only come from educated or middle-class backgrounds? Why is that?
- Are our institutions out of reach for people from poorer communities? Book smart does not always translate to God-gifted.

- How much money and how many resources are we pouring into planting and / or revitalising churches in poor communities?
- How many grants did we give out to people from council estates / schemes in the past year?

Wanting to take the gospel to students, the business communities and the newly minted housing estates is not wrong. Wanting to plant new churches near them is not wrong. What is wrong is ignoring the lost who bring no financial gains to your church, or who only bring more complex pastoral problems. Are you ignoring the least and the last?

Jesus calls us to feed His sheep. Not just the expensive-looking ones. Not just the healthiest ones. Not just the ones with great future prospects. Not just the ones who are easiest to engage with. Not just the ones we feel comfortable with.

All of them. Whichever dark corner of our cities, towns and villages they come from.

I was once approached at a Christian conference and asked the following question: "You're very good at telling us what the problem is. But what is the answer?"

The answer is simple:

We need to plant and revitalise more gospel churches in housing estates and schemes across the UK.

And as we do so, we must rethink pretty much everything about church life, church ministries and church training.

PART IV:

RETHINKING EVERYTHING IN LIGHT OF THE LOCAL CHURCH

SPOTLIGHT:

WHY WE NEED THE CHURCH IN OUR POOREST COMMUNITIES

JOEL KURZ, PASTOR, GARDEN CHURCH, BALTIMORE, USA

Joel pastors a church in Baltimore, one of the poorest and most violent cities in the USA. I asked him to write an essay on this topic for me. "But this is a book about the UK," you may be saying to yourself. Indeed, it is. But the points he makes transfer to every community in every nation on the planet, not least to those who suffer from poverty and deprivation.

Our communities are broken by addiction and violence. Abandoned houses line the streets. Children need mentors. Joblessness and poverty are real problems. Day-to-day ministry is tough.

For many who want to reach these areas with the gospel, it seems natural to ask:

- How can the church be more relevant?
- In what ways can we transform the community?
- What are the best practices for poverty ministry?

However, if you put the following questions to such people, they're likely to think you've lost it:

- Who leads the church?
- What role does the congregation have in authority?
- What is the meaning of church membership?

Several years ago, I was exploring the possibility of helping another ministry in our city. The leader told me up front, "In order to do church among the poor, we need to throw out everything we know about the church and start all over. Forget discussions on church polity, we need to feed the hungry and clothe the naked."

ECCLESIOLOGY MATTERS

Here's what I told him: "Ecclesiology matters for churches in poor communities." Despite what many Christians who are working in hard places may say, good ecclesiology is vital to gospel ministry among the poor. If we want to see impoverished communities reached with the gospel, then we must prioritise building healthy churches.

But wait, why are we talking about *ecclesiology*? Many of our people don't even know what that word means. Many *pastors* don't even know what that word means. Does it really matter?

In order to answer that question, we need to start by defining ecclesiology. Simply put, ecclesiology is the doctrine of the church. These questions (and many others) make up our ecclesiology: *What is the church? Who leads it? Who belongs to it? What's the purpose and mission of the church?*

EXAMPLE FROM HISTORY

Reading books written by dead guys reminds me of the things that Christians in the past took seriously. Recently, I read a book by Charles Octavius Boothe called, *Plain Theology for Plain People.*[290]

As an African American, Boothe was born a slave in 1845. He became the first pastor at Dexter Avenue Baptist Church in Montgomery, Alabama. I can only imagine, given his context, that Boothe faced any number of hardships in his church.

Therefore, it may surprise us to discover that when Boothe talked about healthy ministry, he talked about *the centrality of the church*. He talked about church leadership, the congregation, the need to serve the poor and church discipline. As he addresses what church members should do, he says that they should "attend faithfully the public services of the sanctuary, and duly observe the Lord's Supper. It is also incumbent on the church in the admission of members to see that the ordinance of baptism is properly administered."[291] Can you imagine someone today – serving in a ministry context of poverty and oppression – saying, "Okay church, here are the two things we need to focus on: baptism and communion." It's unheard of. Why did Boothe emphasise the ordinances, church discipline, membership and church leadership? Because he knew that ecclesiology mattered – no matter the context. This is as true today as it was in Boothe's day.

So, why does ecclesiology matter in poor communities? Here are three reasons:

1. ECCLESIOLOGY HELPS CHURCHES ACCURATELY DISPLAY GOD'S GLORY

In the Bible, the church is referred to as a holy nation and a royal priesthood (1 Pet. 2:9). Jesus calls us to be salt and light in Matthew 5:13–15. Paul refers to the church as the temple in which God lives in Ephesians 2:20–22. We're also called a family by Paul in 2 Corinthians 6:18. Perhaps the most shocking analogy is this: the church as Christ's body in Ephesians 1:22–23.

These metaphors help us to see the centrality of the church in God's purposes. It's the primary way He intends to display His glory to the world (Eph. 3:10). Therefore, church polity – how the church is governed – is hugely important. Thankfully, God's Word explains everything for us – from who leads the church, to who constitutes the church, to matters of discipline and accountability, and even how we should approach Him in worship.

So, ecclesiology is our attempt to rightly understand and apply God's principles for His church. Here's the point: churches in poor communities accurately display God's glory as we embrace biblical ecclesiology.

2. ECCLESIOLOGY HELPS CHURCHES BECOME A COUNTERCULTURAL COMMUNITY

As we accurately show off God's glory, we display something else: a countercultural community. Good ecclesiology should lead a church towards a biblical concern for one another, the right and proper use of authority, and a governance where all stand equal before God. Just think about a few differences between the church and the world.

- Out there, we have divisions. In here, we are one.
- Out there, we hide our faults. In here, we are safe to confess our failures to one another.
- Out there, authority is often abused. In here, those in authority know they will answer to God.
- Out there, it's cut-throat. In here, we take responsibility for each other.

- Out there, disagreements are ugly and brutal. In here, we follow God's direction for dissension, disagreement and reconciliation.
- Out there, nobody submits to anyone (except maybe themselves). In here, we submit to God, our leadership and one another.

The church is a small taste of heaven. Just a taste. And yes, it's a taste mixed with toxins at times. Yet even in our failures, the Spirit does something supernatural and we display a new community to those who have otherwise lost hope.

3. ECCLESIOLOGY KEEPS CHURCHES FROM DESPAIR

A right understanding of the church will lead us to a right understanding of our mission in the community. Our job is not to transform a neighbourhood, but to transform a people within the community who will display God's glory to the neighbourhood and the nations. This, after all, is what Jesus instructed: "Therefore go and make disciples of all nations". He tells us in Matthew 28:19.

Without a proper understanding of the church, we might think our job is to end poverty. *It would be amazing if we could!* But what if we are faithful for 30 years and everyone is still poor? Have we failed? Without a proper understanding of the church, we might think our job is to get everyone in the community off drugs and into jobs. *It would be great if we could!* But what if joblessness remains a problem and the drug epidemic gets worse? Have we failed?

Don't get me wrong, I'm all for jobs, addiction ministry and helping people into employment. Those are good works we need to discuss. My point is simply this: only Christ's return will completely change our poorest communities (or any communities for that matter). One day, He'll come back, the wicked will be judged and His kingdom will be made visible.

Until then, the church is a group of strangers and aliens in a foreign land. We're organised and directed by God through His Word. We live as salt and light. As the body of Christ, we testify to the world who He is and what He's done. We are a beacon of hope for the lost. And we are a family of believers, according to Hebrews 10:25 (ESV), who are "encouraging one another, and all the more as [we] see the Day drawing near".

Ecclesiology matters. As we develop healthy churches, we relentlessly and joyfully produce countercultural communities which accurately display God's glory. One day, Jesus will return. Until that day, let us be reminded that Jesus said in Matthew 16:18: "I will build my church". It's *His* church. Let's build and lead them the way He directs.

CHAPTER 1:
WHY LOCAL CHURCHES MATTER

THE LOCAL CHURCH IS CENTRAL TO THE PURPOSES OF GOD

People often say to me: "You're the guy obsessed with the local church." My response is always the same: Jesus was obsessed with the local church far more than I am! In fact, Jesus was so in love with the church that He gave His own lifeblood for her.

The church, both universal and local, is so important to the Lord. We see that all over Scripture. The Bible teaches us that the church is central to the purposes of God. Therefore, it should be central to the life of every true Christian. Paul, writing to the Ephesians in 5:25, 29 (ESV), says: "Husbands, love your wives, as Christ loved the church and gave himself up for her ... For no one ever hated his own flesh, but nourishes and cherishes it, just as Christ does the church."

Jesus loves the church.

We often forget that simple truth. We so often grumble and moan about the church, and yet we read in Acts 20:28 that Jesus has built the church *with His own blood*. The church is built for Jesus, by Jesus and on Jesus. We cannot separate Jesus from the local church.

This is so very important because there are many so-called Christians and, incredibly, even church planters who think that we can. There are an increasing number of people today who think they can live their Christian life at arm's-length from the body of God's people. As if the local church is an interruption in their lives and gets in the way of their personal spirituality. A friend once said to me: "If the gospel is the diamond in the great salvific plan of God, then the church is the metal clasp that supports it, holds it up and shows it in its greatest light for all the world to see."

THE LOCAL CHURCH IS IMPORTANT FOR THE WATCHING WORLD

Paul wrote to the church at Ephesus, saying, "And he put all things under his feet and gave him as head over all things to the church, which is his body, the fullness of him who fills all in all" (Eph. 1:22–23, ESV). The church has been created to be a witness to Jesus in the world. It is *His* head and body here on earth.

When this was written, it was to Jews, Greeks, slaves and free people. People from all walks of life. The same is true whether we are in the schemes of Scotland or a trailer park in the deep south of America. The worldwide church consists of people who have worked all their lives, people who have never worked, people who are fit and well and people who are ill and dying. Men, women and children. Some have been to university and some have never finished high school. The point is that if we claim to follow Jesus, then we are all one in Him, whether we live in Paris, New York or Edinburgh. We all represent Christ here on earth through our local body of believers.

It is this universal body, showcased in local bodies across the world, that is meant to be a light to the nations. We are meant to be countercultural. We are meant to reflect the holiness and justice of God. We are meant to hold forth gospel hope to the lost and hopeless. In fact, we are the only true source of hope and joy for a world that is wasting away. We are called to be salt and light right where we are.

Each Christian is called to imitate Jesus regardless of their income, their personal circumstances or their social status. We can be Christ's ambassadors *right where we are.* We may not have a state-of-the-art building to meet in. We may not have a large congregation. We may not have a great social media presence or a strong music group. But each of us is called to be a light to the world around us.

Who will be the light to our poor communities if it is not local churches, holding out the gospel and passing on the baton? We need flaming bonfires of gospel light burning brightly in the darkness of our schemes and housing estates. We need the gospel light burning so bright in our midst that it reaches into all the dark places of our land. What better place to see this light burn fiercely than in a healthy, gospel-focused, local church community? A healthy, gospel-centred church is a shining beacon of light to the watching world that lives in the shadows.

Why do we need churches on schemes and council estates? The answer to that question is obvious.

THE LOCAL CHURCH IS WHERE THE BELIEVER GROWS MORE LIKE CHRIST

It is primarily in the local church where Christians learn doctrine, receive reproof and are trained in righteousness (Eph. 4:11–13). The local church provides opportunities for growth that are available nowhere else. In our schemes and council estates, people need the concerted time and effort that only a local church can provide. Very often people will turn up on our doorstep having heard the gospel through some para-church ministry. Yet they almost always have large gaps in their biblical knowledge and Christian behaviour. Without a local church committed to patiently and systematically teaching and training them, these people will flounder indefinitely.

I have said a lot about mercy ministries that you may well disagree with. But I guarantee that you will recognise the importance of local churches helping individuals and families go on in life. Working in our communities with people who have complex social and psychological needs means that:

- More than one agency is required to work with an individual and/or family.
- There are no easy solutions.
- Individuals need long-term commitment and attachment to some form of "stable" family/community.

In fact, it is well documented that individuals who have a solid, consistent support base when they leave rehabilitation centres tend to do far better when it comes to their recovery and reintegration back into mainstream society. It is for this reason that I believe the best mercy ministry is a healthy, gospel-centred church established in the areas of greatest need in our society. We all need a local church if we are to grow in Christlikeness.

THE LOCAL CHURCH IS THE PLACE WHERE BELIEVERS MUST SUBMIT THEMSELVES TO SPIRITUAL AUTHORITY

As discussed, many people from many walks of life struggle with issues of authority, though this problem is especially prevalent in our communities of deprivation across the UK. It goes without saying that people who do not trust the civil authorities do not readily accept criticism or input from anybody they regard as an authority figure. This attitude needs to be dealt with immediately. God calls Christians to submit to spiritual authority within the local church (Heb. 13:17). All believers are called by God to put themselves under the care and oversight of elders. A culture that despises any kind of authority needs to see healthy models of leadership and submission. And the place for people to see this modelled best is in the local church.

THE LOCAL CHURCH IS THE BEST PLACE FOR SPIRITUAL ACCOUNTABILITY

We have probably all encountered people who believed they were called to ministry or who even carried out some kind of ministry even though their personal lives were a mess. This happens where people do not have proper spiritual accountability. All Christians need the spiritual accountability and discipline that being a member of the local church brings. It stops us from drifting. It offers a context for encouragement and rebuke. It provides a community to stir one another on to love and good deeds.

THE LOCAL CHURCH IS THE PLACE FROM WHICH DISCIPLINE IS BIBLICALLY ADMINISTERED

The task of disciplining disobedient or unruly Christians belongs to the local church. This is a difficult task, but one given specifically to the church as a means to show the deepest love and concern for the spiritual care of believers (Matt. 18:15–17). Discipline belongs to the church and is one of its most important functions.

Lesslie Newbiginn says this about the church:

It is surely a fact of inexhaustible significance that what our Lord left behind him was not a book or a creed, nor a system of thought, nor a rule of life, but a visible community ... He committed the entire work of salvation to that community.[292]

DOES IT REALLY MATTER WHO DOES THE JOB?

Despite all the protestations, many para-church agencies working in deprived communities are doing so outside any meaningful oversight of local churches (where they exist). In one sense, it is hard to fault them, because of the lack of gospel churches in deprived communities and the complete disinterest in seriously tackling this problem by the broader evangelical church.

Subsequently, these para-church organisations are left to use more affluent, middle-class churches as hunting grounds for young, socially-conscious Christians interested in helping the poor. They then use our areas and paint them in the worst possible light in order to garner the huge financial support needed to continue to promote their particular ministry. A visit to any of their top-end websites will discover that they talk about partnership with local churches, but the reality is this: partnership is rarely happening on the ground. The situation is further exacerbated by the fact that most middle-class church pastors (and pastors of middle-class churches) are overworked and thus are more than happy to "do their bit" for the poor by allowing so-called professionals to do it on their behalf.

Yet, as I have claimed, this approach isn't working. Therefore, what is required is the planting and revitalisation of gospel churches in our poorest communities. And this needs to happen as a matter of urgency and priority, regardless of denomination and creed. We are going to have to work really, really hard to do this. Turning round decades of neglect is not going to happen in five minutes. It's not going to happen by emptying skips and painting fences. We are going to have to think deeply and carefully and come up with a serious plan.

Somebody once said to me: "Who cares who is doing the work, as long as it is getting done. As long as somebody is making Jesus known, isn't that all that really matters?" I think it does matter how the job gets done. I think it matters very much indeed. In fact, I believe the local church should be *the primary agency* for change in our poorest communities. Where there are *no churches*, we should prioritise church planting. Where there are *aging and dying churches*, we should prioritise revitalisation.

In my opinion, any solutions put forward that don't begin from this starting point are doomed to repeat the failures of the past four or five decades.

SPOTLIGHT:

A RADICAL SOLUTION TO THE GREATEST INEQUALITY

STEVE BELL, PASTOR, GRACE CHURCH, ISLE OF WIGHT[293]

"The greatest inequality [in the UK] is a lack of gospel-preaching churches." These words were written by Stephen Kneale in response to a piece on Sky News about how the pandemic is exacerbating the already significant inequalities faced by the poorest communities in our country.[294] As Stephen noted, most of us tend to respond to articles like this with "an immediate emotional response, followed by some hand-wringing and calls of 'what can we do?' before the whole thing is soon forgotten".

As Stephen pointed out, it is worth realising that the greatest inequality in a deprived community is not to do with its *material* poverty caused by a lack of public provision or investment (serious though that is), but with its *gospel* poverty caused by the poor provision of Bible-believing, gospel-proclaiming churches.

So how can we address this need? What can we do differently to the past? How are we as Christians to respond? Is an emotional response, some hand-wringing and calls of "what can we do?" the best we can manage? It seems to me that this is exactly the response that the UK church has usually been guilty of.

As far as I can tell, most evangelical church planting in the UK is at least partially funded by a fairly small number of either national or regional church networks, some wealthier churches and the associated funds/trusts that they can access. I think that there are sufficiently few of these organisations that you could get senior representatives from all of them together in one room.

My suggestion is that this is done and that they agree together that, for the next ten years, all the new church plants that they help to finance in the UK will be in the more deprived communities (either urban or rural) that we have previously neglected, and that they will no longer help fund further new church plants in predominately middle-class or newly gentrified areas.

Of course, this is not to prevent middle-class churches planting in more middle-class areas if they want to and can pay for it themselves. It is simply to recognise that our most materially-deprived communities are also our most gospel-deprived communities. Therefore, going forward, we must be intentional about redressing the balance rather than just doing a bit of handwringing and forgetting.

I realise that this is a radical solution that many might feel just couldn't work. But I can see some distinct advantages to giving it serious consideration.

WHERE WILL WE FIND THE PLANTERS?

We have a serious problem in recruiting church planters who feel able to lead plants in more deprived communities. The language is often used of not feeling "called" to such contexts. However, I think we often use the language of not feeling "called" in order to simply justify remaining within the comfort of our existing (usually white, middle-class) subculture. If we were to agree to reallocate much of the centrally available funds in the way I'm suggesting, this could potentially be a much-needed catalyst to accomplish two further much needed changes.

- Training for ministry that includes much more UK cross-cultural equipping and exposure
- Expanding the routes into ministry to make them more accessible for training up more planters and pastors from within working-class and deprived communities

It has been recognised for years that we need a broader pool of planter/pastors than simply white, middle-class graduates. Plus, we need our white, middle-class graduates to have proper exposure and training for planting in the hard places. However, progress in this area has been painfully slow, so agreement to reallocate much of the funding could be a significant catalyst to drive forward changes in training too.

HUB CHURCHES FUNDING DEPRIVED MINISTRY

Church planting operates somewhat like the Research and Development department of the church. In other words, new contexts stimulate fresh and creative ways of making disciples, which produce ministry "models" to be picked up by others. (Examples would include the great work done to reach city-centre workers through lunchtime talks, or to disciple, train and release graduates through our university "hub" churches.) However, while we've been able to develop some great models for use in university towns and city-centre settings, we have very few models that translate into deprived urban or rural communities. This leaves prospective planters not only feeling culturally outside their comfort zone, but also with few models of how to proceed or other practitioners to advise them. This is slowly changing through organisations like 20schemes and other pastors and planters working in more deprived settings, but if we are to see "hub" churches resourcing work in deprived communities in the same way that they are in middle-class communities, then we need to give them much more investment.

INVEST MORE NOW RATHER THAN MUCH MORE LATER!

It's often said that its harder to plant in deprived communities, and we therefore need to think about how to make the most of our gospel investment. However, it could be said in response that it's our *lack* of gospel investment in deprived communities in the past that has resulted in the need for more investment now. But even if is harder and slower work, it is certainly not because deprived communities are harder to reach with the gospel than middle-class ones. Indeed, the reverse is probably true.

Of course, both the less wealthy and the more wealthy are equally in need of the gospel, yet if Jesus suggests anything in this area (for example, in Luke 4:18 or Luke 6:20–26), it is surely that it's the materially poor and the physically oppressed – those who have little or nothing in this world – that most keenly sense their need of God and so are most open to responding to Jesus's message.

Just imagine what a difference it could make if the handful of networks and trusts that help facilitate much of the church planting in the UK would collectively agree to redress the imbalance and channel a decade's worth of future resources (or more) into the more deprived communities that are so starved of gospel churches. Radical? Yes! But what a wonderful way of demonstrating to the world that the Christian answer to spiritual poverty is not simply handwringing. Instead of asking what we can do, we can say, "Here's what we are going to do."

SPOTLIGHT:

CHURCHES IN POOR COMMUNITIES DON'T EXIST TO SALVE MIDDLE-CLASS CONSCIENCES

STEPHEN KNEALE, PASTOR, BETHEL CHURCH, OLDHAM[295]

A few years ago, the Bishop of Burnley, Philip North, made some comments on mission to the poor. The high church Anglican was speaking to an audience at New Wine and saw his comments picked up in the mainstream media.

This prompted a discussion among a bunch of independent evangelicals. Some wish to push back on Bishop Philip's comments, insisting that evangelicals were doing a grand job of reaching deprived areas. Others accepted that the church at large was not doing a fantastic job but sought to suggest that their group/denomination/affiliates were bucking the trend. Others (predominantly those working in "hard to reach" areas) insisted the Bishop of Burnley was largely correct and that evangelicalism has a class problem, being as it is largely white, middle-class and unwilling to go to deprived communities.

It is interesting to note how some Christians in attractive areas of the country and in affluent churches claim that, even though the broader church is doing badly at reaching the poor, "their people" are the exception to the rule. By contrast, when we speak to pastors on the ground in poor communities, they report that they are both underfunded and, very often, ignored by larger churches and organisations. Clearly the perception in well-heeled, middle-class churches does not match the reality on the ground for those working in deprived communities!

The thing that irks me the most is the sense in which some middle-class and affluent churches, denominations or affiliations use those of us in deprived areas to claim their own part in mission to the poor. By being associated to those in deprived areas through formal and informal affiliations and groupings, they claim (or infer) that *they* are doing great things to reach the urban poor. This is despite the fact that not one of them has sent us one penny of funding or a single worker (which we would prefer) in order to support or bolster our work. They have neither sent these things directly nor have they indirectly given them to us via their contributions to the larger organisations with whom we are associated.

Pastors and planters in poor communities are not here to act as your ecclesiastical equivalent of, "I can't be racist, I've got lots of black friends." You are *not* reaching the poor or doing anything to advance mission in deprived communities simply by being formally or informally associated through denominations and affiliations to those doing this work. In fact, making such a claim is less credible than the "lots of black friends" line because, a lot of the time, we've never met nor had a direct conversation. We don't even know each other and yet, by our association through the same group, you claim a part in a work you've done precisely nothing to advance.

In the New Testament, those who actively prayed, gave money, met practical needs and sent workers were considered gospel partners. If you have done none of these things, in what way have you been a gospel partner? If you haven't done any of these things, what biblical example can you provide of being considered a fellow worker?

At an organisational level, the same applies. It is ridiculous for an organisation to claim it is engaged in mission to the poor simply because some of its member churches happen to be. Take the Church of England as an interesting example. Clearly, they have church buildings in deprived communities (as does the FIEC). But if many of those areas have become deprived since the churches were built, the organisation does nothing to offer funds or workers to such areas, and ordinands (and lay persons) refuse to move to those areas on the grounds of need, in what way is the organisation engaged in ministry to deprived communities? We might say some of their ministers and/or churches happen to be doing that work, but in what way are the organisation *supporting* this? You can't claim to be part of the ministry when, if those churches were not there, it would have literally no impact on your day-to-day working practice, funds or distribution of resources.

The proof that you are engaged in mission to the poor – even if you are not part of a church in a deprived community – is that your prayer meetings are given over to actively praying for those in such areas, your income is significantly reduced because you are giving funds away to those in such communities, and your membership is not as large as it might be because you are sending workers to churches in deprived areas. Whether you are an individual church or a larger organisation, if your finances, human resources and prayer times would bear no discernible difference if all the churches in deprived areas closed down, tell me in what way you are serving in such ministry?

Don't tell me what a wonderful job we're all doing at reaching the poor, deprived and ethnic minorities when the stats simply do not bear it out. Don't tell me you are doing anything to resolve this problem when your church is in an affluent area, full of educated people and your mission partners (if you have any) are not working in deprived communities. Until your cheque clears, the workers you have sent arrive and your regular emails asking me how you can pray for us are becoming burdensome, you are not involved in the work of reaching deprived communities.

It should be to our shame that, for all our talk of doctrinal purity, it is denominations many of us would write off as "liberal" or "compromised" who have actually gone to such communities. Whatever else we may say about them, they are at least committed to the poor. If the gospel that is peddled in many of our deprived towns is sub-optimal (even false), we must surely bear some responsibility for refusing to go and for failing to support those Bible-believing, mission-hearted people that would. You cannot claim to care for the poor if you are happy to see them head to hell because you would not go and reach them, would not support those who would reach them and do nothing but wring your hands while claiming to have done something because you "recognise the problem".

We are not here to salve the consciences of those who will neither come nor support ministry to the poor. We refuse to be patronised and wheeled out as an example of how *other* churches and organisations are burdened by the disgraceful reality that UK evangelicalism is an almost exclusively middle-class affair – a burden they gladly express by their "gratefulness" for us while simultaneously doing nothing to support us. We are here because we love the Lord Jesus, we take seriously His commission, we believe the gospel claim is good news for the poor, and we long to see His kingdom advanced among those He tells us plainly in Scripture will respond. We do not need your hand-wringing or your clarity in "identifying the issue", we need your money, your people, your prayer. Until you genuinely engage in these kind of ways, your talk is simply a means of comforting yourself in your lack of action and you remain part of the very problem you claim to want to solve.

CHAPTER 2:

WE HAVE TO CHANGE OUR GIVING HABITS

A research paper published by the Evangelical Alliance (EA) in 2015 reported the following statistics about evangelical Christians and their personal responses to poverty.[296] The EA asked the question, "How have you personally responded to poverty in the past 12 months?"

- 73% of evangelical Christians gave money to a poverty charity in the previous 12 months
- 70% contributed to a food bank
- 67% donated to an international disaster appeal
- 56% gave money to someone in need
- 55% gave to a UK charity specifically tackling poverty
- 37% volunteered some time to a church project or a Christian charity that tackled poverty
- 31% gave money directly to a street beggar
- 30% bought a beggar food and drink
- 10% opened their home and shared a meal with someone in poverty

There is no question that many evangelical Christians are generous when it comes to giving financially to charities and institutions claiming to fight poverty, but observe how *practically all* of that giving is focused on relief only. There isn't any foolproof way to gauge accurately to whom and to what Christians give their money, and how that money is then spent. I am often advised by believers to apply to this trust or that grant-making body. "They give millions to Christian mission each year", I am told. Well, I don't know where it is going, but I can tell you that it isn't going towards planting and revitalising churches in poor communities. Certainly not in Scotland and the north of England anyway.

I am going to assume, conservatively, that tens of millions of pounds per year is being given to Christian organisations in the poverty sector (for that is what it is) which operate outside the bounds of a local church. In my opinion, that's money that could be better and more strategically used in the service of King Jesus in the building up and strengthening of local gospel churches, the very thing He gave His lifeblood to establish.

We read in Acts 11:29–30 of the churches taking up an offering to help struggling Christians in Judea. A prime example of local churches helping local churches. That's Christians in financially better off congregations helping those in churches that are not. What has happened to UK Christians to make them lose confidence in their local church to distribute their offerings to the right people and places? Why are believers giving millions to organisations who are not strengthening local churches in our poorest communities? We have believers sending more money to televangelists than they do towards the needs of their own local body.

It is criminal.

Of course, our first responsibility is to our own church. But, let me ask you this question: *What is being done with the excess money that is left in your church's budget at the end of each year? Is it just accruing interest? Or is it being put to work for the good of the kingdom?*

Steve Levy, a Pastor from Swansea, Wales, suggests the following:

> *And please could I ask those in leadership in church life, after we have used the money needed to be spent on the work the Lord has called us to, could we – for just one year – give our money to gospel churches where they need it: the poor. Can you imagine what good would come of it? Can you imagine the joy you will feel if the church that you partner with grows?*
>
> *Look at the millions and millions being given to organisations which simply cannot justify their existence from the Bible – many of whom do far more harm than good. And think of the organisation God has set up – the church, how it perfectly meets the needs of the poor that no man-made institution could ever do.*
>
> *It's time for biblical budgetary reform. People will be upset, but Christ will be glorified and the poor in Britain will hear the gospel. Think what might happen if all the money we paid to para-church organisations was paying for gospel churches in the neediest areas of our country.*[297]

Steve has also put his money where his mouth is. For the last couple of years, his church has given a substantial sum of money to go towards gospel ministry in my home church in Niddrie, one of Scotland's most deprived schemes. This act has strengthened relations with our churches. It has strengthened relations with our leaders. As Steve says, "Every time we think of that area, we would thank God for that church. That church gathered by God, bought with Christ's blood, reflecting heaven in a world under God's wrath. Time to switch budgets."[298] What's more, when our church discovered that Steve's church needed to raise funds for building repairs, we made a significant contribution to that fund. This is real gospel partnership in action. This, surely, is the best way for richer, larger churches to partner with those struggling in deprived communities.

Local churches ought to be the places that oversee the administration of financial gifts to other local churches, particularly in deprived communities. It's why we have deacons. They came about in Acts 7 because of complaints of favouritism when it came to helping widows in need. The church dealt with it and came up with a solution. Why, then, are local churches devolving their God-given responsibility for almsgiving to the poor to outside institutions? If the church is entrusted with the perfect Word of God, why is it not entrusted with His money?

REMEMBER JESUS IN OUR GIVING

> *Jesus didn't patronise the poor – he was poor. ... His mum was close to disgrace when pregnant. He was born in a shed and had to make do with cloths instead of proper clothes as a baby. His cradle was an animal feeding trough. Others brought a lamb to sacrifice at their son's circumcision. At his circumcision, his mum could only afford a pigeon. He was a refugee. He grew up in an area from which nothing good came.*[299]

When the Lord saw the poverty and suffering of people, He was always deeply moved. How angry the Lord got with His disciples when they neglected the widow and the fatherless. What shame it brings on us when we do likewise. God has not saved us to erect barriers in order to keep certain people out of our churches and our conferences and our wallets. We have been saved in local churches whose sole aim is to glorify God by bringing the light and life of the gospel of Jesus to the poor and the oppressed.

> *The people of God didn't just help the poor, they welcomed the poor, preached good news to the poor, and largely* were *the poor.*[300]

This leaves us with some questions to answer. If we are so concerned with the poor that we give millions every year to organisations claiming to help them, why do we price them out of everything from church weekends away, conferences and children's camps? How do we justify charging hundreds, sometimes thousands of pounds for families to come to our conferences? How is that not excluding the poor? "There are bursaries", you say. Are there? How many and for how much? How many poor families do you actually know well enough to even invite?

Steve Levy observes:

> *There are camps being operated in the Christian world to which only the cream of society can go, and children from most of the rest of our society are excluded. Thousands of pounds are poured into student ministry, and other projects which are for the educated classes, while ministers in poor areas can hardly survive.*[301]

How are we treating the widow, the fatherless, and the refugee in our churches? Do you even know who is struggling financially among your own people? Do you even care? How are we making sure that they don't feel like second-class citizens among us? If you are part of a wealthy church, how is your congregation directly supporting churches in poorer parts of your city, town or village?

We must take a long, hard look at ourselves and at our giving. Stop defrauding the local church of your financial gifts. If all we have comes from the Lord, then all we have should be given to His bride, wherever she is to be found.

SPOTLIGHT:

HOW CAN WE BETTER HELP CHRISTIANS IN POOR COMMUNITIES TO RAISE MONEY?

JEREMY MARSHALL, BANKER, PHILANTHROPIST, AUTHOR

How can we help churches in deprived areas to raise money? The problem has been explained elsewhere in this book, but what are possible solutions? Where is the money in the first place? Is it with churches, individuals or trusts and foundations or even with banks and Donor Advised Funds, such as Stewardship? And is there potential outside the UK?

Being the son of a pastor, I have three points

- Organise
- Build partnerships
- Think laterally

All, I believe, are biblical principles for church growth and can be found in the New Testament.

ORGANISE

First, there is awareness that the problem even exists. If we look at most churches, they typically spend money on their own needs, something for the denomination if they are in one, and then they give money to support missionaries sent from the church around the world. (I can vividly recall, from my childhood, the pins on maps of the world with pictures of missionaries in remote places.)

Missing entirely was the thought of giving to missionaries in the UK. This, I imagine, reflected the historic sense of the UK as a sending country rather than as one in need of missionaries to its own shores. Today the picture is entirely different and, in fact, many of those countries we once evangelised are now sending missionaries to us.

Despite this, we still remain blind to the massive need among the pagan British.

If we don't recognise the issue, and if it is not brought into the Christian public's eye, then we will never experience a change in our going, our sending or our giving. Let's take the example of student ministry. Some Christians bristle at the amount of resources that student ministries take from the UK church. But it wasn't always like this. After the Second World War, IVF (which then became UCCF) spent a lot of time and effort publicising the need for the growing student population to be evangelised. The end result, over time, was that they not only raised the profile of gospel work among students but that people began to give money to their endeavours.

20schemes operates like this in Scotland, but we have nothing similar for the rest of the UK. (Acts 29 Church in Hard Places, although still in embryonic form may well do so in future years.) We need a UK-wide body that will champion the cause of those working in deprived communities and make the wider Christian body aware of the great spiritual and physical needs that exist. Perhaps an umbrella group of different leaders from these communities could form and begin that process.

Some of you may well say, "Not another para-church organisation. We only need local churches!" But, speaking as a funder and as a board member of a fund-giving organisation, it is bewildering to get so many different appeals for financial help from all kinds of people in all sorts of places. It would be much easier if there was some kind of *clearing house* which would put a stamp on requests and help to inform the broader Christian world of how we can help in a much more informed way.

My second recommendation is that the leaders of churches and church plants in deprived communities need to cultivate relationships with potential donors. Get to know them. Invite them for a visit (much easier in London than Addis Ababa!). Build relationships. Just turning up and saying, "Give us some money," doesn't work. It's about building 2 Corinthians 8 and 9 type long-term partnerships. Not just money, but prayer, advice and even friendship!

BUILD PARTNERSHIPS

What might such partnerships look like?

Individuals: Ask others for their contacts. Ask to speak to wealthy donors who are interested in funding church planting and revitalisation (easier said than done). Ask them for coffee or lunch. Networking and asking for advice sounds daunting for many people in deprived areas, but the wonderful thing about the fellowship of the Christian faith is that, I would hope, anyone who asks another Christian for advice should get it.

Churches: Go to the leadership and say, "Would you be interested in forming a partnership with us?" Think of it as similar to town twinning.

Foundations: Ask them questions before submitting applications. For example, "What kind of applications do you look for?" Admit that you need help and most will be happy to oblige. A good place to start is The Christian Funders Forum.[302] There is no trick to getting a grant. Simply, find a funder that says they fund your sort of ministry. Then read their website, and if you still think you fit what they are looking for, apply by following their guidelines *to the letter*.

If you really don't know where to start, then contact Stewardship (I am a trustee).[303] We are passionate about helping churches in deprived areas. We have also just established a pathway to support church planters. We have lots of donors looking for good ideas. Come and speak to us about how we can help. Some of our training does depend on knowing and having contacts, but we are willing to listen and tailor what we offer to help you succeed.

Our heart is to serve you.

THINK LATERALLY

Be creative and entrepreneurial. There are many ways to "skin the financial cat". 20schemes have started Retrain, where they are starting up and buying small businesses to use as a funding stream for future church plants and workers.[304]

One of the issues for people like me is that once we give money for a church building, it's tied up for a long time, whereas lending money allows it to be recycled for other uses. That's why I and some friends (including Stewardship) recently acquired the Kingdom Bank.[305] It specialises in making loans to churches, often in deprived areas. Between the Kingdom Bank and Stewardship (and many others not mentioned), there is a rich Christian eco-system with a wealth of possible ways of helping.

If you have a building, then maybe there is a way to create funds by renting it out when it is not in use. This can create a flow of people using the building who would not ordinarily come in and also generates a small income stream.

Above all things though, we must throw ourselves on God Almighty and both trust Him and ask for His help. Hudson Taylor, a missionary to China in the 1800s, once said this:

> *God's work done in God's way will never lack God's supply. He is too wise a God to frustrate His purposes for lack of funds.*[306]

Fundraising is hard work, but God will provide and, with God's help, the gospel will flourish among the least, the last and the lost of our land.

CHAPTER 3:

WHY MY FIRST HIRE WAS A WOMAN, AND WHY YOURS SHOULD BE TOO

When I first moved to Niddrie Community Church in 2007, I spent the first six months or so getting to know who was in the congregation (it was very small). I wanted to find out who was who and who was good at what. I quickly discovered that some of the women in the church felt somewhat marginalised and disenfranchised. It appeared that they had been left to take a back seat in the life and ministry of the church and in the local community they were trying to reach with the gospel. They were on the usual rotas: tea, coffee and the flowers, but that was about it.

As I began to get to know the community of Niddrie, it became very clear to me very early on that we needed to hire a community worker, and it needed to be a woman. At that time, the complementarians weren't as loud in the UK evangelical scene as they are now, so it was a bit of a risk to make one of my first hires a woman. I had read many articles and blogs from pastors and church planters talking about growing their leadership teams. Very, very few of them talked about hiring a woman in the early stages of their ministry. Even those that did tended to leave it as one of their later appointments and, even then, only if the money came in. I have seen many a planter's development plans, and often women are just not in them. They will talk about hiring a youth worker, or an executive pastor, or a worship leader before they would even consider a woman.

At 20schemes, we insist that all of our church planters make sure they are employing a mature woman *from the off* as they embark on their church planting and/or revitalisation venture. Here are some of my reasons why.

WOMEN MAKE UP A LARGE PROPORTION OF THE COMMUNITIES WE ARE TRYING TO REACH

In fact, as we have already noted, lone parents make up approximately one-quarter of all families living in Scotland. Unsurprisingly, nine out of ten of these lone parents are women. In the poorest communities in Scotland, a little over half of all the residents are women. That is a lot of vulnerable women with multifaceted pastoral problems (over half of them suffer from a long-term health problem or a disability).

WOMEN IN OUR COMMUNITIES OFTEN FACE MULTIPLE ISSUES WHICH COMPLICATE DISCIPLESHIP

So, for instance, millions of women across the UK have admitted to illegally taking prescription drugs during the past year, and even more have used street drugs in the same period. Tragically, 45% of women in the UK have experienced at least one incident of inter-personal violence in their lifetime.[307] Statistics also reveal that a staggering 54% of all UK rapes are committed by a woman's current or former partner, and half of all rapes are committed by men who once claimed to love them.

Many of these vulnerable and needy women with complex physical, psychological and spiritual problems are in our congregations and are in our communities. They crave love and attention, and require a lot of time as we counsel and disciple them in the Word. Because their emotional needs are often so great, it's simply not wise or prudent for a man to invest serious amounts of time into their lives.

MOST PASTORS ARE MORE LIKELY TO FAIL MORALLY WHEN THEY GET DEEPLY INVOLVED IN COUNSELLING NEEDY WOMEN

While that is a broad generalisation, a survey of the 15 men who have preceded me at Niddrie revealed that one in three of them were removed for offences of sexual immorality. 100% of these men ran into difficulties though intense counselling with the opposite sex. Sadly, our church leaders are not immune to sexual sin and many pastors have fallen in this area with a church member they have been counselling or with somebody they have been evangelising. Counselling and evangelising vulnerable women in the schemes is a minefield. Any form of tenderness or a willingness to listen from a male is almost always misunderstood sexually. (This is true the other way around as well.) A man who listens to them is a very powerful aphrodisiac. Temptation can be, for some, very hard to resist. They aren't used to men listening to their problems. They are used to men *being* the problem.

WOMEN SHOULD ONLY DISCIPLE WOMEN

We realise that there are many ways pastors can counsel members of their congregation safely, but we would suggest having a gifted, trained and mature woman would be one of the most helpful. In many churches, this type of thing is left to the pastor's wife or maybe the wife of an elder. Almost invariably, this is not because of giftedness but is due to the position her husband holds within the fellowship. It is fine if she is trained but can be immensely damaging if she is not. Regardless, the point remains that in crisis situations (a daily occurrence in the schemes) a mature, godly woman can continue the relationship on into deeper, long-lasting friendship in a way a pastor cannot and should not. When we talk of discipleship, we do not mean the odd monthly pastoral meeting but the intense, daily walk with God as women do life together.

But what place for men then?

WE NEED GODLY MEN TO TEACH WOMEN TO TRAIN GODLY WOMEN

Of course, women need the influence of godly men in their lives. The church is to be led by men after all. That much is clear from Scripture. These men have responsibility to teach the whole congregation sound doctrine and to model godliness as per Titus 2. But they have a responsibility to teach women too. These are Paul's instructions in Titus 2:3–5.

> *Likewise, teach the older women to be reverent in the way they live, not to be slanderers or addicted to much wine, but to teach what is good. Then they can urge the younger women to love their husbands and children, to be self-controlled and pure, to be busy at home, to be kind, and to be subject to their husbands, so that no one will malign the word of God.*

Everything we do at Niddrie is overseen by the elders and has the approval of the whole congregation. It is not that we are not involved in the life of women in our church, because we are. Women can see us teach and model godliness in the home and as we preach the Word and lead the meetings. We still counsel couples and single women in certain situations. If with a couple, it is with my wife. If with a single woman, it can be with my wife or it can be with one of our women's workers or a friend she trusts. Also, our women's pastoral worker reports to the elders regularly so that we can pray intelligently for those with specific needs and difficulties. But, at the heart of it all, we, as the male leaders, are ensuring that our women's pastoral workers are being supported and trained to do their job well.

Now, we realise some feel that by equipping women to pastor and train other women, we are not fulfilling the distinctive male-only role of pastor as we should. Some feel that we are confusing people by having women in pastoral positions within the church. When we say that our women's worker "pastors" our women, we don't mean that she is a *pastor*, rather that she assists the pastors by providing day-to-day pastoral care to our women. I am often asked by other pastors how we can trust what is being taught and said if we are not present.

A few things to say here.

We trust our women because, as with the male leaders, we trained them well in the doctrines of the church before we released them into ministry. In fact, it is remarkably offensive to suggest that by giving women responsibility at this level we are opening the church up to serious error. Far more men have led churches astray than women.

The church is not confused about who the pastors are, but is instead built up as women, and men, are involved in "one anothering". The pastor is not seen as the only one who is qualified to minister among the flock that he shepherds. That is a good thing, as one man cannot adequately take on this role, particularly in our cultural context. Even with a small church and multiple elders we would struggle under the weight of pastoral issues in our congregation.

Women are encouraged that they have a serious part to play in the kingdom of God and that they are not just bystanders or there to cook the meals. The local church needs women's workers. Most of the women living in our poorest communities are suffering without the hope of the gospel. They have not heard the good news that can set them truly free from their burdens. Women on schemes need more than women parachuting in to be another worker in their life, perpetuating dependency. They need women who will do life with them every single day of their lives. The harvest is great, the workers are few, and women are being left on the shelf. They shouldn't be.

Employing a woman is not a luxury, as some have suggested to me in the past. Employing more women for ministry should be our highest priority.

CHAPTER 4:

RETHINKING EVANGELISM IN HARD PLACES

TRUST THE GOSPEL AND THE CHURCH

I was once contacted by a group who wanted to come to my church to teach our men how to reach the men on our estate with the gospel. For a small fee, they told me, they would come along on a Saturday and spend five hours or more teaching our men how to be effective evangelists. "Okay", I said. "Tell me the gospel in a sentence." "What?" Came the reply. "Tell me the gospel in a sentence." "Wow. That's a tough one," he said. "If you can't tell me in a sentence, you're no good to me," I said.

"Well," he said, "what material does your church use to evangelise the men in your community?" "The same material we use to evangelise the women – the Bible," I replied. "There's no need to be rude," he said, obviously offended. "I'm not being rude. We don't have a course and we don't use specific material. We often just use the Bible." He hung up, apparently very unhappy with my tone.

Now, maybe I was being a little facetious. My people use a wide array of good resources, including a combination of

Christianity Explored and our own in-house material.[308] But, my point is that we often do just use the Bible.

Our evangelism is very simple and very direct.

- God is Holy
- We are wicked sinners
- His just wrath rests upon us for our wilful rebellion
- Jesus comes and He is perfectly holy
- Jesus dies on the cross and takes upon Himself the full wrath of God
- If we want forgiveness and eternal life, we must repent and believe

Herein lies the problem. Most Christians who ask me how we "do evangelism" don't believe it is that simple. They've lost faith in the power of the gospel. So, when I say we use the Bible to evangelise people, they smile and nod, but I can tell from the body language that they're thinking: "No way is it that simple. If it was everybody would be doing it."

But it really is that simple. We believe that *the gospel is the power of God for salvation to all who would believe*. The poorest communities in the UK really don't need clever strategies, they need to hear the gospel. The best place to hear that gospel is from a local body of witnesses in the church. You can clean their gardens and fill skips with rubbish for the next 100 years, but only the gospel of Jesus Christ has the power to save their souls, and that gospel has to be communicated to them simply, clearly and directly. We don't need a five-hour seminar or a six-week course to understand that.

YOUR CHURCH IS BORING

We tend to get a lot of rubberneckers at our Sunday services (this was pre-Covid), mainly earnest students with a heart for the poor. I remember one young man vividly. He'd heard about us online and followed us on social media and he was excited to come and "experience church with us" (his words). An hour later, he trudged up to me, looking a bit deflated and underwhelmed. "Is that it?" he asked. I don't think he was meaning to be offensive – he'd just been really excited to visit our church. We had prayed and sang and preached, and prayed some more, and sang some more. And then prayed again. He was crushed by the monotony of it. By the normalcy of it. He looked around at our people and said, completely without malice, "But how do you make them sit through that every week? What's the secret?"

They come because they have been saved by the gospel, and not by fancy rhetoric or clever presentations. They come because that is the power of the gospel in action. They stay because they have been taught that the Christian life is more drill than thrill. The Christian life is pretty boring, it has to be said. It's a slow trudge to glory with a few exciting bits in between, if we are lucky. We don't need to whip a crowd into an emotional frenzy in order to win them to Christ. We need to simply preach the gospel to them and let the Holy Spirit do all the heavy lifting.

AM I GOING TO HELL?

Sometimes visitors will request to stay with us for a week or two just to see how we "do life" (their words), and they're equally disappointed when they discover that all we really do in our day-to-day lives is preach the Word, pray the Word and read the Word. We live our lives among our people and we take every opportunity we can to proclaim the gospel to everybody who comes across our path. What is normal to us tends to be an eye-opener to the average middle-class Christian student.

I remember once sitting with a group of students in our cafe in Niddrie, and I asked them what the most common question they got about the faith was? They gave me the usual answers: "Can we trust the Bible? How can you prove the existence of God? Does God hate gays? What about evil and suffering? What about evolution and creation?"

"What do you think the number one question in my community is?" I asked them. "I'll tell you that it is not on your list."

Silence. A couple had a few guesses.

I called over a friend of mine from the community and said to him, "These students have all come here to tell people in Niddrie about Jesus, Joe. Why don't you ask them the question you always ask me?" Joe rubbed his hands together and pulled up a chair. "Well, my partner died a few months ago of an overdose. She left me with the kids. They're in care now though, until I sort myself out. Anyway, she hated God. Said it was all a waste of time. But I sort of believe in Him. And I was told that the Bible says if you don't repent of your sin then you go to hell. So, my question is this: Is my partner in hell now because she didn't believe?"

I pushed my chair back and left them to it. I watched for ten minutes as not one of them would give a direct answer to his direct question. They prevaricated and a couple even looked panicked. I returned to the table to rescue them, and I asked Joe, "Did they answer your question?" "Nah," he said, "I didn't have a clue what some of them were trying to say."

So, I went around the table and asked each one, "Is Joe's

God-hating partner in hell or not? Yes, or no." A couple of braves ones squeaked out a "yes", the majority said "no", and one said, "It's not quite that simple." (There's always one.)

"Tell them what you think, Joe," I said to him. "Well, if what you say about the Bible is true, then she is in hell for her sin. She hated God and she always used to say she'd rather be in hell with her pals anyway."

There we have it. An unbeliever with a consistently better theology of hell than the majority of the people who've apparently come to tell him the good news about Jesus and why He came to earth to live a perfect life and to die a cruel death. It's not complicated at all. In fact, it is very clear. And for those of you thinking it is unfair to base this view on such a small sample, I have posed this question to hundreds of students over the years and the overwhelming majority bottle it when it comes to giving a straight answer to a direct question.

Somewhere along the line, evangelical Christians in the UK have lost touch with the simplicity and straightforward bluntness of the gospel and gospel preaching. And I think they have lost it because the very people who are blunt and straightforward are missing from their congregations in huge numbers. We have to rediscover the simplicity and directness of the gospel if we are to have any hope of making inroads into the places we will find the least, the last and the lost.

How would you have answered Joe's question?

The bottom line is this: People won't respond to a gospel we are too scared to preach. Christians have made a spiritual gift out of cowardice. They call it, "being sensitive" or "not being offensive".

So, don't come into our schemes and council estates with a low-key gospel, high on love but low on justice. Don't come in trying to be our friends and teaching our young people and children all the "positives" of the Bible, without explaining the full gospel of Jesus to them. Showing the love of Jesus by serving at food banks, or starting a holiday breakfast club, or cleaning up gardens – they may all be good things, but they are not the gospel and they do not save anybody.

WE PROCLAIM A FOOLISH GOSPEL

People need to know there is danger up ahead. And we do them no favours by fudging on the gospel. People need a crucified Saviour and they need to know God's forgiveness because, at heart, they are all guilty rebels – lawless ones – who, outside of Jesus, lie under God's holy wrath. They will be scandalised by that news. They will be offended by it. They will be angered by it.

Look what Paul says in 1 Corinthians 1:23, "we preach Christ crucified, a stumbling block to Jews and foolishness to Gentiles". There is never a good way to break the bad news of the good news. Because what we bring to people is serious and they will only fully appreciate the love of God and the good news of Jesus once they realise what they have been saved *from*. The gospel is not a proposition, it is a demand. We are commanded to repent and believe. The alternative is to reject Christ and perish. People respond one of two ways: they think it's foolishness or they believe. It really is that simple.

There is no greater power in the universe than the power of the gospel. *Only the gospel* can transform sinners into saints. *Only the gospel* can break the hardest heart and transform the messiest life. *Only the gospel* can save the vilest offender who truly believes, or the hard-nosed atheist, or the snotty teenager, or the intellectual philosopher. *Only the gospel* has the power to do that. *Only the gospel* can raise the spiritually dead.

I think we are all looking for strategies because, deep down, we're ashamed of the gospel. We lack confidence in it. We think it sounds too easy or too simplistic for cultured and cynical twenty-first-century ears. We think we need to give it a helping hand or to jazz it up a bit.

Years ago, a friend of mine was invited to speak at a big youth event in his town. As he met with the organising committee of the event to discuss the details, he outlined the message he was going to preach from the Bible. There was an awkward silence in the room after he'd outlined his talk. "Is everything okay?" He asked.

Silence.

Then one of the organisers said, "We were looking for a more culturally relevant talk. We were thinking of maybe showing the kids video clips from some modern movies and then basing the talk around that. That way they won't be scared off by the Bible, and they'll probably understand spiritual truths better." My friend was angry. "So, let me get this right, you think that unsaved young people are going to understand the spiritual truths of God and the gospel by *not* using the Bible?"

Embarrassed silence.

"Look," said one of the organisers. "Our job is to help these young people on their spiritual journey towards the Lord." "But they're not on a spiritual journey towards the Lord," my friend replied. "In fact, they are going completely in the opposite direction."

It is not our job to make the Bible more relevant. Or to make the gospel palatable for the masses. We are not allowed to add to God's Word or to take away from it. We can't dress it up and put lipstick on it. The gospel is already perfect. And it is perfect precisely because it is God's invention, not ours. The gospel will remain true for all eternity. It never goes out of fashion. It's so simple a child can understand it. Don't confuse the fact that it is unpopular and unpalatable with being complicated and hard to understand. The only people who want to make it "relevant" are those who are embarrassed by it or ashamed of it – those who think, deep down, that it will never work on its own.

MESS WITH THE GOSPEL AND WE MESS WITH GOD

Look at Romans 1:17. Not only is the gospel *the power of God to salvation* but, in it, *His righteousness is revealed.* Park your bum there for a second! Any desire on our part to meddle with the gospel message means we are, quite literally, meddling with the *very righteousness of God.*

When Paul wrote these words, Rome was the centre of world power and culture. It was where all the poets, musicians, artists, philosophers and great scientists of the world lived. It was a place of many cultures and of great ideals. Can you imagine how the story of a Jewish carpenter boy being the Saviour of the world played out? Not only that, but He was crucified as well! The worst punishment that was reserved for the lowest criminals. What people wanted was clever philosophy and educated arguments. They didn't want this strange story from a little backwater place in the Empire.

The question is, how should Paul start preaching in a city like Rome? Maybe he should start where the people are at? Maybe he should start off by giving them some spiritual lessons from the theatre plays of the day. Remember, as well, that Paul was very highly educated, so he would have more than held his own in any debate. But he doesn't do any of that.

He goes in hard in Romans 1 and 2.

People were lost. People were living in sin. People were unaware that the wrath of God was upon them. People didn't have a clue that eternal damnation waited for them. They didn't realise just how much they needed the good news of Jesus. Paul knew that salvation didn't come about through fancy arguments or clever spiritual talks about the latest play. Salvation could only come about through the preaching of the gospel.

People need the gospel.

It is irrelevant whether they like it or not. Our job is to make it clear and to leave the rest up to God. That's why I don't understand it when Christians ask me about what strategy we use or how we evangelise. We open the Bible and preach the gospel of Jesus Christ. Sometimes we do it formally, as in a Sunday service, but most of the time we are just talking to people about it informally, or maybe doing one-to-one Bible studies. We don't need to go on a training course to learn how to do that.

Maybe some people are more confident than others. Obviously, some are more gifted than others as well. Nor am I saying we shouldn't make good use of booklets or other evangelistic publications. We do. But at the heart of whatever it is we are trying to do in our churches lies the gospel of Jesus, and we should neither mess with it nor be ashamed of it.

SHARE THE GOSPEL. SHARE IT AGAIN. REPEAT.

We certainly shouldn't be subcontracting evangelism in our poorest communities because we have no time for them or simply can't be bothered with them. If we leave it to well-intentioned but poorly taught students and heretical social justice warriors, the church is condemning generations and millions of people in our estates and schemes to hell. You're saying to them: "You don't matter enough for us to do this right and make sure it is getting done properly."

Middle-class Christians have made an idol out of apologetics. They've made a god out of having intellectual debates. We have made idols out of evangelistic strategies and formulas. But none of these things save people. I'm not saying they are wrong in certain instances, but I am saying that nobody ever got converted through apologetics or through a solid philosophical argument. These things might have got people to the church or interested in spiritual things, but that is the limit of their power.

Only the power of the gospel as it is verbally proclaimed can bring a dead soul to life.

We need to have more confidence in the Holy Spirit of God as He works through the Word of God. Many Christians tell me that they don't do evangelism because they wouldn't know what to say if somebody asks them a hard question. If you know the gospel and if you believe it is the power of salvation for all who will believe, then you do know what to say. People think there is some magic key which allows us to open the hearts of the people. There isn't.

There is the gospel. Use that. Preach that. Share that. Trust that. I have a Bible and a church full of converts that says the gospel works. Stop overcomplicating our role in evangelism. We are only the mouthpieces. Stick to the script God has already given us. It's not like we have to memorise new lines or anything. It's all on a plate for us. We speak the words of life. He breathes new life into some. Others get very angry with us. We disciple the new sheep.

Repeat until death.

SPOTLIGHT:

THE PROBLEM OF "IMPOSTER SYNDROME"

AL GOODERHAM, PASTOR, GRACE CHURCH, DONCASTER

Imposter Syndrome. Most of us have felt it. That uneasy feeling because you just don't fit in. That somehow your being there is inappropriate. Many of us find ourselves in places where we feel like we're the imposter and we fear that at any minute we'll be exposed and driven out. I'm not Northern, yet I serve in a northern town. I'm not working class, and yet I serve in an area with many working-class people. Am I an imposter? It's a question I've struggled with.

One of the dangers is that a largely middle-class church in the UK struggles with imposter syndrome when it comes to thinking about serving working-class areas. We think, "I can't go or serve or send because they might think I'm an imposter, that I'm coming riding to the rescue on my middle-class charger." Or we're afraid of how exposed we'll feel, how out of our comfort zone we'll be, or how others ministering there might react to us. Will they be hostile?

I'm middle class but with working-class roots and one temptation is to play that up to justify being here. On one side, my Grandad was a farm labourer – he lived in a tithed cottage where he and my grandma paid no rent until he retired, when they then had to pay the princely sum of 50p a week. They were never wealthy and none of their children went to university. My maternal grandparents were very different, landowner farmers and clearly quite well off, at least back when that was possible in farming. Added to that, my dad had a management job, and we were encouraged to do well at school and sixth-form college and then go to university. I then trained as a teacher and taught for five years before entering ministry in a middle-class church.

So far, so very middle class. I can't pass myself off as working class and, to be honest, I shouldn't even try. What matters isn't what class I can pass myself off as, but that I share Jesus's compassion for people and have His good news to share. But there are some challenges that come with the imposter syndrome.

We planted Grace Church into an ex-RAF base, with lots of social housing and some affluent areas. In many ways, we have all the divisions of a town in a more compressed area. It was an area intensely segregated along base housing lines. And with a slightly unique former Forces feel. It's a hard place to plant, we have seen fruit but it has not been low hanging. It's hard graft.

And, increasingly, I find myself not quite fitting into any social class, feeling like an imposter everywhere. I've quickly adopted the same chips on my shoulder as those we predominantly work alongside – though perhaps with the added zeal of the converted ex-smoker, in terms of class. I see so many privileges that are taken for granted by so many middle-class churches and Christians who don't even stop to think about who they are *not* reaching because of what and how they do things. I see the frustrations in terms of accessibility, expectations, funding, ministry training and so on for the working class and for the churches serving in those areas. I get frustrated at those in the church at large who swallow the media line about the "undeserving poor" and the "feckless welfare spongers" when, for the vast majority, the reality is far from that.

But I also find that I don't quite fit with those we work alongside. We have some shared experiences but have had so many that are very different. My assumptions – and theirs – about childhood, food, bills, schooling, parenting, marriage and so on are so very different. So sometimes I feel like an imposter there too. But – and here's the key – we listen and learn and love and bear with the imposter syndrome we experience. And we seek to apply the gospel again and again in our actions and our conversations, committed to people and the area because Jesus alone saves and He loves these people, no matter which of the estates they are from.

One of the fallacies of the UK church scene is that you only need people with working-class and deprived backgrounds to plant into those areas, or even that you need Northerners to reach Northerners. In some ways, it would be a huge advantage; we long to see more indigenous believers from the estate. But what these areas of immense gospel needs is *people*, of whatever class, who love Jesus passionately and because of that will love and listen and serve everyone in humility. It doesn't need to be people who are class blind – because that's dangerous and there's no such thing, we're all a product of our upbringing. It needs people who will love and commit long-term, who don't see it as a stepping-stone but come with their coffin, who don't assume they know the answers but come with compassionate determination to listen and empower, not assume and solve.

We need people who love Jesus, who show that by loving people, who cross divides, who accept differences, who don't confuse gospel values and cultural or class values. Who will commit to loving and discipling those who are very different from them and train up leaders over the long-term from any and every social background in whatever way they need, not just how we're used to doing it. We need people who are prepared to bear with the imposter syndrome and be between cultures with all its discomfort, for Christ's glory and the salvation of the lost.

CHAPTER 5:

RETHINKING DISCIPLESHIP AMONG STUPID AND ANNOYING PEOPLE (LIKE US)

"If you are a Christian who seeks to live faithfully and to live according to God's Word, you can help in most every situation. You can't necessarily fix the problem, but you can find ways to help them in their struggle. A centrepiece of this discipleship culture are the members teaching one another from God's Word with the goal of growing in personal holiness. You, as a member, are called to counsel the Word to one another. And whether you realise it or not, you are a soldier who sits on the front lines of the battle in this discipleship culture."[309]

Deepak Reju, *The Pastor and Counselling*

DISCIPLESHIP IN THE SCHEMES

Imagine you begin a ministry to the poor in a community near your church and you begin to see people saved. But the kind of people being saved are not the kind of people that your church are used to. Maybe they have criminal backgrounds. Maybe they have come from a background of serious sexual abuse. You see, evangelism and mercy ministry are actually quite easy.

They don't take up too much of our time. Volunteering at a soup kitchen maybe takes up a couple of hours a week. Doing a children's club in a poor community, maybe the same amount of time. But now people are being saved. What are we going to do with them? How are our churches going to cope?

- What do we do with someone who has had an addiction for 20 years and their life is an absolute mess?
- How do we disciple someone who has four children to three different partners and they all live within streets of one another?
- How do we walk alongside someone who has been sexually abused, lived on the street for the last five years and just come out of jail?

Where do we begin? With the drugs, sex, children, family? All of this is going to take a lot more than a few hours a week out of our lives. Discipleship in many churches is nothing more than going to church on a Sunday, maybe the odd prayer meeting and/or Bible study, and meeting up with friends a few times a month for a good gossip. But this approach to discipleship is insufficient for our context of ministry. We live in communities where many people do not work, and so they have a lot of time on their hands. People need constant, daily investment. This is especially true when people have families who are not Christian and face rejection. Or people have had a chaotic life with lots of different issues that need support. What our new Christians need is a new family and the local church has to be it.

The problem of discipleship is worse in UK churches, where most Christians are very closed when it comes to sharing their lives with other people. Many Christians don't want to admit their weaknesses, temptations and secret sin struggles. Much of Christianity in the UK, particularly in theologically reformed churches, is strong on doctrinal truth, but extremely superficial when it comes to their personal lives. People are more than happy to debate the finer points of doctrine with each other all day long. They will talk about the Bible and the sermon and their favourite preacher. But they suddenly shut down when the conversation begins to get personal. They suddenly lose their tongues when asked about how their relationship with Jesus is developing. Or when asked about which specific sins they are currently battling.

Understanding poverty and having a heart for the poor is all well and good, but we need a solid plan of discipleship if we are going to see real growth and development from indigenous Christians in poor communities. So, how do we do it? How do we disciple those we have reached out to once they come to faith in Christ? Well, let's get the basics right.

DISCIPLESHIP MEANS TEACHING THE BIBLE ABOVE ALL OTHER CONSIDERATIONS

Jesus's main ministry to His disciples was to teach them about Himself. He taught them the Word. He taught them about the kingdom of God and what it looked like. He taught them about who He was and why He had come. He taught them about the end and what it was going to look like.

Then, just before His departure, He commands His followers in Mathew 28:19–20, to do exactly the same things that He had modelled to them. "Go and *make disciples*, baptising them and teaching them all that I have commanded" (emphasis mine). So, the first disciples went out into the world to do exactly that: preach the gospel and make disciples. Biblical discipleship is not happening if the gospel is not being preached and the Word of God is not being studied.

Paul said this about his work in Colossians 1:28-29 (ESV): "Him we proclaim, warning and teaching everyone with all wisdom, that we may present everyone mature in Christ. For this I toil, struggling with all his energy that he powerfully works in me." Paul didn't just preach the gospel and then say to his new converts, "Right, here's a Bible, there's a church. Make sure you get yourself along on Sundays and don't forget the midweek prayer meeting."

Paul *agonised over them*. He kicked them up the backside when they were chasing after false doctrines. He encouraged them when they needed comfort. He pointed them again and again to the teachings of Jesus. He was desperate for his brothers and sisters to become mature in Christ. So, if we are serious about making disciples then we need to keep on teaching people until they understand all that Jesus has taught and are able to then teach others.

The biggest lie that Satan has sown in poor communities is that we are incapable of reading or understanding the deep truths of Scripture. But that's not the case. We just need the Word of God. Plain and simple. It is the Word that brings life. It is the Word that convicts sinners. It is the Word that is our spiritual food to help us grow. I know people in the schemes who've never read a book, or finished their schooling who, when they come to Christ, will sit down and listen to a 45-minute sermon without blinking once. They will sit down and listen to a Bible study for an hour. No frills – just wanting to listen to God's Word clearly explained.

Christians from educated backgrounds far too often assume that men and women from poor communities lack intelligence. They confuse poverty and necessity with stupidity and inability. They think that because people never finished high school or they watch reality TV shows that they are a little bit culturally backwards and can't take in deep doctrinal truth.

That is just not true.

People in our communities are thirsty for the Bible. Therefore, we are obligated to feed it to our new-born disciples in much the same way as Jesus did. He didn't water down truth to make it more palatable. He gave His disciples difficult things to think about. In our discipleship we have to teach people *the whole counsel of God*. Shepherds need to feed God's sheep. That doesn't mean that we give all the rich Christians the steak and throw the scraps to the poor. It means that we teach all people the whole counsel of God, all of the time.

Obviously, in deprived communities we can find the challenge almost overwhelming. Where do we start? Do we challenge the addiction, the sexual immorality, the stealing from the local shop, the misuse of money or the gossiping first? People don't turn up to our churches struggling with only one issue. Some issues may be more pressing than others. This is where the beauty of opening the Word of God comes in.

If we commit to teaching people the whole counsel of God, the Holy Spirit will do His work as He prods and convicts those whom we are discipling. It's not our job to be the moral conscience of those in our care. It's our job to teach them the truth persistently and consistently, being faithful to what the Bible says. That's how people change. That's how they become more mature in Jesus.

I remember in the early years of my ministry in Niddrie, we had a flurry of people professing to follow Christ within a short period of time. On the one hand, it was such a blessing to see. On the other hand, it was chaos. These people were, quite literally in some cases, fighting one another over long-held family grudges (a big issue in scheme life). They were gossiping. They were sleeping with one another. They were up to all sorts of mischief. I remember in one elders meeting one of the elders said, "What are we going to do with them?

Christians don't behave like this." "Of course, they do," I said. "Just look at the book of Corinthians."

Another elder asked the question: "But how are we going to stop them disrupting the church so much?" The answer to his question was very simple. We just had to keep on patiently and persistently teaching God's Word to them. We had to keep challenging sin and then let God do His thing. In fact, we decided to do a preaching series on 1 Corinthians. And guess what happened? God challenged a lot of hearts and those who truly were Christians moved on with the Lord, while those who were false just stopped coming. God did His thing through His Word.

That's the beauty of a local church that serves up a hot dish of consecutive, expository preaching for its members, week in and week out. It's a long, slow process, but it's the most effective discipleship method in the universe.

But discipleship is not just sharing the Word of God. There is something else involved too.

DISCIPLESHIP MEANS SHARING LIFE

If we think about how Jesus discipled, it is very different from how it is done today in many churches. Jesus didn't just teach people in a formal setting. He didn't just meet up with the disciples once a week for a quick catch-up over a coffee. He was with His disciples constantly. He shared His entire life with them, not just a few snatched moments when He could make time in His busy schedule.

In Deuteronomy 11:19, Moses commands the people of Israel to teach God's Law to the next generation: "Teach them to your children, talking about them when you sit at home and when you walk along the road, when you lie down and when you get up." In other words, teach your children the Word of God in all of life, not just a few formal scenarios.

In Acts 20:18–20, Paul reminds the Ephesian elders of the example he set them while he was with them.

> *You know how I lived the whole time I was with you, from the first day I came into the province of Asia. I served the Lord with great humility and with tears and in the midst of severe testing by the plots of my Jewish opponents. You know that I have not hesitated to preach anything that would be helpful to you but have taught you publicly and from house to house.*

Paul lived among the people he was discipling. He got to know them. They were a part of his everyday life. He discipled them when life was good and when life was bad. They laughed and cried together. And in every one of these situations, Paul sought to bring the Word of God to bear so that they would grow more Christlike.

He says something similar to the church in Thessalonica in 1 Thessalonians 2:7–8. "Instead, we were like young children among you. Just as a nursing mother cares for her children, so we cared for you. Because we loved you so much, we were delighted to share with you not only the gospel of God but our lives as well." Paul loved the believers he was discipling so much that he shared the gospel with them, and also his life as well.

Truly biblical discipleship is not just about formally teaching the Bible to people either in a congregational setting, small groups or one-to-one situations. It is not less than that, but it is certainly more than that. It is sharing life together. Eating together. Laughing together. Using the everyday moments of life, good and bad, to remind one another of the Word of God, and to consistently and persistently point one another to Jesus. The Lord ate, drank, loved, taught, cared for, walked alongside and loved His disciples. So, when I read Matthew 28:19–20 that's what I hear Him saying.

Making disciples surely means nothing less than pouring your mind, heart and soul into new believers (and mature ones too), with the intention of seeing them become more knowledgeable in the Scriptures and, slowly but surely, becoming like Christ every single day.

It's not very complicated when we break it down, is it? So, what's the issue then? Why aren't more of us engaged in this kind of discipleship? One word.

Time.

THE IDOL OF TIME

The great idol in the lives of so many Christians today is the idol of *time*. We will give money to good causes. We will sometimes pray about the needs of the less fortunate. But the bottom line is that we are all *just so busy*.

You might have picked this book up and be thinking to yourself: "Somebody ought to do something about the lack of gospel witness and churches in our deprived communities." But you are probably not, for one second, thinking that this someone ought to be you. "Where would I find the time?" You say to yourself, "Between my job and my family, and my other commitments, I don't have the time to do any of this stuff. I am happy to give towards somebody else doing it."

Let me encourage you to think of it another way. It's not that you don't have the time. It's that you don't want to do it. It's that you don't feel the issue is urgent. Or if you do, not urgent enough for you to do something about it. It's that you don't believe that millions of people, most of whom live on your own doorstep, are going to hell. It's that you don't see them as important enough to bother trying to save, because you have *other priorities* in your life.

We all find time to do the things we want to do. Go out for a drink with work friends. Have a nice holiday. Spend the weekend with friends from our school days. Go to the gym five days a week. Buy a season ticket for our favourite sporting team. We always have time.

The bottom line is that we just don't want to share it. And we certainly don't want to share it with the type of people described in this book.

Biblical discipleship isn't difficult. It's just costly. A 30-minute Bible study with a colleague over our lunch break is easy enough now and then. But to get involved in the life of somebody who is completely messed up is something else entirely. That would mean sharing our lives with people who are not like us. It would mean not just inviting people to lunch once a month but inviting them into our families. It would mean taking people's burdens upon our own shoulders.

The difficulty is not that we don't understand what biblical discipleship ought to look like. It's not that we are incapable of doing it. It's that *we just don't want to*. We don't want to find the time. We would prefer to get our cheque books out and soothe our consciences that way.

We like our "me" time. We like our leisure time. We have our diaries all mapped out. We don't have room to fit other people into our lives. And especially not people who have a mountain of problems to deal with. We don't want people texting or ringing us every single day for advice. We don't want to have to sit through hours of people talking about their terrible home life. We'll happily serve in a soup kitchen a few hours a week or help at a camp for disadvantaged children once a year. That's it. Duty done. Time to go home, put the TV on and relax.

That's not New Testament discipleship. That's not what Jesus taught His disciples, and it is not what Matthew 28:19–20 means. If our discipleship isn't costly and exhausting, then we are doing it wrong.

Discipleship has to be *all* of life, or it is none.

DISCIPLESHIP REQUIRES PATIENCE AND PERSISTENCE

The original band of 12 disciples were some of the dumbest men in the world at that time. They did and said many stupid things. They fought with one another over who was the greatest or who was Jesus's favourite. Yet Jesus was extremely patient with them. He kept teaching them. He kept walking with them. He kept persisting with them.

If I've learned one thing in over 20 years of pastoral ministry in my context, it is the need for patience in my discipling. There is a reason Jesus calls us sheep and that is because we are stupid. We need to be told the same truth a hundred times, and we still ignore it.

Discipleship can be so *disheartening.*

Discipleship can be so *annoying.*

I have sometimes spent half a day trying to convince someone in my congregation not to follow a particular course of action. I have read the Bible with them. I have prayed with them. I have warned them of the consequences should they sin. I have asked them to repeat back to me what they have heard God say through the Word. I have prayed with them again. The person cries and feels convicted and gets emotional. They thank me profusely for my time and for my wisdom and then they walk out of the door and, within minutes, they go and do the exact opposite of what we'd discussed!

That is the painful reality of discipleship. It is a slow, sometimes discouraging process.

Deep-rooted sin issues don't get dealt with after a week. It takes weeks, months and years of patiently, persistently and consistently teaching the same truths before we begin to see the first bloom of spiritual fruit.

There are so many books available on discipleship right now and they all sound so exciting. We read about all the success stories. All the ones who made it through the ups and downs of their lives. Very rarely do we read a book about all the failures of church life and discipleship. I have never read a chapter of a book that said, "Discipling stupid and annoying people"!

The reality is that many of the people we disciple can quickly become annoying. They can be extremely irritating. Their stories of crime and prison might read well in black and white but dealing with them in real life soon gets boring and monotonous. It is hard to keep a soft heart when dealing with angry, mean, bitter, lazy people who are always looking for excuses for their sin or looking for shortcuts to godly living.

Discipleship like this is just so *tiring*. Teaching the same people the same truths again and again and again. Constantly pointing them to Jesus and urging them to live a life of obedience in the power of the Holy Spirit. Living life day in, day out with people requires bags of patience. It's little wonder that so many Christians don't want to live their lives this way!

Perhaps the hardest part of biblical discipleship is the heartbreak that it so often brings.

DISCIPLESHIP MEANS HEARTBREAK

Jesus's ministry was full of heartbreak. He taught His disciples. He loved His disciples. He shared His life with His disciples. And yet look how many walked away. I think John 6:66 is one of the saddest sentences in the Bible. "From that time many of His disciples went back and walked with Him no more" (NKJV).

Heart-breaking.

Yet a closer look at the New Testament shows us that this is what we are to expect in our discipleship: heart-breaking, soul-crushing disappointment. When we consider the parable of the sower, for example, we discover that 75% of the gospel seed that was sown *failed*. Some of the seed looked like it was producing something, but it was soon swept away. That is a poor success rate when it comes to farming – but that is the life of Christian discipleship in the kingdom of God.

We share the gospel with people. We share life with people. We love people like they are our own family. We invite people into our homes and our lives. They come on family holidays with us. But, before we know it, they are telling lies about us on social media. Once that happens a few times, we begin to wonder whether it is worth all the effort. Maybe the middle class have the right idea after all. Just do a coffee once a fortnight and exchange polite chit chat. It's far less painful.

In Christian discipleship we must steel our hearts for disappointment, but we must not have steely hearts. Like Jesus, we must persevere and keep on teaching the truth. We must be careful not to make people the centre of our lives. We must be careful to ensure that all our hopes do not lie in them making it. People are going to let us down. We are going to let them down.

The only person any of us can truly rely on to never let us down is Jesus.

We must guard our hearts against despair and bitterness. It's so easy to become cynical and jaded when it comes to discipleship. When the next messy convert comes along, we think, *What's the point? Won't this one just turn out like the last one? Why should I bother?* We need to treat each person individually and give them the same amount of time and effort and truth. We need to be consistent across the board.

This is hard.

This leads us to a common pitfall among those who engage in discipleship with those from chaotic backgrounds. Over-discipling.

WE MUSTN'T OVER-DISCIPLE PEOPLE

When Jesus left to go up to heaven, He sent His disciples out into the world in the power of the Holy Spirit. Therefore, everyone we disciple who is truly saved has the Spirit of God within them. They have the Spirit of God to transform them and empower them to live the Christian life. It is easy to forget that truth when we are discipling people with complex social and psychological needs. It's easy for *us* to become their functional saviours.

It's easy to fall into the following sinful pattern of behaviour:

1. They have some form of crisis. Maybe their social security payments have been suspended.
2. They immediately ring you in a panic.
3. You calm them down and then make sure they have some money to buy food for the children.
4. Problem solved. Crisis averted. Life goes on.
5. Another crisis rears its head. They forgot to put money on the electricity meter and it has run out.
6. They ring you in a panic.
7. You calm them down and then put some money on their meter card.
8. Problem solved. Crisis averted. Life goes on.
9. Repeat ad nauseum and ad infinitum.

There are all sorts of issues with this scenario, not least of which is that you have become the saviour in this person's life, not Jesus. Every time they come to a crisis point, they are turning to you and not the Lord. After all, why do they need the Lord when they have you!

This is not to say that we shouldn't help people; we should when it is appropriate. But it is to say that in our discipleship we must teach people that the first port of call in any crisis is God, not us. Let's try the problem another way:

- Somebody has a problem. Their social security has been stopped.
- Ask them if they have prayed about it. If they haven't, encourage them to do so immediately. If they are not sure how or what to pray, show them.
- Encourage them to ring or contact the appropriate people who deal with these things. Never do for somebody what they can do for themselves.
- Almost always the situation gets resolved.
- Check in with them to see how they are. If things are going okay, encourage them to thank God for answered prayer. If they are still struggling, encourage them to pray again.
- If all else fails, step into the breach but help them to come up with some proactive ways they can move forward.
- Pray with them.

It's so, so easy to allow people to depend entirely on us. We rarely admit it, but it gives us a real feeling of power and control. The fact that we can control another human being's life, and that they completely rely on us and our advice, is as intoxicating as any drug. Sometimes, if we are not very careful, we can be guilty of over-discipling people. There's a fine line between being somebody's discipler and their carer.

In our discipleship we must ensure that:

- There is only one Saviour, and it is not us.
- Our motives are grounded in wanting people to mature in Christ for their spiritual good rather than to make us look good to others in the church.
- Don't make decisions for people that they can make for themselves. Even when we think a step is simple, we must let them come to their own conclusions, unless they are obviously sinful.
- Help people to learn from their mistakes. They are going to make many, and they need to know that this is okay, as long as they repent quickly and get back in the race.

CONCLUSION

Biblical discipleship done this way is costly. It means denying self. It means giving up personal space and leisure time. It means giving up a whole way of life. It's stressful. It's painful. It's joyous. It's funny. It's sad. It's exhilarating. It's depressing. It's often thankless.

But Jesus has called us to feed His sheep. All of them. Even the ones in the part of the town that scares you the most. People need the gospel of Jesus. People need churches in which to be properly discipled in order to grow in their faith.

That, surely, includes the least, the last and the lost in the UK.

SPOTLIGHT:

DISCIPLING WOMEN

SHARON DICKENS,
DIRECTOR OF 20SCHEMES WOMEN'S MINISTRY

"We'd gone for a cup of tea and a catch up. I'd been hanging out with Cathy for years. We talked about everything, and this day was no different. She shared about the sadness of losing her child. She always said that she took drugs to dull the pain. We talked and, at some point, I shared the gospel with her. Then she said the saddest thing ever. 'I just need to get myself sorted and then I'll think about Jesus.'"

A question that I get asked a lot is, "How do you engage women?" What they really mean is, "How do I engage with women?" I'm never really quite sure how to answer this because I think it is a bit of a weird question to ask. Am I being asked how to evangelise, or how to meet people? Unless you are one of those rare women who works from home, does all her shopping and banking online, and only talks via text or email, then in some way, somehow, in your everyday life you are engaging with people. Some may even become friends.

I know some people are more adept than others at social interaction, but unless you're Tom Hanks in Castaway and your only pal is Wilson the volleyball, then you are always engaging with others. So, the question we should really be asking is, "Why *don't* I share the gospel with them?" How deliberate are you being about sharing the gospel while you engage the world around you? If you're not intentionally looking for ways to evangelise the lost around you, then why not?

Personally, I'm just not one of those people that can sit down with someone and within minutes share the gospel. I'm not an evangelist. However, just because I don't have the gift of evangelism doesn't mean that I get a special waiver from sharing the gospel. When we are hanging out with people we know (colleagues, friends, family, gym buddies, mums at the school gates) we talk about what we really care about – our children, our hobbies, our pets, our relationships. But many of us find it difficult to get past these superficialities and move on to the deeper spiritual truths of life and death. Why is that? If Jesus is so important to us, why can't we talk about Him?

We make excuses about "lack of opportunities". We worry about offending people. We are scared of being asked a question we cannot answer. But if Jesus is such an important part of our lives, then it should be just as natural, easy and normal talking about Him as it is talking about all the other things going on in our lives.

A couple of years ago, I decided to join the local gym. I wanted to get fit, and I was looking for an opportunity to meet new women from my community. I'd been thinking for a while how I could proactively engage with women in Niddrie who work during the day and who I would never ordinarily get a chance to meet.

So, the local gym was my solution. I started a Pilates class and met a few women there. Over time we got chatting about all the usual things of life. I'd been very intentional in going to the same classes, at the same time, with the same people and praying for each of the women by name. The Lord has been good and I've had several opportunities to share my faith. Nothing was forced. In fact, most of the time the ladies instigate the questions. I try not to be just another face in the crowd. I'm there to get fit but I don't see that as my primary goal. I don't leave Jesus behind when I sign into my class. A deliberately intentional life, always seeking opportunities to share, can bring amazing opportunities to share the gospel.

Let me answer a few questions of my own:

1. Do you know where the women in your community are spending their time?
2. Does your life look exactly the same as everyone else's? Are you distinct?
3. Are you being deliberate about engaging women (or deep down are you hoping no one looks your way or starts a conversation)?
4. Do you have any non-Christian friends? Do you really share the gospel with them or just invite them to church? (It's not the same thing.)
5. Do you pray for the women you meet, by name, asking God to save them and to give you gospel opportunities?
6. What little changes in your life can you make to help you be more intentional about how you engage?

You don't have to be gifted. Being faithful is far more important. We may fumble, we might not get the right words, and we may even get asked a question we don't know the answer to. But real relationships always lead to real opportunities and so we need to be bold when they arise. Who knows what God will do? With prayer and boldness, you will be surprised at how God draws people to Himself through a simple, faithful witness.

DISCIPLESHIP AND ACCOUNTABILITY

I'm from an unchurched background and when I was first saved, I really didn't have a clue what it was all about beyond the fact I was a sinner who deserved hell. Thankfully, Jesus died for my sins because He loved me. I believed everything older Christians told me because *obviously* they knew better than I did.

I remember someone once telling me that God would take my first child from me in punishment for what I'd done before I was saved. Thankfully, there was an older godly woman who counselled me and helped me to unravel what was biblically true. I would go to her with a problem and she would say, "'Let's find out what the Bible says about that," or the dreaded, "What do you think Jesus is trying to teach you though this?" She patiently taught me to rely on Christ and trust the truth of His Word. She's still in my life thirty-two years later and is one of my closest friends.

Discipleship isn't new. As mothers and sisters, we have been teaching the young how to navigate life ever since Eden. When I taught my son to do the laundry, I didn't just hand him the manual for the machine, a box of laundry detergent, the laundry basket and say, "On you go, son." I showed him how to separate the whites from the darks, which button to push and how much laundry detergent to use. I walked him through it. In fact, I walked both my children through all the big life lessons such as cooking, cleaning, personal safety and relationships. I didn't leave them to work things out by themselves. It's what we do as parents. So, why would it be any different for our spiritual children, regardless of their age and sex? Mature Christians have a responsibility to help new believers to grow in the faith.

Yet, when it comes to helping new Christians grow and mature in the faith, most churches do nothing more than hand people a Bible and leave them to their own devices. This is simply insufficient when discipling people from unchurched and chaotic backgrounds. In fact, I don't think it's enough for any Christian, regardless of their background.

Discipleship provides the framework where believers walk through life together with Christ and the local church offers a place to deal with, and face, life's trials and struggles. It's within this context that we encourage each other to rely on Christ and speak biblical wisdom into everyday situations. We can pray, support, example maturity, strengthen one another, bring comfort, admonish and, ultimately, point the believer to Christ. This type of discipleship is costly. The sad truth is many just don't want to pay the price.

Discipleship can be uncomfortable, especially when we have to challenge someone we love. We need to speak the truth in love and not be fearful of challenging sin. If we truly love someone, we will gently tell them what they need to hear even though we know they won't like it (and maybe not like us afterwards). We must encourage them to think through their actions, helping them to become more aware of their sin and the temptation they struggle with. We need to prepare them to fight temptation, flee from sin and run to Christ.

We need to be patient. Change is often slow. Sin is an ongoing battle in our own lives – and we cannot expect it to be any different for those we are discipling. We must patiently repeat the same truths day after day. It's repetitive. It's often frustrating. But it's necessary.

Sometimes we wonder if the people we are discipling are even saved! How many times has God had to repeat Himself to us? Seven? Seventy times seven? We need to patiently disciple, with love and perseverance. Keep speaking, keep encouraging, keep pointing them to Christ and keep praying for and with them. Philippians 1:6 says, "being confident of this, that he who began a good work in you will carry it on to completion until the day of Christ Jesus."

Sadly, there will be those who walk away, never to return. People who we poured our lives into. People who started well but didn't last the course. People who will break your heart. People who shared your life but now walk past you in the street. It's a sad reality – the parable of the sower paints the picture. In those heart-breaking moments, it's easy to feel dejected, like it's all a pointless waste of time. But we need to continue to faithfully share the gospel, invest in the next generation and watch God build His church.

CHAPTER 6:

RETHINKING THEOLOGICAL TRAINING AND THE LOCAL CHURCH

As I have established, as local churches have either aged, shut or moved out of town, the housing estates and schemes of the UK are largely spiritual wastelands. We have been left with several generations of people not only untouched by the good news of Jesus Christ, but also with a major shortage of indigenous leadership at a local church level.

Para-church organisations have largely failed at establishing, discipling and training young men and women to stay within and/or establish healthy, gospel-centred, local churches in our communities. That is not to say that para-church organisations have not seen fruit. It is just that this fruit has not been tied directly to the local church (largely because they just don't exist in these areas). Therefore, what we need in the UK right now is a church revitalisation and planting movement that incorporates indigenous training into its DNA.

The problem we have is bigger than we think. Believe it or not, the demise of working-class leaders in our churches can even be partly laid at the door of Margaret Thatcher!

THE LEADERSHIP GAP – WHY MAGGIE IS (INDIRECTLY) TO BLAME!

In the 1980s, the Conservative Government, led by Margaret Thatcher (The Iron Lady) encouraged millions of council tenants to buy their own homes. The consequence of this policy was positive, in that many working-class people could buy their own house at an affordable price. It gave people a certain dignity and financial security to own their own home, particularly among a section of society used to making others rich and financially secure.

However, problems arose when people began to get on the property ladder and discovered that the house they bought dirt cheap from the government was actually worth tens of thousands more on the open market. That meant that people could sell up and move to a more respectable side of town. Over the decades, as the homeowners have moved out and moved up, it has affected, for example, the sense of community that once existed.

Now, I am not arguing for the existence of the once "noble poor", claiming that the poor are without error or fault, because that is a fantasy. But there were organisations that used to be at the heart of almost every council estate prior to the Thatcher years in the 1980s. Ian Gilbert says this: "Organisations which have traditionally provided community cohesion, such as trade unions, cooperative societies and social clubs have declined."[310]

It is important that we grasp this change because it has had a devastating effect on the church and the gospel in poor communities all across the UK. Who would have been the natural church officers and spiritual leaders in poor communities up to the 1950s and 1960s? The shop floor steward, or the Miners' Union leader. But upward mobility meant that, within a generation, many of these men were gone – and they left behind a leadership vacuum on our estates and schemes. Churches that were booming in the 1950s and 1960s have been in terminal decline since then. There are no males. There are no Christians. There are no converts. There are no leaders. Even if somebody does become a Christian, there are no local churches to disciple and equip them and so they too are forced to leave and go to the middle-class-dominated church in town and assimilate to their culture. Once there, it is virtually impossible for them to rise to any sort of leadership responsibility in a system that is locked out to their class.

In the 1970s, the Lausanne Covenant on World Evangelism, published a manifesto which included the following statement, concerning leadership training and development:

> *We also acknowledge that some of our missions have been too slow to equip and encourage national leaders to assume their rightful responsibilities. Yet we are committed to indigenous principles, and long that every church will have national leaders who manifest a Christian style of leadership in terms not of domination but of service. We recognize that there is a great need to improve theological education, especially for church leaders. In every nation and culture there should be an effective training programme for pastors and laity in doctrine, discipleship, evangelism, nurture and service. Such training programmes should not rely on any stereotyped methodology but should be developed by creative local initiatives according to biblical standards (Col. 1:27–28; Acts 14:23; Tit. 1:5, 9; Mark 10:42–35; Eph. 4:11,12).*[311]

We who are trying to revitalise or plant churches in the UK's most deprived communities have to face up to a grim reality. Those of us from council estates and housing schemes across the UK stand at the edge of a spiritual precipice. We have few Christians willing to come to our aid. We have little money being handed our way. We have few healthy churches and we have practically no leaders either now, or coming through the current theological training systems.

That means we may not see future church leaders coming from our communities for several decades. Therefore, any plan we have for reaching, discipling and producing healthy churches in our poorest communities needs to take these factors into account. We are going to have to do the training ourselves. We are going to have to take back theological training and put it into the hands of our churches, as small and weak as they may be.

We ought to be looking to the five-year-old child on our estate and asking ourselves: *What can we do not only to reach this child and their family, but to build a long-term, theological training pathway that will develop them as the future leaders of the church 20 years from now?*

But, as we do that, we are going to have to work out how we can survive in the long-term. Many of us are overstretched and underfunded. We need to get creative if we are going to achieve our goal of providing a solid, theological education for a future generation of council estate and housing scheme pastors, evangelists and women's workers.

Three things come to mind:

1. We are going to have to rely on a generation of "cultural outsiders" (British, American or otherwise) to help us in a fledgling church revitalisation and church-planting movement in the UK.
2. We are going to have to train these outsiders to be on the look-out for "cultural insiders" as they make

the transition to indigeneity. These insiders will be people who have been saved from our estates and schemes, who may well need to leave their own community, but we can use their insider knowledge for other communities.

3 Ultimately, we are going to have to train a new generation of "culturally indigenous" leaders.

We have started the process with our Ragged School of Theology, our in-house theological training programme for men and women that we have been developing, in various forms, for the past decade. We have recently partnered with Union College, in Wales, to improve the course which we will open to students UK-wide in the coming years.

We offer a three-year Ministry and Theology Certificate to compete with any theological institution in the UK. It includes specialist electives concerning ministering to women, youth work, preaching and counselling, all within a housing scheme context. Our lecturers are either converts from housing estates or have worked and/or are pastoring in housing estates.

We are not ratified by any secular institution, but we are ratified in an unofficial capacity by Union which, in effect, guarantees the quality of the training that we offer. We aim to be the training hub for scheme ministry, particularly in Scotland, but also to the rest of the UK (when it comes to council estates). The training is offered either in person or online. People have the luxury of studying for half a day a week and not having to leave their contexts whatsoever. Thereby, their local churches and/or plants retain their most gifted people as they learn on the job. In this way, the local church is not weakened, it is strengthened.

What we are doing is not new and it is not radical by any means. This is how people have been doing training in the two-thirds world for decades. The issue is getting the Western evangelical world to get down off their high horse and accept that our kind of vocational training is just as reliable and effective – if not more so in some cases – than their so-called "scholarly approach" to theological training. In other words, three years training with the RST is going to be more than adequate to prepare anybody for the rigours of pastoral ministry in our communities. In fact, they will probably be better prepared than those who take the higher educational route.

As part of their training, we give our younger converts ministry responsibilities more quickly than is often the case in middle-class churches. Often, the middle-class approach to leadership training is, "Prove yourself and then we will see", but a better way, we think, within scheme culture is, "Take responsibility until you prove you are unable." In other words, we give local converts responsibility more quickly and release them into areas of service and teaching (not just chair stacking). Alongside this, they are shadowed by a mentor. In other words, we are equipping them from behind and from the side, not just up front. We walk with them and talk with them and live with them.

That is how Jesus did it with the disciples.

We are constantly looking for people with high leadership potential. For example, drug dealers, or at least those who didn't use their own stash, often make great leaders. They are self-starters and entrepreneurial. What they need is character and that comes with the work of the Holy Spirit, time and teaching.

We need the gospel to go viral before we establish our leadership structures. It will only go viral if new converts are released early, not over-discipled or mollycoddled and not expected to live up to some super idealism imposed from cultural outsiders. The early church was a bit of a mess, but the gospel also went viral as it fell into the hands of ordinary people. Let it loose and mop up the mess afterwards. Far too many leaders are control freaks. Of course, we will face the accusation of promoting people too quickly. This is a favourite one of cultural outsiders. Leadership development requires practice as much as knowledge and character.

Jesus allowed the early disciples to engage with Him in ministry. They failed, they misunderstood Him and they let Him down, but none of that suggested they weren't ready. Knowledge is good, but it is insufficient on its own. Remember, Bible college students who think they can preach a good sermon are no good if they can't understand the basic principles of cross-cultural communication and culture.

Cultural insiders and indigenous people are not going to look like outsiders. They won't be polished or have Bible college education, but that doesn't mean that they can't lead.

We need to be working out how to combine contextualised theological education that is helpful for our people and is overseen, governed and assessed on the ground by the local church.

SPOTLIGHT:

A RESPONSE TO MEZ

MIKE REEVES, PRESIDENT OF UNION SCHOOL OF THEOLOGY, WALES

Many of Mez's questions and concerns have also been on my mind. I agree that theological colleges have too often been entrenched and self-referencing instead of serving the local church and meeting her needs. Spiritual and pastoral formation has therefore suffered, and paper qualifications have been taken as an automatic passport into pastoral ministry.

Before suggesting a way forward, I think a distinction may help. We tend to talk today about "training" for pastoral ministry, but I suggest there are actually three components to a good preparation for ministry: training, education and formation. Training develops the necessary hands-on skills needed for pastoring a local church. Education builds knowledge of God, His Word, our own lives and the world. Formation shapes the Christlike character that is essential for Christian ministry. If any of these pieces are missing, the church will suffer through neglect or starvation.

As Mez shows, a good deal of *training* for pastoral ministry tends to be done best in the context of the local church. He is quite right, then, to warn of the dangers of separating preparation for ministry from the local church. However, *education* usually requires a bigger context.

When education is limited to one man (a local pastor) trying to pass on his education to his assistant(s), there is a necessary trickle-down loss. There is leakage. The assistant will receive only a percentage of the education his pastor has, and with nothing to balance out the quirks and eccentricities he has learned. If that is the only model of education the church has, it will get weaker, generation after generation. This was precisely how the great Puritan movement gradually died: once a force for the reformation of the church, bit by bit it lost the ability to say anything to the world.

So what is the way forward?

On the one hand, local churches cannot abdicate their responsibility and hand over all ministry preparation to the colleges. That way lies dislocation, and the training and formation errors Mez has outlined. On the other hand, neither should they imagine that they can do everything themselves (just as they don't imagine they can produce by themselves all the Bibles, songs and books they use). Those who do usually betray either a lack of appreciation for education or a worrying sectarian mindset. Instead, local churches and colleges need to *work together*, with the college actively serving the local church.

This is possible: it is what Union School of Theology is doing as it partners with the Ragged School of Theology and local churches around the world. What we have found is that the partnership enables us to address these issues together and provide a theological education that is both robust and contextualised. Working together, we are learning to prepare people for ministry in a way that is not dislocated or dysfunctional. We are still learning, but this way we can get the best of both worlds, neither making do with inadequate training, nor providing education that fails to be fit for purpose.

CHAPTER 7:

RETHINKING MERCY MINISTRY AND THE LOCAL CHURCH

"For disadvantaged people to flourish into their full, God-given potential, they must leave behind dependencies that impede their growth. Initiatives that thwart their development, though rightly motivated, must be restructured to reinforce self-sufficiency if they are to become agents of lasting and positive change."[312]

Robert D. Lupton, *Toxic Charity*

This is a quote from one of my favourite books, provocatively entitled, *Toxic Charity: How churches and charities hurt those they help (and how to reverse it)*. The book is written by Robert D. Lupton who is the founder of FCS Urban Ministries.[313] His aim is to help Christian churches to think more carefully about the kind of help they think they are giving to the poor and oppressed, particularly in the two-thirds world. According to Lupton, *good intentions* while admirable are often dangerous and counterproductive to those we are seeking to help, particularly if we have not thought through the implications seriously beforehand.

According to Lupton, instead of encouraging dependency, we should be looking at ways in which our giving and/or helping can produce more independency.

At Niddrie, we are constantly assessing and reassessing all of our ministries and outreach initiatives. We have tried (and failed) with several local initiatives in order to help those struggling financially. During the global pandemic of 2020–21 we were handing out up to 600 food parcels a week to the families of children at risk. However, once the government restrictions eased and people were able to get out more, we brought the initiative to an end instead opened a cheap food stall twice a week in our building, using stock donated to us by local supermarkets. We didn't want to keep people overly dependent on us, but we also wanted to give them affordable options if they couldn't afford supermarket prices.

DEVELOPING EMPLOYMENT INITIATIVES

For many years, 20schemes has desired to create a back-to-work employability project as part of our on-going discipleship. We wanted to move people out of relief mode and into becoming members of society that contribute, instead of just taking. As a church, we want to grow our disciples to become not only mature Christians and faithful church members, but also active and constructive citizens of society. Work is an important element in all of that.

Years ago, we were discipling a young woman who had a number of issues both before and after she became a Christian. She had received the help of social workers, drug workers, health visitors and many more people in her chaotic life for over a decade. At one point, we estimated that she had cost the Scottish government half a million pounds. All that expense and effort and she had not changed her behaviour in the slightest. If anything, she had deteriorated over the years.

But along comes Jesus and He transforms her from the inside out. Praise God, she's now a mature Christian woman, drug-free, an active church member and also a productive member of her community. She's in a job that cares for some of the most vulnerable people in society with severe learning difficulties. She now has a lovely family and it brings us great joy to see how God has redeemed not just her soul, but her whole life.

Thankfully, she isn't the only one. We have helped people go to university, learn to drive, take computer qualifications, and much more. We've partnered with Christian businesses who have given young Christian's work experience or provided assistance for them while they volunteer for other organisations. We have discipled and prepared many people to go on to employment or go as fully equipped missionaries.

RETRAIN

Recently, we launched a new initiative called Retrain. This ministry has a number of objectives including:

- Finding meaningful employment for new believers
- Helping new believers start up small businesses
- Buying small businesses to employ new believers

Retrain has a number of purposes as we look to the future:

- Putting new Christians back into the workplace as salt and light
- Raising money through the profits to develop and train more indigenous interns for our Ragged School of Theology
- Raising money through profits to help the funding of more church plants and revitalisations in Scotland's poorest communities

In other words, our mercy ministry has objectives and purposes bigger than just meeting immediate relief in the lives of people who are struggling. We want them to come to know Jesus. We want them to be baptised and join our church. We want them to be able to access theological training and discipleship. We want them to have the option to pursue vocational ministry in the schemes if God has gifted them for that. Or to work for God in the workplace if He has gifted them for that.

Retrain, like the Ragged School of Theology, is just another way the local church can enable new believers not stick at being victims and consumers, but know that God has called them to something so much more than that.

Of course, we face many hurdles in what we are trying to do. Sadly, the advent of the welfare state and the huge upsurge in the drug culture (prescribed and otherwise) have left us with a (hardcore) subculture with no work ethic, no drive and no family support system. People have no motivation to work hard whatsoever because, ultimately, they know the state will bail them out, as it has done for generations. Generally, people are happy getting by "with their Giros" and subsidising their income with the odd bit of work here and there, legal or otherwise.

Niddrie is not Africa or some other two-thirds world nation where many people will work hard, doing almost anything, in an effort to provide for their families. People who think nothing of working 18-hour days. Of course, the advantage in many of these countries (and I saw it first-hand in Brazil) is that people aren't subject to the same tight governmental regulations and financial restraints when it comes to business start-ups and entrepreneurial endeavours. But, still, ask the average Niddron who comes into our cafe what their dream is, and they will look at you blankly. As for a stable support system, forget it. The abused child of yesteryear dragged up by an alcoholic dad and a Valium-loving mother is now a parent themself. It is tragic. How do we even begin to put into practice some of our "community stimulus" ideas when individualism and familial breakdown is pretty much the standard on our scheme for so many of those who need our help and support? The answer is at once obvious, yet appears to many, at first glance, to be trite and far too simplistic. I will state it, nonetheless.

We must continue to preach the only, true saving gospel of the Lord Jesus Christ loudly and clearly, praying for deep, personal spiritual revival and renewal in the minds and hearts of our listeners.

There it is. Read it again.

We must continue to preach the only, true saving gospel of the Lord Jesus Christ loudly and clearly, praying for deep, personal spiritual revival and renewal in the minds and hearts of our listeners.

We must preach Christ and Him crucified. We must never present Him as a self-help option or as someone who has come to make their life better or to give them another handout. He came to call all of us to "deny self and pick up our cross *daily*". He is calling all of us to a life of *ongoing repentance*. I truly believe that only a move of God's Holy Spirit in a person's life is going to motivate them towards a life of constructive independency.

Before that happens, they need to be born again. No spiritual renewal equals no physical and communal renewal. Fact. Now, many of my dearest and most respected friends will argue that the main job of the church is to proclaim the gospel and leave the rest of this stuff up to the state or other outside agencies. I wholeheartedly agree.

The issue comes in dealing with the new believer who has spent the last 30 years of his life in a drug-induced daze, sponging off the state and living at home with his girlfriend and three children. Oh, and not to mention the other four children he has to three other women on the scheme. He now becomes our "problem" as we work out what biblical discipleship looks like for him. *How do we encourage him to begin to make a positive contribution to society instead of just taking all the time? How can we disentangle him from a benefits system that actually leaves him financially better off unemployed?*

At Niddrie, we have seen first-hand that the only way a person can be stimulated to move away from the benefits system and into the workplace is through the power of God's Holy Spirit. Not only does He save lost souls, but He is the great motivator when it comes to the complete turnaround of lives. That's why we have seen long-term drug addicts get their first job(s) for decades. *And the support system they need but don't get at home?* The local church. The local body of believers that encourages them, rebukes them, corrects them and helps keep them motivated.

Our love and discipleship does not stop because they have moved into the workplace. At Niddrie, we are looking for people to move to independency almost from the moment they come to faith. In the early days, we encourage people to volunteer in the community cafe and to help with the maintenance of the building as a first step on the ladder. Those who are after a free ride soon get fed up and leave, but those who really want to move on with their lives stay and work hard. The next step is often a voluntary job in the community one day a week. They are baby steps, but they are steps in the right direction. It is about the only system we have in place at the moment to separate the wheat from the chaff. It is a long-term objective, but we are beginning to see the early signs of fruit.

I do know that however we structure things here, we need to:

1 Keep the gospel the main thing

2 Keep the local church as the centre of all we are doing

3 See all projects as a means for gospel proclamation and/or ongoing discipleship

4 Ensure that all income generated is reinvested into the community

5 Plan a timetable to ensure future, indigenous leadership.

DO MORE GOOD, BETTER

According to Lupton, ancient Hebrew wisdom describes four levels of charity:

> *The highest level is to provide a job for one in need without his knowledge that you provided it. The next, lower level is to provide work that the needy one knows you provided. The third level is to give an anonymous gift to meet an immediate need. The lowest level of charity, to be avoided, if at all possible, is to give a poor person a gift with his full knowledge that you are the donor.*[314]

It is an almost indisputable fact, especially among those of us who work in deprived communities, that handouts do not help people out of poverty. In fact, they breed contempt on the part of the recipient, who begins to feel that they deserve our charity and ultimately that we owe it to them. It also breeds dependency and demotivates those being helped. Yet, local churches continue to persist with the model of charity that means handing out free clothes and food and so on.

We need to build models of ministry that are two-way and reciprocal at every level. By all means open a soup kitchen but have those in attendance helping to serve or prep what's on offer. Instead of giving out clothes, set up a small online business and employ people to run it. There are many ways we can change what we do to help people in need. The issue is that this takes times and effort. Much of the love in local church is easy love. It's far easier to hand stuff out and wish people well on their way, than stop, think and develop a strategy that will help people in the long-term. As Lupton says, "Serving people is different from developing people."[315]

So, how do we make our ministries to the poor better? Lupton says this: "If we are to rightly care for those in need, the responsibility lies with those with the resources to create systems built on interdependency rather than dependency."[316]

A good first step is to serve fewer people better than more people poorly. How about capping the numbers to your food bank or your soup kitchen? Instead of feeding 40 homeless people once a week, maybe, drop down to 5–10 people. Focus all your time and energy on them. Make 5–10 real friends and really get to know them, rather than 40–50 acquaintances that you know hardly anything about.

Some people still ask the questions: *Why does all this matter so much? Why are you picking holes in mercy ministry? What have you got against food banks? What does it matter who is helping people and how they are helping people as long as they are helping people?*

In his brilliantly insightful book, *The Alternative: Most of what you believe about poverty is wrong,* Mauricio L. Miller says, "Shallow understanding from people of good will is more frustrating than absolute misunderstanding of people from ill will."[317] In other words, it matters because most of our mercy ministry is damaging the poor, not helping them. It is perpetuating poverty rather than resolving it.

THE WORSE WE MAKE IT SOUND, THE MORE IT LOOKS LIKE WE ARE HELPING THEM

Mauricio says this about working with poor people in his city: "To qualify for my programs people had to highlight their weaknesses, their deficiencies. The more helpless you presented yourself to be, the more eligible you were for services."[318] He then cites the example of two young gang members who were trying to get out of their difficult situation. One of the lads had a record for robbery and the other had no criminal record. But, because of restrictions on Mauricio's funding, he could only accept the lad with the criminal background because he qualified as *the neediest*.

The other lad was not accepted because his lack of lawbreaking meant he didn't fall within their "needy parameters". Mauricio began to realise that he was, in effect, rewarding criminal behaviour. Alongside this, in his experience, the more needy he could paint a community, the more funding he received. The more funding he received, the more people he could employ to "help" these *needy people*. "Poverty Pimping" is what he calls it, and it is rife among agencies seeking to help the poor and needy (including, incidentally, those of us who plant and revitalise churches too).

One of his big assertions is that the welfare system does not help people escape (financial) poverty. The problem lies in the fact that "benefits are reduced as your income goes up and almost disappear if you earn more than poverty level income".[319] He's right. It's the same in the schemes. So, for example, a young couple with three children get their rent and rates paid by the state. They also receive child benefits and JSA (Job Seeker's Allowance). In order for them to live at the same level as they currently live under that system, they need to be earning close to £1,800 per month *after tax*! When both are barely literate and unskilled, that is never going to happen. Even if one of them does happen to get a low-paid job, it affects their benefits so dramatically that they end up losing money when they work. Therefore, they have no motivation to get a job. It's not about laziness for them. It's about simple economic mathematics. They're not sponging off the system.

They're trapped by it.

When we make ministry to the needy areas all about handouts and us serving them, rather than real partnership and relationship, it perpetuates the "them and us" mentality and reinforces the class divide. We often want to help people out of pity and love. But often our pity and love actually disempowers them. We do for them what we should be helping them to do for themselves. After all, how did they survive until we came along on our white horses? There are no easy answers to these questions.

But there is gospel hope. Now, more than ever, the UK's poor need the hope of gospel churches.

CHAPTER 8:

EXPOSITORY SERMONS AND THE POOR

One of the things I constantly hear is that in order to succeed on a housing estate, preaching needs to change. It needs to be shorter. It needs to have one point. It needs to be more conversational.

You are absolutely right. Preaching does need to change. It needs to be *expositional*. It needs to be faithful to the biblical text. It needs to be doctrinal. It needs to be practically applied.

One of the biggest lies that trendy, right-on Christians tell is this one. That somehow, we cannot handle this kind of preaching and teaching in our poorest communities. That we don't have the stomach for it. That it is above and beyond our capabilities to understand, or even be interested in. That it is all too much for us.

They are wrong.

We need fish, chips and mushy peas, not hummus and couscous salads. We want proper food, not bitesize snacks.

At Niddrie, our people will easily sit through and digest a 35- to 40-minute expository message. Yes, some of it may be hard for them to understand, but the brain is like any muscle – when it is regularly exercised it becomes stronger. I also run a midweek Bible study which is 60–90 minutes of me teaching through a book of the Bible verse by verse. People love it and they come prepared to learn, regardless of their level of literacy. Those who can write make notes and those who don't listen intently.

SPOTLIGHT:

GOSPEL-CENTRED PREACHING IN HARD PLACES

ANDY PRIME, PASTOR,
GRACEMOUNT COMMUNITY CHURCH, EDINBURGH[320]

I've been in ministry for about 10 years. The first half of that decade I preached largely in chinos, a V-neck sweater and boat shoes. The second half of that decade I've preached largely in tracksuit bottoms, T-shirts and trainers. That's not down to a change in personal stylist but due to a change in ministry context. I've moved from being on staff at a large, city-centre church to a small, local church in a housing scheme. The context change has led to a wardrobe change.

Being asked to write this article has forced me to scrutinise what else has changed about my preaching ministry other than my outfit. It forced me to re-watch some of the videos from those first five years. And as many of you know, listening to your own voice is always misery. But listening back to sermons from your first five years in ministry? That's absolute torture. If I believed in purgatory, I think my purifying recompense would be to have to listen to my entire back catalogue.

But here's what some of this suffering yielded: in some core ways there's not that much difference.

WHAT'S THE SAME

The image of God: After all, every single human being – regardless of race, gender, class, health and age – is created in the image of God. Far more unites us than divides us. Fallen humanity has a perverted inclination to draw lines, create divisions, form cliques and build walls in order to keep those who are different from us away from us. But God's design in creation and redemption delights in togetherness. Gospel-centred preaching to image-bearing humans will hold the same rough shape regardless of context.

The clarity of Scripture: Because of my belief in the clarity of Scripture, my preaching in the last five years hasn't been dumbed down. Preaching in a hard place is still Word ministry. The clarity of Scripture isn't muddied by context, and the command to preach is not gagged by context. I've heard some churches in areas like ours describe their services as "short and fun" as if "long and serious" was beyond people here. A hard place doesn't equal a stupid place. I know stupid rich people, and I know intelligent poor people. But if being a Christian in a hard place is going to be hard, then shallow, superficial stuff on a Sunday won't cut it. To go hard in a hard place, we'll need to go deep in preaching.

Gospel centrality: Our conviction on the centrality of the gospel itself means that the content of my preaching has been the same over the last ten years.

I've moved to a setting where there are more social needs. But more *social problems* don't require a *social gospel*. The greatest need of every single person I've met in the last 10 years has been salvation from their sins. And the only hope for every person I've met in the last 10 years has been the Lord Jesus Christ. So, regardless of context, we proclaim Him. And we proclaim Him from all the Scriptures.

Give me a football anywhere in the world. I'll find some players, we'll know the rules and we'll play the same game. The same thing's true of preaching. It doesn't matter where you plonk down a pulpit, I'll preach to fellow image-bearers, I'll do it from the Scriptures and it will be about salvation in Jesus. Doesn't matter where in the world you play it, it's still the same beautiful game. Doesn't matter *where* in the world you preach it, it's still the same urgent ministry.

So, the silhouette's the same. Some of the details, however, are definitely different. No doubt, some of that's simply due to my growth as a preacher. If your preaching hasn't progressed over the course of a decade, then you're probably an appalling preacher. Other changes, however, are specific to preaching the gospel in a hard place.

WHAT'S CHANGED?

Fundamental to any communication is the principle that *who you're speaking to* impacts how you speak to them. Dialogue between different people differs. I speak differently to a toddler than I do to a colleague. I speak differently to someone who has grown up speaking English than I do to someone who's just learning English. I speak differently to my mates than I speak to a judge in court. Language changes. Tone changes. Speed changes. Words change. Sometimes, it may happen naturally. Other times, it's painstakingly hard. But at all times it's necessary.

Although most preaching is entirely monologue, good preaching feels like dialogue. Your preaching prep must keep your listeners in mind. And so, because the people I'm now speaking to has changed, my preaching has necessarily changed. If it didn't, I'd be preaching in vain.

As preachers, we're often quick to speak and slow to listen. But I think that the key to being a preacher who people will listen to in a hard place is being a preacher who listens to them about what makes life hard.

So here are the two unbelievably basic things that have changed my preaching over the last five years.

LISTENING TO PEOPLE'S STORIES

I'm from a culture where questions are a normal and critical part of any communication. In my current culture, however, too many questions make you sound like a police officer or a social worker. Instead, conversation revolves around stories being shared. The storyteller remains in control of how much they self-reveal, rather than questions assaulting them into unconsented revelation.

This impacts how you preach. My tendency in preaching would be reduce everything in Scripture – from narrative to poetry – into a stereotypical, three-point, logic-driven, question-and-answer style sermon. That's probably not helpful (or faithful!) preaching in any context, but least of all, mine. It's taught me to respect the genre, preserve the tone and unfold the stories in a way that's faithful to whatever text I'm preaching rather than what's just natural to how I've been trained to think and communicate in my culture.

But beyond the story-telling culture at large, the story of both my community and individuals in my church have impacted how I preach. What do I mean? Well, here's a few examples.

- Story after story has revealed a matriarchal culture. This has impacted how I preach through what the Bible says about headship, submission and women in ministry.
- Story after story has revealed a suspicion of people in authority. This has impacted how I preach

through what the Bible says about eldership and church governance.

- Story after story has revealed that a large percentage of the community have suffered as victims of abuse. This has impacted how I explain that all humanity are guilty rebels facing the punishment of a holy God.
- Story after story has revealed fathers who were either absent or abusive. This has impacted how I preach on the Fatherhood of God
- Story after story has revealed endless relapses in the life of a Christian addict. This has impacted how I preach on repentance and Christ's victory over sin.

I didn't hear stories like these in my first five years. But upon hearing them, if they don't impact how I preach, I'm giving my community the impression that God's not really for them. But He is. And thankfully, in the Bible, you don't have to look far to find families and churches that fall into the same mistakes we do, and need the same powerful, saving grace we need.

Hear me right. I'm not saying the stories in our community change what we believe or what we teach. Instead, they shape *how* we approach these truths pastorally so that we can apply them sensitively in our preaching.

It also means the majority of my illustrations come from within the community rather than outside of it. It means the emotional range of my preaching tries to match the emotional range of my community. It means my level of vulnerability seeks to reflect how much credibility the culture places on transparency and openness.

I also endeavour to scrutinise my sermon notes to ensure that every word is in the vernacular of my community. At the heart of the Reformation was a zealous drive to get the Word of God and the preaching in the pulpits translated from Latin into the language of the people. Strangely, many people today who love the Reformation still seem to go about quoting Latin phrases. (I'll resist from ending this article with a "SDG".)[321] But you don't have to speak in Latin to be incomprehensible. You can speak a dialect of Christian jargon in English, and you might as well be speaking Latin. The people I've come to know through the stories I've listened to are those who need to hear the gospel in a way they can understand. I'm called to preach for the people in my community that aren't in the room yet, but if they were to walk in, they'd understand every single word.

LISTENING TO PEOPLE'S QUESTIONS

The lecturer at seminary who taught our preaching class taught us what have become two of the most important questions in my preaching prep: "What's the biggest objection a Christian would have to this text?" and "What's the biggest objection an unbeliever would have to this text?" The usefulness of these questions lies at the heart of why good preaching feels like dialogue, even though it's largely a monologue. As you study a text, you try to discern what your hearers' strongest objections to the text will be. Good preaching raises such questions, tackles them head-on, and then answers them.

A change in context often means a change in questions. In my first five years, in coming to a text like the Passover in Exodus 11–12, the predominant question in my head would probably have been something like, "How can God harden Pharaoh's heart and still hold him accountable for his wickedness?" That's a legitimate question, and one you'll probably have to answer. But an unbeliever probably has more basic questions, like "How can you love a God who kills babies?" You might even get asked, "What's an Exodus?" and "Who's Moses?" We forget that people don't know what we already know.

The questions people are asking in Gracemount are different to the questions I had to answer before. I was used to the theoretical, apologetic questions that largely came from an atheistic and sceptical point of view. In Gracemount, I've never had to convince someone of God's existence or the reality of the afterlife. Instead, almost every question I've been asked has come from trauma rather than theory.

I remember caring for a mum whose son died. Her first two questions to me: "Is he in hell because he hadn't been baptised?" and "If I commit suicide, will I go to hell too?" They reveal not only a supernatural worldview, but also cultural Catholicism.

What about the lad who's reading the Bible with me? He asks questions like, "If I become a Christian, will I have to forgive my dad for all the ways he abused me?" Or the hyper-vigilant, paranoid addict whose main questions when we're preaching through Exodus are about the conspiracy theories surrounding aliens being the builders of the pyramids. Or the Christian who questions whether or not their mental health struggles caused by drug use prevent them from usefulness in the church. Or the daughter who wants me to confirm that what the local Spiritualist medium told her about her Catholic mum being in heaven is true.

If I fail to address these questions, or if I somehow communicate that they're "weird", I'm giving my community the impression that God's not really for them. But He is. And so, they're the questions I must dialogue with in my preaching.

Here's my task as a preacher in a hard place: to preach the gospel of the Lord Jesus Christ to those asking these questions and living these stories. So, my preaching in my hard place may not even work in your pulpit in your hard place, because the stories and how they're told will be different, and the questions and why they're asked will be different. Sermons preached in hard places will probably be sermons whose usefulness is limited to their postcode.

See, it's not my job merely to preach the gospel. The task of a preacher isn't simply to place raw ingredients in front of his hearers and expect them to cook the meal from scratch. It's to provide a fully cooked meal for the hearers to feast. A sermon devoid of application is like the church at Sardis in Revelation 3. It gives the appearance of life, but it's dead.

Many people in our community feel forgotten by those in authority. They feel like the government is miles out of touch. They feel like no one listens to them. The feel like no decisions made in parliament are ever going to make any difference where they are. That attitude filters its way into the church, which I partly understand. Many churches have abandoned our communities, and so it does seem like that.

PRACTICAL ADVICE

So, here's some practical ways that we as elders have sought to ensure that our preaching lands on our hearers.

Service structure: We've adopted an order of service where the preaching happens near the beginning. We have a call to worship. We sing. We pray. And then we preach. Part of the reason for that is that we want people to feel in the weekly rhythm of our gathering that God is God, and as such He has the authority and right to speak first. And then everything we do is in response to that. We think that's a helpful model for our people to then mimic in their daily devotions: hear God speak in the pages of the Bible first, and then worship and pray in response to that.

But the other reason for front-loading the sermon is to model and further explain how these truths are then applied. We don't want to just preach, sing and then leave. We want to preach, dwell and further apply. So, following the sermon we sing songs that directly respond to what's been preached. Following the songs, we read from another passage of Scripture that draws out specific applications. Following the reading, we usually have some kind of related corporate response to read together – that may be the Lord's Prayer, the Apostles' Creed, the Ten Commandments, or a confession of sin. Following this, we'll pray through these applications of the sermon. The revelation of God in the preaching directs our prayers, and so models, especially to new believers, how we ought to pray.

This is just another way of saying that the liturgy of our Sunday gatherings all aims at dialoguing with our own specific congregation about how the specific text we've looked at today answers our specific questions and can transform our specific stories. So we preach first, in order to allow time to show how God's authority is not only for our good, but it's for us personally.

Weekly devotions: We provide a handout for our sermons each Sunday. On one side, there are simply some of the main headlines from the sermon to aid engagement and memory. On the other side, we list devotions for Monday to Saturday that again flow from the sermon. There may be other passages to read and pray through, or songs to sing and reflect on, or verses to memorise and use, or prompts to encourage other members, or specific items of local or international interest to pray for. But they all relate to the sermon. We want to help people drill deep into the Scriptures and meditate on their relevance to their everyday lives. And there's not many off-the-shelf devotional materials written for our context. So we write them ourselves.

We encourage those in our congregation who are in one-to-one discipling relationships to use these devotions when they meet. We've started using our mid-week Bible studies to continue to study the passages and truths preached on Sunday.

The purpose of a sermon isn't complete until its truths are believed and applied. And so the job of the preacher isn't complete when he shuts his Bible and steps out of the pulpit.

So, if I had to say all this in a tweet: Make your sermon monologues feel like dialogues, by listening hard to people's stories and questions, and then labouring hard to connect the living Word to your specific hard place.

ADDENDUM

If I could recommend one book, check out Charles Spurgeon's *Practical Wisdom (Plain Advice for Plain People)* published by the Banner of Truth. In the preface, Spurgeon writes

> *I have written for ploughmen and common people. Hence refined taste and dainty words have been disregarded for strong proverbial expressions and homely phrases. I have aimed my blows at the vices of the many and tried to inculcate those moral virtues without which men are degraded. Much that needs to be said to the toiling masses would not well suit the pulpit and the Sabbath; these lowly pages may teach thrift and industry all the days of the week in the cottage and the workshop; and if some learn these lessons, I shall not repent the adoption of a rustic style.*[322]

We need more present-day pastors and authors to adapt their style for those in the hardest places. And if I can disagree with Spurgeon for a second, we need it in the pulpit and on the Sabbath as well.

CONCLUSION

In many ways this is not a conclusion but, hopefully, the beginning of a new conversation. My intention in writing this book has not been to offend, but to generate fruitful discussion. Many things have been left unsaid. In truth, this work could have been twice the length it now is. But, I want to leave you, the reader, with four things to think about:

First, I want to lay to rest the lie that suggests only working-class people can be effective in working-class communities. Paul was a Jew of Jews and yet was used greatly in reaching the Gentiles. For that reason, I asked my (upper) middle-class co-pastor, Andy, to write about this in the hope that it would persuade more middle-class men to come and pastor in our estates and schemes.

Secondly, I want to leave us with a challenge from the Bible to help us reflect about what action we should now take given the information revealed in the book.

Thirdly, I want to inspire some of you to forsake all and to come to work alongside us in the most beautiful of mission fields.

Finally, my friends and I, from estates and schemes across the UK, wanted to write a letter to the UK church seeking your help and understanding about our work among the least, the last and the lost.

SPOTLIGHT:

CAN A MIDDLE-CLASS PASTOR REALLY BE EFFECTIVE ON A COUNCIL ESTATE/SCHEME?

ANDY CONSTABLE, CO-PASTOR,
NIDDRIE COMMUNITY CHURCH, EDINBURGH

Paul says this to the church in Ephesians 2:13–18:

> *But now in Christ Jesus you who once were far away have been brought near by the blood of Christ. For he himself is our peace, who has made the two groups one and has destroyed the barrier, the dividing wall of hostility, by setting aside in his flesh the law with its commands and regulations. His purpose was to create in himself one new humanity out of the two, thus making peace, and in one body to reconcile both of them to God through the cross, by which he put to death their hostility. He came and preached peace to you who were far away and peace to those who were near. For through him we both have access to the Father by one Spirit.*

The Bible clearly teaches that the gospel breaks down all cultural barriers. As a middle-class man on a housing scheme, I can personally testify to that. I am not from a scheme. In fact, I look like I should be on Downton Abbey rather than on a council estate in Scotland! I was brought up in London in a loving, Christian, middle-class home. My dad worked in insurance while my mum was a full-time mum. My parents brought me up to know the truths of the gospel.

However, I didn't become a Christian till I was 18. As I grew into my teens, I rejected the faith of my parents. I didn't think that Christianity or the church was relevant to my life. I didn't see that I was a *sinner* and in need of a *Saviour*. But God used two events in my teenage years to bring me to Christ.

The first was a holiday camp where I met a Christian who had been converted from a Muslim home. *Why would a lady leave her faith and family to come to Christ? Why would she leave a comfortable life to be abused physically and mentally by her parents?* Her reason? She had realised that salvation came through Christ alone. It was then that I began to see that I needed the forgiveness of Christ.

The second thing that happened was hearing a powerful sermon on Isaiah 1 at my home church. I don't know what it was that night, but it felt like every word of that sermon was written for me. The pastor said that we had rebelled against God and that the only way to receive forgiveness for ours sins was through faith in Jesus Christ. He also said that we needed to not just believe upon Jesus, but also make Him Lord of our lives.

That night I was heavily convicted. I wasn't a drug taker or a heavy drinker. I've never had a physical fight with anybody in my life. But I still realised the deep sin in my life and that I had rebelled against God. I had tried to do things my own way. I had disrespected my parents. I had been a selfish, self-focused teenager. I realised that I was guilty of pride, lust, anger, jealousy and envy.

I was a sinner.

But I also understood that once I had repented of my sin and put my faith and trust in Jesus Christ, that in that moment He had forgiven every one of my sins. As the preacher quoted from Isaiah 1:18 that night: "Though your sins are like scarlet, they shall be as white as snow", I also realised that if I was going to follow Christ that I needed to do it properly. It was *all or nothing*. I knew that I couldn't be like the people of Israel who knew the truth and yet just blatantly disobeyed. I needed to pick up my cross and follow Him.

One of the first books I read as a Christian was a book called, *Don't Waste Your Life* by John Piper.[323] In it the author said that living for Christ is the best thing in the world. In fact, he wrote that doing anything else was a *waste* of time. In the book, he quotes an old hymn which says: "Only one life will soon be past only what's done for Christ will last"![324]

All I wanted to do from that moment on was tell people about Jesus.

Seven years and a university degree later, I found myself as an intern in Niddrie. I was 25, enthusiastic, idealistic and very naive. I didn't have a clue about pastoral work and I certainly had no idea about scheme culture. I went to a private school in the city of London. I like hummus. I am a cultural outsider if ever there was one! Even worse (particularly when working in a Scottish scheme), I am English! That's two cultural barriers to get over!

I've got no street experience at all. I was one of those guys you duped in town for £30 to get a bag of heroin. I didn't know anything about Valium, I thought everyone was telling the truth and that the guy who was gouching (high on drugs) was just a little bit ill. I was a polite and well-meaning but pretty clueless intern.

But I've been on staff for 10 years now and I understand a little bit more about what is going on. I've made some deep personal friends in Niddrie. I have been involved with discipling men who have come to Christ from Niddrie. I have made many mistakes. I've been cheated and hurt by relationships, but I understand the culture far more than I used to. I realise that not everyone is telling me the truth. I have contextualised my preaching and think I have adapted. It's been a tough time, but one in which I have grown in my faith and been changed by God. The gospel has broken down cultural barriers and allowed me to be used by God in some small way in Niddrie so far.

I firmly believe that God can use the middle class in our housing estates and schemes.

GOD USES US DESPITE OUR DIFFERENCES

We see racial and cultural diversity all over the New Testament. Jesus chose 12 disciples with very different ways of seeing the world. They may all have been Jewish, but they were from a wide range of backgrounds: Matthew was a despised tax collector who undoubtedly would have been wealthy. He had a decent job working for the Romans. He probably would have voted Conservative, lived in a nice town house and sent his children to a private school.

Simon the Zealot, on the other hand, was a revolutionary. He hated the government and wanted to overthrow it. He probably didn't have a job and he probably would have signed on the dole. He would have lived in a poorer area of Israel, somewhat like a housing estate. Ordinarily these two men would have been arch-enemies. Simon would have viewed Matthew as a money-grabbing traitor to his own people.

Yet Jesus chose these two men and put them together on a team. Actually, He did more than that. He commanded them to *love one another*. This must have been difficult. Yet they both followed Christ. They both were transformed by His grace. They were both used to bring the gospel to the nations.

These weren't the only differences between the disciples. Peter was a hot head with a big mouth and Thomas was a facts man but also a bit of a doubter. James and John were a bit like the Kray twins! "Repent or burn" would have been their motto!

Jesus chose these vastly different men to work together in gospel unity. They were a pretty useless team to start with. But, in the end, God used them powerfully to spread the gospel.

GOD USES OUR CULTURAL DIFFERENCES TO DEMONSTRATE THE POWER OF THE GOSPEL

Jesus says this in John 13:34–35: "A new command I give you: love one another. As I have loved you, so you must love one another. By this everyone will know that you are my disciples, if you love another." How will people know that we are His disciples? By the way that we love one another. We often don't appreciate how powerful it is when unbelievers see Christians from housing estate and middle-class backgrounds worshipping God together in friendship and love. All too often in our world, we retreat into our cultural cliques and stay there.

The church is meant to run counter to this behaviour. In the church we are all added into the mix and told to get along. In our church in Niddrie, we have people who have been through the social work system *and* social workers. We have policemen *and* those who have been in jail. We have former drug addicts *and* those who have never touched a drug in their life. We have those who have been on the dole all their adult lives *and* others who've worked all their adult lives. We are all united under the banner of the gospel of Jesus.

When we view our lives through the prism of the cross, we realise that we are *all* sinners and we *all* need Jesus. Once, Gentiles and Jews kept away from one another, but in Christ the dividing wall of hostility was broken between them. The same has to apply to the class system of the UK. If we cannot come together under the gospel of Jesus, then how else will our divisions be healed?

The problem is that this sounds great on paper, but the reality is easier said than done. It's one thing to preach unity, but another to practise it. In the UK, we have to confess that as middle-class Christians we have been guilty of neglecting the least, the last and the lost in our own countries. In fact, we can often look at the housing estates around us with a mixture of fear and snobbish disdain. Sometimes all we see are drug addicts and thieves, rather than potential brothers and sisters in Christ.

Sometimes our snobbery has been much more subtle. We don't mind using a working-class person for their testimony, but we wouldn't even consider them for further training and ministry within our churches. Ask yourself the following questions:

- How many people are we training in our churches who are *not* tertiary educated?
- How many of our leaders come from these communities?

I suspect I know the answer for the vast majority of UK evangelical churches. We have work to do if we are to tear down the barriers that we have built up, for the sake of gospel witness. We shouldn't just be interested in using people as trophies of grace, we should be training the next generation of church leaders. If we think of Simon and Matthew, both these men were leaders in the church. I suspect that only Matthew with his money and contacts would have any hope of a church internship in the modern UK church.

THE DANGER OF REVERSE SNOBBERY

We must also watch for reverse snobbery when it comes to these matters. A snob is someone who looks down their noses at other people, and this is not just a middle-class sin. The working (and non-working) class are as guilty of snobbery as anybody else. They look on chino wearers with the same disdain that the middle class do with tracksuit-wearing chavs. Anybody not from a housing estate is immediately labelled as stuck-up by those who have been born and bred on one. There are some working-class Christian leaders who think that men like me shouldn't be allowed to work in these communities because of our more privileged background.

Christians, regardless of background, must work hard to fight against this sin. We honour Jesus by working together. If we want to reach the least, the last and the lost of the UK, then middle-class and working-class people are going to have to come together. Those watching on will see the truth of the gospel we proclaim by the way that we love and honour one another.

WE DON'T KNOW HOW BLIND WE ARE UNTIL WE MEET SOMEBODY WHO CAN SEE MORE CLEARLY

There is a lot about my middle-class culture that is sinful and idolatrous. But the same can be said for council estate and scheme culture. We can only see the weaknesses in our own culture when we mix with others who are not like us and don't see the world or think in the same way that we do. Just being around people of a different class and culture starts to chisel off the ungodly bits of our culture and help us to reflect Christ better. If we just remain within our own cultural bubbles then we become blind to our weak spots. We think *our* way is the *right* way to live. We think that our way is the only way to think.

But when we are forced to question our culture, the way we do things and what we believe about the world, it is then that we experience personal and spiritual growth. For example, I didn't realise just how individualistic and self-absorbed my middle-class cultural sensibilities were until I experienced the community life of a housing scheme. We live in fenced off houses and live our lives largely through diaries and planned appointments. It's not all bad or wrong, but it can be very restricting and controlling. Housing scheme and council estate culture is very different. Real community, good and bad, is here for all to see. People look after one another. There is always someone to talk to. People are much more flexible and will drop things to help you out. People will stop in the street and talk to you very honestly and openly, sometimes for a long time!

But scheme culture is not perfect. It is full of idols and sin. It is a very gladiatorial culture. Pride runs deep and grudges can be held between families over generations. Arguments can happen quickly and degenerate into violence with little provocation. Sometimes it's good having someone around who is polite and calm to take the edge off. It's hard to stay mad at a person who refuses to argue!

COUNCIL ESTATES AND HOUSING SCHEMES NEED MIDDLE-CLASS PEOPLE AS MUCH AS OUR MIDDLE-CLASS CHURCHES NEED THEM

In the church at Niddrie, I am part of a diverse team of people. We have middle-class men and women. We have housing scheme men and women. We have a short beanie wearer from Ireland! We have a posh guy from London. All of us have different personalities and temperaments and ways of seeing the world. But we learn from one another and balance each other out. Although sometimes painful, our frustrations with one another are great for our sanctification.

GOD CAN USE FAITHFUL PEOPLE ANYWHERE AND AT ANYTIME

Maybe you're a middle-class person reading this, thinking to yourself: *Could I make it in one of these communities? Would the people accept me?* The short answer is: yes, of course. You don't need to have a gangster testimony to make it on a scheme. You don't need to have grown up in a scheme to minister fruitfully in a scheme.

People have been sharing the gospel cross-culturally since Jesus sent out His first disciples. Paul was a Jew of Jews whose most fruitful ministry was with the Gentiles, a people as far from him culturally as they could possibly be! The gospel overcomes all barriers and is the power of salvation for everyone who believes, whatever their background. All we have to do is be willing for God to use us.

That's the real problem. It's not that middle-class Christians like me can't have an effective ministry among the least, the last and the lost of the UK. It's that we don't want to go.

We just don't care enough about the souls who live in these places.

Maybe you think that the best people to reach scheme people are people like Mez. It's certainly true that he has an advantage in terms of understanding the culture, language and worldview. Evangelising and explaining the Bible within this culture comes more naturally to him. His testimony book has gone out into hundreds and hundreds of homes. He has a connection with local people that runs deep.

But he will admit that I need him to do the work just as he needs me. We are a team. We work together with our complementary characters and gift sets. However, the middle class do run into difficulties when they try to minister into these communities without any help from cultural insiders. It doesn't make the work impossible – for nothing is impossible with God – but it certainly makes it harder.

So, if you're a middle-class Christian, let me give you seven things I've learned – from one middle-class Christian to another.

First, we have to be *teachable* if we are coming to these communities as a cultural outsider. If we are not, then it is going to be very difficult to break through the cultural barriers. This is not our natural territory and insiders can smell it a mile away.

Part of this will be to see the invisible cultures differences that exist between us. There are some major do's and don'ts in scheme culture. I remember when I first came to Niddrie and I would get alongside somebody and automatically invite them round for dinner. Not a single person ever turned up! People here socialise at pubs, at football matches and maybe round the TV for a big sporting event. I was used to a middle-class culture where we have dinner parties and invite people for food. I had to adapt quickly.

It's not much different from entering a Muslim context. If we did that, then we would take our time to learn the language, find out about the culture and ask questions in order to gain more understanding. The added barrier in scheme culture is that they don't take well to being questioned and so things take much longer to work out.

Secondly, if we are going to reach out to a housing scheme or a council estate, then we must *live there*. We will have no discernible impact if we live outside the community that we are seriously trying to reach. If we drive in or offer a couple of weekly groups, people may grow to like us, but they will never accept us as more than a posh-do-gooder, and there are plenty of them to be found in our communities.

Thirdly, we middle-class people need to be *patient*. It's going to take time to build relationships. It has taken Mez seven years to build enough trust in his neighbours that they now speak to him instead of ignoring him in the street – and he is a cultural insider! Families have lived alongside one another in these communities for many generations. Therefore, if we are going to commit to work in a scheme, then we need to really commit for a long time before we see any fruit.

Fourthly, if we are going to work in a scheme, then we need to *respect the culture*. Too often people come into a scheme because they have come to "help poor people". We come in and we highlight all the bad stuff so that we can write back to our prayer support about the terrible drug addicts that we are trying to help. Of course, there will be bad things but there will also be a lot of good, because God's common grace extends even into the darkest corners of the UK. I failed to appreciate this fully when I first came to Niddrie. But, over the years, I have come to deeply respect, admire and love the rich cultural heritage of my community. There is a deep pool of musical, literary and amateur dramatics talent.

We must never allow ourselves to forget that people are God's image bearers – no matter how damaged – and they are certainly not our pet projects, whom we use to boost our own self-esteem.

Fifthly, people will forgive you many sins if you are *authentic* to who you are. It sometimes pains me to watch middle-class people come into our culture and pretend to be more than they are. I remember a young man from years ago who came with a mission team and he was desperate to share about his drug addict background with some of our locals in the community cafe that we run. So, he began to tell his story of how he overcame a serious drug addiction. When he had finished speaking one of the locals asked him what his battle had been with. Cough medicine was his answer! Unfortunately, that teenage lad is remembered in our scheme years later for all the wrong reasons! As cultural outsiders, we have to adapt but we don't have to get tattoos or go on a bender in order to identify with people. I'm still my goofy old self and people take it or leave it.

Sixthly, one of the big things required for this work is a *sense of humour*. If you cannot laugh at others and yourself, then you are not going to have a very comfortable experience. We can't take ourselves too seriously.

Lastly, this kind of work requires *sacrifice* and *perseverance*. Many of us feel more at home socialising with friends in a nice city-centre bar or a coffee shop than we do on a council estate or housing scheme. That's only natural. But, in time, if we stick at it, we become more comfortable in our new culture. I couldn't imagine living anywhere else but a scheme now! Remember what Jesus said to His disciples: "everyone who has left houses or brothers or sisters or father or mother or wife or children or fields for my sake will receive a hundred times as much and will inherit eternal life" (Matt. 19:29).

CONCLUSION

We need to work harder as Christians in our churches to reflect the diversity of our nation. That will never happen if we neglect the least, the last and the lost communities of the UK. We need middle-class Christians to forsake all and to plant and revitalise gospel churches in council estates and housing schemes all across our land.

We don't want to have middle-class churches and working-class churches. We want to plant gospel-centred churches that contain the rich diversity of not just the classes, but the different ethnicities that make up the modern UK. We have a responsibility to Jesus to do better and we will have to work hard to bridge the great divide that currently exists between the evangelical church in the UK and its working-class population.

Finally, can I make a plea to my working-class brothers and sisters on behalf of my own middle-class community? Please bear with us. I know we can be a bit geeky, a bit aloof and a bit patronising. But please be patient with us as we learn from you. We need your help to adapt to the culture and climate of your communities. We have our blind spots, but we have our good side too. Lots of middle-class people like me, for example, have lots of middle-class friends and family with lots of money – and that can come in handy when you are running a church on a housing estate or a scheme!

WHAT DOES GOD WANT FROM US IN THE LIGHT OF ALL THIS?

MEZ MCCONNELL

As we have demonstrated, the UK is a group of nations that have great disparities between the haves and the have-nots. The gap between the richest and poorer members of our society is growing year on year.

What is true for the world is also true for the church. We may talk about social justice and loving the poor, but the reality is that many of our poorest communities are thrown to the spiritual wolves of heretical whack job charismatics, prosperity churches and other fringe lunatics as evangelicals focus on the educated and elite classes. They may well feel sorry for the poor, but they live in fear and suspicion of the communities in which they grow up. Churches may well run some form of mercy ministry, but very often that is where the care stops.

God is not happy with the current status quo.

He wants us to do more than shake our heads or throw our hands up in the air in despair, saying, "what can we do?" What we can do is listen to what He tells us in Micah 6:8.[325]

> *He has told you, O man, what is good; and what does the* Lord *require of you, but to do justice, and to love kindness, and to walk humbly with your God?*

When Micah wrote these words, the world was in turmoil. The people of God were not living up to His expectations. They were not caring for the poor and the needy. By not taking *them* seriously, God's people were not taking *Him* seriously.

Micah 6:8 asks one very simple question of all of us. *What does God require of us?* What does God require of His people as we live in this world of such sin and inequality? In Micah 6, God's people are angry with God. They can't understand why they are constantly under attack from their enemies. So they charge the Lord with unfaithfulness and injustice. The synagogues are full of worshippers bringing their offerings to God. They are sacrificing their best to please Him. Their tithes are being paid on time.

Yet still His people suffer.

So, the people are demanding answers. "We are doing our bit, so why are you not doing yours?" That's the nature of their grievance. "Why are you being so unfair to us?" Sarcasm drips from their tongues in verses 6 and 7:

> *With what shall I come before the Lord, and bow myself before God on high? Shall I come before him with burnt offerings, with calves a year old? Will the Lord be pleased with thousands of rams, with ten thousand rivers of oil? Shall I give my firstborn for my transgression, the fruit of my body for the sin of my soul?*

In other words, what more do we have to do to please you? That's the implication here. How far are we supposed to go in order to win your approval – sacrifice our children? The people are claiming that they are doing everything they can to please Him, yet He's just not satisfied.

God reminds them in verse 2 that the Creator does not answer to His creation – rather, the creation is answerable to its Creator. "Hear, you mountains, the indictment of the LORD, and you enduring foundations of the earth, for the LORD has an indictment against his people and he will contend Israel." *You* don't accuse *me*, He says. *You* don't bring charges against *me*. *I* will bring my charges against *you*.

"How have I wearied you?" The Lord asks them in verse 3. "How have I have burdened you?" In verse 4, His words are full of irony as He reminds them how quickly they forget all that He does for His people: "I brought you up from the land of Egypt and redeemed you from the house of slavery." He reminds them that it was He who brought them into a land flowing with milk and honey. They had left Egypt in a mess and yet entered the Promised Land as a nation. "I gave you leaders", He tells them at the end of verse 4. "I rescued you from your enemies", He reminds them in verse 5.

The people of God are unhappy with the Lord, but the Lord is unhappy with His people. That's the context behind God's question in verse 8. "You ask what I require of you. Let me tell you", He says to them in verse 8. Listen carefully.

- Do justice
- Love kindness
- Walk humbly

The synagogues were full and the altars overflowing with sacrifices, but they were indifferent to the poor. That's what angered God. It angers Him still. Invite any prophet to dinner and he will wax lyrical about two topics concerning the nature of God: (a) His righteousness and (b) His justice. A cursory trip through the history of the Jewish people in the Bible will show up a couple of consistent faults in their worship of God. In fact, they were so prone to these two errors that God had to send prophet after prophet to them to remind them of their responsibilities. What were these two main faults?

- They practised outward righteousness, yet their hearts were far from the Lord.
- They either abused or neglected the most vulnerable members of society (women, children, lepers, etc.).

I am sure if we'd been alive in Micah's day, we would have been impressed by the sheer pageantry of temple worship. We would have been dazzled by the priest's robes and all the sights and sounds and smells. We may well even have been impressed by the piety of the Jewish religious leaders, those solemn looking men who took their faith so seriously. Yet that's not how Jesus viewed them in Matthew 23:23, when He said this to them:

> *Woe to you, scribes and Pharisees, hypocrites! For you tithe mint and dill and cumin, and have neglected the weightier matters of the law: justice and mercy and faithfulness. These you ought to have done, without neglecting the others.*

Note that they're not rebuked for fulfilling their religious duties. Jesus was upset with them because, despite all the outward religious piety, they were neglecting the needs of the less fortunate. They had perfected all the outward forms of religion, saying all the right things, offering all the right sacrifices, singing all the right songs, praying all the right prayers, perhaps even raising their hands in worship to the praise of their God. Yet Christ condemns them in the strongest possible terms.

There is a phrase bandied around in some Christian circles which says that "God hates religion." It just isn't true. God loves religion. God hates *empty* religion. He hates a religion devoid of love and mercy and kindness. Of course, it is good to go to church, to pray, to go on to the mission field, to give money, even to plant churches. But we can do all those things *heartlessly*. James 1:27 tells us:

> *Religion that is pure and undefiled before God the Father is this: to visit orphans and widows in their affliction, and to keep oneself unstained from the world.*

God's people in Micah's day were living with a false sense of what it meant to please Him. They thought God would declare them righteous if they would only keep doing their religious duty. In effect, they'd ripped the heart right out of the faith. Isaiah says almost exactly the same thing in Isaiah 1:10–15 to those living in his day, guilty of similar sins.

> *Hear the word of the Lord, you rulers of Sodom! Give ear to the teaching of our God, you people of Gomorrah! "What to me is the multitude of your sacrifices?" says the Lord; I have had enough of burnt offerings of rams and the fat of well-fed beasts; I do not delight in the blood of bulls, or of lambs, or of goats. When you come to appear before me, who has required of you this trampling of my courts? Bring no more vain offerings; incense is an abomination to me. New moon and Sabbath and the calling of convocations – I cannot endure iniquity and solemn assembly. Your new moons and your appointed feasts my soul hates; they have become a burden to me; I am weary of bearing them. When you spread out your hands, I will hide my eyes from you; even though you make many prayers, I will not listen."*

The Lord is not interested in a heartless religiosity. So, what were the people to do, if the Lord refused to accept their offerings or hear their prayers? He tells them in verses 16 and 17.

> *Wash yourselves; make yourselves clean; remove the evil of your deeds from before my eyes; cease to do evil, learn to do good; seek justice, correct oppression; bring justice to the fatherless, plead the widow's cause.*

In New Testament terms, we think we can get away with a couple of church services on a Sunday (if we are really spiritual) and maybe an appearance at the weekly prayer meeting. We maybe put a few pound coins in the offering plate and support our favourite charity. Some of us may read these words with a sense of relief. We help the poor. We operate a food bank. Maybe, some of us are on a first name basis with the man who begs outside the bank, or the Romanian woman near Asda. But what do we know of their lives? Their personal plights? How have we sought justice on their behalf?

I've been involved in church planting and revitalisation for almost 20 years. I've spoken at conferences around the world. One thing seems to unite the modern church planter and pastor, regardless of country and culture: Hardly any of them are called to the poorest, most deprived and downtrodden areas in their cities, towns and villages. For a God so obsessed with righteousness and justice for the poor, I am amazed at just how few modern men and women He is calling to the task. Maybe, He has changed His mind and He now just wants us to focus on students or the more upmarket end of our societies?

Or maybe, just maybe, we are not listening to Him.

Then there are the lies that we tell ourselves. We dampen down our consciences by telling ourselves that we will plant in a rich church, let's call it a hub church. We will reach the rich to reach the poor. We have already discovered how that usually works out. If I actually received a pound for all the rich church leaders who said they were going to help our ministry, I wouldn't have to fundraise ever again!

Invariably, we will tell ourselves anything to ease our conscience over the fact that hardly anybody is going to the poorest communities of the UK and practically nobody is giving up their comfortable lives to go to live and die on our council estates and schemes for the sake of Jesus. We tell ourselves that somebody else will do it. Anybody else.

Just not us.

Indifference to the poor and the vulnerable is as big a sin in the eyes of the Lord as outright injustice. We live in such a dangerous generation. We can sit in front of our televisions and watch the greatest disasters in history unfold before our eyes, with a sandwich in one hand and a beer in the other. We may feel a slight twinge of empathy for immigrants in those terrible camps, but if it gets too much we can always switch over to the sports channel or our favourite reality TV show.

Without realising it, UK Christians have become deaf and hard-hearted to the needs of the least, the last and the lost in our nation. It happened in Micah's day. It happened in Isaiah's day. It happened in Amos's day. It happened in Jeremiah's day. It happened in Jesus's day. Time and again God had to send prophets to wake His people from their slumber. They were the ones with the megaphones, shouting to be heard above all the religious regalia and self-satisfied spiritual smugness that was going on.

This time God is shouting to His people through the prophet Micah. He shouted to His people then and He is shouting to us today. Those of us who claim to take our Bibles seriously need to open our ears and listen. Many of us accuse the liberals of taking scissors to the Bible when it comes to penal substitution or issues of sexual morality. But aren't some of us guilty of taking scissors to the Bible when it comes to our treatment of the poor? He is asking all of us:

Do you really want to know what I want from you? What will make me happy?

ACT JUSTLY

Literally *do* justice. Where is the justice of the modern-day church? How are we to practice justice? Should we take the knee against racism? Should we march on parliament? Should we start a social media campaign? What does "doing justice" look like in our churches? In the context of Scotland, our church is *doing justice* by planting and revitalising churches in the poorest communities in our country. We have seen the need. We have heard the Lord. And so we are compelled to take the gospel to these places.

What is your church's vision for the least, the last and the lost where you are? Which church will take the light of the gospel to the darkest corners of your town, city or village if you don't? Let me tell you who does have a vision for these communities.

Satan.

He loves hanging out in these communities. He loves to see prosperity heretics move in. He loves a mad charismatic with little grasp of the gospel. He really likes the Spiritualists. He has a real soft spot for all the witches' covens and the tarot card readers.

What state does the UK church have to be in to see that Satan and the hordes of hell have a better plan to reach the least, the last and the lost than we do? How can we sit idly by as he blinds the minds of millions upon millions who (mistakenly) think that hell is what is happening to them now?

The best way our churches can *do justice* is to take the righteous gospel of Jesus Christ into all of our communities. What could be more just than introducing people to the gospel of Jesus so that they can be declared righteous by faith? Without that knowledge they will remain under His righteous wrath, and if they do not turn from their sins in repentance and faith, then they will one day discover that the hell of this life was merely a pale shadow of the reality of eternal hell to come.

First, then, *do justice*. Secondly, we are to *love mercy*.

LOVE KINDNESS

Of course, mercy and love go together. God's love goes hand in hand with every single word in the Bible. Note that God doesn't say: "Act mercifully." He says, "*Love* mercy." How are we to love mercy? What does it mean to "love" mercy?

In Matthew's gospel, Jesus speaks to His disciples concerning the huge crowds following Him. He says to them: "I have compassion on the crowd because they have been with me now three days and have nothing to eat. And I am unwilling to send them away hungry, lest they faint on the way" (Matt. 15:32). Jesus didn't just feel bad for them. He loved them so much that He does something about it. On this occasion, He lovingly and mercifully fed them.

The Old Testament had some radical laws about loving mercy and helping those in need. In Leviticus 25:35 we read: "If your brother becomes poor and cannot maintain himself with you, you shall support him as though he were a stranger and a sojourner, and he shall live with you." That is a merciful love that is so counter-intuitive to many in our culture and, even more tragically, to many in our churches.

There are some Christians who are suspicious of anything that smells remotely of socialism. They get twitchy around biblical themes like this. I remember speaking at one church about our responsibility to the poor in society and I was approached by a well-dressed man at the end. "The problem with that message," he said to me (without any introduction), "is that it is almost childish in its simplicity. I have paid hundreds of thousands in taxes over the years. How much have *you* paid?" "Well, not hundreds of thousands, obviously," I replied. "My point exactly," he continued. "Therefore, I have been far more generous and merciful and loving to the poor than you have." "Well, hang on a minute," I said. "Let me ask you a question. Do you love paying taxes?" "It's my duty as a good citizen and it's a good witness to the Lord," he responded. "Yes, but do you *love* it? I mean, really love it. Were you giddy with excitement each month to find out how much tax you had to pay? And if it seemed a bit low to you, did you ring the tax man to offer to pay more to help the less fortunate in society?" "Don't be ridiculous," he said.

That's my point. No one loves to pay taxes. No one is begging to pay more. In fact, most people pay accountants to work out how they can pay less. Paying our taxes is a legal obligation. A duty. It is something we have no choice over. We are obligated to do it.

God is not interested in a religion of obligation; He wants it to come from the heart. He wants our mercy to be something deeply and profoundly heartfelt. We shouldn't give out of a sense of legal or moral obligation. The Lord loves a cheerful giver.

Justice and merciful love are issues of the heart, not of the wallet. Christians don't love mercy by being forced to do acts of compassion because there's no other resort left to them. They do it even when they don't have to. Especially when they don't have to. We should be known as those who love to help others and who give little thought to personal cost. What is it to us to give up our holiday and even our homes to those who are struggling or in need of company and some compassion? It should be nothing to those of us who know that this life is nothing more than a waiting room for the next.

Maybe you pastor a church in a rich community and are wondering how best to help your poorer neighbours. Maybe you are a member of a church with a decent job and you are wondering the same thing. Here's what you can do to practice justice and to love mercy.

Support church planters and pastors in poor communities.

If there are none in your city, or town or village, then find someone who is looking to do these things. And when you do, joyfully and lovingly give your money to those in our poorest communities, be prepared to do it for a very, very long time. Do it cheerfully without any hope of a return on your investment. Give your money to local church leaders, planters and pastors.

Give until it hurts.

So, do justice and love mercy. Finally, God says, walk humbly.

WALK HUMBLY

If we are trusting in Jesus Christ today, regardless of who we are and where we are from, God has been lovingly merciful and gracious to us. If He had treated us with His pure and godly justice, then we would have been doomed for ever.

Justly doomed.

But He humbled Himself in love, and He saved us when He bore our sins on the cross and took upon Himself the full wrath of God that we justly deserved. How much more, then, should we extend that same mercy, love and justice to others? How can we look at another human being and think to ourselves: "They deserve nothing from me"? How much more should we remember with all humility that every single good thing we have in our lives comes from Him. It is not a result of our industry, but rather His grace and mercy.

Saving religion is marked by a faith that constantly asks, "What can I do to serve the one who has saved me and who has shown undeserving mercy to me? What can I do to show my gratitude to Him for giving me spiritual life? How can I show justice and mercy to my fellow man and how can I walk humbly with my God?"

The humble soul does not divide the world into the deserving and the undeserving. The humble soul realises there's only the undeserving when it comes to all things spiritual. Does that council estate near us *deserve* a church? No. Does your community *deserve* one? Does that loud-mouthed, boorish, dole-dossing man who's always shouting things at us on the way to church *deserve* our charity? No. Do you *deserve* the Lord's charity?

Humility has a way of levelling the playing field for all of us.

Let me ask you some questions. *What causes you to lie awake at night worrying*? Is it your exam results? Is it your job? Maybe it's your children's education. Will you be able to get them into that good school? Do you worry about getting a good holiday this year? Have you got too much to do?

What about the plight of poor families on the estate not far from you? The one you tell your children not to go near. What about the millions in the UK with no access to a gospel church? What about the poor pastor/planter working under enormous pressure with very limited resources? Do you worry about how he will pay the bills and feed his children?

Does that keep you awake at night? Do you worry about what university you or your children should go to, or do you worry about those who will never get a chance to go to university?

Who lies awake worried about the least, the last and the lost in our nation?

CALL TO THE UK CHURCH: THE BEAUTIFUL HARVEST FIELD

MEZ MCCONNELL

What's it really like living and working in the schemes? It's brilliant. It's home. It's where a spade is a spade (for the brave anyway).

It's the place of twitching curtains when the sound of raised voices rings around the street. It's the place of the white van with the ladders on the roof. It's the place of the burned-out bikes on nearby fields. It's the smell of hash as you walk past hooded youths congregated at children's parks. It's the sight of the junkies collecting their prescriptions at 9 a.m. in the morning and then selling them at 9:05 a.m. It's the sight of the elderly lady on her way to the post office for her pension. It's dodging the motability scooters winding their way to Lidl.

It's sharing a joke with the window cleaner as he does your windows or listening to the latest local gossip from the hairdresser. It's watching the man who used to come to your church for a while, and who professed Christ, slumped into a heroin-induced coma on the steps of the church. It's watching the half-starved children, heads down, on their way to a failing school system and returning home to a barrage of abuse and sub-nutritional microwave meals.

It's listening to the screams of your neighbours as they batter each other senseless and scream obscenities at three in the morning. It's sharing Jesus as often as you can with desperate people. It's hearing the news of yet another suicide or dead body found in the street. It's watching known drug dealers driving around in expensive motors when they've never done an honest day's work in their life. It's seeing the pattern of abuse and hopelessness being passed on to the next generation.

It's hard.

It's gruelling.

It grinds away at your soul.

It's getting up every single day, seeking the Lord, guarding your heart against your own sinful proclivities, fighting the constant urge to give up, putting all of these things aside and getting on with the work of the kingdom. It's the daily grind of evangelism and discipleship, followed by moments of great encouragement as people profess faith. It's then followed by moments of profound sadness as you realise that most of them confessed faith but never really possessed it.

There is something proudly depressing about seeing a man who lived with you for 12 months lying in his own vomit in the local park, with a needle sticking out of his arm. There is the deep grief of seeing a man who you baptised and who sang Christian songs so loudly and out of tune that it made people uncomfortable, completely comatose and being urinated on by eight-year-old children.

WHAT'S IT LIKE BEING A WORKING-CLASS CHRISTIAN IN THE UK?

It's going to middle-class conferences and overhearing middle-class pastors deny the existence of class in our country, and then talk sneeringly of those working for Jesus in these communities.

It's being told you have a chip on your shoulder. It's being told you exaggerate the problem. It's being told that the system isn't broken because, *after all, you're a pastor, aren't you?*

It's listening to it from people who won't lift one finger to help you, regardless of what you say. It's being told that the church has a heart for the poor, and yet receiving nothing from them. It's being told not to hold a conference about the UK church and the poor without inviting middle-class speakers. It's being told not to bite the hand that never feeds you. It's being told that you only wear a beanie or informal clothing to make a point, rather than it being your preferred clothing of choice.

What is it about UK Christians that causes them to burst into tears and express outrage for South American street children on the one hand, and yet tut loudly as they're forced to step over the homeless man on their way to get a pint of milk? We say that we love the poor of this world and yet we ignore them on our own doorsteps.

We don't need the UK church to come to our storm-tossed communities waving their little spiritual torches, so that they can lead us to the safety of their middle-class lighthouses. We need our own gospel lighthouses. We need healthy churches. We need church plants. We need revitalised churches. We need the light of life full-time. We need supplies for the battle. We need frontline troops. We need money. We need infantry. We need prayer warriors. We need encouragement. Don't send us your children to be babysat and amused for two weeks and then call it mission. Send us your best. Send us your brightest. Come and live with us. Come and celebrate with us. Come and die with us. Leave worldly ambition behind. Leave upward social mobility behind. Leave your pension behind. Leave your children's education behind. Leave it all and follow Jesus.

Many years ago, I took a group of young people on a trip to Uganda to work with street children. And every person came back from that trip determined to follow Jesus more seriously. One young man in particular stood out. He had plans for university and a great career. His parents were successful business people and they lived in a big house on the outskirts of the city. So big, the place had a stream running through its back garden. He told me that he wanted to go to Bible college and train to be a missionary. I was so encouraged. A couple of days later I had a knock at the door and two angry parents were standing there. I invited them in and they went nuts at me. How dare I tell their son it was okay to be a missionary. These were influential people in the church and the father was even a church officer! I was confused. Surely, becoming a missionary for Jesus was a high calling. The highest calling.

They looked at me as if I was stupid. "It's okay for people like you," his mother screamed at me (thus giving the game away). "My son has options. Maybe if they don't work out, then he could think about full-time missionary service. But we are not going to let him throw his life away." "Wow!" I said, "Throw his life away! Are you joking me? How is serving Jesus as a missionary throwing your life away?" They stormed out and that was the beginning of the end for me in that church. Their son went on to university and has since forged a successful career. But he is nowhere with the Lord. His family chose educational success and upward mobility over full-time missionary service. I sometimes wonder if they regret it. I suspect they haven't even thought of it like that.

But that's how almost every middle-class Christian child is raised. Education and career. Anything else is madness. And all we have produced is a theologically conservative, spiritually-neutered generation of believers who've been convinced to water down the hard sayings of Jesus. "He says this, but what he really meant was that." And if you do pursue Bible college, then make sure you take an upwardly mobile position afterward: Intern, Pastoral Assistant, Youth Worker, Assistant Pastor and then the glory of Co-Pastor and Senior Pastor. And we hide it all behind a veneer of middle-class respectability and risk averseness.

Attempting great things for God is viewed as being foolish and unwise. Playing it safe is seen as the spiritual thing to do. And what's it left us with? An anaemic faith, with pulpits full of anaemic communicators, throwing cold water on the dreams of the young. Wonderfully crafted sermons with pithy middle-class illustrations, without a call to arms for gospel warriors.

And it's why so many of our young swallowed the Mark Driscoll approach to biblical manhood – all MMA fights, craft beers and tattoos. We need solidly biblical, gospel-loving young people to forego university and the call of upward social and financial mobility and lay down their lives for Jesus in the spiritual wastelands that are the UK's housing estates and housing schemes. If you are reading this, wondering what you should do with your life and thinking, "Maybe I'll take a gap year or work for some student ministry or para-church organisation."

Forget that.

Come and work in a council estate. Come and join the spiritual revolution that is slowly happening in the UK. Come and give your life to that. Forget the call to middle-class respectability. Forget the sensible option. Forget your career or future stock options and pension plans. Follow Jesus into the coalface of the spiritual war in our country. Come and migrate to the spiritual wastelands of the UK and work long hours, in difficult circumstances, with some beautiful glimpses of gospel light, with many discouragements and little financial reward. And then die here. Nameless and forgotten by all but Him who we serve: King Jesus.

If you're a church leader or in church leadership, partner with us – *really* partner with us. We don't want lip service. We need sacrificial partnering, costly praying, generous giving, deep fellowshipping. Will your church calendars, your church budgets and your church prayer meetings reflect the crying needs in our schemes and estates?

If you lead a church in a privileged area, if you have lots of young people in your church family, are you teaching them the Word of God in all its fullness? Are you teaching them to do justice, love kindness and walk humbly in relation to the least privileged in our society? Are you encouraging people to give their lives in service to Christ in some of the most unreached parts of our country, whatever the cost? How will the least, the last and the lost believe in Him of whom they've never heard? And how are they to hear if no one tells them?

A story is told of the time Thomas Guthrie met Thomas Chalmers when he first moved to Edinburgh. Guthrie was looking down over the Cowgate (a slum at the time), horrified by the drunken men and women and the young street children wandering the streets, dirty and hungry. A hand was laid on his shoulder and he turned around to find the famous preacher and social reformer, Dr. Thomas Chalmers. Guthrie recalls:

> *Hopeful of success, he surveyed the scene beneath us, and his eye, which often wore a dreamy stare, kindled at the prospect of seeing that wilderness become an Eden, these foul haunts of darkness, drunkenness and disease, changed into "dwellings of the righteous where is heard the voice of melody". Contemplating the scene for a little in silence, all at once, with his broad Luther-like face glowing with enthusiasm, he waved his arm to exclaim, "A beautiful field, sir; a very fine field of operation."*[326]

A beautiful field indeed. It is my field and I hope to persuade you that it could be your field too.

APPENDIX 1:

ONLINE RESEARCH RESOURCE

This code will lead you to the online research resource:
This page is password protected. To access the page, please use the following password: **leastlastlost**

Alternatively, here is the website address:
https://20schemesequip.com/least-last-lost/

APPENDIX 2:

A RESPONSE FROM THE FIEC

JOHNNY PRIME, ASSOCIATE NATIONAL DIRECTOR, FIEC

This book is the product of hours and hours of research and we have been very pleased to be able to play a small part in supporting 20schemes in their mammoth task. The FIEC was founded in 1922; today, it is made up of around 630 churches throughout England, Scotland and Wales. We are united in the biblical good news of our Lord Jesus and committed to working together to reach Britain for Christ.

In recent years there has been a growing conviction in the FIEC that if we are to reach Britain for Christ, a priority must be to work together more deliberately to reach areas and communities where there is little, if any, gospel witness. That includes our poorer communities, whether such communities are found in cities, rural areas or coastal towns. In many ways this reflects the origins of the FIEC. Many of the original FIEC churches were mission halls and churches planted in poorer communities with a passion to share the grace of the Lord Jesus.

We are seeking to take seriously the fact 45% of the UK population are not middle class; and that the majority are without opportunity to hear the gospel in their community. We also recognise that those already serving in these areas are best placed to help our family of churches to shape the way ahead.

We have much to learn, but the FIEC is seeking to encourage work in poorer communities in a number of ways.

INFORMING

As a family of churches, we are committed to sharing information that we hope will lead to prayer and action. Over the last 10 years we have sought to highlight places in the UK where there is little or no evangelical witness. We are grateful for the way the information we have shared has stimulated prayer for gospel advance. It has been encouraging to see how the Lord has been answering prayer with churches being planted. More recently, we have been seeking to highlight the need for deliberate planting and revitalisation of churches in poorer areas.

GATHERING

The annual FIEC Leaders' Conference has become a main gathering point for leaders of FIEC churches. At a recent conference a few years ago, we gathered together those leading churches in deprived communities to start a conversation about what could be done to better reach these communities. The ongoing conversation with those already working in these areas needs to continue as the message of this book is taken on board. One outcome of that conversation was a bursary scheme established to fund the attendance at the Leaders' Conference by those working in poorer areas. We are hoping and praying for productive conversations at future Conferences that result in meaningful support for those working among the least, the last and the lost.

CONNECTING

A fruit of getting folk together has been connecting churches for mutual support and encouragement. For example, a church in South London is now partnering with a church in the North-East, helping to fund a women's worker and joining together for Zoom prayer meetings. Other FIEC churches in more affluent areas have made similar connections. These are mutually beneficial partnerships for the advance of the gospel. It is the kind of partnership we see between the churches in the New Testament – and we hope to see many more partnerships like this developing.

DISTRIBUTING

Over recent years the FIEC has been entrusted with funds from various sources for the work of training and mission in the UK. We have been able to distribute these funds for the honour of the Lord Jesus. Over the last three years it has been a privilege to allocate £650,000 for work in postcodes that fall within the 20% most deprived areas of the country. On one level, it is a drop in the ocean, but it is a pattern we pray we will be able to continue as further funds are entrusted to us. The work of churches in poorer areas will always need ongoing financial support.

ENCOURAGING

Part of our work is encouraging churches to look beyond the borders of their immediate locality to poorer areas with no gospel church. Perhaps I can illustrate with how this worked out for an FIEC church where I was serving in Enfield, North London. The London Borough of Enfield has a population of 340,000 (bigger than some cities!), but with few gospel churches. Western Enfield is more middle class and eastern Enfield is working class with some of the most deprived council wards in London. As the local church in Enfield town prayed for the borough, we prayed for opportunities to plant churches in eastern Enfield. This led to the planting of Silver Street Community Church in one of the most deprived and ethnically diverse areas in London. A number of key families took the step to move to live in the area and God has been pleased to bless the establishment of a diverse gospel community within a diverse local community. The Enfield churches are now considering planting a church in another part of eastern Enfield. This is the kind of mindset we want to encourage and facilitate.

ENVISIONING

We also want to envision those training for ministry to consider gospel work in "unfashionable" places. Many of those being trained for ministry are from large city-centre, student churches. We praise God for their work with young people and the way many hear the call to serve the Lord Jesus while they are students. But if we are to reach Britain for Christ, we need a new generation of those converted and trained in the "fashionable" places to be willing to go to the "unfashionable" places, to learn how to do church there, and to settle down and make these places home for the long haul of planting or revitalising churches that will reach the lost.

As we read the New Testament, we discover that the Apostle Paul had the ambition to preach the gospel where Christ was not known (Rom. 15:20). Christ is largely unknown in huge swathes of the UK and particularly in deprived areas. How important it is for independent churches to work together to make Christ known in places like this. Please pray for us.

ENDNOTES

Foreword

1 Emphasis mine.

2 Entry for 27 May 1742, *The Journal of the Reverend John Wesley*.

3 Morgan, G.C., *The Practice of Prayer* (Fleming H. Revell, 1906), p.12.

4 Luke 5:32, KJV.

Introduction

5 Luke 14:25–27.

6 Luke 14:33.

7 A non-alcoholic drink favoured by many UK Christians!

8 See www.20schemes.com for more information.

9 The Fellowship Of Independent Evangelical Churches, www.fiec.org.uk.

10 Ten of Those, www.10ofthose.com; Christian Focus Publications, www.christianfocus.com.

11 The Union School of Theology, www.ust.ac.uk.

12 Joslin, R., *Urban Harvest: Biblical perspectives on Christian mission in the inner cities* (Evangelical Press, 1982).

13 Joslin, *Urban Harvest*, p.2.

14 Church In Hard Places is an initiative of Acts29 which seeks to train and support church planters in some of the world's poorest countries, https://www.acts29.com/church-in-hard-places/.

15 McGarvey, D., *Poverty Safari: Understanding the anger of Britain's underclass* (Luath Press Limited, 2017), p.125.

16 The original source for this quote is unknown.

17 We will discuss this further when we think about mercy ministries in more detail.

18 Our research has been conducted in partnership with the FIEC and has therefore focused on FIEC churches but we trust that the results will be useful to evangelical churches from other denominations.

Part I – Chapter 1

19 John-Baptiste, A., "When Council Estates were a Dream", BBC News, 4 July 2019, https://www.bbc.co.uk/news/extra/iZKMPd0wjP/council_housing.

20 Barnes, C., "Not Fit For Purpose", The National Archives, 30 August 2013, https://blog.nationalarchives.gov.uk/not-fit-for-purpose/.

21 For further details, see "The History of Council Housing", University of the West of England, 2008, https://fet.uwe.ac.uk/conweb/house_ages/council_housing/print.htm.

22 "History of Council Housing", UWE.

23 Emma at HASpod, "When and Why Asbestos Was Banned in UK Construction", HASpod, 10 April 2018, https://www.haspod.com/blog/asbestos/when-why-asbestos-banned-uk-construction.

24 "Urban blight" is defined by the *Collins Dictionary* as "the decay and deterioration of an urban area due to neglect or age".

25 According to the *Cambridge Dictionary*, "to squat" is "to live in an empty building or area of land without the permission of the owner". On my housing estate, empty houses/flats were also called squats.

26 A term generally ascribed to Ruth Glass to describe the social changes she saw in London in the mid-1960s when the poor were displaced from their homes to make way for the middle class who bought them cheaply and immediately refurbished and modernised them. See MacRury, J., "Gentrification describes a brutal and often violent process", Geographical, 25 March 2020, https://geographical.co.uk/opinion/item/3629-gentrification-and-urban-inequality-the-displacement-of-bame-and-migrant-communities.

27 Glass, R. et al., *London: Aspects of Change,* a Centre for Urban Studies report (ed. MacGibbon and Kee, 1964). Quoted in "Ruth Glass and 'Coining Gentrification'", *The Bartlett Review*, 2019, available at https://www.ucl.ac.uk/bartlett/sites/bartlett/files/ucl.125_bartlett_issueone_digital.pdf.

28 The term "problem people" is also used by politicians and outsiders to describe those who are guilty of committing a large proportion of petty and/or serious crime in our communities.

29 Ginsburg, N., "The Privatization of Council Housing", Critical Social Policy 25(1), 2005, pp.124. See also, Pawson, H. and Fancie, C., *Maturing Assets: The Evolution of Stock Transfer Housing Associations* (Policy Press, 2003), pp. 35–36, https://www.jrf.org.uk/report/evolution-stock-transfer-housing-associations; Pawson, H. et al., *The Impacts of Housing Stock Transfers In Urban Britain* (The Chartered Institute of Housing and the Joseph Rowntree Foundation, 2009), p.112, https://www.jrf.org.uk/report/impacts-housing-stock-transfers-urban-britain.

30 Pawson et al., *Impacts of Housing Stock Transfers In Urban Britain,* p.112.

31 Pawson, H. and Fancie, C., *The Evolution of Stock Transfer Housing Associations,* Joseph Rowntree Foundation, 10 September 2003.

32 The John Rowntree Foundation (JRF) is another source of data we have used and looks primarily at trends. Despite some limitations, their research has proved to be innovative and helpful. According to the JRF, "Poverty is when your resources are well below your minimum needs ... Poverty means not being able to heat your home, pay your rent, or buy the essentials for your children. It means waking up every day facing insecurity, uncertainty, and impossible decisions about money. It means facing marginalisation – and even discrimination – because of your financial circumstances. The constant stress it causes can lead to problems that deprive people of the chance to play a full part in society." See "What is Poverty?", Joseph Rowntree Foundation, https://www.jrf.org.uk/our-work/what-is-poverty.

33 Pawson and Fancie, *Evolution of Stock Transfer Housing Associations.*

34 Pawson and Fancie, *Evolution of Stock Transfer Housing Associations*.

35 Pawson and Fancie, *Evolution of Stock Transfer Housing Associations.*

36 McDonnell, J., "Labour Pledges to Wage War on Poverty", Labour Party, 19 November 2019, https://labour.org.uk/press/labour-pledges-to-wage-war-on-poverty-to-reverse-the-damage-of-a-decade-of-austerity/.

37 Definition of "poverty", *Cambridge Dictionary*, https://dictionary.cambridge.org/dictionary/english/poverty.

38 Definition of "poverty", *Oxford Learner's Dictionary*, https://www.oxfordlearnersdictionaries.com/definition/american_english/poverty.

39 Definition of "poverty", *Collins Dictionary*, https://www.collinsdictionary.com/dictionary/english/poverty.

40 Definition of "deprived", *Oxford Learner's Dictionary*, https://www.oxfordlearnersdictionaries.com/definition/english/deprived.

41 Definition of "deprived", *Oxford Learner's Dictionary*, https://www.oxfordlearnersdictionaries.com/definition/english/deprived.

42 "Measuring Poverty", Child Poverty Action Group, https://cpag.org.uk/child-poverty/measuring-poverty.

43 The Social Metrics Commission (SMC), https://socialmetricscommission.org.uk. According to the SMC, 14.3 million people in the UK live in poverty. In fact, 12.1% of the total UK population (7.7 million people) live in what they call "persistent poverty". This means that more than one in ten of the UK population lives in persistent

poverty. The SMC is very helpful because it enables us to understand lifestyle choices and a household's ability to live, what they deem, a comfortable life. They have a well-researched process for identifying "comfort" but it still remains somewhat of a mystery when it comes to processing the data faithfully. The SMC is more interested in tracking the trajectories and trends of the UK's lifestyle choices, rather than seeking to explain how and when people and households fall into deprivation. Again, there is some criticism around how they use their metrics and data, and a particular weakness is the feeling that they have seriously underestimated the cost of living in the UK by as much as 40%! To their credit, though, the SMC has allowed us to track, and gain some insight into, the emergence of the so-called "working poor".

44 "English Indices of Deprivation 2019 Research Report", UK Government Ministries of Housing, Communities and Local Government, 26 September 2019, https://www.gov.uk/government/statistics/english-indices-of-deprivation-2019.

45 "Council Conclusions on 'Combating Poverty and Social Exclusion: An integrated approach'", European Commission Employment, Social Affairs & Inclusion, 27 June 2016, https://ec.europa.eu/social/main.jsp?catId=751andlangId=en.

46 "Campaigning For an End to Child Poverty", End Child Poverty, https://www.endchildpoverty.org.uk. This source is helpful for locating child poverty *by region* within the UK. The data is also useful for corroborating the locations *where* people experience material deprivation. According to the ECP: "A child is deemed to be growing up in poverty if they

live in a household whose income is 60% below the median income", https://www.endchildpoverty.org.uk/faq-on-local-child-poverty-research/.

47 The Index of Multiple Deprivation (IMD) ranks every small area in England from 1 (most deprived area) to 32,844 (least deprived area). These reports, used by each country within the UK, serve as a baseline when it comes to demonstrating deprivation. The IMD reports are particularly helpful in locating areas *where* material deprivation is most likely to be experienced. However, they are heavily focused upon *income* as determinative of one's deprivation. Their weakness lies in the fact that statisticians are just not able to interview and assess the income of every household in the UK. The IMD's data is very helpful for *locating an area* where people experience deprivation, but not necessarily people *in* deprivation. This means that some households could live in a "deprived" community, such as my own, and yet live a comfortable, financially secure life.

48 "Deprivation and Poverty", Nottingham Insight, https://www.nottinghaminsight.org.uk/themes/deprivation-and-poverty/.

49 "Deprivation and Poverty", Nottingham Insight.

50 Dorling, D., *So You Think You Know About Britain? The surprising truth about modern Britain* (Constable and Robinson, 2011), p.134.

51 Beed, C. and Beed, C., "Recent Christian Interpretations of Material Poverty and Inequality in the Developed World", *Journal of Markets & Morality* 16(2), 2013, p.1.

52 "Sustaining Human Progress: Reducing Vulnerabilities and Building Resilience", United Nations Development Programme Human Development Report, 2014.

53 "Committing to Child Survival: A promise renewed", United Nations Inter-Agency Group for Child Mortality Estimation (UN IGME). UNICEF, 2014.

54 "Progress on Drinking Water and Sanitation: 2014 Update", World Health Organization and UNICEF Joint Monitoring Programme (JMP), 8 May 2014.

55 "WPF (World Food Programme) says Hunger Kills More Than AIDS, Malaria, Tuberculosis Combined", Relief Web, 4 June 2009, https://reliefweb.int/report/world/writethru-wfp-says-hunger-kills-more-aids-malaria-tuberculosis-combined.

56 McGarvey, *Poverty Safari*, p.94.

57 "English Indices of Deprivation 2019", UK Government.

58 "English Indices of Deprivation 2019", UK Government.

59 We will look at the thorny issue of what constitutes poverty from a biblical perspective in the second half of the book.

60 There are a growing number of people who avoid homelessness by rotating through the homes of family and friends, sleeping on their couches and in guestrooms. See, for example, "Sofa Surfers: The young hidden homeless," 21 December 2017, sec. UK, https://www.bbc.com/news/uk-42427398; Jenkins, C., "The Hidden Homeless: Britain's young sofa surfer surge," Channel 4 News, 4 December 2014, https://www.channel4.com/news/sofa-surfing-hidden-homeless-britain-youth-benefits.

61 This is reflected both in gentrification and the privatisation of public housing. See Harris, J., "The End of Council Housing", *The Guardian,* 4 January 2016, https://www.theguardian.com/society/2016/jan/04/end-of-council-housing-bill-secure-tenancies-pay-to-stay; Murie, A., "Shrinking the State in Housing: Challenges, transitions and ambiguities", *Cambridge Journal of Regions, Economy and Society* 11(3), November 2018; Stephens, M., et al., "2018 UK Housing Review: Autumn Briefing Paper", Chartered Institute of Housing, March 2018, https://researchportal.hw.ac.uk/en/publications/2018-uk-housing-review-autumn-briefing-paper; Ravetz, A., *Council Housing and Culture: The history of a social experiment* (Routledge, 2001).

62 "What is Poverty?", Compassion, https://www.compassion.com/poverty/what-is-poverty.htm.

Chapter 3

63 All of the testimonies in this chapter are based on real people, some of whom have had their names changed to protect their identities.

64 "World Economic Outlook Update: A weakening global expansion", International Monetary Fund, January 2019, p.8, https://www.imf.org/en/Publications/WEO/Issues/2019/01/11/weo-update-january-2019.

65 Dorling, D. and Thomas, B., *Bankrupt Britain: An atlas of social change* (The Policy Press, 2011), p.7.

66 Dorling and Thomas, *Bankrupt Britain*, p.17.

67 Dorling and Thomas, *Bankrupt Britain*, p.28.

68 Jensen, E., "Understanding the Nature of Poverty", *Teaching With Poverty In Mind: What being poor does to kids' brains and what schools can do about it* (ASCD, November 2009), https://www.ascd.org/books/teaching-with-poverty-in-mind?chapter=understanding-the-nature-of-poverty.

69 Cassidy, J., "The Real Cost of the 2008 Financial Crisis", *The New Yorker*, 17 September 2018, https://www.newyorker.com/magazine/2018/09/17/the-real-cost-of-the-2008-financial-crisis.

70 Leisering, L. and Leibfried, S., *Time and Poverty in Western Welfare States: United Germany in Perspective* (Cambridge University Press, 2001).

71 Jensen, "Understanding the Nature of Poverty", *Teaching With Poverty In Mind.*

72 "Facts About Poverty", Urban Ventures, https://urbanventures.org/facts-about-poverty.

73 "Facts About Poverty", Urban Ventures.

74 Kidd, Dr. D., "Lifting heads, Not Ripping Up Roots" in Gilbert, I., *The Working Class: Poverty, Education and Alternative Voices* (Independent Thinking Press, 2018), p.233.

75 "Types of Poverty", Richmond Vale, 15 March 2016, https://richmondvale.org/en/blog/types-of-poverty.

76 "Relative vs Absolute Poverty", Habitat for Humanity, https://www.habitatforhumanity.org.uk/blog/2018/09/relative-absolute-poverty/.

77 Francis-Devine, B., "Poverty in the UK: statistics", UK Parliament House of Commons Library, 31 March 2021, https://commonslibrary.parliament.uk/research-briefings/sn07096/, emphasis mine.

78 "Chapter 2: Eradication of Poverty", World Summit for Social Development Programme of Action, United Nations, 1995, https://www.un.org/esa/socdev/wssd/text-version/agreements/poach2.htm.

79 Francis-Devine, "Poverty in the UK".

80 Jensen, "Understanding the Nature of Poverty", *Teaching With Poverty In Mind.*

81 Jensen, "Understanding the Nature of Poverty", *Teaching With Poverty In Mind.*

82 "Types of Poverty", Richmond Vale.

83 Jensen, "Understanding the Nature of Poverty", *Teaching With Poverty In Mind.*

84 "Measuring Poverty", The World Bank, last updated 16 April 2021, https://www.worldbank.org/en/topic/measuringpoverty.

85 The Social Metrics Commission.

86 Chart adapted from "Guide on Poverty Measurement", United Nations Economic Commission for Europe, 2017, p.81, http://www.unece.org/fileadmin/DAM/stats/publications/2018/ECECESSTAT20174.pdf.

87 Family types are taken from the HBAI dataset once SMC poverty indicators (assessed at the sharing unit level) have been allocated to each benefit unit.

88 "Ch2: Eradication of Poverty", UN World Summit.

89 "Ch2: Eradication of Poverty", UN World Summit.

90 "Who Is At Risk of Poverty?", Child Poverty Action Group, https://cpag.org.uk/child-poverty/who-risk-poverty.

91 "Who Is At Risk of Poverty?", Child Poverty Action Group.

92 "Who Is At Risk of Poverty?", Child Poverty Action Group. The overall number of women who are low paid (3 million) is still much higher than the overall number of men who are low paid (1.9 million).

93 "Who Is At Risk of Poverty?", Child Poverty Action Group.

94 "Who Is At Risk of Poverty?", Child Poverty Action Group.

95 Di Meglio, E., ed., *Living Conditions In Europe: 2018 Edition* (Eurostat: European Commission, 2018), p.26, https://doi.org/10.2785/39876.

96 Compare methodologies in the following reports: *Measuring Material Deprivation in the EU: Indicators for the whole population and child-specific indicators* (Eurostat: European Commission, 2012), available at https://doi.org/10.2785/33598; Smith, T., et al., The English Indices of Deprivation 2015 Research Report, UK Government: Department for Communities and Local Government, 2015), available at https://www.gov.uk/government/statistics/english-indices-of-deprivation-2015. For example, the EU looks at metrics such as owning a car, home, quantity of clothes, and other specifics to calculate material deprivation. Conversely, UK countries use the seven categories of deprivation: income, employment, health and disability, education/skills/training, barriers to housing, crime, and living environment (each with sub-domains).

97 Stephens et al., "2018 UK Housing Review", p.11. See also the important study the CIH report cites from: Bramley, G. and Fitzpatrick, S., "Homelessness in the UK: Who is most at risk?" *Housing Studies* 33(1), 2018, pp.96–116, https://doi.org/10.1080/02673037.2017.1344957.

98 Stephens et al., "2018 UK Housing Review", p.11, emphasis mine; Bramley and Fitzpatrick, "Homelessness in the UK".

99 Stephens et al., "2018 UK Housing Review", p.11; Bramley and Fitzpatrick, "Homelessness in the UK".

100 "A New Measure of Poverty for the UK", Social Metrics Commission, September 2018, p.81, https://socialmetricscommission.org.uk/wp-content/uploads/2019/07/SMC_measuring-poverty-201809_full-report.pdf; "Measuring Poverty 2019: A report of the Social Metrics Commission", Social Metrics Commission, July 2019, https://socialmetricscommission.org.uk/wp-content/uploads/2019/07/SMC_measuring-poverty-201908_full-report.pdf.

101 "New Measure of Poverty for the UK: 2018", Social Metrics Commission, p.81.

102 "New Measure of Poverty for the UK: 2018", Social Metrics Commission, pp.77–78.

103 Statistics adapted from "Measuring Poverty 2019", Social Metrics Commission. For comparison, see earlier report for 2016/17 analysis and note the considerable increase in costs (about 25%) – Table 9: Poverty Lines, "New Measure of UK Poverty 2018", Social Metrics Commission, p.78. SMC derived their analysis from the Family Resources Survey and HBAI dataset (2016/17).

104 For an explanation of "equivalised", see "Chapter 3: Equivalised income", Office National Statistics, https://www.ons.gov.uk/peoplepopulationandcommunity/personalandhouseholdfinances/incomeandwealth/compendium/familyspending/2015/chapter3equivalisedincome.

105 "Households Below Average Income: An analysis of the UK income distribution 1994/95–2016/17", UK Government Department for Work and Pensions, 22 March 2018, p.5, https://assets.publishing.service.gov.uk/government/uploads/system/uploads/attachment_data/file/691917/households-below-average-income-1994-1995-2016-2017.pdf.

106 I am indebted to Donald Hirsch for his kind conversations and insights, though any fault or error in judgement is my own.

107 Hirsch, D., "The Cost of a Child in 2019", Child Poverty Action Group, September 2019, p.11, https://cpag.org.uk/sites/default/files/files/policypost/CostofaChild2019_web.pdf.

108 "New Measure of Poverty for the UK 2018", Social Metrics Commission, p.111; "Measuring Poverty 2019", Social Metrics Commission, p.5.

109 "Feeling The Pinch", End Child Poverty, January 2017, p.1, http://www.endchildpoverty.org.uk/images/Feelingthepinch/ECP-FeelingThePinch-final-report.pdf.

110 "Feeling The Pinch", End Child Poverty, p.1.

111 Miller, C. and Clarke, D., "Nearly Half of Children Living in Poverty in Some Areas Of Devon", Devonlive, 25 January 2018, https://www.devonlive.com/news/devon-news/nearly-half-children-living-poverty-1115648.

112 "Child Poverty", Joseph Rowntree Foundation, https://www.jrf.org.uk/data/child-poverty.

113 Hirsch, "The Cost of a Child in 2019".

114 Bourquin, P., et al., "Big Increases in In-Work Related Poverty Rate Are About Much More Than Just Low Pay", 18 June 2019, https://www.ifs.org.uk/publications/14196.

115 Bourquin et al., "Big Increases in In-Work Related Poverty Rate".

116 Castelow, E., "Witches in Britain", Historic UK, https://www.historic-uk.com/CultureUK/Witches-in-Britain/.

117 Elliot, L., "How Poverty has Become the Scourge of Those in Work", *The Guardian,* 9 February 2020, https://www.theguardian.com/business/2020/feb/09/how-poverty-has-become-the-scourge-of-those-in-work.

118 "UK Poverty Increases Despite Low Unemployment: Report", The Hindu BusinessLine, 7 February 2020, https://www.thehindubusinessline.com/news/world/uk-poverty-increases-despite-low-unemployment-report/article30759064.ece.

119 The Youth Training Scheme (YTS) was an on-the-job training course in the United Kingdom for school leavers aged 16 and 17 and was managed by the Manpower Services Commission. In 1989, it was renamed Youth Training and was placed under the management of local training and enterprise councils.

120 "Poverty in Later Life", Age UK, May 2021, https://www.ageuk.org.uk/globalassets/age-uk/documents/reports-and-publications/reports-and-briefings/money-matters/poverty_in_later_life_briefing_2021.pdf.

121 "Later Life in the United Kingdom 2019", Age UK, May 2019, https://www.ageuk.org.uk/globalassets/age-uk/documents/reports-and-publications/later_life_uk_factsheet.pdf.

122 For a brief explanation of the difference between the three, refer to: "Migrants, Asylum Seekers, Refugees and Immigrants: What's the difference?" International Rescue Committee, 22 May 2019, https://www.rescue-uk.org/article/migrants-asylum-seekers-refugees-and-immigrants-whats-difference?gclid=EAIaIQobChMIoLf4.

123 Hodgkinson, H.L., "Grasping Demographics: Get ready for them now", *The Education Digest* 68(4), December 2002), p.4–7; "Measuring UK Poverty 2019", Social Metrics Commission; Sefton, T. et al., "All Kids Count: The impact of the two-child limit after two years", Child Poverty Action Group, 2019, pp.42–51; Bridge, G., Butler, T. and Lees, L., eds., "Mixed Communities Gentrification by Stealth?" Policy Press, 2012, https://doi.org/10.1332/policypress/9781847424938.001.0001.

124 "Family Resources Survey 2014/15", UK Government Department for Work and Pensions, 28 June 2016, https://assets.publishing.service.gov.uk/government/uploads/system/uploads/attachment_data/file/531242/family-resources-survey-2014-15.pdf.

125 Hughes, C. and Kenway, P., "Foreign-born People and Poverty in the UK", Joseph Rowntree Foundation, 29 July 2016, https://www.jrf.org.uk/report/foreign-born-people-and-poverty-uk.

126 Hughes and Kenway, "Foreign-born People and Poverty in the UK".

127 This contrasts with a poverty rate of 19% for UK-born people. See Hughes and Kenway, "Foreign-born People and Poverty in the UK".

128 In contrast to 24% of children form UK born families. See Hughes and Kenway, "Foreign-born People and Poverty in the UK".

129 Hughes and Kenway, "Foreign-born People and Poverty in the UK".

130 The names have been changed to protect identities.

131 Brewer, M., Etheridge, B. and O'Dea, C., "Why are Households that Report the Lowest Incomes So Well Off?", *The Economic Journal*, 127(605), October 2017, p.F46–F49, https://doi.org/10.1111/ecoj.12334.

132 "Why the Majority of the World's Poor are Women", Oxfam, https://www.oxfam.org/en/why-majority-worlds-poor-are-women, emphasis mine.

133 "6: Child Poverty in Scotland: Priority groups – lone-parent families", Public Health Scotland, August 2020, p.4, http://healthscotland.scot/media/3133/child-poverty-in-scotland_priority-groups_lone-parent-families_briefing.pdf.

134 Taulbut, M., McCartney, G. and Davis, M., "Lone Parents in Scotland, Great Britain and the UK: Health, employment and social security", NHS Scotland", November 2016, p.5, https://www.scotpho.org.uk/media/1157/scotpho161123-lone-parents-scotland-gb-uk.pdf.

135 Taulbut, McCartney and Davis, "Lone Parents in Scotland, Great Britain and the UK".

136 Taulbut, McCartney and Davis, "Lone Parents in Scotland, Great Britain and the UK".

137 "Child Poverty in Scotland – lone-parent families", Public Health Scotland, p.10.

138 Taulbut, McCartney and Davis, "Lone Parents in Scotland, Great Britain and the UK", p.10.

139 "Child Poverty in Scotland – lone-parent families", Public Health Scotland, p.10.

140 "Child Poverty in Scotland – lone-parent families", Public Health Scotland, p.8.

141 "Child Poverty in Scotland – lone-parent families", Public Health Scotland, p.8.

142 Tweed, E., Miller, R. and Matheson, C., "Why are Drug-related Deaths Among Women Increasing in Scotland? A scoping of possible explanations", The Scottish Government Social Research, June 2018, p.4, https://www.gov.scot/binaries/content/documents/govscot/publications/research-and-analysis/2018/06/drug-related-deaths-women-increasing-scotland-9781787810129/documents/00537548-pdf/00537548-pdf/govscot%3Adocument/00537548.pdf.

143 Tweed, Miller and Matheson, "Why are Drug-related Deaths Among Women Increasing in Scotland?", p.8.

144 Tweed, Miller and Matheson, "Why are Drug-related Deaths Among Women Increasing in Scotland?", p.12.

145 Tweed, Miller and Matheson, "Why are Drug-related Deaths Among Women Increasing in Scotland?", p.12.

146 Interviewee 128 in Tweed, Miller and Matheson, "Why are Drug-related Deaths Among Women Increasing in Scotland?", p.13.

147 McDaid, S. and Kousoulis, A., "Tackling Social Inequalities to Reduce Mental Health Problems: How everyone can flourish equally", Mental Health Foundation, 2020, p.10,

https://www.mentalhealth.org.uk/sites/default/files/MHF-tackling-inequalities-report_WEB.pdf.

148 McLean, J. et al., "The Scottish Health Survey 2017 edition: A National Statistics Publication for Scotland" vol. 1, 2017, p.66.

149 McLean et al., "The Scottish Health Survey 2017 edition", p.66.

150 McLean et al., "The Scottish Health Survey 2017 edition", p.76.

151 "Period Products (Free Provision) (Scotland) Bill", The Scottish Parliament, https://www.parliament.scot/bills-and-laws/bills/period-products-free-provision-scotland-bill.

152 Grierson, J., "Domestic Abuse Killings 'More Than Double' Amid Covid-19 Lockdown", *The Guardian*, 15 April 2020, https://www.theguardian.com/society/2020/apr/15/domestic-abuse-killings-more-than-double-amid-covid-19-lockdown.

153 "Rape and Sexual Assault: What health workers need to know about gender-based violence", NHS Health Scotland, p.8, http://www.healthscotland.scot/media/2463/gbv-rape-and-sexual-assault-march2019-english.pdf.

154 "Domestic Abuse and Stalking Charges in Scotland, 2019–20", Crown Office and Procurator Fiscal Service, 8 September 2020, https://www.copfs.gov.uk/media-site-news-from-copfs/1902-domestic-abuse-and-stalking-charges-in-scotland-2019–20.

155 "Domestic Abuse and Stalking Charges in Scotland", Crown Office and Procurator Fiscal Service.

156 Harkins, D., "Child Abuse Cases in Scotland Soar as Sex Offence Figures Rise By a Third", *Daily Record,* 10 August 2020, https://www.dailyrecord.co.uk/news/scottish-news/child-abuse-cases-scotland-soar-22494408.

157 "Violence in Scotland", Zero Tolerance, https://www.zerotolerance.org.uk/vaw-facts/.

Chapter 4

158 "Poor Law Reform", UK Government, https://www.parliament.uk/about/living-heritage/transformingsociety/livinglearning/19thcentury/overview/poorlaw/.

159 Watson, Dr. S., "Ch 2: Activism – Educating the Working Class" in Gilbert, *The Working Class*, p.16. However, these terms were first coined by Pierre Bourdieu in his 1986 work, *The Forms of Capital*. See "The Forms of Capital", Marxists Internet Archive, https://www.marxists.org/reference/subject/philosophy/works/fr/bourdieu-forms-capital.htm.

160 "Cultural Captial vs Economic Captial vs Social Capital" *(sic.)*, Language as Bourdieuan Capital in the Era of Globalization, 25 March 2015, https://languageascapital.wordpress.com/2012/03/25/cultural-captial-vs-economic-captial/.

161 "Social mobility, movement of individuals, families, or groups through a system of social hierarchy or stratification. If such mobility involves a change in position, especially in occupation, but no change in social class, it is called 'horizontal mobility.' An example would be a person who moves from a managerial position in one company to a similar position in another.

If, however, the move involves a change in social class, it is called 'vertical mobility' and involves either 'upward mobility' or 'downward mobility.' An industrial worker who becomes a wealthy businessman moves upward in the class system; a landed aristocrat who loses everything in a revolution moves downward in the system." From https://www.britannica.com/topic/social-mobility.

162 "National Statistics Socio-economic Classification", Office for National Statistics, Standard Occupational Classification 2020, vol. 3, 2020, https://www.ons.gov.uk/methodology/classificationsandstandards/standardoccupationalclassificationsoc/soc2020/soc2020volume3thenationalstatisticssocioeconomicclassificationnssecrebasedonthesoc2020.

163 Over one year unemployed is classified as long-term.

164 Wheeler, B. et al, "Life in Britain: The office", Danny Dorling's blog, http://www.dannydorling.org/books/lifeinbritain/pdfs/Report_7_The%20office.pdf.

165 Wheeler et al, "Life in Britain: The office".

166 Davidson, G., "Insight: The full story of Scotland's exam results shambles", *The Scotsman,* 9 August 2020, "https://www.scotsman.com/education/insight-full-story-scotlands-exam-results-shambles-2936974.

167 Scottish Qualifications Authority, https://www.sqa.org.uk/sqa/70972.html.

168 Davidson, "The full story of Scotland's exam results shambles".

169 A popular way to deal heroin, cocaine and other drugs. They are placed at the bottom of a cone and covered with ice cream.

170 Manstead, A.S.R., "The Psychology of Social Class: How socioeconomic status impacts thought, feelings, and behaviour", *British Journal of Social Psychology*, 57, 2018, p.267, https://bpspsychub.onlinelibrary.wiley.com/doi/pdf/10.1111/bjso.12251.

171 Booth, R., "Secret Pontins Blacklist Prevented People With Irish Surnames From Booking", *The Guardian*, 2 March 2021, https://www.theguardian.com/uk-news/2021/mar/02/secret-pontins-blacklist-irish-surnames.

172 All of the testimonies in this chapter are based on real people, some of whom have had their names changed to protect their identities.

173 Interestingly, some of the older respondents self-consciously referred to themselves as working class, whereas the younger ones did not.

174 Beckett, A., "The Right To Buy: The housing crisis that Thatcher built", *The Guardian*, 26 August 2015, https://www.theguardian.com/society/2015/aug/26/right-to-buy-margaret-thatcher-david-cameron-housing-crisis.

175 Radio Rentals was formed in 1932 to allow people to rent radios, funnily enough. The cost of a new "wireless" as they were often called back then was too steep for most normal people, so it was more affordable to rent a radio set on a monthly basis. As the years went by and television sets became the medium of choice for people to entertain themselves, Radio Rentals moved into renting out both television sets and video recorders.

176 Kerbie was a popular children's game played by two children. One stood on one side of a road and the other on the other side. They would throw a ball and hope to hit the edge of the kerb so that it bounced back to them. If it did, and they caught the ball, they earned a point.

Chapter 5

177 "Profile: John Prescott", BBC News, 27 August 2007, http://news.bbc.co.uk/1/hi/uk_politics/6636565.stm.

178 "Most People In Britain Today Regard Themselves Working Class", University of Oxford, 30 June 2016, https://www.ox.ac.uk/news/2016-06-30-most-people-britain-today-regard-themselves-working-class.

179 Manstead, "The Psychology of Social Class", p.268.

180 O'Brien, L., "Britain Now Has 7 Social Classes – and Working Class is a Dwindling Breed", *The Independent*, 3 April 2013, https://www.independent.co.uk/news/uk/home-news/britain-now-has-7-social-classes-and-working-class-dwindling-breed-8557894.html. The researchers say: "We use the term 'precariat' as a reflection on the existence of a significant group characterised by high amounts of insecurity on all of our measures of capital." See "Largest Class Survey Reveals Polarized UK Society and the Rise of New Groups", ScienceDaily, 3 April 2013, www.sciencedaily.com/releases/2013/04/130403104218.htm.

181 Watson, "Ch 2: Activism" in Gilbert, *The Working Class*, pp.18–19.

182 "Largest Class Survey Reveals Polarized UK Society", ScienceDaily.

183 Hoggart, R., *The Uses of Literacy: Aspects of working-class life* (Penguin Books, 1958), p.xxi.

184 Payne, R.K., *A Framework For Understanding Poverty* (AHA Process Inc, 1996), p.9.

185 Woodrow, F., "Classlessness" in Gilbert, *The Working Class,* p.211.

Chapter 6

186 In this chapter, as elsewhere in the book, I will use the terms "council estate" and "housing scheme" interchangeably. A council estate is where traditional working-class communities have historically lived – in Scotland, they are known as housing schemes.

187 "Drug Deaths in Scotland Reach New Record Level", BBC News, 30 July 2021, https://www.bbc.co.uk/news/uk-scotland-58024296.

188 Poverty porn includes TV programmes, articles and books about poverty and poor people that do not address the issues behind the poverty but present it as a form of entertainment – for example, the TV shows, *Benefits Street* and *The Scheme*.

189 "Gypsy Roma Traveller History and Culture", The Traveller Movement, https://travellermovement.org.uk/about/gypsy-roma-traveller-history-and-culture.

190 The real population may be different as some members of the community do not participate in the census.

191 The Traveller Movement, https://travellermovement.org.uk.

192 "Although Travellers speak English in most situations, they often speak to each other in their own language; for

Irish Travellers this is called Cant or Gammon and Gypsies speak Romani, which is the only indigenous language in the UK with Indic roots." See https://travellermovement.org.uk/about/gypsy-roma-traveller-history-and-culture.

193 This is according to unofficial research done by a local housing association.

194 John 4:35.

Chapter 7

195 Hoggart, *Uses of Literacy*, p.8.

196 According to the Urban Dictionary, one definition of a NED is: "non educated delinquent live in Glasgow stand around drinking Buckie and pissing in letterboxes. They are members of young teams." See https://www.urbandictionary.com/define.php?term=NEDs. The term was added to the *Collins Dictionary* in 2005 and has two definitions: "1. a hooligan; 2. a young working-class person who dresses in casual sports clothes." Note the phrase "working-class".

197 *Jeremy Kyle Show*, ITV1, https://web.archive.org/web/20071113034824/http://www.itv.com/jeremykyle/. Recording and broadcasting was suspended in May 2019 following the death of a participant.

198 If they like you. Otherwise, you just get stared at.

199 *Trainspotting* is a critically acclaimed 1996 film based on the life of a young Edinburgh born drug addict called Renton who was trying, unsuccessfully, to escape his addiction and start a new life in London.

200 "The Scale of Economic Inequality in the UK", The Equality Trust, https://www.equalitytrust.org.uk/scale-economic-inequality-uk.

201 "Household Income Inequality, UK: Financial year ending 2020", Office for National Statistics, 21 January 2021, https://www.ons.gov.uk/peoplepopulationandcommunity/personalandhouseholdfinances/incomeandwealth/bulletins/householdincomeinequalityfinancial/financialyearending2020.

202 Lloyd-Jones, D.M., *The Christian and the State in Revolutionary Times*, Westminster Conference, 1975, p.103.

203 Joslin, *Urban Harvest*, p.3.

Chapter 8

204 Lewis, O., "The Culture of Poverty", *Scientific American*, October 1966, https://meylindasp.files.wordpress.com/2014/06/lewisoscarthe-culture-of-poverty.pdf.

205 Lambert, T., "A Brief History of the British Police", Local Histories, last revised 2020, http://www.localhistories.org/police.html.

206 It describes old mining and single-industry towns who have historically voted Labour despite the age and occupations of their residents making them more likely to vote Conservative according to national trends. Brooke, S., "Does the 'Red Wall' Really Exist – and will Labour win it back?", 22 February 2021, https://www.examinerlive.co.uk/news/local-news/red-wall-really-exist-labour-19868934.

207 Devine, T., "The Strange Death of Labour Scotland", *New Statesman,* 2 March 2016, https://www.newstatesman.com/politics/uk/2016/03/strange-death-labour-scotland.

208 Goodwin, M. and Heath, O., "Brexit Vote Explained: Poverty, low skills and lack of opportunities", Joseph Rowntree Foundation, 31 August 2016, https://www.jrf.org.uk/report/brexit-vote-explained-poverty-low-skills-and-lack-opportunities.

209 Catholics, especially, still see some merit in having their children baptised.

210 Hoggart, *Uses of Literacy*, p.10.

211 Hoggart, *Uses of Literacy,* p.42.

212 Hoggart, *Uses of Literacy,* p.114.

213 Hoggart, *Uses of Literacy,* p.114.

214 Hoggart, *Uses of Literacy,* p.71.

215 According to the *Cambridge Dictionary* a blended family is "a family that consists of two adults, the child or children that they have had together, and one or more children that they have had with previous partners". See https://dictionary.cambridge.org/dictionary/english/blended-family.

216 Quoted in the University College London research: "Children in Poverty at Greater Risk of Childhood Traumas", UCL, 9 July 2020, https://www.ucl.ac.uk/news/2020/jul/children-poverty-greater-risk-childhood-traumas.

217 "Looked After Children: Statistics briefing", NSPCC Learning, 2021, https://learning.nspcc.org.uk/research-resources/statistics-briefings/looked-after-children.

218 Hoare, G., Boswell, K. and Kail, A., "Tackling Child Abuse in Scotland: A guide for funders", R.S. MacDonald Charitable Trust, May 2016, p.3, https://www.thinknpc.org/wp-content/uploads/2018/07/Child-abuse-in-Scotland-a-guide-for-funders1.pdf.

219 McGarvey, D., *Poverty Safari*, p.12.

220 Hoggart, *Uses of Literacy*, p.24.

221 Hoggart, *Uses of Literacy*, p.131.

222 From McGarvey, D., *Poverty Safari*, p.193, quoting Vance, J.D., *Hillbilly Elegy: A Memoir of a family and culture in crisis* (Harper Press, 2016).

223 Bennett, T. et al. *Culture, Class, Distinction* (Routledge, 2009).

224 Morgan, J., "Struggling Northern Towns Look to Rugby League for a Sense of Rebellion", iNews, 30 January 2020, https://inews.co.uk/news/long-reads/rugby-league-rebellion-brexit-struggling-northern-towns-391661.

225 Quoted in Pinxten, W. and Lievens, J., "The Importance of Economic, Social and Cultural Capital in Understanding Health Inequalities: Using a Bourdieu-based approach In research on physical and mental health perceptions", *Sociology of Health and Illness*, 36(7), 2014, https://onlinelibrary.wiley.com/doi/pdf/10.1111/1467-9566.12154.

226 Tinson, A., "What Geographic Inequalities in COVID-19 Mortality Rates and Health Can Tell Us About Levelling Up", The Health Foundation, 7 July 2021, https://www.health.org.uk/news-and-comment/charts-and-infographics/what-geographic-inequalities-in-covid-19-mortality-rates-can-tell-us-about-levelling-up.

227 Triggle, N., "Is Covid At Risk of Becoming a Disease of the Poor?", BBC News, 25 February 2021, https://www.bbc.co.uk/news/health-56162075.

228 Triggle, "Is Covid At Risk of Becoming a Disease of the Poor?".

229 Tinson, "Geographic Inequalities in COVID-19".

230 Tinson, A. and Tallack, C., "Deprivation and Excess Deaths", The Health Foundation, https://www.health.org.uk/news-and-comment/charts-and-infographics/deprivation-and-excess-deaths.

231 "Mental Health Statistics: Poverty", Mental Health Foundation, https://www.mentalhealth.org.uk/statistics/mental-health-statistics-poverty.

232 Boardman, J. et al., eds., *Social Inclusion and Mental Health* (Royal College of Psychiatrists Publications, 2010).

233 Dickens, S., *Relationships: How do I make things right?* (Christian Focus, 2020), https://www.christianfocus.com/products/2866/relationships-how-do-i-make.

Part II – Chapter 1

234 "African countries once had large textile industries – and some critics blame the flood of cheap second-hand clothes from abroad for the continent's shrunken textile sector." See Reality Check team, "Reality Check: Why some African countries don't want charity clothes", BBC News, 27 July 2018, https://www.bbc.co.uk/news/world-africa-44951670.

235 Graves, R.L., "Breaking Generational Poverty Through Collaborative Efforts", Doctor of Ministry Thesis, Asbury Theology Seminary, May 2017, p.25, https://place.asburyseminary.edu/cgi/viewcontent.cgi?article=2112andcontext =ecommonsatsdissertations.

236 Nnamani, Amaluche Greg., "Dialetics of Poverty and Oppression: From an African and theological perspective", *Bulletin of Ecumenical Theology,* vol.12, 2000, https://dsc.duq.edu/beth/11/.

237 Almsgiving was a sacred obligation in Israel. The inner circle of disciples around Jesus regularly gave alms to the begging poor (John 13:28–29).

Chapter 2

238 Graves, "Breaking Generational Poverty Through Collaborative Efforts", p.30.

239 It is important to note that gleaning was also used negatively in the Old Testament in reference to killing men in battle, as in Judges 20:45. There is also the sense in which we glean from the pages of Scripture when we read the Bible and seek to feed on its spiritual riches.

Chapter 3

240 DeYoung, K., "Obligation, Stewardship, and the Poor", 9Marks, 1 July 2012, https://www.9marks.org/article/journalhow-should-we-think-about-our-obligation-help-poor/.

Part III – Chapter 1

241 Wright, P., "Obituary: Ivan Illich", *The Lancet*, 11 January 2003, https://doi.org/10.1016/S0140-6736(03)12233-7.

242 Corbett, S. and Fikkert, B., *When Helping Hurts: How to alleviate poverty without hurting the poor and yourself* (Moody Publishers, 2014).

Chapter 2

243 McGarvey, *Poverty Safari*, p.125.

244 I am using the term "mercy ministry" as any church-based work that seeks to reach the poor of their city/neighbourhood by offering free handouts.

245 McGarvey, *Poverty Safari*, p.105.

246 McGarvey, *Poverty Safari*, p.125.

247 Saul, N. and Curtis, A., *The Stop: How the fight for good food transformed a community and inspired a movement* (Melville House Publishing, 2013).

248 Butler, P., "Food Banks are 'A Slow Death of the Soul'", *The Guardian*, 25 September 2013, https://www.theguardian.com/society/2013/sep/25/food-banks-slow-death-soul.

249 Butler, "Food Banks are 'A Slow Death of the Soul'".

250 Butler, "Food Banks are 'A Slow Death of the Soul'".

251 John is a real person whose name I have changed to protect his anonymity.

Chapter 3

[252] The entire article can be read here: Frame, J., "Proposal for a New Seminary", The Works of John Frame and Vern Poythress, 23 May 2012, https://frame-poythress.org/proposal-for-a-new-seminary/.

[253] Frame, "Proposal for a New Seminary".

[254] Frame, "Proposal for a New Seminary".

[255] Frame, "Proposal for a New Seminary".

[256] Frame, "Proposal for a New Seminary".

[257] Frame, "Proposal for a New Seminary".

Chapter 4

[258] Florida, R., *The New Urban Crisis: How our cities are increasing inequality, deepening segregation, and failing the middle class – and what we can do about* it (Ingram Publisher Services, 2017), p.xii.

[259] Florida, *New Urban Crisis*, p.xix.

[260] Florida, *New Urban Crisis*. Also, Prynne, J., Bar-Hillel, M. and Watling, L., "London's £3bn Ghost Mansions", *Evening Standard*, 14 February 2014.

[261] Florida, *New Urban Crisis*, p.8.

[262] Florida, *New Urban Crisis*, p.8.

[263] Florida, *New Urban Crisis*, p.19.

[264] Florida, *New Urban Crisis*, p.65.

[265] McConnell, M., "The Silliness of Social Engineering", 20schemes, https://20schemesequip.com/the-silliness-of-social-engineering/.

266 Amadeo, K. "Why Trickle-Down Economics Works in Theory But Not In Fact: The shortcomings of supply-side economics", The Balance, 29 March 2021, https://www.thebalance.com/trickle-down-economics-theory-effect-does-it-work-3305572.

267 Including Tim Keller and others.

268 Acts 29, https://www.acts29.com.

269 As quoted in Strivens, R., "C.H. Spurgeon on 'Top-Down' Evangelism", Robert Strivens blog, 25 April 2021, https://robertstrivens.wordpress.com/2021/04/25/c-h-spurgeon-on-top-down-evangelism/.

270 Florida, *New Urban Crisis*, p.136.

271 This is the edited version of an article by David Robertson, a Free Church minister in Scotland, now living in Australia.

272 MacPherson, H., "How the Church of Scotland's Disruption of 1843 Unfolded", *The National,* 10 December 2019, https://www.thenational.scot/news/18090228.church-scotlands-disruption-1843-unfolded/.

273 "Scotland Ministries", Mission to the World (MTW), https://www.mtw.org/teams/europe/dundee-scotland.

274 McCaffrey, J.F., "Thomas Chalmers and Social Change", *The Scottish Historical Review*, 60(169), April 1981, pp.32–60, https://www.jstor.org/stable/25529400.

275 Entry for 3 March 1834, Bonar, Rev. A.A., ed., *The Life and Remains, Letters, Lectures, and Poems of the Rev. Robert Murray McCheyne* (Robert Carter, 1847), p.26.

Chapter 5

276 As many will have heard Dick Lucas, former Rector of St Helen's Bishopsgate, say on many occasions.

Chapter 6

277 Adams, R., "University Applications from 18-year-olds at a Record High", *The Guardian,* 16 August 2019, https://www.theguardian.com/education/2019/aug/16/university-applications-from-18-year-olds-at-record-high.

278 Arnett, G., "UK Became More Middle Class Than Working Class in 2000, Data Shows", *The Guardian,* 26 February 2016, https://www.theguardian.com/news/datablog/2016/feb/26/uk-more-middle-class-than-working-class-2000-data. This correlates with those in C2DE occupations.

279 Taken from a talk at a pastor's conference in Yorkshire in 2016.

280 For more information refer to www.20schemes.com/retrain.

281 "Middlesbrough had the largest share of the most deprived areas", from "England's Most Deprived Areas Named as Jaywick and Blackpool", BBC News, 26 September 2019, https://www.bbc.co.uk/news/uk-england-49812519.

282 Funding the Family Business, http://www.fundingthefamilybusiness.org.

283 This material originally appeared as a blog post and is reproduced with permission: Kneale, S., "We Have a Problem Resourcing the Church in Deprived

Communities", Building Jerusalem blog, 25 August 2017, https://buildingjerusalem.blog/2017/08/25/we-have-a-problem-resourcing-the-church-in-deprived-communities/.

284 Leong, D.P., *Race and Place: How urban geography shapes the journey to reconciliation* (IVP, 2017).

285 Leong, *Race and Place*, p.137.

286 Leong, *Race and Place*, p.141.

287 Leong, *Race and Place*, p.142.

288 Leong, *Race and Place*, p.144.

289 Leong, *Race and Place*, p.163.

Part IV – Chapter 1

290 Boothe, C.O., *Plain Theology for Plain People* (1890, reprinted by Lexham Press, 2017).

291 Boothe, *Plain Theology*, p.120.

292 Newbigin, J.E.L., *The Household of God: Lectures on the nature of the church* (SCM Press, 1953), pp.24–25.

293 This material originally appeared as a blog post and is slightly edited and reproduced with permission: Bell, S., "Guest Post: A Radical Solution to the Greatest Inequality", Building Jerusalem blog, 23 February 2021, https://buildingjerusalem.blog/2021/02/23/guest-post-a-radical-solution-to-the-greatest-inequality/.

294 "Covid-19: 'I Had My Head Down in Shame': A pandemic life in one of the UK's poorest towns", Sky News, 17 February 2021, https://news.sky.com/story/covid-19-i-had-my-head-down-in-shame-a-pandemic-life-in-one-of-the-uks-poorest-towns-12219505.

295 This material originally appeared as a blog post and is reproduced with permission: Neale, S., "Churches in Deprived Communities Don't Exist to Salve the Conscience of the Middle Classes", Building Jerusalem blog, 8 August 2017, https://buildingjerusalem.blog/2017/08/08/churches-in-deprived-communities-dont-exist-to-salve-the-conscience-of-the-middle-classes/.

Chapter 2

296 A copy of the full record can be found at: "21st Century Evangelicals: Good news for the poor?", Evangelical Alliance, 29 May 2015, https://issuu.com/evangelicalalliance/docs/21st_century_evangelicals_-_poverty.

297 Taken from an article Steve wrote for 20schemes: Levy, S., "The Best Way to Give to the Poor is Through the Church", 20schemes, 2 June 2014, https://20schemesequip.com/the-best-way-to-give-to-the-poor-is-through-the-church/.

298 Levy, "The Best Way to Give".

299 Levy, S., "Jesus and the Church: the best hope for the poor", 20schemes, 26 May 2014, https://20schemesequip.com/jesus-and-the-church-the-best-hope-for-the-poor/.

300 Levy, S., "Are Our Churches Really Keeping the Poor at Arm's Length?", 20schemes, 19 May 2014, https://20schemesequip.com/are-our-churches-really-keeping-the-poor-at-arms-length/.

301 Levy, "Are Our Churches Really Keeping the Poor at Arm's Length?".

302 Christian Funders Forum, https://christianfundersforum.org.

303 Stewardship, https://www.stewardship.org.uk.

304 20schemes, https://20schemes.com.

305 Kingdom Bank, https://www.kingdom.bank.

306 J. Hudson Taylor was born on 21 May 1832 in Barnsley, Yorkshire, and served as a pioneering missionary to inland China.

Chapter 3

307 Walby, S. and Allen, J., "Domestic Violence, Sexual Assault and Stalking: Findings from the British Crime Survey", Home Office Research Study 276, March 2004, http://nomsintranet.org.uk/roh/official-documents/HomeOfficeResearchStudy276.pdf.

Chapter 4

308 We have a series called *The First Steps*, published by Christian Focus, https://www.christianfocus.com/series/168/first-steps.

Chapter 5

309 Pierre, J. and Reju, D., *The Pastor and Counselling: The basics of shepherding members in need* (Crossway, 2015).

Chapter 6

310 Cameron, D., "Social Mobility: The Trojan Horse of inequality" in Gilbert, *The Working Class*, p.187.

311 Stott, J.R.W., *The Lausanne Covenant: An exposition and commentary* (Lausanne Committee for World Evangelization, 1975), sec. 11: Education and Leadership,

https://lausanne.org/content/covenant/lausanne-covenant#cov.

Chapter 7

[312] Lupton, R.D., *Toxic Charity: How churches and charities hurt those they help (and how to reverse it)* (Harper Publications, 2011).

[313] Focused Community Strategies, https://www.fcsministries.org.

[314] Lupton, *Toxic Charity.*

[315] Lupton, *Toxic Charity.*

[316] Lupton, *Toxic Charity.*

[317] Miller, M.L., *The Alternative: Most of what you believe about poverty is wrong* (Lulu Publishing, 2017).

[318] Miller, *The Alternative*, p.5.

[319] Miller, *The Alternative*, p.36.

Chapter 8

[320] This material originally appeared as a blog post and is reproduced with permission: Prime, A., "Gospel-Centered Preaching in Hard Places", 9Marks, 31 March 2020, https://www.9marks.org/article/gospel-centered-preaching-in-hard-places/.

[321] *Soli Deo Gloria* – Glory to God alone.

[322] Spurgeon, C., *Practical Wisdom (Plain Advice for Plain People)* (1869, republished Banner of Truth, 2009).

Conclusion

[323] Piper, J., *Don't Waste Your Life* (Crossway Books, 2018).

[324] Studd, C.T., "Only One Life".

[325] The English Standard Version is used throughout this chapter.

[326] Guthrie, D.K. and Guthrie, C.J., *Autobiography of Thomas Guthrie, D.D. and Memoir by His Sons* vol.2 (Robert Carter & Brothers, 1875).

ACTS 29 | CORE COMPETENCIES
Able To Teach
The Importance of Preaching and Teaching in a Church Plant
Philip Moore
DAILY
C.H. SPURGEON
FAITH
NINE WAYS TO BE